T0328306

Business-to-Business Marketing

Reviews

Prof. Anayo D. Nkamnebe PhD, Professor of Marketing, Nnamdi Azikiwe University Nigeria. President, the Academy of Management Nigeria (TAMN)

This book is a must-read for scholars and practitioners interested in gaining insightful state-of-the-art knowledge about the working dynamics of the B2B marketing environment in Africa. The continent of Africa is predominantly constructed as a consuming region, thus promoting an overly skewed consumer-centric marketing (B2C). Ironically, the enormous marketing opportunities for B2B marketing in Africa are buried beneath the dormant potentials of "Rising Africa" market, which await empirical, context-specific and case-by-case expose. Four African scholars used this book to break the iceberg! They masterfully domesticated extant B2B marketing theories within the African context and render B2B marketing discourse in authentic narratives, which significantly differentiates it from what authors from other climes present. Indeed, the book serves as Africa's B2B marketing gold standard! I unreservedly recommend the book as reference material for B2B marketing in Africa to both scholars and managers.

Dr Kofi Q. Dadzie (Associate Professor), J. Mack Robinson College of Business, Georgia State University, Atlanta, USA. Immediate Past President, Academy of African Business and Development (AABD); Area Editor of *Journal of Business and Industrial Marketing*.

Africa has been waiting for this book. *Business-to-Business Marketing: How to Understand and Succeed in Business Marketing in an Emerging Africa* will fill a significant gap in research, teaching, consulting and management of B2B in Africa.

This book integrates recent empirical research, marketing concepts, theories and frameworks with rich case materials grounded in the African B2B context.

Over the past several decades, there has been a dramatic increase in the number of business schools and accompanying programs and student admissions at academic, MBA, executive MBA, certificate and diploma levels. However, much of the existing textbooks in use in Africa do not reflect the empirical reality that students face in the African context.

This book provides comprehensive material suitable for undergraduate, MBA, MSc and post-graduate courses (part of or the whole book). It presents both the traditional and evolving topics to enable professors to guide their students through the whole gamut of knowledge required from undergraduate to post-graduate courses in B2B. It has an excellent level of integration of theory, practice and context. While it is based on an academic format, it is easy to read and understand. I believe that this book will also be useful on the office shelves of B2B managers – a kind of "African Kotler" of B2B. It is a book that managers can refer to for insight when formulating strategies and developing action plans. Consultants will find it a useful reference when preparing reports and lectures. Likewise, leaders of government institutions and non-governmental organisations should find the book very insightful for seeing their organisations through a marketing lens. That is likely to lead to better revenue outcomes through understanding the marketing approach to fulfilling their objectives by providing improved value through their products and services.

I strongly recommend the book for B2B courses in the continent and about the continent and for consultants and managers in the B2B field.

Business-to-Business Marketing
How to Understand and Succeed in Business Marketing in an Emerging Africa

Dr Richard Afriyie Owusu
Associate Professor, School of Business and Economics, Linnaeus University, Sweden

Dr Robert Ebo Hinson
Professor, University of Ghana, Legon, Ghana

Dr Ogechi Adeola
Associate Professor, Lagos Business School, Pan-Atlantic University, Nigeria

Dr Nnamdi Oguji
Business Development Expert, KONE Corporation, Finland

A PRODUCTIVITY PRESS BOOK

First published 2021
by Routledge
600 Broken Sound Parkway #300, Boca Raton FL, 33487

and by Routledge
2 Park Square, Milton Park, Abingdon, Oxon, OX14 4RN

Routledge is an imprint of the Taylor & Francis Group, an informa business

© 2021 Richard Afriyie Owusu, Robert Ebo Hinson, Ogechi Adeola, and Nnamdi Oguji

Library of Congress Cataloging-in-Publication Data
A catalog record for this title has been requested

ISBN: 9780367201470 (hbk)
ISBN: 9780367770884 (pbk)
ISBN: 9780429259777 (ebk)

Typeset in Garamond
by codeMantra

Contents

SECTION 1 CHARACTERISTICS OF THE BUSINESS-TO-BUSINESS MARKET

SECTION 2   MARKETING AND PURCHASING IN THE BUSINESS-TO-BUSINESS MARKET

SECTION 3   COMPETITIVE ASPECTS OF THE BUSINESS-TO-BUSINESS MARKET

SECTION 4 STRATEGIC ALLIANCES AND COLLABORATIVE RELATIONSHIPS MANAGEMENT IN THE BUSINESS-TO-BUSINESS MARKET

List of Figures

List of Tables

Preface

Background

While over half of the economic activities of modern economies occur in the business-to-business (B2B) market, there is relatively less research and teaching of the subject compared to the business-to-consumer (B2C) market. The dynamics of the B2B market are more complex than those of the B2C market. For instance, the activities on the B2B side of a product such as a motor vehicle built in South Africa are complex and lengthy before a new model reaches the consumer, and it continues after its introduction to the market. The process involved in the B2B sphere includes the development of basic research and technologies by universities, consulting firms and companies in many countries, integration of existing technologies, acquisition of patents, acquisition of standards and approvals from authorities, manufacturing in South Africa, logistics and distribution to various showrooms around the country.

Due to the increased competition in B2B, companies are concentrating on developing core competencies. Their aim is to become very competitive in a few areas where they can continue to be among the best. Moreover, global business marketing has expanded from the importation of raw materials to outsourcing core parts of production globally. Therefore, B2B has evolved into positioning the firm to collaborate in value chains and networks, rather than owning all parts of a value chain.

Successful B2B marketing and purchasing should be based on strategic planning. B2B marketers and purchasers should be professional staff as they are responsible for large budgets of their employers. They have to be more strategic and negotiate more intensely, as they have high responsibilities for their decisions. There are fewer buyers and suppliers. A B2B supplier might have a few major buyers that buy up to 90% of their products. B2B purchases are often components and inputs to the production process and are, thus, critical in terms of quality, just-in-time deliveries and product development. Just-in-time logistics approaches have reduced fixed costs but raised the importance of coordination and information-sharing between organisations in the value chain.

As African markets grow, the role of B2B in generating innovations; developing products; building efficient value chains; interacting with foreign companies that are entering African markets; competing in the outsourcing markets; and developing and marketing business services, systems, solutions and public–private partnerships for industrial projects is critical for the continued development of African economies. The lack of infrastructure and advanced home-grown technologies calls for the ability to innovatively purchase and market systems and projects by governments, institutions and African companies, for example, through various forms of public–private partnerships in projects.

Unfortunately, our research and experience show that there is very little knowledge of B2B marketing and management. In too many business schools, engineering faculties and universities, B2B marketing and management is not a core course but an elective. The large proportion of current managers and technical staff who are involved in B2B have not taken a course in the subject.

This has to change, as experience and research from the highly developed economies show that successful B2B marketing and management cannot be taken for granted.

Globally, B2B research has been picking up momentum in the past few decades. Besides, research approaches such as strategic management, selling and purchasing strategies, relationship marketing, business networks, business ecosystems and supply chain management are being developed and applied to research and consulting. Very little of the research has, however, focused on the African business markets, and limited knowledge of how companies can succeed in the African B2B market exists. In a review of one of the leading African business journals (*Journal of African Business*) and two leading B2B journals (*Industrial Marketing Management* and *Journal of Business-to-Business Marketing*) over 10 years, we found <10% of the articles on B2B in Africa. We have not found any specific textbook on B2B in Africa.

Furthermore, in a recent analytical literature review of aspects of B2B relationships, Oguji and Owusu (2014) found only 19 articles published on sourcing in Africa in 40 scholarly journals over 33 years. In another review, Oguji et al. (2021) found only 22 relevant articles on international joint ventures and acquisitions in Africa from all peer-reviewed academic journals up to 2017. As a result, there is a paucity of published materials available for teaching business marketing in African universities and business schools.

Objectives

The objective of this book is to provide a comprehensive, state-of-the-art understanding of B2B marketing and management and to apply this knowledge to the African environment in order to help students, managers, consultants and others to develop strategic approaches to B2B in Africa.

Conceptual analyses as well as cases and applications to the African business market are provided. As a result, it is useful for academic and professional programmes as well as providing insights for managers to enhance their strategy development and competitiveness of their organisations.

Structure and Contents

This book covers the characteristics of the B2B market, competitive strategy from both the transactional and relational points of view, marketing and purchasing strategies, and topical issues such as project business, outsourcing, capacity development and business services. It covers all the topics necessary for a comprehensive understanding of contemporary concepts and practice of B2B marketing and management. It analyses private, governmental and non-governmental organisational aspects of B2B. B2B collaborations, networks, relationship marketing, B2B marketing mix, strategic alliances and emerging issues like big data analytics are thoroughly analysed.

All topics are developed with African examples, and the analyses are based on African cases and realities. This book thus provides both broad and deep knowledge necessary for successful B2B marketing and management in Africa.

Intended Readership

This book can be used for undergraduate, graduate and post-graduate courses in business programmes in Africa, as well as African business programmes in universities outside Africa. At the undergraduate levels, professors can choose parts of the book that they find most relevant, for example Parts 1–4.

At the graduate or post-graduate level, professors can use the entire book. Graduate and post-graduate students will find specific topics useful for a broad understanding of their topics and formulating the focus of their research. This book provides a fundamental reference point for knowledge and discussions when writing theses or articles on B2B in Africa. It can also be used for executive MBA courses. For practising managers, this book is a reference for applicable concepts, models and cases of B2B that will inform and motivate their strategy formulation and decision-making. Executives of government and private institutions, as well as non-governmental organisations, will gain a new insight into marketing management that will motivate them to improve their performance.

Why Read This Book?

In summary, this book is the gold standard of B2B knowledge about Africa for B2B marketing managers in Africa and those outside Africa who want to understand the African B2B market. As it covers the range of relevant contemporary B2B concepts and frameworks, applies them in the African context and provides African examples and cases, the reader will gain

a. Excellent understanding of contemporary concepts and models of B2B marketing
b. Ability to analyse the organisation's B2B environment
c. Ability to develop relevant competitive and collaborative B2B strategies
d. Excellent understanding and ability to analyse the organisation's positions in, and develop strategies for its networks, supply chains, clusters and business ecosystems
e. New insightful understanding of their positions in business markets and how to strategise to improve their performance, particularly for executives and leaders of public institutions and non-governmental organisations.

Finally, this book combines an excellent mix of academic research/theories/models with practical examples and cases. It is built on current research results, the considerable research on African business of the four academics, and many years of working in and consulting for companies and organisations in and outside Africa.

Acknowledgments

We thank the following experts for contributing cases to the book:

Dr Adele Berndt, Associate Professor, Jönköping International Business School, Jönköping University, Jönköping, Sweden

Mr Christopher Boafo, PhD Candidate, African Centre for Career Enhancement and Skills Support (ACCESS), Faculty of Economics and Management, Leipzig University, Germany

Ms Emma Nkonoki, PhD Candidate, University of Turku, Finland

We thank the following experts for their constructive comments on drafts of the book:

Professor Johan D. E. Jager, Tshwane University of Technology, Pretoria, South Africa.

Professor Charles Blankson, G. Brint Ryan College of Business, University of North Texas, Denton, Texas.

Professor Kofi Dadzie: J Mac Robinson College of Business, Georgia State University, Atlanta, USA

Professor John Kuada, Aalborg University, Department of Business and Management, Aalborg University, Aalborg, Denmark

Professor Chantal Rootman, Department of Business Management, Nelson Mandela University, Port Elizabeth, South Africa

Professor Samuel Famiyeh GIMPA, School of Business, GIMPA University, Accra, Ghana

Professor Anayo D. Nkamnebe, Unizik Business School, Nnamdi Azikiwe University, Awka, Nigeria

Professor Nnamdi Madichie, Unizik Business School, Nnamdi Azikiwe University, Awka, Nigeria

Dr Richard Glavee Geo, Associate Professor, Norwegian University of Science and Technology, Trondheim, Norway

Dr Ato Dadzie, Senior Lecturer, School of Business, GIMPA University, Accra, Ghana

Dr Ebenezer Adaku, Senior Lecturer, School of Business, GIMPA University, Accra, Ghana

Dr Kwame Adom, Senior Lecturer, University of Ghana Business School, Legon, Ghana

Dr Ibn Kailan Abdul-Hamid, Senior Lecturer, University of Professional Studies, Accra, Ghana

Dr İlke Kocamaz, Assistant Professor, Marmara University, İstanbul, Turkey

Dr William Degbey, Lecturer, School of Business and Economics, University of Turku, Finland

Dr Mahmoud Abdulai, Senior Lecturer, University of Ghana Business School, Legon, Ghana

Dr Lawrence Akwetey, Senior Lecturer, London School of Commerce, London, UK

Dr Imoh Antai, Assistant Professor, Jönköping International Business School, Jönköping University, Jönköping, Sweden

Dr Kuthea Nguti, Lecturer, Strathmore University Business School, Nairobi, Kenya

Mr Kojo Kakra Twum, Lecturer, School of Business and Economics, Presbyterian University College, Okwahu, Ghana

Mr Philip Mampukia Yakubu, PhD Candidate, Department of Business and Management, Aalborg University, Denmark

Mr Christopher Boafo, PhD Candidate, ACCESS, Faculty of Economics and Management, Leipzig University, Germany

Mr Isaiah Adisa, Olabisi Onabanjo University, Ogun State, Nigeria

Mr Onyeunoegbunem Calyxtus Enweazu, University of Lagos, Nigeria.

Thanks for secretarial support to

Ms Rahmat Surakat, MSc Student, School of Business and Economics, Linnaeus University, Kalmar, Sweden.

Authors

Dr Richard Afriyie Owusu is an Associate Professor of Marketing and International Business at the School of Business and Economics, Linnaeus University, Sweden. He is also the Research Leader of the Global Mind Knowledge Platform and a member of the Academic Council at Linnaeus University. During his academic career of over 15 years, he has taught and researched, among others, B2B marketing; international business; and business development, management and entrepreneurship in Africa, in universities in Europe, Africa, Australia and the USA.

He has published over 30 scientific articles and book chapters spanning international market entry strategies, acquisitions and joint ventures, international project business, business networks and business in Africa. He has participated in several corporate projects such as Globalization of Finnish SMEs (GlobFinn), and Brands, Innovation and Globalization of Finnish Companies (BIG). He contributed to the Ghana Export Strategy (2010–2015) while consulting for Omega Strategic Resources Limited. Currently, Dr Owusu is also a partner of Foresight Consulting, a consulting partnership dedicated to promoting successful business in Africa.

Dr Robert Ebo Hinson is a marketing communications practitioner, turned scholar. He holds a DPhil in Marketing from the University of Ghana and a PhD in International Business from the Aalborg University Business School. In his marketing communications career (1998–2003), he managed advertising budgets for brands such as Acer, Canon, LG, Microsoft, Mercedes Benz and Peugeot. In 2004, he also worked as the Marketing Communications Advisor to Cal Bank IPO, a bank that was eventually listed on the Ghana Stock Exchange. There was an oversubscription of shares by over 250%, making it one of the most successful IPOs in Ghana to date. Since turning scholar in 2003, he has served as Rector of the Perez University College, Winneba, Ghana, the Acting Director of Institutional Advancement at the University of Ghana, Legon, and twice as the Head of the Department of Marketing of Entrepreneurship at the University of Ghana Business School, Legon. Dr Hinson is also an Extraordinary Professor at the North West Business School in South Africa. He is one of the leading marketing scholars in Africa and has served on notable local and international boards. In 2019, he was listed as one of the top 100 speakers in Ghana by the Speakers Bureau Africa (https://speakersafrica.com/top100-3/).

Dr Ogechi Adeola is an Associate Professor of Marketing and Head of Department of Operations, Marketing and Information Systems at the Lagos Business School, Pan-Atlantic University, Lagos, Nigeria. She commenced her career with Citibank Nigeria, spending about 14 years in the Nigerian financial sector before moving to academia. Dr Adeola holds a doctorate in Business Administration (DBA) from Alliance Manchester Business School, Manchester, UK. She is a 2016 Visiting International Fellow, The Open University Business School, Milton Keynes, UK; a 2017

Paul R. Lawrence Fellow, Chicago; a guest lecturer at the University of Ghana Business School; and Associate Dean, University of the People, Pasadena, CA, USA.

Dr Adeola has published academic books and papers in top scholarly journals with her co-authored articles winning Best Paper Awards at international conferences in 2016–2019, consecutively. She is a Fellow of the Institute of Strategic Management, Nigeria, and the National Institute of Marketing of Nigeria.

Dr Nnamdi Oguji is an experienced professional with over 8 years' experience working for KONE as business development expert and managing global supply chain projects for KONE Corporation, Helsinki, Finland. In parallel, Dr Oguji completed his PhD in Economics and Business Administration in 2015 from the University of Vaasa, and continues his research in international business and supply chain and thematic areas within this field that integrate digitalisation and big data.

Over his tenure in KONE Corporation, Dr Oguji has helped KONE set up big data-based technologies in Finland and India, and leveraged big data analytics for customer insights, offering development, pricing and competitive intelligence, supply chain excellence and driving sales and profitability. During this same time, he has taught in several universities in Finland as a guest lecturer on the application of big data in international business and supply chains. He also has publications in several ABS-ranked journals.

Introduction

Introduction and Learning Objectives

In this introduction, we will define marketing, illustrate its various parts and functions, and provide a summary of the evolution of marketing knowledge.

At the end of this introduction, the reader will

- Understand the definition of marketing as an organisational and scientific discipline and practice
- Understand the evolution of marketing knowledge and practice
- Understand the approach to B2B marketing used in this book
- Understand the scientific approach that is necessary to improve B2B management and marketing strategies to compete in an ever-competitive global business environment.

What Is Marketing?

In this section, we introduce the reader to the general subject of marketing and briefly describe the evolution of marketing knowledge and practice.

The world's leading marketing academy, the American Marketing Association (AMA), defines marketing as "the activity, set of institutions, and processes for creating, communicating, delivering, and exchanging offerings that have value for customers, clients, partners, and society at large" (American Marketing Association, 2017).

According to Kotler (2018), marketing as an academic discipline started in the early 1900s and has gone through several phases of evolution. Kotler and Levy (1969) broadened marketing to include the activities of traditionally non-business entities like government and societal institutions, organisations and even nations (see also Fox & Kotler, 1980; Kotler & Armstrong, 2010). McKenna (1991) emphasised that the changes in the market, technology and consumer demanded a new definition and practice of marketing. "Marketing is now everything, and everything is now marketing" (p. 69). Marketing should concentrate on dialogue with the customer, provide value to the customer, follow the developments in technology, use technology, and should be integrated and practised in the whole organisation, not just the staff of the marketing department. Various other contributions summarised below have enabled the understanding of marketing to improve and be dynamic over the period. Therefore, the definition of marketing by the AMA initially focused on firms, profits and a limited list of marketing mix tools but has been reformulated several times to encompass the developments in research and practice (Booms & Bitner, 1980; Grönroos, 1994, 2006).

Kotler and Armstrong (2010, p. 29) make both a "broad definition" similar to the definition of the AMA above and a "narrow definition" that focuses on "business contexts". The "broad definition" states that "…marketing is a social and managerial process by which individuals and organisations obtain what they need and want through creating and exchanging value with others". The "narrow" definition specifies "…profitable, value-laden exchanges with customers". In contrast to Kotler and Armstrong's "narrow definition" focusing on profit-making companies, Kotler (2018), and the AMA emphasise that marketing is not undertaken only by profit-making companies but also by non-profit-making organisations, government agencies, institutions and non-governmental organisations. They emphasise that marketing is not only about sales, branding or advertising. It is a complex process that includes assessing the needs of the market; developing products and services to meet the needs; advertising, branding and other promotion activities; pricing; interacting with customers or other parties; and ensuring mutual value to the organisation and other parties.

Kotler and Armstrong (2010), Grönroos (1994, 2017a), and Sheth and Parvatiyar (1995) emphasised the importance of building relationships with other parties and customers for successful value creation. Thus, Grönroos (1994) proposed a paradigm shift in marketing, from a focus on the "four Ps" to a broader set of "Ps" that encompass relationships and place relationship building and management at the centre of marketing. Other contributions on the importance of exchanging value through services in addition to goods have culminated in the work of Vargo and Lusch (2008) that proposes a "services dominant logic" to marketing in place of the "goods dominant logic". According to them, "marketing should be defined as providing a service, that is: – a process of using the organisation's resources for the benefit of, and in conjunction with another party" (see also Furrer et al., 2020; Grönroos, 2017a,b; Parasuraman et al., 2002; Vargo et al., 2020; Zeithaml et al., 2018).

The definitions above imply that there are different kinds of parties in marketing, apart from the business seller/marketer and customer/purchaser. The AMA talks about "…exchanging offerings that have value for customers, clients, partners, and society at large". The definition does not mention profit for the parties. On the other hand, while both Kotler and Armstrong, and Grönroos add "profit" to their descriptions of the objectives of marketing activities for companies, they emphasise "value" as the end purpose for both parties. Thus, they do not mean profit specifically in the profit-and-loss accounting sense for the marketer in the short term. That is, they do not imply that companies and organisations must get more revenue than their costs in every deal, but that value should be exchanged in every deal or over time. Value is defined as "mutual benefit" by the AMA, Grönroos, and Kotler and Armstrong. Thus, the definitions emphasise marketing as an exchange. Valuable exchange for all parties must benefit all of them because if the purchasers are not satisfied, they may not return for new purchases. If the marketer earns a large profit at the expense of the purchaser, it may be short-lived, because, in a competitive global market, the purchaser can easily find better exchanges. Value to purchasers will satisfy them and let them come back, which will guarantee the marketer continued sales and, thus, long-term survival (Grönroos, 2017b; Keränen & Liozu, 2020). Thus, the objectives of marketing as "for-profit" include maintaining the company in the long term, not just making a short-term accounting profit. Additionally, marketing is also done by organisations and institutions that were not founded to make profits. Their marketing activities are, thus, to provide value to them and their publics, e.g. "hospitals, museums…and even churches" (Kotler & Armstrong, 2010, p. 52).

The assessment of value to the firm itself and the other firms in the exchange is complex. It reflects the challenges facing today's marketing managers, entrepreneurs, salespersons and B2B companies (Mahajan, 2017). How does the marketing manager know what the purchaser values, how the purchaser will use the product, and thus what prices, product, place, promotion, staffing and marketing process to use to create value for the purchaser? Each party decides the value it perceives; thus, the marketer does not control the value perception of the purchaser (Grönroos, 2017b; Hallberg, 2017; Kotler, 2017). Reviews of the research by Debnath et al. (2016) and Sota et al. (2018) confirm the complexity and multifaceted nature of value, thus making competitive strategy more challenging than ever.

Moreover, Kotler (2018, p. 18) argues that "a non-profit organization is also after 'profit', but it defines it in a broader way". Some non-profit organisations may need to gain surplus revenue to advance their goals. They may, at least, have to break even, because making losses means that they cannot continue to exist.

While the above trends and scholars encompass the nature of marketing generally as a science and management function, value, relationships, networks and services have always existed in B2B research and practice (see Anderson et al., 1994; Holm et al., 1999; Hadjikhani & LaPlaca, 2013; Keränen & Liozu, 2020; Mattsson, 1997; Möller, 2013). Hadjikhani and LaPlaca emphasise that the practice and study of B2B are as old as other aspects of marketing.

Other research and managerial evolution that shaped the development of B2B Marketing emanated from strategies (e.g., pricing, telemarketing, direct mail and event marketing) in business markets (Laric 1980; Rao & Rabino, 1980), and the early development of relationship management and value exchange research in B2B (Johanson & Mattsson, 1987, Mattsson 1973; Page & Siemplenski 1983). With increasing competition in the '90s, following the technological developments and advent of computers and the internet, the nature of B2B marketing was further transformed with the enabling communication technologies. From 2000, advanced IT-enabled applications, e.g., software and computer programming enabled systems (e.g., artificial intelligence, machine learning) and applications (e.g., Salesforce), as well as social media platforms (Facebook, YouTube, Twitter and LinkedIn), led to integrated marketing in B2B, and have continuously increased the complexity and heterogeneity of the discipline.

While B2B marketing has evolved over the years, its practice varies across regions of the world. For example, Karjalainen & Salmi (2013) suggest differences between the continental purchasing strategies and tools of companies in Western Europe compared to North America. While Europeans emphasise a reduction in prices and total cost of ownership as strategic objectives, North Americans place greater emphasis on compliance with social and ethical guidelines. Similarly, Dadzie, Johnston and Pels (2008) showed that while B2B marketing practices in West African nations conform with the Contemporary Marketing Practice (CMP) framework where firms practise both transactional marketing and relationship marketing simultaneously, differences exist in the intensity and scope of B2B marketing practices in Ghana and the Ivory Coast compared to Argentina and the USA.

The Changing Tools of Marketing

Borden (1964) and McCarthy (1960) summarised the tools of marketing as the "marketing mix" – a categorisation of the tools that marketers use to achieve their goals. They listed them as the "4Ps" – product, price, promotion and place. Booms and Bitner (1980) and Grönroos (2006), among other scholars, have emphasised that more tools should be added, and some have suggested 7Ps, by adding "people", "process" and "physical evidence". Each of these categories contains several tools. In this vein, Håkansson and Snehota (1989), Grönroos (2006), Sheth and Parvatiyar (1995), and Johanson and Vahlne (2011) criticised previous marketing theory and practice for emphasising "transactions" instead of "relationships". They implied that, based on the old marketing mix approach, companies were too fixated on their competitiveness and profits to the detriment of the purchaser and other parties. Instead, they proposed that companies should consider mutual benefits, thus assuming the interests of the other parties in the market. The era of "relationship marketing" was, therefore, highlighted, and a "paradigm shift" was suggested for marketing (Grönroos, 2006; Sheth & Parvatiyar, 1995). Since then, academia and industry practice have widened the definition and approach to marketing, as emphasised in the previous sections.

The paradigm shift was aided by the advent of computer power and communication technologies, leading marketers to build databases of customers and apply relationship marketing through loyal customer programmes. The massive developments in communication and digital technologies have given marketers new ways to communicate and reach their publics (Debnath et al., 2016; Sota et al., 2018). Social media has provided new vast platforms for companies and organisations to reach and be reached by their publics (Agnihotri et al., 2016). User-generated content and social media allow other parties in the market to provide their experiences of a company in the market and for the company to reach a broader range of market actors (Owusu et al., 2016). We are now in the era of digital marketing and globalisation with vast possibilities but also dangers for the B2B company.

Another approach to the content and functions of marketing is summarised in the five "philosophies" or "concepts" of marketing (Kotler & Armstrong, 2010): the marketing concept, the production concept, the product concept, the selling concept and the societal marketing concept. While the marketing concept was seen as the foundational concept for marketing because it emphasises competitiveness and success, the societal marketing concept is currently seen as equally important as it highlights what value companies bring to society. We will discuss these concepts of marketing concerning B2B further in the chapters of this book.

In the midst of the above, concerns about environmental degradation and corporate social responsibilities are adding new demands on B2B companies and organisations (Cheng & Sheu, 2012; Kotler, 2011). Companies are being asked to support fair trade, responsible consumption or "demarketing" (Kotler, 2018; Kotler & Levy, 1971). Some of these demands are made by non-profit organisations and governments and meant to change how for-profit companies do their marketing.

The most recent crisis (the health pandemic, Covid-19) has thrown local and global markets into serious difficulties while also opening up opportunities in the use of digital technologies (Ratten, 2020). While sudden political, social, natural and health crises and pandemics are not new, the Covid-19 pandemic is relatively unique and is having severe unexpected effects on business all over the world, particularly on service industries and supply chains (Kabadayi et al., 2020; Jiang & Wen, 2020). However, various strategies are suggested for firms to manage it and for researchers to provide management solutions to the emerging problems (Craighead et al., 2020; Finsterwalder & Kuppelwieser, 2020; Moosmayer & Davis, 2016; Wenzel et al., 2020). We are, thus, in an era of more significant challenges, complexities and potentials. What that will mean for the practice and science of marketing remains to be seen.

Conclusion

The practice and theory of marketing have evolved from a transaction-oriented approach, and a focus on the marketer's profit-making, to a relationship and mutual value-oriented approach. Marketing is undertaken not only in for-profit companies but also organisations and institutions that were not initially established to make profits. Therefore, the concepts of mutual value and win-win relationships are considered more encompassing for today's marketing thought and practice.

A focus on mutual value and win-win relationships is regarded as a better approach, even for for-profit companies. According to B2B researchers, these practices and concepts have existed in B2B for a long time. Thus, B2B research and practice have learnt from and contributed to the evolution of general marketing thought.

The evolution of marketing thought and practice shows that it is essential for B2B researchers and practitioners to recognise the broadness and complexity of marketing and not to reduce it to "sales" or "advertising" alone as the term tends to be used in everyday language. Furthermore, new unexpected challenges like the Covid-19 pandemic can disable firm strategies and relationships, and require a dynamic new approach to survive.

Marketing management is, therefore, a complex, multifunctional and multi-tasking set of activities and processes for achieving a company's or organisation's value objectives or goals. On the whole, as the definitions above show, marketing involves many activities internally within the firm and externally concerning the market where there are various "…customers, clients, partners, and society at large" (American Marketing Association, 2017). This generic characterisation is suitable for both B2B and B2C marketing.

In the following chapters, we will discuss further the concepts described above, developments concerning the B2B market and how B2B companies can apply them to improve their competitiveness.

Part 1 helps the reader to gain a deep understanding of the characteristics of the B2B market. It consists of Chapters 1 and 2. Chapter 1 covers the features of the B2B market using the established concepts of marketing, and Chapter 2 covers concepts of strategy and how to develop a competitive strategy in the B2B market. The chapter ends with a description of aspects of B2B markets in four African countries. Each chapter ends with an African case study.

Part 2 covers marketing and purchasing strategies in the B2B market. It consists of Chapters 3–5. Chapter 3 covers the marketing mix strategies for the B2B organisation. Chapter 4 covers specifically selling strategy of the marketing organisation, while Chapter 5 deals with the buying strategies of the purchasing organisation. Each chapter ends with an African case study.

Part 3 discusses aspects of the B2B market that are important to creating competitive niches. It consists of Chapters 6–9. Chapter 6 covers strategies of business services, Chapter 7 covers supply chains and sourcing strategies, and Chapter 8 covers strategy for systems and project business. Chapter 9 ends the section by covering the roles and characteristics of governments, institutions and non-business actors in B2B. Each chapter ends with an African case study.

Part 4 focuses on collaborative strategies and relationship management in the B2B market. It includes Chapters 10–12. Chapter 10 deals with forms of strategic relationships and governance structures in the B2B market. Chapter 11 focuses on how to develop collaborative relationships between buyers and sellers in the African B2B market. Chapter 12 focuses on positioning, brand-building and creating loyalty in the African B2B context. Each chapter ends with an African case study.

Part 5 focuses on capacity development of B2B organisations in Africa. It consists of Chapter 13 that focuses on how to develop sales and marketing capability in the African B2B context.

Part 6 covers emerging issues in B2B marketing. It consists of Chapter 14 which covers the evolution and impact of globalisation, big data and strategies of servitisation and value co-creation in African B2B markets. This book concludes with a summary of the evolution of African B2B markets, relevant developments in the African and global economies, and strategies for successfully competing locally and internationally.

References

Agnihotri, R., Dingus, R., Hu, M. Y., & Krush, M. T. (2016). Social media: Influencing customer satisfaction in B2B sales. *Industrial Marketing Management*, 53, 172–180.

Anderson, J. C., Håkansson, H., & Johanson, J. (1994). Dyadic business relationships within a business network context. *Journal of Marketing*, 58(4), 1–15.

Borden, N. H. (1964). The concept of the marketing mix. *Journal of Advertising Research*, 4(2), 2–7.

Booms, B. H., & Bitner, B. J. (1980). Marketing strategies and organisation structures for service firms. In W. R. George & Donnelly, J. (Eds.), *Marketing of Services* (pp. 47–51). American Marketing Association, Chicago.

Cheng, J. H., & Sheu, J. B. (2012). Inter-organisational relationships and strategy quality in green supply chains: Moderated by opportunistic behavior and dysfunctional conflict. *Industrial Marketing Management*, 41(4), 563–572.

Craighead, C. W., Ketchen Jr, D. J., & Darby, J. L. (2020). Pandemics and supply chain management research: Toward a theoretical toolbox. *Decision Sciences*, 51(4), 838–866.

Dadzie, K. Q., Johnston, W. J., Pels, J. (2008). Business-to-business marketing practices in West Africa, Argentina and the United States. *Journal of Business & Industrial Marketing* 23(2):115–123.

Debnath, R., Datta, B., & Mukhopadhyay, S. (2016). Customer relationship management theory and research in the new millennium: Directions for future research. *Journal of Relationship Marketing*, 15(4), 299–325.

Finsterwalder, J., & Kuppelwieser, V. G. (2020). Equilibrating resources and challenges during crises: A framework for service ecosystem well-being. *Journal of Service Management*, 31(6), 1061–1069.

Fox, K. F., & Kotler, P. (1980). The marketing of social causes: The first 10 years. *Journal of Marketing*, 44(4), 24–33.

Furrer, O., Kerguignas, J. Y., Delcourt, C., & Gremler, D. D. (2020). Twenty-seven years of service research: A literature review and research agenda. *Journal of Services Marketing*, 34(3), 299–316.

Grönroos, C. (1994). Quo Vadis, marketing? Toward a relationship marketing paradigm. *Journal of Marketing Management*, 10(5), 347–360.

Grönroos, C. (2006). On defining marketing: Finding a new roadmap for marketing. *Marketing Theory*, 6(4), 395–417.

Grönroos, C. (2017a). Relationship marketing readiness: Theoretical background and measurement directions. *Journal of Services Marketing*, 31(3), 218–225.

Grönroos, C. (2017b). On value and value creation in service: A management perspective. *Journal of Creating Value*, 3(2), 125–141.

Hadjikhani, A., & LaPlaca, P. (2013). Development of B2B marketing theory. *Industrial Marketing Management*, 42(3), 294–305.

Håkansson, H., & Snehota, I. (1989). No business is an island: The network concept of business strategy. *Scandinavian Journal of Management*, 5(3), 187–200.

Holm, D. B., Eriksson, K., & Johanson, J. (1999). Creating value through mutual commitment to business network relationships. *Strategic Management Journal*, 20(5), 467–486.

Johanson, J., & Vahlne, J. E. (2011). Markets as networks: Implications for strategy-making. *Journal of the Academy of Marketing Science*, 39(4), 484–491.

Jiang, Y., & Wen, J. (2020). Effects of COVID-19 on hotel marketing and management: A perspective article. *International Journal of Contemporary Hospitality Management*, 32(8), 2563–2573.

Johanson, J., & Mattsson, L. G. (1987). Interorganizational relations in industrial systems: A network approach compared with the transaction-cost approach. *International Studies of Management & Organization*, 17(1), 34–48.

Kabadayi, S., O'Connor, G. E., & Tuzovic, S. (2020). The impact of coronavirus on service ecosystems as service mega-disruptions. *Journal of Services Marketing*, 34(7), 909–920.

Karjalainen & Salmi (2013). Continental differences in purchasing strategies and tools. *International Business Review* 22, 112–125.

Keränen, J., & Liozu, S. (2020). Value champions in business markets: Four role configurations. *Industrial Marketing Management*, 85, 84–96.

Kotler, P. (2011). Reinventing marketing to manage the environmental imperative. *Journal of Marketing*, 75(4), 132–135.

Kotler, P. (2017). Philip Kotler: Some of my adventures in marketing. *Journal of Historical Research in Marketing*, 9(2), 118–126.

Kotler, P. (2018). Why broadened marketing has enriched marketing. *AMS Review*, 8(1–2), 20–22.

Kotler, P., & Armstrong, G. (2010). *Principles of marketing*. Pearson Education, London.

Kotler, P., & Levy, S. J. (1969). Broadening the concept of marketing. *Journal of Marketing*, 33(1), 10–15.

Kotler, P., & Levy, S. J. (1971). Water resources sector strategy: Strategic directions for World Bank Engagement.

Laric, M. V. (1980). Pricing strategies in industrial markets. *European Journal of Marketing*. 14, 303–321.

Mahajan, G. (2017). Value dominant logic. *Journal of Creating Value*, 3(2), 217–235.

Mattsson, L. G. (1973). Systems selling as a strategy on industrial markets. *Industrial Marketing Management*, 3(2), 107–120.

Mattsson, L. G. (1997). "Relationship marketing" and the "markets-as-networks approach": A comparative analysis of two evolving streams of research. *Journal of Marketing Management*, 13(5), 447–461.

Mattsson, L. G. (1995). Firms, "Megaorganizations" and markets: A network view. *Journal of Institutional and Theoretical Economics (JITE)/Zeitschrift für die gesamte Staatswissenschaft*, 151(4), 760–766.

McCarthy, E. J. (1960). *Basic marketing: A managerial approach* (revised edition). Richard D. Irwin, Homewood, IL.

Möller, K. (2013). Theory map of business marketing: Relationships and networks perspectives. *Industrial Marketing Management*, 42(3), 324–335.

Moosmayer, D. C., & Davis, S. M. (2016). Staking cosmopolitan claims: How firms and NGOs talk about supply chain responsibility. *Journal of Business Ethics*, 135(3), 403–417.

Oguji, N., & Owusu, R. (2014). Africa a source location. Literature review and implications. *International Journal of Emerging Markets*, 9(3), July 2014, 424–438.

Oguji, N., Degbey, W. Y., & Owusu R. A. (2021). International joint ventures research on Africa: A systematic literature review, propositions, and contextualization. *Thunderbird International Business Review*, 63(1), 11–26. https://onlinelibrary-wiley-com.proxy.lnu.se/doi/epdf/10.1002/tie.21993.

Owusu, R. A., Mutshinda, C. M., Antai, I., Dadzie, K. Q., & Winston, E. M. (2016). Which UGC features drive web purchase intent? A spike-and-slab Bayesian Variable Selection Approach. *Internet Research*, 26(1), 22–37.

Page, A. L., & Siemplenski, M. (1983). Product systems marketing. *Industrial Marketing Management*, 12(2), 89–99.

Parasuraman, A., Berry, L., & Zeithaml, V. (2002). Refinement and reassessment of the SERVQUAL scale. *Journal of Retailing*, 67(4), 114–139.

Rao, S., & Rabino, S. (1980). Product-market strategies in the minicomputer industry. *Industrial Marketing Management*, 9(4), 325–330.

Ratten, V. (2020). Coronavirus and international business: An entrepreneurial ecosystem perspective. *Thunderbird International Business Review*, 62(5), 629–634.

Sheth, J. N., & Parvatiyar, A. (1995). The evolution of relationship marketing. *International Business Review*, 4(4), 397–418.

Sota, S., Chaudhry, H., Chamaria, A., & Chauhan, A. (2018). Customer relationship management research from 2007 to 2016: An academic literature review. *Journal of Relationship Marketing*, 17(4), 277–291.

Vargo, S. L., & Lusch, R. F. (2008). From goods to service (s): Divergences and convergences of logics. *Industrial Marketing Management, 37*(3), 254–259.

Vargo, S. L., Lusch, R. F., Akaka, M. A., & He, Y. (2020). Service-dominant logic. In *The Routledge Handbook of service research insights and ideas* (pp. 3–23). Routledge, Abington.

Wenzel, M., Stanske, S., & Lieberman, M. B. (2020). Strategic responses to crisis. *Strategic Management Journal*, 36(2), 216–234.

Zeithaml, V. A., Bitner, M. J., & Gremler, D. D. (2018). *Services marketing: Integrating customer focus across the firm*. McGraw-Hill Education, New York.

American Marketing Association (2017). Retrieved August 8, 2020, from https://www.ama.org/the-definition-of-marketing/.

CHARACTERISTICS OF THE BUSINESS-TO-BUSINESS MARKET

1

Introduction and Learning Goals

In Part 1, we will describe the characteristics of the business-to-business (B2B) market and explain the foundational strategies and philosophies of marketing as they apply to the B2B sphere. Each chapter ends with an African case study.

Chapter 1

The Business-to-Business Market

INTRODUCTION AND OBJECTIVES

In this chapter, we will define and describe the business-to-business (B2B) market, the differences between B2B and the business-to-consumer (B2C) markets, and the parties in the market.

At the end of this chapter, the reader will understand the following:

■ The characteristics of the B2B market
■ Core marketing concepts in the B2B context
■ The different parties involved in the B2B market and their roles in the market
■ Similarities and differences between B2B and B2C marketing.

1.1 What Is Business-to-Business Marketing?

Following the definition of marketing by the American Marketing Association (AMA) mentioned in the introduction, B2B marketing can be defined as "the activity, set of institutions, and processes for creating, communicating, delivering, and exchanging offerings that have value for *business-to-business* customers, clients, partners, and society at large". Paraphrasing the relationship marketing paradigm, B2B marketing can be defined as the development, management and maintenance of interactions, relationships and networks between companies and organisations (see Hadjikhani & LaPlaca, 2013). Thus, B2B marketing includes various aspects of the functions and behaviours of companies, organisations and institutions that are actors in the business market. All these actors undertake B2B marketing in multiple ways both internally and externally towards "B2B suppliers, customers, clients, partners and society at large". In this book, our emphasis is the inter-organisational aspect that is the relationships with other parties. We will only briefly, at times, analyse the actors, activities and resources used internally to achieve the inter-organisational value creation and exchange.

In the following section, we will summarise how B2B marketing is done, using the extended marketing mix ("7Ps"), and the philosophies of marketing (see Ellis, 2010; Ford et al., 2011; Grönroos, 2017, 2006, 1994; Johanson & Vahlne, 2011; Kotler & Armstrong, 2010).

1.1.1 What Are the Key Components of Business-to-Business Marketing?

In the following two sections we describe the key components of B2B marketing using the marketing mix factors and the philosophies or concepts of marketing.

1.1.2 Marketing Mix Factors in Business-to-Business Marketing

Product: There are several aspects of the product in general – quality, innovation, features, durability, goods, services, etc. (Kotler & Armstrong, 2010). Companies and organisations have a product or service which they sell/provide/offer to and buy/demand/need from other companies. For example, the South African power production company ESKOM produces electrical power, heating and energy that it supplies to companies and organisations in South Africa and other neighbouring countries. ESKOM builds various power production facilities, transformer stations, connection lines and software to ensure that it can supply power to government departments, factories, office complexes, universities, etc. The company plans its power production to ensure a right mix of different production sources – coal, nuclear, solar, wind, etc. As power demand grows and ESKOM has to deal with the challenges and requirements of environmental degradation, it might undertake product innovation – e.g. innovate more efficient solar, wind and geothermal energy technologies.

On the other hand, ESKOM purchases products that go into its production. It purchases technologies, combinations of products and services (systems) that go into its power production (e.g. transformer stations), and projects (full power production stations purchased from another company that plans, builds and delivers them as complete functioning facilities). Product strategies will be discussed in more detail in Chapter 3.

Price: The aspect of the price includes the quoted price of a product, discounts and credit terms (Kotler & Armstrong, 2010). The Kenyan telecommunications company SAFARICOM sells mobile communication, digital communication, and related products and services to other companies and organisations. As a private company, it may have to pay dividends to its owners so that they continue to invest in the company. To maintain and raise its share price, it cannot continue to lose money forever. Thus, it must break even, which means charging its customers at least to cover its cost or make profits, which means charging prices to provide a margin above its costs. While being considered a leading telecommunications company, it has current and potential competitors. Thus, while SAFARICOM must charge a price as to break even or make profits, it also has to match the prices of competitors. It might consider older customers for discounts, and new customers for entry prices to get them to experience the company's products for the first time. It might provide payment periods that will enable the customers to receive products and pay later. SAFARICOM, on its part, buys equipment (systems) from suppliers like SAMSUNG and networks in the form of projects from suppliers like ERICSSON, NOKIA or HUAWEI. The company's pricing decision is, thus, complex and has to take account of a myriad of factors and parties that impact its market. Pricing strategies will be discussed in more detail in Chapter 3.

Place: The strategy of place is to determine where the company should locate its offices, sales and purchasing facilities to reach its customers in the best way (Kotler & Armstrong, 2010). The nature of place is changing with online access and modern communication technologies. As ECOBANK considers how it can better serve its business and organisational customers across the continent, it considers where it should set up new offices. This decision considers the cost of offices and the business prospects in different cities and countries of Africa, as well as the role of digital and mobile communication in providing access to its business and organisational customers. As banking is increasingly being done in Africa on mobile phones and online, the company could consider a mix of physical offices and online presence as well as applications and technologies that will enable business customers to choose to do business with the company safely and smoothly either online or by coming to the banking hall. Place strategies will be discussed in more detail in Chapter 3.

Promotion: This includes advertising, public relations, personal selling and sales promotion activities (Kotler & Armstrong, 2010). In 2017, former Gambian minister Momodou Sabally launched a consultancy company called Pen's Den Consulting. The question for such a company is how to advertise and publicise itself locally and internationally to companies, organisations, international multilateral organisations and governments, among others, to inform them of the company's services. Should the company depend mainly on the personal networks and public image of the founder, contact possible customers and partners by phone and email, or depend mostly on its online presence to spread the word about what it can offer and gain customers? Promotion strategies will be discussed in more detail in Chapter 3.

People: A company or organisation consists of people in different positions. The quality of staff, expertise, ability to deal with customers, ability to provide product and service quality, and exceeding customer expectations in interactions are vital for its competitiveness (Kotler & Armstrong, 2010). As EY expands its management consulting in Africa, it has to employ qualified, innovative and motivated staff to promote and sell its services to companies and governments. Some of these qualities are already available in the staff they employ, and others can be developed through training after employment. In the final analysis, the quality of the company's products and services will be achieved through the people who work for it. People strategies will be discussed in more detail in Chapter 3.

Process: How the company delivers its products and services to customers, how it is organised internally to achieve its marketing goals, how interactions and relationships are developed with its publics, are aspects of the process strategy (Kotler & Armstrong, 2010). Digitalisation has brought new possibilities to B2B processes, and B2B companies are fast adopting digital communications for managing their value creation processes. Process strategies will be discussed in more detail in Chapter 3.

Physical Evidence: The concept of physical evidence was developed, particularly concerning services. As discussed in Chapter 6, as a result of the intangibility and other characteristics of business services, marketers need to show evidence of the quality of the potential service and their ability to deliver the promise (Booms & Bitner, 1980; Grönroos, 2017; Kotler & Armstrong, 2010). Therefore, physical evidence is the ability to convince the purchaser that the marketer will provide the promised value. This is more important in B2B than B2C. As discussed in Chapter 8, many B2B sales are systems and projects, whose characteristics and quality cannot be shown in the initial negotiations but only promised. The B2B marketer shows "physical evidence" through reputation and references, among others (Salminen & Möller, 2006).

The 7Ps are integral parts of every B2B marketing organisation. Every B2B company has to have a product, price it, have selling points, promote it, have people/staff to deal with customers, and have a process for doing that. Institutions and organisations that are dealing with B2B companies have to implement similar strategies. What differentiates different B2B companies, institutions and organisations are the components of each part in the organisation's strategy. How much emphasis does a B2B company place on product, price, process, people, etc. that provide value to the customers and give it a competitive advantage, as compared to a government agency or organisation? Many industrial companies are known to concentrate on their product characteristics and believe that "a quality product sells itself". In that situation, they may not invest very much in process and people, for example. On the other hand, government institutions and organisations may be more concerned about their nearness to the public, and the services they provide than making profits. Therefore, they may invest more in product, place, people and process than price.

1.1.3 The Marketing Philosophies/Concepts in the Business-to-Business Marketing Context

The Marketing Concept: According to the marketing concept, companies would succeed best by meeting their customers' needs better than their competitors (Kotler & Armstrong, 2010). This requires that companies understand what their customers and other important actors want and provide these better than their competitors. This means that the customers are satisfied, and all aspects of the product, price, place, promotion, people and process are altogether better than their competitors. ECOBANK should ensure that the customers would not leave for competing banks as a result of the competitors offering better information, access, longer-term financial support, etc. Besides companies, ECOBANK has to deal with regulators, and they have to meet all requirements of the regulators. To implement the marketing concept, the company has to invest in its strategy to continuously understand the dynamics of the market, the moves of competitors and the demands of other parties in the business market. Winston and Dadzie (2002) studied to what extent "top managers" emphasise market orientation in Nigeria and Kenya. Their results indicated high management commitment to the marketing concept in both countries. However, the extent of commitment differed between locally owned (mainly African) and international firms as well as on the basis of the level of competition among the firms in the industry. On his part, Okoroafo (2004) found out that foreign businesses in sub-Saharan Africa practised higher market orientation than African businesses. However, their African competitors have realised the significance of customer-focused marketing and are adjusting to being able to compete better. Okoroafo advises that marketing orientation should be practised through the entire organisation. Staff who have direct links with clients should be motivated and trained adequately to implement the marketing concept.

The Production Concept: According to the production concept, B2B firms would invest in the quality of their production process. They would see that as the main factor to provide value to their customers and be competitive (Kotler & Armstrong, 2010). Thus, a company like Dangote Cement in Nigeria would invest in the quality of its production process, seeing that as most important to produce and supply quality cement to building contractors. Dangote Cement would believe that investing in the production process would give it the ability to compete better than some of the other concepts.

The Product Concept: According to the product concept, the B2B company would invest in innovating and providing the market new products and offers. They would look beyond current products and try to fill market needs by finding new products and services or developing new feature of products that customers demand (Kotler & Armstrong, 2010). A financial services company would invest in providing new investment and banking services for its corporate clients. The aim would be to stay ahead of the competition, gain new corporate customers and keep old customers satisfied. They would invest in relevant product innovation strategies, seeing them as their panacea to success.

The Selling Concept: According to the selling concept, the B2B company would invest in its selling processes and strategies. The company would see the selling strategies as the best way to gain customers, keep them and provide value to the market (Kotler & Armstrong, 2010). Training and investing in the sales force and promotion strategies would be seen as the best way to beat the competition.

The Societal Marketing Concept: According to the societal marketing concept, the B2B company should consider the needs of society as essential, even while it pursues its profit objectives (Kotler & Armstrong, 2010). The needs of society have been summarised, for example, as a corporate social responsibility (CSR). Recently, environmental degradation has raised concerns about the effect of industrial companies on society. Which timber trees should timber companies harvest in Gabon and Congo, and in which forests (EIA, 2019)? How can mining companies in Africa ensure that their mining activities do not destroy the environment? What should they do to ensure that they give back to society and that their host communities are not alienated? How much should they give back to society in terms of taxes and support for poor communities? Such issues are becoming increasingly important.

The marketing concept was the first concept that was formulated, and it was meant to encompass the total objectives and processes of marketing. Therefore, in many senses, the other concepts emphasise different aspects of the marketing concept. B2B companies may concentrate on the marketing concept precisely or combinations of the other concepts. For example, Dangote Cement has an overall strategy of producing cement of the right quality and price, and promoting its brand and product to provide value and satisfaction to contractors and builders. The company develops product characteristics that meet African needs (product concept) and ensures quality in production (production concept). It is building factories in various African countries and recruiting traders to sell its products all over Africa; promoting its products through advertising and corporate branding; and providing competitive prices, discounts and payment periods to contractors (selling concept). Furthermore, it makes contributions to society in the form of philanthropies and reducing dangerous emissions (societal marketing concept). Conversely, there are other B2B manufacturing companies known for concentrating on their engineering (production concept) and technical product quality dimensions (product concept), but not selling or societal marketing concepts because they believe that "a quality product sells itself".

(For more on the marketing philosophies described above, see Kotler & Armstrong, 2010).

1.2 Parties in the Business-to-Business Market

While we use the term "business to business" (B2B), the business market includes both for-profit and non-profit organisations. As we stated in the introduction, marketing is defined broadly. Furthermore, the marketing function of institutions, public organisations and non-profit organisations has been emphasised by the definition of marketing by the AMA and by marketing authorities like Kotler (2018, 2011), Fox and Kotler (1980), and Kotler and Levy (1969). In the B2B literature, understanding the nature of different types of B2B actors is emphasised as crucial for developing a strategy towards them (Ellis, 2010; Ford et al., 2011; Hadjikhani & Thilenius, 2005). In the following, we will classify parties in the business market using their profit, funding sources and their type of production status.

1.2.1 Profit/Funding Status

On the bases of their profit/funding status, we can differentiate between business actors, non-business actors, and political or institutional actors.

Business actors are B2B companies whose objective is profits. Their owners and financiers expect not just to cover their costs, but to make profits. Profits are an opportunity cost for their investments because the owners could have invested in other companies or assets that would increase in value and give them returns. Some owners may have a long-term perspective and may take losses in the short term, but must make profits in the long term. The reality for a business actor is that a lack of profit will reduce its share prices, which will reduce the value of the company and the likelihood of new investments in the long run, as owners and shareholders will sell off their shares to reduce their losses. Competitors can easily buy up the company if its share value falls too low. Business actors might also have taken loans and have to pay back the loan plus interest. Therefore, the behaviour of business actors must be profit-oriented in the long term. In order to reach their objectives and be competitive, companies like Oando and Arik Air of Nigeria, Safaricom of Kenya, and Sasol and Shoprite Holdings of South Africa must generally use profit-oriented strategies in their dealings with other business parties. However, they have to deal with other parties in the business market, including non-business and institutional actors. Therefore, their profit-oriented strategies have to be altered by consideration of the objectives of the other types of actors. The critical question is, what is the best overall strategic approach to achieve its profit objectives? Our summarised answer from our research and consulting is that the B2B company should use a mix of transactional and relationship strategies based on its combination of marketing mix and marketing philosophy concepts that suit its type of business, its national and international business environment. We will discuss these critical questions more extensively in the coming chapters.

Non-business actors are parties that are active in business markets but have non-profit objectives. They are non-governmental organisations and idealistic organisations that want to impact how B2B companies achieve their goals (Hadjikhani & Thilenius, 2005). The Environmental Investigations Agency (EIA), an NGO, recently published a report on illegal harvesting and trade in timber in Congo and Gabon. The report led the Government of Gabon to take steps to streamline the timber export sector. The work of EIA affects companies in the timber and natural resources industry. Greenpeace is known all over the world, and among its objectives is to impact how companies do business in Africa (https://www.greenpeace.org/africa/en/). Many small and local NGOs exist in African countries, and they interact with and impact businesses, e.g. mining companies in their localities. Some of these have been established to support development in their village, local council or region (e.g. Apire Town Development Committee in Ghana); to support other development objectives like Green Cameroon; or even to establish ethnic-based associations to support the development of their areas like the Ogoni Youth Federation in Nigeria. NGOs may be non-political or political, and their aims are varied. These NGOs may be financed by members' fees, local and foreign donations and, sometimes, financial support from businesses that are active locally or even outside the region to meet their CSR objectives. Firms have to relate to these non-business actors sometimes in buying or selling situations, but more often in negotiations, legitimacy, legal and corporate reputation issues. (See Chapter 9 for details on the nature and role of non-business actors in B2B.)

The third type of party in the business market is the **institutional or political actor**. These are often based on the significant roles of every government – legislative, supervisory and development of the country. Government agencies, departments and authorities are, thus, established that make business rules, supervise and participate in business activities to ensure development. For example, recently, as many African countries liberalised their economics and aimed at economic growth, they set up new agencies, companies and authorities to streamline natural resource exploration and extraction. For example, the Government of Ghana set up the Ghana

National Petroleum Commission (GNPC) in 2011 when it became clear that new technologies could find and exploit hydrocarbon resources in the country. Thus, the GNPC's objective is to regulate, manage and coordinate the upstream hydrocarbon sector. Similar regulatory authorities exist in Ivory Coast, Nigeria, Kenya, Mozambique, Angola, etc. Government agencies and authorities with political and legislative functions like ministries, police, military and the judiciary are different in their statuses, powers and behaviours from agencies like the GNPC. Full governmental institutions like the Ministry of Trade, Industry and Investment in Tanzania, and the South African Defence Forces that have political purposes are different from other institutions and termed political actors/institutions. There are other government or publicly established or funded agencies, parastatal companies and government authorities that are not established to make a profit but are run according to some level of business principles, in order to bring in some revenue for their funding. Such institutional actors interact with businesses with some business principles in negotiations, oversight, procurement and product/service provision (see also Jansson, 2020; Meyer & Peng, 2016, 2005; North, 1990, 2005; Scott, 1995; Williamson, 2000). (See Chapter 9 for details on the nature and role of institutional and political actors in B2B.)

1.2.2 Are Government-Owned Companies Business or Institutional/Political Actors?

In many African countries, the government owns companies in infrastructure-related areas, production or other areas considered essential to the economy. Governments also invest in companies in sectors that are deemed critical for national ownership, or to make profits to contribute to government revenues, e.g. mining and oil exploitation in most African countries. In some countries, government companies exist in purely business areas like factories. Some government companies in the utilities and infrastructure sectors were inherited from the colonial governments. In some other countries, there was a socialist approach, which believed that the government should own the major companies to ensure economic development and social justice, e.g. Tanzania and Zambia. Recently, many African countries have sold the whole or parts of government companies to divest and liberalise the economy. Whether these kinds of companies and parastatals that work in the purely business sectors or even government authorities like the Rwanda Housing Authority should be classified as business or institutional/political actors are not precise. However, the reality of these government-owned companies/parastatals is that they have some power/backing of a government that business actors have to take into account when dealing with them. In the final analysis, what we want to communicate in this book is how to relate to and work with various parties in the business market. Therefore, it is vital to correctly strategise when dealing with government-owned companies/parastatals or purely institutional/political actors, as their objectives and mode of working will be different. (See Chapter 9 for details on the nature and role of institutional actors in B2B.)

1.3 Functions or Types of Business-to-Business Producers

1.3.1 Who Are Producers?

What do we mean by B2B production and who are B2B producers? As discussed in the introduction, marketing science defines production as the provision of value that can be exchanged.

Production or products are not only tangible, that is producing a computer, but also intangible, for example, the software or codes that allow the computer to run; transporting, storing, selling and servicing the computer. Therefore, the term "product" represents both goods and services. It is, however, useful to classify different types of producers because their functions or type of production impacts their strategies, which we will discuss in more detail later in this book. We should note, however, that many marketing authors use the terms "goods and services" and "products and services" to differentiate between physical products and services.

Manufacturers are companies that produce value through some physical manufacturing or factory processes. These are traditional industrial firms like the Tema Cocoa Processing Factory in Ghana, which produces cocoa paste and chocolates, or the Zambian government-owned Indeni Oil Refinery for which the Zambian government was seeking private sector participation in 2019.

Intermediaries (middlemen, distributors, transporters, etc.) are companies that enable value creation between two or more B2B companies or represent B2B companies in different markets. They are often criticised for taking fees and sometimes considered as not "producers". However, they are often indispensable for ensuring business deals. There are many types of intermediaries depending on the risk they take and the kind of commission/fees they take. They make it easier for other B2B parties by undertaking the contacts, representation and negotiation on the other parties' behalf, assuring either or both parties of the authenticity of the other party and the deal, and getting a fee for their work. They are often experts in the market, e.g. foreign markets. **Distributors** are also middlemen, and they include **wholesalers**, **agents** and **retailers**. They move products from sellers to buyers; they stock products and add value through repackaging, rebranding and adding characteristics that are valuable for specific markets.

Consultants provide various types of advice and ideas to enable companies and organisations to achieve their objectives. They range from managerial, technological, through financial to legal consultancy. Consultants develop expertise in the field, and while, like middlemen, they are often criticised as not being "producers", they are often invaluable for many B2B companies at many stages of their value creation processes.

Bankers and financiers provide banking and financial advice to B2B companies. They enable B2B companies to invest, to plan financially and to get support to overcome periods of low revenues. On the other hand, when companies lose the trust of bankers and financiers, they could be declared bankrupt, which often ends their business.

Private institutions and not-for-profit organisations play "business" roles or are able to influence the B2B company. Local African NGOs are widespread and have objectives of promoting the development of their areas and supporting other causes. They lobby and interact with local companies and central authorities to influence the work of the companies in various ways. Mining and oil extraction companies that disregard these groups and the welfare of local communities may incur the negative actions of these parties. The case of Shell Oil Company in Eastern Nigeria is a well-known example of infamy of a rich multinational company (Reuters, 2018).

Public institutions as regulators and legislators influence and deal with B2B companies in (1) business deals, e.g. buying supplies of equipment and technology for government departments and agencies, or buying infrastructural services and technologies for power stations, road building, etc.; and (2) regulation and supervision of B2B companies, e.g. making and implementing rules for how companies treat their waste, or approval of products by, for example, the Medicines Control Authority of Zimbabwe. Companies have to communicate, negotiate and maintain legally acceptable relations with these institutions as an integral part of their business. (See Chapter 9 for details on the nature and role of institutional actors in B2B.)

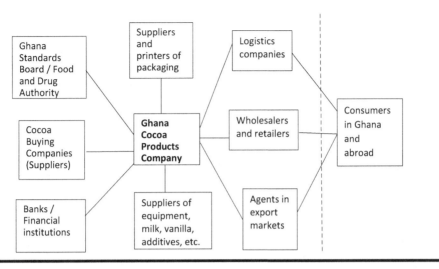

Figure 1.1   The B2B market relationships of Ghana Cocoa Products Company (CPC).

Figure 1.1 illustrates the parties in the business market on the left side exemplified with the Cocoa Processing Company (CPC) located in Tema, Ghana (https://www.goldentreeghana. com/). The company has to deal with other types of B2B companies and other parties in the B2B market to produce and get its products to the final consumer. The company does not own cocoa farms and is, therefore, dependent on the supply of quality cocoa from buying agents. It has to source equipment, milk and additives from other manufacturers. Public institutions, like the Food and Drug Authority, exist nationally and internationally to grant the company licenses and approve its products. To reach the final consumer, it depends on transporters, distributors and foreign agents. Thus, successful management of the company demands more than managing its internal staff, production and product development. The other parties are critical to its success. In the subsequent chapters, we will further discuss the various aspects of marketing relationships and strategies with other B2B parties.

1.4 Similarities and Differences between Business Marketing and Consumer Marketing

Figure 1.1 shows the boundaries of business marketing (B2B) and consumer marketing (B2C). While B2B is about marketing activities with other parties in the business market, B2C is about marketing activities with the consumer, i.e. the individual who buys products and services for consumption.

1.4.1 Companies and Organisations as Opposed to Individual Consumers

The fact that the parties in B2B are companies and organisations and not individual consumers changes their buying and selling behaviours in many ways. While companies and organisations may also make purchases for their final use, e.g. a government agency buying fruits and beverages for the daily use of their staff, their buying behaviour is fundamentally different from that of individuals or families. While organisations are run by people who undertake the negotiation, communication, buying or selling, the purchasing manager is bound by the rules of his employer. He does not pay for purchases from his income, unlike what he might do for his family. As a result, the processes of search, negotiation and closing the deal are different.

1.4.2 Professional Buyers and Sellers and Many Actors Involved in a Firm's Purchases

Due to the strategic and managerial structures and processes of firms and organisations, B2B marketing and purchasing are often carried out by trained and experienced professionals or those working in the marketing function. They have different names in companies and organisations like sales department, marketing department, purchasing department, supply chain department, corporate communications, etc. As a result, the marketing processes are planned and followed up through established and documented procedures by staff professionally trained for those tasks. The level of interaction, intensity and bureaucracy of the organisational marketing process varies with the type of buying or selling, e.g. whether a repeat buying from a previous supplier or project buying from a new project marketer. However, as Johnston and Bonoma (1981, p. 143) proposed, organisational buying is done by a "buying centre" consisting of many groups and levels of influences and staff in the organisation (see also Johnston & Lewin, 1996; Owusu & Welch, 2007). Negotiations with, buying from, and selling to suppliers and clients follow the organisation's strategy and is accountable to senior managers, owners, or boards of companies and organisations. Therefore, the nature of B2B marketing differs vastly from B2C, as the B2C individual or family decide and take responsibility for their own decisions. Emotional and "irrational" buying is a characteristic of consumer behaviour and not of B2B.

1.4.3 Fewer Buyers and Fewer Sellers

In contrast to the large number of potential customers for B2C, B2B has innately a much smaller number of buyers and sellers. For example, although Africa's arguably best airline, Ethiopian Airlines, has millions of possible B2C customers and tens of thousands in their frequent flier lists, their B2B sales have a much smaller number of companies and organisations. This means that Ethiopian Airlines can develop closer and more intense relationships with companies that buy flights for their staff than for an individual customer who flies to Addis Ababa once every few years. A department store has thousands of customers coming in every day but a much smaller number of companies and organisations that take supplies of fruit and food packages for their staff. The department store can employ key account managers to manage relationships with some large B2B buyers and groups of buyers. The B2B relationships can, therefore, be closer and be managed more carefully compared to B2C relationships.

1.4.4 Large Amounts Bought and Sold at the Same Time

Due to their budget, their professional/business approach, strategic and planning perspectives, and the small number of buyers and sellers, organisations buy and sell large amounts at a time. Even when organisations buy relatively routine items like fruits and beverages for their staff, they usually reach agreements for supply over a period, e.g. a year. Sellers to organisational buyers have fewer buyers than when they sell to consumers. This means that companies that are selling all or most of their products and services in the B2B market are often dependent on a much smaller number of buyers, and hence, even losing a single buyer may be the difference between success and failure. Small and medium-sized B2B companies may be manufacturing or servicing specific components within a supply chain and, thus, dependent on very few buyers. In this situation, keeping each account is critical. Many selling firms, thus, employ key account managers, each of whom has a number of customers to manage and keep satisfied. Contract negotiation periods are, therefore, intense and critical as negotiations are undertaken over quality, price, service, delivery schedules, etc., all of which the seller has to get right in competition with other bidders.

1.4.5 *Close and Intense Interactions and Relationships*

Due to the need to negotiate technical, economic, logistics and other details, as well as the need for strategic planning, strong or long-term relationships between B2B companies are useful. Relationships provide trust and collaboration, which connects B2B parties into networks and supply chains; success for many B2B parties is based on relationships, networks and their supply chain. The Cocoa Products Company should build good relations with cocoa buying companies, which would also benefit from good relations with farmers. Downstream in the supply chain, the Cocoa Products Company should develop relationships with companies that use cocoa products as inputs, agents and grocery chains in the consumer countries. When such relationships work well, each point in the supply chain is dependent on the excellent work and trust of the other. The B2B side of the supply chain is also described as a network because it has no specific leader, and the companies are both independent and dependent on each other for their success. Increased competition, the complexity of products and globalisation have increased the importance of networks, as companies specialise in specific areas of competence and outsource the rest. Currently, some of the world's biggest companies like Apple and Amazon outsource a large part of their products and services, and their success depends on collaboration with their network partners. The world's leading companies plan their new product development with suppliers, sub-contractors and other network members to remain competitive. On the other hand, while outsourcing was a strategy from the design and innovation stage of Boeing's Dreamliner aircraft, it was blamed for the problems the plane faced with bad batteries (Washington Post, 2013). Therefore, as B2B networks get more complex, the performance of each member is critical for each other one.

1.4.6 *Project and System Purchases*

B2B parties often prefer to buy combinations of products, services, technologies and training as systems or project buying. This requires that the buyer and seller undertake intense and prolonged interactions to clarify what exact combination is needed and other aspects of the deal like supply, installation and payment schedules. Project business is also the purchase and sale of infrastructure solutions like road and power systems where many of the buyers are governments or government agencies. Due to the size of the purchase, and the technological, product and service complexities, they involve lengthy negotiations, long periods of delivery and construction, and new technologies and business environments that create unique challenges for both buyer and seller. They often involve sub-contractors, suppliers, consultants and government agencies in a temporary business network that has to be managed successfully (Owusu & Welch, 2007; Owusu, 2002). (See Chapter 8 for a detailed discussion of project and systems business.)

1.5 Conclusion

In this chapter, we have clarified what B2B marketing is, the different parties involved and the differences with B2C marketing. B2B marketing is about exchanging value with other B2B parties, but the modus operandi differs with different kinds of parties. We have applied the core concepts of marketing to create a background for the rest of the book in order to develop an understanding of successful B2B marketing in a more competitive global market. As we believe that Africa's development starts with business growth, B2B companies become the foundation of this growth as they occupy most of the value chain. To be competitive both locally and internationally, they should understand the type of parties they deal with and what strategies are required. In the following sections, we will delve in more detail into aspects of B2B marketing.

Case Study: Crispy Kreme of South Africa: A B2B or B2C Company?

Author: Dr Adele Berndt, Jönköping International Business School, Sweden.

For people from different parts of the world, there are many ideas about Americans and their lifestyle. If you were to ask people about Americans and their food preferences, they would identify burgers and other types of fast food, including doughnuts. In the USA, there is a general perception that the doughnut is a "patriotic sweet treat" yet changing food tastes means that it is also viewed as an indulgence. Despite this, there is an international market for doughnuts, and this includes South Africa (SA), which is one of Krispy Kreme's (KK) new markets. While SA is the initial entry point into Africa, developing the entry model will also impact their success in other parts of Africa. One critical decision is how to produce a quality product and then ensure it reaches the customer efficiently.

DOUGHNUTS IN AMERICA AND THE HISTORY OF KK

While reports suggest doughnuts were eaten by the Egyptians and Native American tribes in previous centuries, it was in the First World War that soldiers received them from volunteers. Upon returning home to the USA, it became a challenge to find them. Initially, doughnuts were made by hand, but their popularity led to the invention of machines to manufacture doughnuts more efficiently.

In 1937, Vernon Rudolph bought a yeast-raised doughnut recipe from a French chef and rented a building in Winston-Salem, NC, USA. He used this recipe to open a doughnut factory, initially selling them to grocery stores, but due to customer demand, these were sold through a serving window at their factory. The Original Glaze® doughnut became their signature product, and their bowtie logo was registered as a trademark in 1955.[1] By 2015, KK had over 1000 stores opened throughout the world, including Canada, the UK and South Africa. It is estimated that every day, KK makes about 5 million doughnuts that are retailed through these outlets.

KRISPY KREME (KK) IN SA

The decision was made to enter South Africa through KK Doughnuts SA (Pty) Ltd – their first entry into the African continent. Shareholders in this private company are Fournews (Pty) Ltd and

---

[1] https://www.krispykreme.co.uk/our-history (accessed 15 July 2019).

Table 1.1 Mission, Vision and Brand Positioning

Mission	To use our unlimited passion and knowledge to create a fun-filled magical experience, by serving desirable doughnuts and premium coffee at value for money and accessible to all
Vision	To be South Africa's favourite sweet treat destination while providing a joyful experience serving hand-crafted doughnuts, made fresh daily
Brand positioning	Hand-crafter moments for everyone

Source: **Krispy Kreme (2019).**

John & Gerry's Brands (Pty) Ltd who have previous food franchising experience with brands such as News Café, Smooch, Moyo and Café Fino.[2] Gerry Thomas is the CEO of KK Doughnuts SA (Pty) Ltd, and they are responsible for opening the required number of outlets, as agreed to in the master franchise as well as the development of the brand.[3]

This development includes the management of the existing stores (16) in SA as well as the opening of more stores.[4] In introducing this business into SA, a mission, vision and brand positioning was formulated, as reflected in Table 1.1. KK aims to enhance the lives of customers through their product which includes both doughnuts and beverages.[5]

THE BUSINESS OF DOUGHNUTS

There is a complex process that ensures KK can sell doughnuts and a wide range of suppliers and intermediaries in producing quality products.

THE PRODUCTION OF DOUGHNUTS

The first step in producing doughnuts is to prepare batches of doughnut mix (imported from the UK) according to the secret recipe (which includes yeast) to ensure that the doughnuts are light and puffy ("clouds of happiness"), as described on the KK website.[6] Once the dough is mixed, the dough needs to prove to so that it can rise, after which it is fried and glazed. The doughnuts are made fresh at the point of sales, and one store (the Rosebank store) has production capacity up to 1320 doughnuts per hour.[7] Another factory in Sandton can produce 3240 dozen doughnuts an hour, which serves as a distribution hub for other Gauteng stores and other retail partners.[8]

KK makes use of a hub and spoke system of production and distribution. The hub is responsible for the manufacturing of products which are then supplied to between five and ten stores. One

---

[2] Schroeder, E. (2015). Krispy Kreme to open 31 shops in South Africa, 19 May. *Food Business News.* https://www. foodbusinessnews.net/articles/6067-krispy-kreme-to-open-31-shops-in-south-africa (accessed 4 July 2019).

[3] Nedbank Franchising (2016). Make Krispy Kreme Happen, 1 September. https://www.entrepreneurmag.co.za/ advice/franchising/franchisee-advice/make-krispy-kreme-happen/.

[4] Anon (2019a). Businesstech. Krispy Kreme to launch in Cape Town 16 May. https://businesstech.co.za/news/ business/317368/krispy-kreme-to-launch-in-cape-town/ (accessed 4 July 2019).

[5] Anon (2019a), ibid.

[6] https://www.krispykreme.com/about (accessed 4 July 2019).

[7] Anon (2015). Businesstech. Krispy Kreme launches in South Africa: Everything you need to know, 25 November. https://businesstech.co.za/news/business/105185/krispy-kreme-launches-in-south-africa-everything-you-need-to-know/ (accessed 4 July 2019).

[8] Sanchez (2015).

such production hub is located in Linbro Park, Sandton. As KK expands, more of these systems will be needed to satisfy demand.

While KK is known for its glazed doughnuts, some product adaptations have been introduced into SA. The adaptions to the local market are seen with KK offering six doughnuts in SA that are not sold elsewhere, such as the milk tart and Bar One doughnuts.[9]

SUPPLIERS OF INGREDIENTS FOR KK

While KK imports the doughnut mix, other ingredients (such as those for the toppings) are sourced locally.[10] The suppliers of the ingredients in the UK are carefully selected due to their significance to the final product. For the toppings, using locally produced and sourced ingredients enables KK to not only support the local industry but also maximise their profits.[11] The choice of local suppliers is also due to the customisation of varieties to the SA market.

THE DISTRIBUTION OF DOUGHNUTS

KK's distribution strategy includes the development of their own stores where they can manage the customer experience as well as various partnerships with other organisations such as Pick n Pay, Total Bonjour & Engen Quickshops. In the case of the stores, these tend to be located in malls as the malls can provide the required foot traffic (foot count) that stores need to be profitable.[12] Providing the customer with ease to get the product is the reason for the partnerships. Fresh products are delivered once daily while still providing the anticipated product quality. In other markets, these partnerships account for up to 40% of KK's profits.[13]

It is possible to order online via their website, but there is a minimum order of 20 dozen boxes (or three cake stand packages). Furthermore, there is a lead time of 2 days (and an R350 delivery fee) to fill the order. Thus, this does not serve as a solution for the individual consumer wanting their doughnuts immediately.

RETAIL PARTNERS IN THE DISTRIBUTION OF DOUGHNUTS

All customers cannot get to one of their 19 KK retail stores[14] (located conveniently), which has contributed to the decision to use other retail intermediaries including Pick n Pay, Total Bonjour & Engen Quickshops. The nature of doughnuts is that they are often purchased as impulse products; thus, while they are getting their cars filled with fuel, they can buy some doughnuts. KK packages their products which are distributed to these "Doughnuts-On-The-Go" outlets, specifically petrol station forecourt stores and selected Pick n Pay stores which increases the accessibility to the product.[15]

[9] Anon (2019b). Businesstech. Krispy Kreme launches in South Africa: Everything you need to know, 25 November. https://businesstech.co.za/news/business/105185/krispy-kreme-launches-in-south-africa-everything-you-need-to-know/ (accessed 4 July 2019).

[10] Ibid.

[11] Krispy Kreme (2019). https://mediaupdate.co.za/marketing/135669/krispy-kreme-south-africa-set-for-expansions (accessed 15 July 2019).

[12] Sanchez, D. (2015). Lines out the Door as Krispy Kreme opens in South Africa. *The Moguldom Nation*, https://moguldom.com/107576/lines-out-the-door-as-krispy-kreme-opens-in-south-africa/ (accessed 4 July 2019).

[13] Anon (2018). Franchising: New on-the-go offering from Krispy Kreme. https://bizmag.co.za/franchising-new-on-the-go-offering-from-krispy-kreme/ (accessed 22 July 2019).

[14] Anon (2020). Krispy Kreme remains triumphant despite international brands taking strain in the South African market, 26 January. https://www.cbn.co.za/featured/krispy-kreme-remains-triumphant-despite-international-brands-taking-strain-in-the -south-african-market/ (accessed 2 February 2020).

[15] Ibid. (2020).

Petrol stations are owned by franchisees through agreements, and all franchisees are required to operate their businesses complying with the franchise agreement. Forecourt stores are known not only for their location but also for their operating hours, which is often 24 hours a day. Engen is a fuel brand that has the most significant footprint in South Africa, operating more than 1000 service stations, selling 25% of the fuel sold in SA and serving 143 million customers.[16] Engen is committed to satisfying customer needs and is always investigating new ways to grow their markets.

Another partnership is with NetFlorist, an online florist and gift store. Doughnuts can be ordered for occasions, but in this instance, it requires one-day lead time to ensure that doughnuts are freshly produced. There are a number of ordering restrictions with regard to assortment and quantity, and initially, it was also limited to the Johannesburg region.[17]

KK's as a Retailer

To be most satisfying, a doughnut needs a cup of coffee (or other drink), which explains the rest of the menu offering in KK stores. The company sells an assortment of hot and cold beverages such as coffees (lattes, cappuccino and teas) as well as specialist cold drinks known as chillers. This range includes Kremey Chillers (fruit and an indulgent selection) as well as frozen lemonades and iced lattes.

With KK being a premium brand, this is reflected in the price of their doughnuts. A single glazed doughnut costs R8.95, a dozen cost R89.95, and assorted doughnuts cost R10.95 for one or R99.95 for a dozen.

THE FUTURE

Gerry Thomas poured over the latest results and customer insights. Their operation in South Africa has made it to the top ten in the KK group after just 3 years.[18] Anyone would be satisfied. While the progress and future developments are fascinating, it is now time to focus on the next challenge ahead.

If KK is to be a success, they need to expand to other parts of SA and into the rest of Africa. This is going to require development in many different areas, including HR and developing production hubs to distribute the product in their many other outlets.

1.6 Questions

1. Is KK a B2B, B2C firm or both?
2. Comment on the importance of relationships with business partners in the development of their distribution strategy.
3. KK has implemented a network distribution system. Draw KK's supply chain/network and comment on the suitability of this form of distribution for doughnuts, especially for KK's proposed expansion into other African countries.
4. Comment on the potential conflict in the distribution channel between forecourt stores and KK's retail outlets.
5. What precisely is the B2B marketing decision facing KK as it attempts to expand into other African countries?

---

[16] Anon (2019c). Engen scoops 9th consecutive top brands win, 30 September. https://www.cbn.co.za/featured/engen-scoops-9th-consecutive-top-brands-win/ (accessed 2 February 2020).
[17] Anon (2017). Krispy Kreme SA partners with NetFlorist, 29 May. https://www.mediaupdate.co.za/marketing/135576/krispy-kreme-sa-partners-with-netflorist (accessed 2 February 2020).
[18] Ibid.

References

Booms, B. H., & Bitner, B. J. (1980). Marketing strategies and organisation structures for service firms. In J. Donnelly, & W. R. George (Eds.), *Marketing of services* (pp. 47–51). American Marketing Association, Chicago, IL.

Ellis, N. (2010). *Business to business marketing: Relationships, networks and strategies.* Oxford University Press, Oxford.

Environmental Investigation Agency (EIA) (2019). Toxic trade. Forest crime in Gabon and the Congo and Contamination of the U.S. Market. Available at: https://content.eia-global.org/posts/documents/000/000/830/original/Toxic_Trade_EIA-web.pdf?1553480150.

Ford, D., Gadde, L. E., Håkansson, H., & Snehota, I. (2011). *Managing business relationships.* Wiley, Chichester.

Fox, K. F., & Kotler, P. (1980). The marketing of social causes: The first 10 years. *Journal of Marketing*, 44(4), 24–33.

Greenpeace Africa (2020). https://www.greenpeace.org/africa/en/, Accessed: May 5, 2020.

Grönroos, C. (1994). Quo Vadis, marketing? Toward a relationship marketing paradigm. *Journal of Marketing Management*, 10(5), 347–360.

Grönroos, C. (2006). On defining marketing: Finding a new roadmap for marketing. *Marketing Theory*, 6(4), 395–417.

Grönroos, C. (2017). Relationship marketing readiness: Theoretical background and measurement directions. *Journal of Services Marketing*, 31(3), 281–225.

Hadjikhani, A., & LaPlaca, P. (2013). Development of B2B marketing theory. *Industrial Marketing Management*, 42(3), 294–305.

Hadjikhani, A., & Thilenius, P. (2005). *Non-business actors in a business network: A comparative case on firms actions in developing and developed countries.* Elsevier, Amsterdam, New York etc.

Jansson, J. (2020). *International Business Strategy in Complex Markets.* Edward Elgar Publishing, Cheltenham, UK.

Johanson, J., & Vahlne, J. E. (2011). Markets as networks: Implications for strategy-making. *Journal of the Academy of Marketing Science*, 39(4), 484–491.

Johnston, W. J., & Bonoma, T. V. (1981). The buying center: Structure and interaction patterns. *Journal of Marketing*, 45, 143–156.

Johnston, W. J., & Lewin, J. E. (1996). Organisational buying behavior: Toward an integrative framework. *Journal of Business Research*, 35(1), 1–15.

Kotler, P. (2011). Reinventing marketing to manage the environmental imperative. *Journal of Marketing*, 75(4), 132–135.

Kotler, P. (2018). Why broadened marketing has enriched marketing. *AMS Review*, 8(1–2), 20–22.

Kotler, P., & Armstrong, G. (2010). *Principles of marketing.* Pearson Education, London.

Kotler, P., & Levy, S. J. (1969). Broadening the concept of marketing. *Journal of Marketing*, 33(1), 10–15.

Meyer, K. E., & Peng, M. W. (2005). Probing theoretically into Central and Eastern Europe: Transactions, resources, and institutions. *Journal of International Business Studies*, 36(6), 600–621.

Meyer, K. E., & Peng, M. W. (2016). Theoretical foundations of emerging economy business research. *Journal of International Business Studies*, 47(1), 3–22.

North, D. C. (1990). A transaction cost theory of politics. *Journal of Theoretical Politics*, 2(4), 355–367.

North, D. C. (2005). The contribution of the new institutional economics to an understanding of the transition problem. In A. Shorrocks (Ed.), *Wider perspectives on global development* (pp. 1–15). Palgrave Macmillan, London.

Okoroafo, S. C. (2004). Marketing orientation, practices, and performance of Sub-Saharan African Firms. *Journal of African Business*, 5(2), 163–172. DOI: 10.1300/J156v05n02_09.

Owusu, R. A. (2002). Project marketing to Africa: Lessons from the case of IVO Transmission Engineering and Ghana's national electrification scheme. *Journal of Business & Industrial Marketing*, 17(6), 523–537.

Owusu, R. A., & Welch, C. (2007). The buying network in international project business: A comparative case study of development projects. *Industrial Marketing Management*, 36(2), 147–157.

Reuters (2018, September 23). Timeline: Shell's operations in Nigeria. Retrieved August 8, 2020, from https://www.reuters.com/article/us-nigeria-shell-timeline/timeline-shells-operations-in-nigeria-idUSKCN1M306D.

Salminen, R. T., & Möller, K. (2006). Role of references in business marketing–towards a normative theory of referencing. *Journal of Business-to-Business Marketing*, 13(1), 1–51.

Scott, P. (1995). *The meanings of mass higher education*. McGraw-Hill Education, New York.

Washington Post (2013, January 18). Is outsourcing to blame for Boeing's 787 Dreamliner woes? Retrieved August 22, 2020, from https://www.washingtonpost.com/news/wonk/wp/2013/01/18/is-outsourcing-to-blame-for-boeings-787-woes/?noredirect=on.

Williamson, O. E. (2000). The new institutional economics: Taking stock, looking ahead. *Journal of Economic Literature*, 38(3), 595–613.

Winston, E., & Dadzie, K. Q. (2002). Market orientation of Nigerian and Kenyan firms: The role of top managers. *The Journal of Business & Industrial Marketing*, 17(6), 471.

1.7 Insights into Some African Business Markets: Kenya, South Africa, Tanzania and Ghana

1.7.1 Kenya's B2B Market – Examining the Tourism Sector

Author: Dr Adele Berndt, Jönköping International Business School, Sweden.

When thinking about the tourism sector in East Africa, it is easy to focus on the final consumer who arrives in the country to enjoy the sunshine, beaches and wildlife. This seasonal industry comprises many entry-level jobs which may not always provide viable career options (Karanja, 2015). Behind the scenes is a range of business services which are necessary if any organisation is to be successful and provide excellent service and a clear focus on customers and customer satisfaction. These B2B providers serve an integral role in all areas of this industry.

1.7.1.1 Tourism – a B2B Perspective

Services currently make up ~47.5% of the Kenyan economy and, similar to other economies, are becoming more critical to the economy. Tourism services make up around 10% of the country's GDP, despite having experienced numerous challenges in recent times such as increased competition, terrorism and questions regarding the sustainability of the development associated with tourism (CIA The World Factbook, 2017; Frost et al., 2004). The operation of a successful supply chain contributes to competitiveness while also impacting service quality. For example, having a supplier that provides excellent products (or services) such as textiles or food can mean that the accommodation offered to guests is more comfortable and perceived as superior or luxury.

1.7.1.2 Government

At Kenya's independence in 1963, the economy depended on the export of tea and coffee to generate foreign reserves. However, due to the potential fluctuation in the prices of these products, the decision was made to focus on the environment and specifically "nature-based tourism" (Sanghi et al., 2017). This decision required the commitment of the government to provide the environment for the development of both leisure and business tourism.

In 1965, the Kenyan government set up the Kenyan Tourist Development Corporation (KTDC) whose purpose was to supervise the industry and the development and monitoring of accommodation (e.g. lodges and hotels) and transport in the tourism sector (Frost et al., 2004). The Ministry of Tourism and Wildlife was established to manage tourism and conservation efforts in the various national parks within the country, thereby increasing the contribution to the economy (Frost et al., 2004; Ministry of Tourism and Wildlife, 2020). Its significance is due to the impact on the employment of local people and the development of skills necessary to provide excellent service.

Supporting the development of infrastructure includes various activities necessary to help tour operators and accommodation providers, and consists of the development of transport and communication infrastructure such as roads, airports and internet access. International airports which are under the control of the Kenyan Airports Authority (KAA) make it possible for 40 international airlines to fly into Nairobi, bringing tourists mainly from Europe (Frost et al., 2004).

Tourism also impacts other aspects of the economy, including agriculture and local communities, as these facilities are built in rural areas and impact those living in these communities (Frost et al., 2004). Community partnerships are developed with local communities through community conservancies. The conservancies pay rent to the owners of the land and employ residents while also implementing social development programmes in the area (Kenya Tourism Board, 2016). Tourism also contributes to community-based enterprises by community members who derive the benefits of these enterprises (Manyara & Jones, 2007).

1.7.1.3 Tour Operators

Tour operators provide an essential service for tourists, bring business and leisure tourists into Kenya, and assist Kenyans to travel themselves – the so-called inbound and outbound tour operators (Ngesa & Cavagnaro, 2010; Sanghi et al., 2017). Many of these tour operators are micro-enterprises (employing less than five people) who provide services on a seasonal basis (Ngesa & Cavagnaro, 2010). These operators need to interact with a range of suppliers themselves, including airlines and lodges, matching the needs of customers with a range of suppliers.

1.7.1.4 Accommodation Providers

Accommodation is offered by numerous providers including hotels and lodges with foreign chains, forming a part of this sector. These services require many physical and skills resources to provide excellent service to guests. Examples include sheets, linen and toiletries, which need to be sourced as well as food items for the efficient operating of restaurants and food services. Training and development are provided by diverse providers, including colleges and in-house (or corporate training) to improve the front and back office delivered to customers. This includes training in customer service, food preparation and wildlife guiding, as well as in indirect services such as car rental (Karanja, 2015).

1.7.1.5 Other Tourist Services

Underpinning the tourism industry are various restaurants, souvenir producers and transport operators (e.g. taxis). Similar to the accommodation and transport providers, B2B enterprises play a role in providing the necessary support to organisations. While wildlife is often the core focus of tourism, the development of these supporting services such as museums and other heritage sites can improve the tourism experience (Karanja, 2015).

1.7.1.6 Future Developments

Future developments in issues relating to sustainability will impact both the future of the tourism industry in Kenya as well as the business services offered. Increasingly, the use of the internet and e-commerce to purchase and transact business will require improved development in infrastructure. The internet, however, also makes it possible for consumers to contact various service providers directly, thereby eliminating other organisations in the distribution channel.

Sustainability issues will continue to receive extensive attention, as too many tourists can also negatively impact the tourism experience. Kenya has created ecotourism labels that are focused on four principles, including environmental conservation, education and empowerment, social responsibility, and cultural and heritage preservation (Kenya Tourism Board, 2016). One such rating scheme is the Global Sustainable Tourism Council (GSTC) scheme. This rating scheme requires reviewing by an accreditation panel and should the accommodation be evaluated as meeting these requirements they will be required to maintain these standards. Similar schemes provide confidence for customers regarding the operator and the management of the business.

The entire industry, being customer-focused, requires an extensive range of B2B products and services, covering a range of industries and sectors. With Kenya forming part of a broader East African region, the potential for the development of the sector and associated enterprises into other countries also needs acknowledgement.

References

CIA The World Factbook (2017). Retrieved June 2, 2020, from https://www.cia.gov/library/publications/the-world-factbook/geos/tz.html.

Frost, F. A., Shanka, T., & Street, K. (2004). *Tourism strategies and opportunities in Kenya and Ethiopia-a case approach*. Curtin Business School, Bentley, West Australia.

Karanja, F. N. (2015). How to increase and attract more tourists into Kenya through experiential marketing (Doctoral dissertation), Nova University Lisbon.

Kenya Tourism Board. (2016). Sustainable tourism report 2016. Retrieved January 27, 2020, from http://ktb.go.ke/wp-content/uploads/2016/11/KTB-Sustainable-Tourism-Report-2016.pdf.

Manyara, G., & Jones, E. (2007). Community-based tourism enterprises development in Kenya: An exploration of their potential as avenues of poverty reduction. *Journal of Sustainable Tourism*, 15(6), 628–644.

Ministry of Tourism and Wildlife. (2020). Retrieved June 2, 2020, from http://www.tourism.go.ke/vision-mission-mandate/.

Ngesa, F., & Cavagnaro, E. (2010, October). Sustainable tour operating practices: Setting up a case study of inbound tour operators in Kenya. Paper presented at EuroCHRIE conference, 25–27 October 2010.

Sanghi, A., Damania, R., Manji, F. N. M., & Mogollon, M. P. (2017). Standing out from the herd: An economic assessment of tourism in Kenya (No. AUS16758, pp. 1–72). The World Bank.

1.7.2 The Motor Industry Development Programme in South Africa

Author: Dr Adele Berndt, Jönköping International Business School, Sweden.

It is vital for policymakers in developing countries to understand how various industries such as mining and the automobile industry are equipped to compete internationally. This understanding enables policymakers to support these industries, impacting the lives of citizens and the development of other associated businesses and suppliers. The motor vehicle (or automotive industry) is one such industry within the economy of many countries, including developing economies. Globally, the motor industry has become more competitive with customers having broader choice and knowledge, increased demands regarding pricing and shorter product lifecycles (Tolmay, 2017). This increases the importance of the supply chain and B2B activities.

1.7.2.1 The Motor Vehicle Industry in South Africa

The motor vehicle industry is viewed as an important part of the production output of a country as the product is valuable in international trade, serving as a key sector of most economies (Humphrey & Memedovic, 2003). The South African motor industry exports to 151 countries, supporting the view that the industry is vital to the economy and international trade. In South Africa, it is estimated that the automotive sector contributes around 6.4% of GDP, with 4% associated with the manufacturing of the vehicles and 2.4% associated with the retail aspect of vehicle sales (naamsa.co.za). It earns ZAR 207 billion from the export of these products, which is ~15.5% of the country's exports (naamsa.co.za). The sector also employs more than 110,000 people which in turn contributes to the development of another 457,000 jobs in several related industries (naamsa.co.za).

Multiple Original Equipment Manufacturers (OEMs) assemble vehicles in SA (e.g. VW, Ford and BMW), all of which are divisions of global OEM brands. This means that strategic decisions impacting these plants are made in other countries such as the USA, Germany and Japan (Naude & Badenhorst-Weiss, 2012). Many of the OEMs have located their plants close together to be close to component manufacturers and other key suppliers in the supply chain. Two examples are Uitenhage and Port Elizabeth (where Mercedes Benz, VW and Opel are based) and Rosslyn outside Pretoria (where BMW, Nissan and Ford are based) (Tolmay, 2017). By locating their plants close together, this provides numerous benefits to component manufacturers and to the attraction of skills such as HR.

When discussing the sector, the focus tends to be the OEMs such as the major vehicle products (e.g. Ford and BMW), but many associated businesses can be identified, such as component manufacturers (Naude & Badenhorst-Weiss, 2012). In recent times, the shift has been made from focusing on individual OEMs to their entire supply chain due to the acknowledgement of the importance of all the components in their global competitiveness (Tolmay, 2017).

1.7.2.2 Supplier Relationship in This Industry

Building relationships with suppliers is vital for all industries. In the case of the OEMs, both local and international suppliers contribute to the vehicle build quality, coming from a range of countries and cultural backgrounds. As supply chains in the automotive industry are viewed as relatively similar, relationship quality can be developed to provide a competitive advantage, business expansion and customer retention (Tolmay, 2017).

1.7.2.3 The Motor Industry Development Programme (MIDP)

South Africa's history is a complicated one, with the policy of apartheid impacting the development of international trade, with many countries boycotting the country and all products manufactured in the country. To support these industries, protective trade barriers (i.e. import duties) were in place. This meant that manufacturers were protected as importing components was expensive due to these duties. With the change in politics during the late 1980s and early 1990s, the government developed policies to assist automotive manufacturers in increasing exports and globalisation efforts (Black, 2001).

Implemented in 1995, the MIDP was a programme that had the aim of reducing various tariffs for imports related to the motor vehicle industry and simultaneously providing support for exports (Barnes & Black, 2013). The objective is to improve efficiency, thereby lowering costs, hence being globally competitive. It was done by giving manufacturers export credits which can be used to reduce the import duties of various items (www.just-auto.com/analysis/an-overview-of-the-south-african-automotive-industry_id86764.aspx). An additional objective of this programme was to provide "high-quality, affordable vehicles" for consumers (Barnes & Black, 2013). Subsequent changes were made to the programme in 1998 and 2002, which resulted in the reduction of export assistance (Barnes & Black, 2013), prior to the programme ending in 2013. It was replaced by the Automotive Production and Development Programme (APDP) which was scheduled to run until 2020, which has similar aims to those of the MIDP while also being WTO (World Trade Organisation) compliant (Bronkhorst et al., 2013). These changes have reinforced South Africa's position as the leading producer of right-hand-drive vehicles for OEMs (ibid).

1.7.2.4 The Impact of the MIDP and APDP

The impact can be seen in various ways. First, the focus is on local content and local suppliers. In vehicle manufacturing, the components installed are critical, and hence, selecting the right suppliers is an important task. With material costs accounting for 75%–85% of the final price of a vehicle, component suppliers impact the OEMs, resulting in increased pressure to manage costs. Using imported components from established organisations can be viewed as the easiest way. Yet, the use of imported parts impacts the development of the local sector, including employees and an impact on the country's import levels. For this reason, policymakers attempt to support local content programmes. Second, there has been a development of associated industries due to changes in the market such as the development of catalytic converter providers who supply the South African market (Bronkhorst et al., 2013). Furthermore, the increased demand for electric and hybrid vehicles is changing automotive manufacturing and the components needed (ibid), which will continue to impact the development of suppliers and industries.

1.7.2.5 Broad-Based Black Economic Empowerment (BBBEE) and Suppliers

Due to the history of the country, policymakers have developed legislation (the Broad-Black Economic Empowerment Act 53 of 2003) that aims to stimulate economic participation by black people in the South African economy (Attorneys, 2014). It impacts the ownership of organisations as well as the choice of suppliers, based on their BBBEE status. This BBBEE status is measured using points gained based on several elements including management control, skills development and supplier development. An organisation's status can range from non-compliant (<40 points), through level 8 (more than 40 but <55 points) to level 1 (more than 100 points) (Attorneys, 2014, p. 11). Regarding new enterprise and supplier development, this involves evaluating suppliers in terms of their BBBEE status (Attorneys, 2014). Thus, before signing a procurement contract, they would be required to assess the suppliers BBBEE status, which in turn impacts their status. For example, Company A would evaluate their suppliers (Suppliers D, E and F), with their BBBEE status serving as an essential criterion in awarding the contract.

References

Attorneys, W. (2014). *Amendments to the BBBEE act and the codes explained* (pp. 1–23). Werksmans Attorneys, Johannesburg.

Barnes, J., & Black, A. (2013). The motor industry development programme 1995–2012: What have we learned? *In International Conference on Manufacturing-Led Growth for Employment and Equality*, South Africa (pp. 1–38).

Black, A. (2001). Globalisation and restructuring in the South African automotive industry. *Journal of International Development*, 13(6), 779–796.

Bronkhorst, E., Steyn, J. L., & Stiglingh, M. (2013). The automotive production and development programme: An analysis of the opinions of South African stakeholders. Retrieved June 13, 2020, from https://www.just-auto.com/analysis/an-overview-of-the-south-african-automotive-industry_id86764.aspx.

Humphrey, J., & Memedovic, O. (2003). The global automotive industry value chain: What prospects for upgrading by developing countries. *UNIDO Sectorial Studies Series Working Paper*.

Naamsa (2020). Press release: Naamsa releases May 2020 new vehicle stats, 1 June 2020. Retrieved June 13, 2020, https://naamsa.co.za/SalesStats.

Naude, M. J., & Badenhorst-Weiss, J. A. (2012). Factors inhibiting the South African automotive industry from fully contributing to local economic development. *Journal of Contemporary Management*, 9(1), 48–65.

Tolmay, A. S. (2017). The correlation between relationship value and business expansion in the South African automotive supply chains. *Journal of Transport and Supply Chain Management*, 11(1), 1.

1.7.3 Evolution of the Tanzanian Innovation Ecosystem

Author: Ms Emma Nkonoki, University of Turku, Finland [19]

According to Jackson (2011, p. 2), "innovation ecosystems are complex relationships that are formed between actors or entities whose functional goal is to enable technology development and innovation". Such actors include material and human capital resources that make up the institutional entities of the ecosystem. "Innovation ecosystems are complex networks of interactions between the actors from industry, government and academia that underlie the innovative activities and performance in the area" (Jucevicius et al., 2016, p. 430). The innovation ecosystem comprises two distinct, but interlinked economies: the research economy, which is driven by fundamental research, and the commercial economy, which is driven by the marketplace or companies.

The actors in the Tanzanian innovation ecosystem are innovation spaces, funding agencies, academic institutions, development partners, the public sector, the private sector and civil society. The first wave of innovation spaces started in 2010 with Buni Innovation Hub, Dar Teknohama Business Incubator, Kinu Innovation Hub, etc. in Dar es Salaam. Right after that, funding agencies began to come in actively, e.g. TanzICT – The Information Society and in 2013 ICT Sector Development Project in Tanzania in 2011, and HDIF – Human Development Innovation Fund. Private sector involvement started to increase around 2015 with a wave of startups and funding instruments being introduced into the ecosystem. Corporate-sponsored programmes aiming at

---

[19] MSc; Innovation and Development. Innovation Expert at FINGO, Finland; PhD Candidate at the University of Turku, Finland.

supporting the ecosystem in business started and continued to become active, e.g. Hackathons and Bootcamps.

The first innovation week in Tanzania was organised in 2015 by the HDIF with financial aid from the UK. Since then, many other innovation- and technology-related events have been held. As new actors continued coming, the ecosystem became bigger. More innovation hubs, accelerators and incubators were started around the country, e.g. Kiota Hub in Iringa, Ndoto Hub in Dar es Salaam, Kili Hub, Mbeya Living Lab, Sahara Accelerator and Anza Accelerator. The main objective of these innovation activities was capacity building and skills development of communities. By 2018, the leading innovation and technology events managed to attract many other players to be active members of the ecosystem, for example, higher education institutions and organisations from the public sector. During the same year, the government under the Commission for Science and Technology published a national guide to advancing discovery, creativity and indigenous knowledge. The strategic plan for science and technology emphasises issues of creativity and innovation. This guide, therefore, contributes to the implementation of the strategic plan for science and technology.

Despite a lot of progress and success, there are still some challenges facing the growth and stability of the ecosystem. These include lack of funding; lack of appropriate policies and regulations governing creativity, innovations and the positive development of the ecosystem; lack of academic institutions with competent innovation and entrepreneurship programmes; and weak involvement of the private sector.

1.7.3.1 The Role of New Ventures in the Innovation Ecosystem

Startup companies are the essential stakeholders of any innovation ecosystem. "A startup is a new and active business entity which did not formerly exist" (Luger & Koo, 2005, p. 18). Startups are the main catalysts of economic development and the emergence and advancement of industries (Schumpeter, 2008). The end goal of the ecosystem is economic growth. The kind of growth triggered by new solutions to social challenges will not be achieved if there are no new ventures. This proves the fact that most developing economies find themselves relying heavily on startups. According to Bajwa et al. (2017), software startup companies build software-intensive products and services within limited time frames and with few resources. These companies tend to look for the most sustainable and scalable business models (see also Giardino et al., 2014). Sutton (2000) defines software startups as organisations that are challenged by limited resources, immaturity, multiple influences, vibrant technologies and turbulent markets. Several software startups are prominent in the Tanzanian innovation ecosystem, and several financiers and donors are supporting them to enable them to establish and scale up.

1.7.3.2 Case – Magilatech

Magilatech is a software development and security auditing startup company in Tanzania that started in 2012. It was a team that won the first Hackathon in Dar es Salaam on software development in 2011 that later decided to join forces and form this startup. The prize came with a tech mentoring programme. The main focus was to solve societal challenges using technology through innovation. The company has since grown and is collaborating with different actors. Different stakeholders of the Tanzanian innovation ecosystem contributed and are still contributing to

Magilatech's growth and scaling through partnerships and collaboration. The startup's first incubation programme was done under the Dar Teknohama Business incubator (DTBi) which is an entity that works under the Tanzanian Commission for Science and Technology (Costech).

The main aim of DTBi was promoting the growth of ICT-based emerging startup companies. The company received more training, international exposure and support from the Information Society and ICT Sector Development Project (TanzICT). Moreover, some foreign embassies have done collaboration work with the startup company. It is clear that public sector actors were almost the first ecosystem actors to contribute to the growth and early success of Magilatech. In terms of other ecosystem actors, between 2013 and 2014, the startup signed several app contracts with the private sector, public sector and academia. The startup has been able to impact society through a B2B model.

Magilatech launched Tigobackup, a mobile security application performing a full content backup on mobile devices and antitheft commands for one of the biggest telecommunication companies in Tanzania – Tigo. Magilatech developed Airtel Visomo, which is an application used at VETA (Vocational Education Tanzania). The application allows students to learn all courses provided by VETA through their phones. The startup has also got much support from the Tanzania Communication Regulatory Authority (TCRA). This was the first entity to facilitate the startup's journey to the international arena. Through cooperation with the University of Dar es Salaam, they managed to get more visibility and thus gain more clients and other collaboration contracts. Magilatech is also working with the grassroots communities through a system called Pact-Vicoba, which influences the daily lives of people through village community banks. They also provide payment automation for non-governmental organisations. The company also assists other startups in developing products and has continued to expand locally and internationally (Magilatech, https://www.magilatech.co.tz/).

1.7.3.3 Conclusion

The main challenges at the moment include regulatory challenges, e.g. getting licenses from the Tanzania Cybercrime Authority, funding, interaction within the ecosystem, developing stronger relations with universities and local industry. However, the startup company remains optimistic in its operations and the future. According to the CEO of Magilatech, "we are in a transformational state as a country, development is coming, but slowly, the most important thing is to survive the pace".

References

Bajwa, S. S., Wang, X., Duc, A. N., & Abrahamsson, P. (2017). "Failures" to be celebrated: An analysis of major pivots of software startups. *Empirical Software Engineering*, 22(5), 2373–2408.

Giardino, C., Unterkalmsteiner, M., Paternoster, N., Gorschek, T., & Abrahamsson, P. (2014). What do we know about software development in startups? *IEEE Software*, 31(5), 28–32.

Jackson, B. D. J. (2011). What is an innovation ecosystem? *National Science Foundation*, 1(2), 1–13.

Jucevicius, G., Juceviciene, R., Gaidelys, V., & Kalman, A. (2016). The emerging innovation ecosystems and "Valley of death": Towards the combination of entrepreneurial and institutional approaches. *Engineering Economics*, 27(4), 430–438.

Luger, M. I., & Koo, J. (2005). Defining and tracking business startups. *Small Business Economics*, 24(1), 17–28.

Magilatech. Retrieved August 15, 2020, from https://www.magilatech.co.tz/.

Sutton, S. M. (2000). The role of process in software startup. *IEEE Software*, 17(4), 33–39.

1.7.4 Business Relationships in an Enterprise Cluster of Informal Artisans in Ghana

Author: Christopher Boafo, Leipzig University, Germany [20]

1.7.4.1 Introduction

Enterprise clustering is found among many informal artisans and tradespeople in Africa. They operate in the sectors of carpentry, garage mechanics, foundry works, leatherworks, pottery making, etc. Schmitz gives a simple definition of an enterprise cluster as the geographic and sectoral agglomeration of firms (Schmitz, 1998). From a management perspective, the principal components of a cluster comprise geographic concentration, the interconnection of firms and institutions, presence of both competition and cooperation, and specialisation (Eisingerich et al., 2010; Porter, 2000). Many studies have reported the success of clusters around the world (e.g. Adesida & Karuri-Sebina, 2016; Brache & Felzensztein, 2019; Felzensztein et al., 2019).

According to Zeng (2008), clusters are of two categories. One type of cluster is spontaneously developed by the enterprises. Initially, this type of cluster was meant to be local. However, nowadays, some of these clusters also operate beyond their location. The second category of clusters is created via public policies (Zeng, 2008). Accordingly, the geographic scope of such clusters may be within a city, regional or even interregional (Porter, 2000).

Studies conducted in Africa (e.g. Adeya, 2008; Ali & Peerlings, 2011; Gatune, 2016; Iddrisu et al., 2012; Yoshino, 2010) acknowledge that artisanal clusters host many enterprises that operate in the informal sector. Some cluster-based informal artisans are found to sell to foreign markets through an early and stage-wise approach of internationalisation (Boafo & Dornberger, 2019). Among the most reported African cases in literature is Suame Magazine (in Kumasi, the second largest city of Ghana). In most cases, the artisanal firms are housed in simple structures in clusters. They adopt traditional technologies and informal management and marketing strategies. The term "workshop" characterises their workspace better than the "factory" (Yoshino, 2010).

1.7.4.2 The "Suame Magazine" Cluster

The Suame Magazine is a spontaneous natural cluster that dates back to 1920. The enterprise cluster covers a landscape of 20 square miles, and it is known for craftsmanship, apprenticeship training and entrepreneurship development in Ghana. Studies have established that Suame Magazine fulfils all the fundamentals of cluster success that include agglomeration, specialisation, labour pooling, internal linkages, external linkages and scale (Gatune, 2016; Iddrisu et al., 2012). The average firm size of five workers dominates the cluster, and a minority of more sophisticated engineering workshops generally have seven to ten workers (Adeya, 2008; Gatune, 2016). Iddrisu et al. (2012) demonstrate that firms in Suame have higher technical skills and better equipment than other clusters in the West African sub-region. In terms of learning and skills acquisition, apprenticeship in this cluster involves a highly social and situated form of learning (Jaarsma et al., 2011; Mano et al., 2012). Simply defined, the method of apprenticeship is learning-by-doing that involves the master craftsman who acts as the teacher, and the learner being the apprentice. Besides, some artisans also acquire skills through technical or vocational education, self-coaching, industrial attachments and experiences from previous employment. The key sectors involve vehicle

---

[20]MBA (Small and Medium Business Studies); PhD Candidate, African Centre for Career Enhancement and Skills Support (ACCESS), Faculty of Economics and Management, Leipzig University, Germany.

repair and maintenance, manufacturing, metalworking, machinists, sale of engineering materials and accessories, and sale of automobile spare parts. An estimated 11,830 enterprises are found in this cluster (Iddrisu et al., 2012). Beyond the nationwide market, the cluster attracts and serves clients around 17 foreign markets across the globe. These include countries in the Middle East, West Europe and North America (Boafo & Dornberger, 2019). In the next paragraph, we discuss how a successful artisan interacts among firms in distinct sectors in the cluster.

1.7.4.3 Interactions and Relationships among Suame Cluster Enterprises

In the Suame Magazine cluster, the firms in different sectors interact from innovation through production to marketing of products and repair services. A typical case study is Montals Engineering, which was established in 1996 and currently has 42 workers, including apprentices. Montals manufactures LPG gas ovens, biomass stoves, dryers and LPG warmers. The owner reports that his firm has thrived through daily personal interactions with other firms in the sector. "Normally, I meet other entrepreneurs that I can trust to share a new design of products. They do likewise", says the owner-manager. The frequent interactions improve their original ideas for new product development.

Furthermore, most inputs (e.g. scrap metals, spare parts) and support services are sourced from firms in the cluster. For this, the entrepreneur reports that one will have to establish good personal relationships and build trust with other firms. The limited firm resources make sub-contracting play a vital role in their production. The contracting firms often offer some technical support to help the suppliers to improve the quality of their supplies (Zeng, 2008). The division of labour among specialists is highly developed in this cluster (Iddrisu et al., 2012). As the owner recounts, "I source my scrap metals (i.e. raw material) from a scrap dealer, then to a machinist for design parts, and foundryman for specialised services. By the time a complete product is finalised, it would pass through the hands of many other craftsmen". A similar approach is the work of a mechanic (vehicle repairer) who sources spare parts from a dealer in the cluster and then requests for the services of welders and machinist when needed. Usually, most orders of inputs and sub-contracts are made on credit and payments are made at a later date. The interviews show that establishing B2B interactions and maintaining business relationships demand social relation skills.

The data show that building strong social networks in the cluster strengthens collaboration and wins the support of other artisans. This is very important for the sustainability of their informal business since the cluster currently faces a surplus of new entrants due to low entry barriers and low level of technology (Iddrisu et al., 2012; Zeng, 2008). The majority of firms produce or provide the same products or services. This has resulted in intense competition and a decline in profit margins (Yoshino, 2010). Moreover, beyond the firm-level relationships, the informal artisans through their trade associations have established relationships with non-government organisations and government institutions. The current active associations include the "Foundrymen Association", "Association of Micro and Small Metal Industries", "Suame Garages Association" and "Magazine Mechanical Association". The key support services have taken the form of capacity development through training in necessary skills and new technologies. Over the years, these have been provided by four public institutions – the "Suame Intermediate Technology Transfer Unit", "National Vocational and Technical Institute", "Kumasi Technical University" and "Kumasi Technical Institute".

References

Adesida, O., & Karuri-Sebina, G. (Eds.) (2016). *Innovation Africa: Emerging hubs of entrepreneurship* (1st ed.). Bingley, Emerald.

Ali, M., & Peerlings, J. (2011). Value added of cluster membership for micro enterprises of the handloom sector in Ethiopia. *World Development*, 39(3), 363–374. DOI: 10.1016/j.worlddev.2010.07.002.

Adeya, C. N. (2008). The Suame manufacturing cluster in Ghana. In D. Z. Zeng (Ed.), *Knowledge, technology, and cluster-based growth in Africa* (pp. 88–170). The World Bank, Washington, DC.

Boafo, C., & Dornberger, U. (2019, August 28-29). *The Internationalisation Degree of Urban Informal Enterprises in Ghana: An Extension of Internationalisation Theories* [Paper Presentation]. 23rd McGill International Entrepreneurship Conference, Southern Denmark University, Odense, Denmark.

Brache, J., & Felzensztein, C. (2019). Geographical co-location on Chilean SME's export performance. *Journal of Business Research,* 105, 310–321. DOI: 10.1016/j.jbusres.2017.11.044.

Eisingerich, A. B., Bell, S. J., & Tracey, P. (2010). How can clusters sustain performance? The role of network strength, network openness, and environmental uncertainty. *Research Policy*, 39(2), 239–253. DOI: 10.1016/j.respol.2009.12.007.

Felzensztein, C., Deans, K. R., & Dana, L. P. (2019). Small firms in regional clusters. Local networks and internationalisation in the Southern Hemisphere. *Journal of Small Business Management,* 57(2), 496–516. DOI: 10.1111/jsbm.12388.

Gatune, J. (2016). Suame Magazine: The evolving story of Africa's largest industrial cluster. In O. Adesida, & G. Karuri-Sebina (Eds.), *Innovation Africa: Emerging hubs of entrepreneurship* (pp. 397–425). Emerald, Bingley.

Iddrisu, A., Mano, Y., & Sonobe, T. (2012). Entrepreneurial skills and industrial development: The case of a car repair and metalworking cluster in Ghana. *Journal of the Knowledge Economy*, 3(3), 302–326. DOI: 10.1007/s13132-011-0047-6.

Jaarsma, T., Maat, H., Richards, P., & Wals, A. (2011). The role of materiality in apprenticeships: The case of the Suame Magazine, Kumasi, Ghana. *Journal of Vocational Education & Training,* 63(3), 439–449. DOI: 10.1080/13636820.2011.572173.

Mano, Y., Iddrisu, A., Yoshino, Y., & Sonobe, T. (2012). How can micro and small enterprises in Sub-Saharan Africa become more productive? The impacts of experimental basic managerial training. *World Development,* 40(3), 458–468. DOI: 10.1016/j.worlddev.2011.09.013.

Porter, M. E. (2000). Location, competition, and economic development: Local clusters in a global economy. *Economic Development Quarterly*, 14(1), 15–34. DOI: 10.1177/089124240001400105.

Schmitz, H. (1998). Fostering collective efficiency. *Small Enterprise Development*, 9(1), 4–11. DOI: 10.3362/9781780440835.

Schumpeter, A. (2008). *The theory of economic development: An inquiry into profits, capital, credit, interest, and the business cycle.* Transaction Publishers, London.

Yoshino, Y. (2010). *Industrial clusters and micro and small enterprises in Africa.* The World Bank, Washington, DC.

Zeng, D. Z. (2008). Knowledge, technology, and cluster-based growth in Africa: Findings from 11 case studies of enterprise clusters in Africa. In D. Z. Zeng (Ed.), *Knowledge, technology, and cluster-based growth in Africa* (pp. 1–13). The World Bank, http://elibrary.worldbank.org/content/book/9780821373064.

Chapter 2

Strategy in the Business-to-Business Market

INTRODUCTION AND OBJECTIVES

In the Introduction and Chapter 1, we defined marketing and business-to-business (B2B) marketing, and discussed their evolution and characteristics as science and practice. In this chapter, we will discuss broadly how business marketing managers can apply strategy, competition and relationship management models in their business. Just as in the previous sections in Part 1, we will discuss the broad outlines of these issues as they will be discussed in more detail in the subsequent chapters.

At the end of this chapter, the reader will understand the following:

- The nature of strategy in B2B markets
- How to develop and implement a strategy
- Competitive and collaborative strategies in B2B marketing.

2.1 Strategy for the Business-to-Business Market

2.1.1 What Is Business Strategy in B2B Markets?

The word "strategy" is common in everyday language, where people talk about their strategy in different situations. There are, thus, various meanings attached to the concept. The term is essential in marketing science and practice, and we will therefore clarify its definition in this chapter.

A strategy is a comprehensive long-term set of plans for achieving specified aims of a company. Thus, a strategy is not single plans, single planning activities or programme of activities. Planning, plans and programmes of activities are part of the strategy or the strategy development process. A strategy provides unifying themes for all parts of a company to achieve set objectives. Thus, it gives coherence and direction to the actions of individuals and organisations. Thereby, strategy provides a consistent purpose and a recognisable path over a period (Grant, 2016; Mintzberg, 1987; Porter, 2008, 1996; Reeves et al., 2016; Sull et al., 2015). A typical B2B company will have several departments apart from the marketing department. In addition to marketing, department, it may have manufacturing, finance, human resources and other departments. Each of these departments, due to their different roles, can have their strategies to achieve their specific objectives. It is, however, important that all the parts of the company understand the final goal – which is to provide value to its B2B partners, receive value in return and establish a good position in a successful business network or supply chain (Holm et al., 1999; Johanson & Mattsson, 2011; Keränen & Liozu, 2020).[1] Thus, all parts of the company should understand the various facets of value and its provision to business customers, the nature and process of value received from suppliers, and how to establish an appreciated position in the business network or supply chain. Through a strategy that makes sure that both the "full-time marketers" (staff of the marketing department) and "part-time marketers" (staff of other departments that contribute to value exchange with B2B parties) are aware of the marketing strategies, the company will create an integrated and joint strategy through all departments to succeed in its business (Grönroos, 1994).

2.1.2 Plan, Tactics and Strategy in B2B

It is essential to differentiate between plans, tactics and strategy. Plans are input into strategy or parts of a strategy; planning is activities in the process of developing strategy. Different departments and managers will make plans for their functions; top management will meet to review the plans submitted by various managers and departments, and they will consult the President/CEO/board before final decisions are made. As stated above, a strategy is the long-term objectives to be achieved, and tools or tactics are formulated steps to achieve them. Therefore, tactics are steps or stages to execute strategy. A well-formulated strategy should clarify plans and tactics (Grant, 2016; Porter, 2008, 1996). For example, the strategy of a B2B company might be broken down into yearly plans, e.g. 2-year plans that will be reviewed against the background of the long-term strategy and what has been achieved to date, to decide what changes should be made towards achieving the strategy. The following case company illustrates how a long-term business strategy can be developed over time.

The strategy of Dankwa Telecom might be formulated as "Achieving Market Leadership of the African Telecom market by 2050". In this case, the company has 30 years to achieve the strategy. The final strategy will consist of the components mission, vision, plans and tactics. Each of these components and the tactics and sub-strategies they add up to will be drawn for different parts of the company and different strategic goals, e.g. sales, profitability, promotion, relationship quality, supply chain position, network position, brand position, product quality and service quality. The long-term strategy is thus a rhythmic combination of various parts. In Figure 2.1, the market entry strategy might be formulated as starting with the biggest economies. Another aspect of the strategy would be dynamism; that is, a part of the strategy would be to follow market changes and make necessary changes; for example, leave and enter markets when necessary. Periodic analyses and analyses of different components will lead to changes, all with the goal of "Achieving Market Leadership of the African Telecom Market by 2050".

Several essential factors on the components of Dankwa Telecom's strategy are not under its control. Competition, the business environment and the strategies of institutional actors are very much beyond the control of the company. No matter how well the company does its part, a good strategy requires that it continually follow up and evaluate these factors that are outside its control, and adjust its mission, vision, plans and tactics to achieve its strategic goals.

---

[1] See Chapter 1 for a fuller discussion of the concept of value.

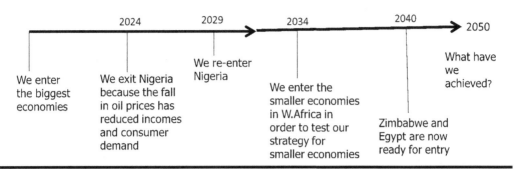

Figure 2.1 **Conquering the African Telecoms market: strategic planning and implementation of Dankwa Telecom.**

2.1.3 Strategic Planning in B2B

In many African companies, the strategy is made at the top or top-down. This is due to the African business culture that emphasises high power distance between the management and the workers. In high power distance cultures, subordinates accept the high level of power of their bosses, and they accept that top management makes decisions without consulting them (Darley & Blankson, 2020; DeBerry-Spence et al., 2008; Hofstede, 1983: see also: Hofstede: http://geert-hofstede.com/the-hofstede-centre.html http://www.geerthofstede.nl/). In African high power distance companies, top managers consider their expertise highly. They do not see the lowest level of workers as able to provide useful input to their strategy-making. They believe that their experience, education and analyses are adequate for formulating strategy. Therefore, the strategy is crafted from the top. This means that it may not necessarily take cognisance of what is happening on the company floor or how the lowest level of staff experience or feel about the strategy.

2.1.4 Current Position and Long-Term Strategy in B2B

A B2B actor should differentiate between its current position in the market and its strategy. As Table 2.1 shows, the current position of a B2B company is crucial to its survival and cannot be subjugated to the strategy. A company can go bankrupt if its current position is terrible despite an excellent strategy. The ability to correctly analyse its current position enables the company to understand its position in a network, supply chain, cluster or ecosystem (see Section 4.6). To be appreciated and maintain its position in these essential B2B relationships, the company has to provide a unique value proposition, i.e. give and receive value to and from its partners. The unique value proposition the company is providing has to be dynamic and be amenable to short-term plans and tactics, as well as "keeping an eye on the ball", i.e. the long-term strategy. Current positioning enables the firm to understand what it is doing and achieving. To analyse the current position, the firm should talk to its partners and use information based on ongoing interactions and relationships. Current positioning enables the company to audit its achievement of the strategy thus far, and success and failure in terms of goals and revenues. Analysing current position also involves analysing the business environment, network, supply chain, cluster or ecosystem and, thus, understanding its current state, and changes against expectations and forecasts in the strategy. There is, thus, a close relationship between the current position and long-term strategy, as shown in Table 2.1.

Table 2.1 Current Position and Long-Term Strategy for the Nana Poku Aluminium Products Company (NAPAP)

Continued analyses of current position; current competition	Long-term strategy formulation
Where is the company competing? **Product:** What type of aluminium products is the company supplying to wholesalers, retailers and builders? Do these products currently meet the needs of the customers, and what products should it invest in to remain competitive in the medium and long terms? Is the company providing services and advice to its customers to ensure that the products supplied meet the real needs of the customers and services to provide the longest possible lifetime value? **Place:** At what points are the products supplied? What distribution and logistics strategy should the company use. Should NAPAP establish supply points nearer its customers or insist that the customers should take delivery at its factory? *How is NAPAP competing? What is its competitive advantage?* **Price:** How does the company's price relate to the quality of its products, as well as the competition? What pricing strategy is NAPAP using? How do the customers evaluate the price? How do the prices of its products compare to the prices of its suppliers? Is it breaking even or making profits? **Promotion:** How much is the company spending on advertising, public relations, personal selling and sales promotion? What brand position is the company able to achieve compared to its competitors and its strategy? **Process:** How is the company interacting with the customers? How is the company building and maintaining relationships with the customers? How is the company interacting with other B2B parties like institutions, government agencies and NGOs? **People:** Are the company's staff able? Are they well trained? What training is currently provided to ensure that the competencies of staff are improved? Are the sales staff trained to provide the customers with quality interactions and maintain good relationships? Are the purchasing and engineering staff coordinating well with their suppliers of aluminium ingots, sand, water, etc.? Do the staff of other departments (apart from marketing), e.g. production, understand their role in ensuring value to the customers and other b-to-b parties? **Continuous Business Environmental Analysis:** Who are the company's competitors? What new producers have emerged? What is the nature of government policy towards imports, for example, cheap Chinese imports and how does this impact NAPAP's competitiveness? What is the company's business environment, network, supply chain, cluster or ecosystem	**Vision Statement:** What does NAPAP Aluminium Products Company want to become? The company should decide on what it wants to become. Does it want to remain an SME concentrating on aluminium products for current customers or add new innovative products to its offer? How many services should it add to its offer. **Mission statement and performance goals:** What is the purpose of the company? What are the core philosophies, and underlying goals of the company? What does the company want to achieve? Is the core goal of NAPAP to remain a regional employer that develops and maintains a strong position in the local supply chain only or to become a national or pan-African company? How will NAPAP attain its objectives? Plans and strategies; guidelines, e.g. yearly plans; yearly evaluations leading to necessary re-organisations? Growth strategies including sourcing capital, networks, acquisitions, etc. How to compete against the increasing cheap imports, e.g. from China

Source: The framework is adapted from Grant (2016, p. 20).

2.2 Formulating Strategy in B2B

To formulate strategy, B2B companies need the following inputs:

- Expertise, knowledge and understanding of the business, forecasts and excellent analyses. Expertise, knowledge and understanding of the business will be based on the "people (P)" of the marketing mix mentioned previously. The owners of the company or recruited management should have the right training and capacity to apply their training, experience and analytical abilities to formulate a realistic and correct understanding of the company concerning its market.

- The "people (P)" also requires that management should be open to access knowledge, expertise and experience from other levels and departments of the company in order to get a full, integrated picture of what is going on at all levels of the company. All relevant departments of the company should be consulted for their data, experiences and input so that the formulated strategy takes cognisance of all relevant aspects. Bick and Nicolaus (2011) found out that engineering firms in South Africa practise internal marketing geared towards giving their staff adequate knowledge about their products and services to be able to promote and sell the company's products or services to gain competitive advantages. The study by Mahmoud et al. (2010) of pharmaceutical firms in Ghana showed that the development of the staff was an important strategy to meet the demands of regulators and provide value to organisational customers

- To achieve the full promise of the "people P" (staff expertise), African B2B companies should move away from the high power distance business culture (Darley & Blankson, 2020; DeBerry-Spence et al., 2008; Hofstede, 1983: see also: Hofstede: http://geert-hofstede.com/the-hofstede-centre.html http://www.geerthofstede.nl/). They should develop a system for integrating the views and experiences of the lower-level staff in strategy development, i.e. abolish the top-down strategy formulation culture.

- Reliable data of the company, the industry and competitors are required. It is well known that statistics and data are not readily available in Africa due to the weakness of institutions that should keep data. The informal nature of a good number of African companies means that some of the parties a company does business with do not keep data and cannot provide the data when needed. Many companies are still keeping their information in the form of paper files that become difficult to retrieve and analyse. The use of computers is growing fast, but various infrastructure problems like power outages, older computers without adequate memory and computer illiteracy of staff reduce their use for data storage (Barnard, 2020).

- An understanding and evaluation of the role of relationships and partners like suppliers, customers and collaborators in developing technology, products and services is necessary. Due to the position of companies in supply chains, a good strategy has to take integrate the fact that "No business is an island", which means that no B2B company can do everything on its own and no B2B company is fully responsible for the success of its products and services (see Section 4.6) (Johanson & Vahlne, 2011; Hakansson & Snehota, 2006). Thus, the ability to understand, analyse and coordinate with the partners is critical in formulating a good strategy. The alternative is a strategy to find new partners, which would mean being able to position itself in another supply chain, implying a new set of parties and conditions to start to work with. Kuada and Mensah (2020) found that in the emerging solar energy industry in Ghana, products, process and functional upgrades are achieved among collaborative partners through the transfer of technical know-how between partnering organisations. As indicated in their studies, foreign knowledge is attractive, and as such, the local firms devise deliberate strategies to get their employees trained every year by their foreign partners. This ensures a close interaction with their B2B partners.

■ An understanding of the business environment and how it might change is essential. The industry and national business environment do impact the company, but for many B2B companies, the international business environment is also relevant. The variables to analyse and follow, thus, become many. In the national business environment, change of government policy, change of governments and developments in the national economy are variables that are difficult to know thoroughly. Keeping data, the ability to analyse and previous experience do help in these endeavours.

■ An understanding of national government policy and how it might change. With democratic elections in many African countries, changes in government policies after elections do happen. Besides, unexpected changes like military coups, whimsical decisions of dictators or civil unrest make strategy formulation difficult. It is common in democracies even in stable, prosperous countries that a new government may be elected on a platform of change, or they may want to make their imprint on the policy, which may mean policy changes that might change the conditions of the business.

■ Using consulting companies is a way to get data and analyses that the company is not able to obtain on its own. Consulting companies can become partners in strategy formulation. They specialise in the business, work with many different actors in the industry, have previous experience of similar cases, have or can collect data, and have experts who can develop models and forecasts. They can be useful, even though this has to be weighed against their costs. Big international consulting companies like McKinsey and EY are active in Africa and collect both national and international data and can provide a critical service. There are also local African consulting companies like M-Bendi of South Africa, Asoko Insight and Foresight Consulting[2] that have data, and analytical expertise about the local industry, economic environment, international business and business strategies, and can partner companies to develop their strategies.

■ Integration of the Corporate Strategy Department into the rest of the company. Many large B2B companies establish a corporate strategy department whose role is to formulate and evaluate strategies. It may also be a Strategy Director with a small staff. The use of a strategy department formalises strategy formulation and provides top management speedy information and a reference point to discuss strategy. It is crucial, however, that the strategy department consults other departments and makes recommendations based on input from all departments. The strategy formulation process described above can be applied in the context of Figure 2.2. That summarises the strategy formulation process.

■ A strategy director or department that sees itself as "the expert" and does not embed itself in the work and experiences of other departments will become removed from the reality of the company and suggest or formulate strategies that might not be realistic for the company. In spite of the establishment of a Corporate Strategy Department, strategy formulation should not be top-down but should involve the knowledge and experiences of

---

[2] Foresight Consulting is registered in Finland and has a presence in the European Union, Ghana and Nigeria (http://www.foresightconsultings.com/).

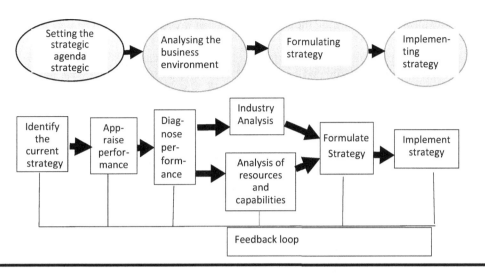

Figure 2.2   The strategy formulation process. (Adapted from Grant (2016), p. 23.)

both high and low levels of staff. All staff that are in direct contact with other B2B actors (like salespeople, management and negotiators, and those that contribute to the quality of products and services like engineering and production, but not in direct contact with external B2B actors) must be heard in the strategy formulation process in order to integrate all relevant inputs.

The overarching components of the strategy process are thus setting the strategic agenda; analysing the business environment; formulating the plans, tactic, vision, mission and objectives that make up the strategy; and implementing the strategy. Sub-components include identifying the current strategy; appraising the current strategy; diagnosing recent and ongoing performance; industry analysis (the company's competitors, relationships and networks, ecosystem, etc.); analysis of the company's resources and capabilities; analysis and formulation of strategy; and its implementation. A good strategy must be continuously appraised and analysed through a feedback loop that connects implementation with each stage of the process.

2.3 Strategy in Micro-, Small and Medium-Sized Enterprises, and Entrepreneurial Companies

Micro-, small and medium-sized companies (MSMEs) in Africa are defined as companies with a staff of under 99. Micro-companies are defined as having a staff of under 6, while MSMEs have a staff of 6–99. The definitions of these companies vary between countries. For example, in the European Union (EU), MSMEs have a staff of under 250 and a turnover of under 50 million euros, while these limits are higher in the USA and China. Most micro-enterprises and MSMEs are entrepreneurial companies because one or a few individuals often own them, often a family or group of private investors, or heavily influenced by the owners. They are usually run by the owners, and their entrepreneurial instincts, drive and ambitions are the main push for the activities of the companies (Easmon et al., 2019; Paul et al., 2017). Many such companies are family companies where family members are running the company, and they are passed on from parents to children. In African countries, it is still a fact that some of these companies may not be formally registered but might be doing profitable business with other companies (Adom & Williams, 2014; Fu et al., 2018). For example, grain mills that provide milling services to bakeries and the bakeries that supply pastries and bread to local shops in small towns and villages may not be registered in the national company registry. This phenomenon is speedily changing as local councils are ensuring that these micro-enterprises and MSMEs register, pay their due taxes and treat their staff according to the law. Research has shown that these companies contribute about 70% of the GDP and employ approximately 85% of the manufacturing workforce (Asare-Kyire et al., 2019; Abor & Hinson, 2005; Mamman et al., 2018; Ribeiro-Soriano, 2017; International Labour Organization, 2018). Therefore, they are crucial for innovation, supply chains, sourcing and relationship management in African B2B.

The number and contribution of micro-, SME and entrepreneurial companies are similar in highly developed countries and parts of the world, like in the EU (European Union, 2015). Ninety percent of all companies in the EU are micro-enterprises and MSMEs, and they generate three-quarters of all jobs in the EU. Many of these company are family firms. Most of the very successful and competitive global EU global giants grew from family firms, examples being the originally Swedish Tetra Pak, and IKEA and the German Mercedes Corporation. The success of these companies provides examples for African micro-enterprises and MSMEs to grow and take the continent along with them. The Swedish company Norden Machinery that is one of the world's leaders in manufacturing advanced packing machinery was an SME until it was purchased by the Italian company Coesia Group. Despite its purchase, it has been allowed to run itself almost as before with its Swedish suppliers, management and business culture. The company exports 97% of its production. Its success is linked to local SME suppliers with whom it collaborates on product and technology development. Its SME suppliers provide most of the input which is then assembled and customised to different B2B customers around the world (https://www.nordenmachinery.com/en/about-us). Thus, while Norden Machinery has outgrown the EU definition of SME in terms of the number of staff, many of its suppliers are local MSMEs and its success is partly dependent on the successful strategies, management and technical abilities of its partner MSMEs. In the same vein, the success of German industry, technology and exports is partly due to the success of its MSMEs (the "Mittelstand"), which is described as "the heart of the German economy" consisting of the companies that collaborate with and supply the major global German industrial names like Mercedes, Siemens and VW (https://english.bdi.eu/topics/germany/the-mittelstand/).

These European MSMEs have been successful for over 100 years and enabled Europe to achieve its economic and technological competitiveness. They provide examples for African micro-enterprises and MSMEs. The critical question is: how should African micro-enterprises and MSMEs formulate strategy, and how can they emulate the success of EU MSMEs?

As a good number of African micro-enterprises and MSMEs are informal and entrepreneurial, their formulation of strategy tends to be unwritten, unstructured and even ad-hoc (Benjamin & Mbaye, 2012; Boafo & Dornberger, 2019; Adesida et al., 2016; La Porta & Shleifer, 2014). In the town of Mufundi in Tanzania, grain milling is an essential value-added business that serves other businesses like bakeries, street food kitchens, restaurants and school kitchens. The local staples "ugali" and "uji" restaurants depend on the promptness and quality of the mills to be able to compete effectively against substitutes like rice and rice porridge. Despite the high importance of this relationship and its long-term nature, there are no formal strategies or written contracts. Therefore, when the mill that "Bupe Restaurant" uses suddenly breaks down, customers will suddenly have to go to the next mill located in the adjacent neighbourhood, which may not be able to serve them because it may want to serve its established customers first.

One strategy of SME foodstuff buying companies in Africa has been to build relations with farmers through paying upfront, buying from a large number of farmers and establishing good relations with traditional leaders in the community. Consequently, farmers get obliged to sell to them. Besides, when problems crop up on one farm, they are likely to get supplies from other farms. Moreover, by building good relations with local traditional leaders, they establish legitimacy in the farming communities which enables them to solve problems with farmers by using traditional mediation, i.e. the intervention of elders and local chiefs when necessary.

2.4 Contents of Business-to-Business Strategy

2.4.1 Planned, Emergent and Realised Strategy

A good strategy for a modern company should be planned, as shown in Table 2.1 and Figure 2.2. However, as a large number of African B2B companies are micro-enterprises, MSMEs and entrepreneurial companies, they do not necessarily formulate strategy formally or write strategy documents. Therefore, while the owners have a strategy, they do not necessarily have a formal written strategy in the form of written vision, mission, plans and tactics. However, a lack of formally written strategy is not the same as a lack of strategy. While planned strategy should be well thought out and include ideas about the components mentioned in Table 2.1 and Figure 2.2, the analysis of position should feed into the review of a long-term strategy as noted in Table 2.1 and Figure 2.2. This means that changes in the assumptions of the long-term strategy, and the business and industry competition, force an emergent strategy on the company. Thus, while the company may maintain a large part of its planned mission and vision, it should review the temporary strategy, thus creating an emergent strategy. Therefore, the realised strategy, in the long run, may differ from the initially planned strategy.

In the final analysis, whether a strategy is formally planned and written or not, it is confronted by the reality of the African business environment, which is generally unpredictable and unstable, as it is impacted by internal forces of changing economic policy, economic growth and corruption and inefficiencies, social (in)stability and industry competition. It is, therefore, important that the business owners or managers appreciated the importance of strategic planning as well as the emergent and realised components of the firm's strategy. Therefore, when evaluating or analysing achievements, all three aspects have to be considered to get a good understanding of performance and how it should feed into the next steps.

2.4.2 Strategic Fit in B2B

Strategic fit in B2B requires that the B2B company understand and develop its internal environment and match this with the external or industry setting. As in Figure 2.3, the foundation of the company is its vision, goals and values, structure and systems, resources and capabilities. The beginning of a good strategy is achieving a fit between these internal components and the industry environment, which consists of customers, competitors and suppliers.

When these aspects are in good shape, the company can develop a core competence, which makes it attractive to organisational partners. Thus, understanding the industry environment, following it and being dynamic in strategy formulation and change are critical to success.

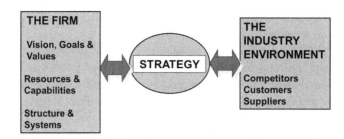

Figure 2.3 Strategic fit: aligning the firm's strategy with the industry environment.

(Source: Grant (2016), p. 10.)

2.4.3 Understanding the Industry and Business Environment

The industry environment is defined more narrowly to consist of other actors within the same industry (Grant, 2016; Porter, 2008). Thus, the industry environment of a maize-buying company would be other maize-buying companies that are current or potential competitors, customers (e.g. restaurants) who buy maize for various products like the East African staple and ugali, and the farmers who produce the maize.

Beyond the industry environment, there is a broader business environment as shown in Figure 2.4. The wider business environment may be affecting the B2B firm directly and indirectly. It determines the direction of the overall economy, total national income, government policy towards the industry and others, the global economy, decisions that affect market access, etc. Nwankwo (2000) stated that the African business environment was challenging but changing, and he suggested caution and changes that should be implemented as well as how companies should strategise for it. Owusu and Habiyakare (2011) studied how the South African business environment changed and how that impacted the entry of foreign firms. They found that the foreign B2B firms generally pursued carefully phased strategies, even in cases where they had a moderate-to-high level of trust in the economy. However, government policies like the "Broad-based Black Economic Empowerment Programme" affected the strategies of some firms in terms of expansion beyond the required 50 staff for implementing a certain level of the necessary employment and equality measures.

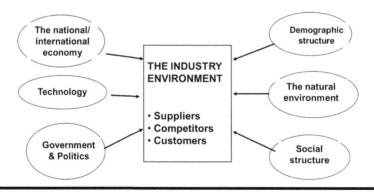

Figure 2.4 Industry and business environment of a B2B company.

(Source: Grant (2016), p. 10.)

The specific industry structure is sometimes seen as more critical for a company as some have argued that the wider business environment affects all firms in the same industry equally, and the most immediate opportunities and challenges come from the specific industry structure and related forces (Porter, 2008). Thus, irrespective of the current business situation, the maize-buying company can lose its position in the market against competitors. It will fail in its business if the farmers it buys from do not produce good-quality maize, and if its customers are having problems paying for its supplies. However, the wider African business environment (government policies, income, infrastructure, etc.) will affect consumption of the final product – banku, ugali, etc., which will affect all industry players (Nwankwo, 2000). We strongly believe that the B2B firm must analyse the wider industry environment as well. Developments in the broader industry environment can affect the profitability of the industry in general and worsen competition. Figure 2.4 combines Porter's five forces (Porter, 2008) (the "industry environment" in the figure) or "industry structure" according to Porter, with the overall national and international business context.

2.5 Segmentation, Targeting and Positioning (STP) in B2B

It is sometimes argued that B2B companies do not need to focus on STP strategies due to the small number of B2B actors. Some studies imply that as B2B firms are usually positioned in some supply chains and business networks, their concern should be providing the required value to their immediate network (Johanson & Vahlne, 2011; Hakansson & Snehota, 2006). However, as Kotler and Armstrong (2010) and Ellis (2010) emphasise, STP should not be disregarded because it is about continuing to consider new customers, suppliers and new networks to work with. It should be part of the ongoing strategy formulation and analysis. As discussed earlier, a good strategy requires dynamism and agility, which STP helps to achieve. Therefore, B2B companies should not reject STP. The questions to ask and deal with are as follows:

Segmentation: Who are the new customers, suppliers and other parties in the market? Which of them are suitable partners for our business? Which new products and services shall we develop? What level of services shall we offer our clients? How shall we classify them? How similar or different are they? What capabilities and core competencies do they have? The company should then analyse them, categorise them and clarify the similarities and differences between them.
Targeting: Which parties should the company select to contact and develop relations with?
Positioning: What marketing strategies should the company use? What core competencies, products and services should the company offer them or seek from them? How should the company position itself in its supply chain or network? What pricing and promotion strategies should it use?

In Chapter 3, we will delve deeper into marketing mix strategies for B2B companies.

2.6 Modes of Collaboration and Competition in Business-to-Business Markets

As we have previously discussed, researchers have found that B2B marketing management consists of building and managing relations with groups of firms with which the B2B party is embedded in relationships that make its business possible and competitive (Hakansson & Snehota, 2006; Johanson & Mattsson, 2011; Möller & Halinen 2017). The firm is located in supply chains (also called value chains) and embedded in networks. Some of these relationships are deliberately developed by some of the parties, while some other parties are brought in through their existing relationships and new business opportunities (Partanen & Möller, 2012; Owusu & Welch, 2007) and sometimes as a result of their location in clusters (Felzensztein et al., 2014). These relationships in value chains, networks and clusters, where the firm depends on others for supplies and for onward selling of its products, services and technologies, or for different kinds of support and collaboration that are necessary for its survival, have become essential for the competitiveness of firms. Some researchers emphasise that nowadays, competition is no more between single companies but between supply chains, clusters and networks. That is, no firm is competing alone anymore but competing with the support of its supply chain and networks (Porter, 2000, 1998; Bengtsson et al., 2010; Kothandaraman & Wilson, 2001). Other researchers have found that these supply chains, networks and clusters include competitors who are competing and collaborating simultaneously, that is "coopeting" ("coopetition") (Bengtsson & Kock, 2000; Galkina & Lundgren-Henriksson, 2017). The foregoing means that B2B strategy has to be developed by considering the firm's position in its supply chain, network or cluster. It also means that B2B strategy is no longer developed within the firm alone but in interaction with the other parties in the firm's relationships. The corn mill entrepreneur in a small African town might source his mill from a local mechanical manufacturer or might buy an imported mill. The mill must be suitably located in order to be easily reachable by local restaurateurs, bakeries and shop owners. The mill is operating in a supply chain that includes the mill manufacturers, the local restaurants, bakeries, shops, etc. For the mill to succeed and compete well, it must consider the needs and interests of its customers. If the mill entrepreneur concentrates only on his profits in his place, promotion, pricing and other strategies, without considering the needs and interests of the bakeries and restaurateurs, he may lose business to a new or existing entrepreneur. While competing against other mills, it would be useful for the mill owners to collaborate as much as the law allows. While every country has, laws aimed at ensuring that businesses do not illegally collaborate by fixing prices and dividing up markets, a fair amount of collaboration strategies between competitors is legal. If Dufie Mill's machine breaks down due to a broken part, Abrafi Mill could agree to loan that part which it has in stock for Dufie Mill to fix its machines and continue its business. Dufie Mill can return the favour next time. Besides, when Dufie Mill gets so much business that some of its customers might be delayed and not get their milled grain in time to cook dinner in their restaurant, an agreement can be made with Abrafi Mill to outsource some of the waiting work. By so doing, the two competitors will be competing and cooperating simultaneously, that is coopeting. In their study, DeBerry-Spence et al. (2008) found that Ghanaian and Ivorian B2B companies use both transactional marketing and relationship marketing. They found that the market context and the characteristics of the firms influenced their marketing strategies, for example, a much lower level of data-based marketing compared to Argentinian and American firms. They found a higher level of transactional marketing among Ghanaian and Ivorian B2B firms than among Argentinian and American firms. The study implied that as competition increases, West African firms are likely to adopt more relational and network marketing strategies than they do now.

In subsequent chapters, we will dig deeper into the concepts and strategies of B2B collaboration like relationship and network management, acquisitions, joint ventures and outsourcing. In the rest of this chapter, we will briefly define and discuss the primary forms of business strategy collaboration and competition.

2.6.1 Supply Chain or Value Chain

The flow of products, services, technologies and value through the B2B system is referred to as the supply chain or value chain (Carter et al., 2015; Christopher, 2011). These concepts are used to depict the significant relationships (marketing, purchasing, negotiation, interdependence, collaboration and coopetition that exist in the B2B market) (Johanson & Vahlne, 2011; Hakansson & Snehota, 2006). In fact, with globalisation and the tightening of competition, supply chains and value chains have become more critical for each of the companies, for the national as well as the global economy (Leuschner et al, 2013; Mena et al., 2013).

As Figure 2.5 shows, the supply chain is represented as the flow of goods with the "upstream" and "downstream" sides. Upstream represents the beginning of the flow, using the metaphor of a stream. Thus, the timber industry in Liberia starts from the forestry companies that husband the forest, plant teak trees and provide space for legal harvesting of wood. The timber harvesters supply timber to the mills. The mills make various kinds of sawn timber that are purchased by furniture and carpentry companies that then supply builders, furniture shops, etc. Each firm in this chain is dependent on the other firms as suppliers or purchasers (Leuschner et al., 2013; Manhart et al., 2020; Mena et al., 2013). The business of the forestry companies (upstream) will not do well if the carpenters and furniture manufacturers do not provide competitive products and services that can compete against imports from Italy, Scandinavia or China. Likewise, the wholesalers and retailers of wood products (downstream) depend on good forestry and legal harvesting of quality wood by the forestry companies. If the wholesalers and retailers choose to promote foreign products instead of local ones, the local forestry firms in Liberia will lose customers.

The term "value chain" is also used to analyse the value creation processes inside a company, where the business of a company is analysed in terms of "primary activities", "manufacturing

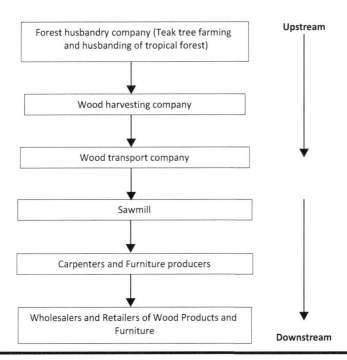

Figure 2.5   The supply chain or value chain for local wood industry products in Liberia.

activities", "supporting activities" and "sales activities". In this book, we are concerned with the B2B activities, that is the interrelationships between firms and other parties in the business market. Therefore, in this chapter, we use the value chain in its inter-organisational meaning as synonymous with the supply chain. When using the "value chain", we are describing each stage in the supply chain as a creation or addition of value, i.e. additions of value from upstream on the way downstream to the final customer. If value is not added or if value is subtracted at any stage, the result will be lower competitiveness of this supply chain, which will hurt the firms in it.

2.6.2 Network

Unlike the flowing stream metaphor of the supply/value chain, the network uses a "spider web" or net metaphor to depict the interdependence, collaboration and interaction among parties in the B2B market (Hakansson & Snehota, 2006; Möller, 2013; Möller & Halinen, 2017). Thus, the parties depicted in Figure 2.6 include the parties in 2.4. However, the network theory extends interest to all other parties that influence or impact the success or failure of each company or the whole supply chain. Thus, the network is defined as interrelationships and interdependence between parties in the B2B market. It implies the embeddedness of B2B parties in relationships and business-related activities.

As explained in Chapter 1, the parties in the B2B market consist of companies, organisations and institutions, including both for-profit and not-for-profit organisations. Institutions can be private or public institutions. Private institutions can be corporate responsibility guardians like Wildlife Conservation Society or Greenpeace; public institutions can be the Ministry for Environment. In representing or analysing the network, the student or researcher looks at it from the perspective of one of the parties, which puts one party in the centre as the focal party from which the interrelationships are analysed.

The business network theory recognises the importance of relationships between the companies for the success of each company. Actors, resources and activities (ARA) are proposed as the summary content of the relationships (Ellis, 2010, p. 138; Lenney & Easton, 2009; Cantù et al., 2012).

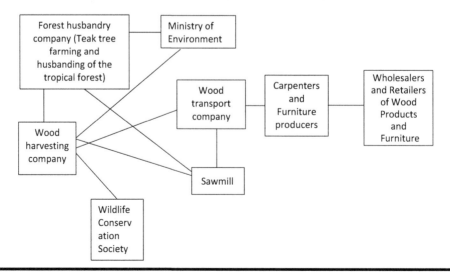

Figure 2.6   The wood and furniture industry network in Liberia.

Actors are both firms and individuals working for the firms in the B2B context. Thus, relationships and relationship management occur at both the individual and firm levels. Personality, personal and social relationships contribute to business relationships. In relationship management, business culture becomes a mediator; that is, what is the right way to establish and maintain relationships between business partners in a specific African country? Business relationships are maintained by not only the quality of products between the firms but also the social and cultural aspects of relationship management (Grönroos, 2017; Möller & Halinen, 2017). Concerning non-business and institutional actors, lobbying and negotiation are the oils of the relationship. African business culture is a combination of traditional relationship management culture, law and legal relationship management, as well as profit-making considerations (Darley & Blankson, 2020; DeBerry-Spence et al., 2008). Social relationships are a fundamental part of African culture. Friendships, family and ethnic ties, traditional social relationship building and Africa's unique culture of enduring, open, cordial and win-win social relationships ("Ubuntu") have formed the African business culture (Berrou & Combarnous, 2012, 2011; Mbigi, 2005). African entrepreneurs use a combination of the relationships mentioned above, and business relationships management in Africa incorporate the informal aspects of African culture. The differences between traditional business culture, law and bureaucracy are lines drawn in the sands of African deserts. Therefore, social relationships and traditional relationship management are the foundations of African B2B management (Darley & Blankson, 2020; DeBerry-Spence et al., 2008).

In Karam's (2003) study of architectural firms in Cape Town, he found that they moved from an initial dislike of marketing to practising B2B marketing by getting involved in professional and social organisations for exchange of professional ideas and information about the market. They developed links with other firms to get contracts through referrals. He further stated that the professional and civic organisations the firms actively participated in provided both peer influence and marketing knowledge, contacts and references.

2.6.3 Clusters

Throughout economic history, there has been a natural tendency for entrepreneurs and firms to develop and assemble near each other. In the pre-globalisation days, this was partly because of the existence of natural or entrepreneurial resources in particular geographical areas. The exploitation of the resources and value addition was easier to do when the firms were near each other. The firms, thus, became a cluster. A business cluster is, therefore, a geographically bounded number of firms and entrepreneurs who are linked to each other in various ways by being located near each other (Bettis-Outland et al., 2012; Eisingerich et al., 2010, p. 241; Felzensztein et al., 2014; Porter, 2000, p. 15). Clusters based on natural resources and entrepreneurship are, for example, the wood and furniture industry cluster of the Kumasi metropolis in Ghana. A spontaneous natural cluster of wood and furniture industry developed in the city based on the tropical forest wood and the entrepreneurial abilities of the natives as well as the cosmopolitan area with immigrants from other parts of the country, other West Africa African countries, the Middle East and Europe. A more bounded cluster in Kumasi, Ghana is the "Suame Magazine" which has been called "Africa's largest industrial cluster" (Adesida et al., 2016). In order to support the woodworking and furniture industry cluster of Oforikrom–Anloga in Kumasi (which was starting to create severe environmental degradation of nearby streams and pollution in a very densely populated area), the Government of Ghana built the Sokoban Wood Village cluster and encouraged/forced most of the companies and entrepreneurs to move there. This became an officially organised cluster of firms. The Bonwire–Adanwomase Kente cluster is another spontaneous informally evolved cluster based on entrepreneurial skills in the area. The firms and entrepreneurs in the clusters are linked in supply/value chains and networks. They supply to, buy from, support each other financially and technically, and achieve unplanned and planned advantages from their aggregation in a geographical area. Therefore, the cluster combines Figures 2.5 and 2.6. For example, the reputation of the Bonwire–Adanwomase Kente cluster is global, with tourists coming from all over the world to visit and buy their handicrafts. Products of the cluster can be found in tourist markets all over Africa. This provides business for each individual handicraft maker, and the cluster as a whole can promote/brand/advertise itself to the whole world. Therefore, each company in the cluster benefits from the geographical aggregation (Felzensztein et al., 2014). Social and business relationships are critical aspects of the success of business clusters all over the world (Berrou & Combarnous, 2011, 2012). As stated earlier, these are integral aspects of African business culture.

Many of the entrepreneurs in these clusters, just as in African economies, in general, are informal (Adom & Williams, 2014). In African countries, most informal firms are open entrepreneurships with public names, shops and offices that innovate and produce products and services that are sold legally. Informal firms interact with some state institutions and are recognised by local and national authorities as contributing to employment and the national economy (Boafo & Donberger, 2019; Benjamin & Mbaye, 2012).

2.6.4 Ecosystems

Recently, the originally biological sciences concept of the ecosystem has been introduced into B2B management. Just like the network, interdependence, interrelationships and co-evolution are critical for B2B parties according to the business ecosystem perspective (Adner, 2017; Rong et al., 2015). It has similarity with the markets-as-networks theory (Möller & Halinen, 2017) that states that B2B firms are embedded in networks that the whole B2B market of nations and globally is one interconnected web of relationships and networks. Thus, the concept is similar to the network, but its proponents emphasise that it will help to improve the understanding of interrelationships between businesses, their surrounding actors and the environment, that is how interrelationships and interdependencies affect all parties, and it is, therefore, not redundant (Rasmussen & Petersen, 2017; Williamson & De Meyer, 2012). Strategy for the B2B firm in the business ecosystem would thus consider these interrelationships, interdependence and co-evolution (Ojala et al., 2018). Some researchers emphasise that there are differences in definition as well as application. The ecosystem integrates the business environment and the role of silent and inactive actors and aspects of the industry and business environment more readily than the network. While the markets-as-networks theory implies that all direct links are critical and indirect links are necessary to analyse, the ecosystem perspective reflects a more substantial level of co-existence, based on its ecological and biological background. This means that indirect links might be more critical from an ecosystem perspective than it is from a network perspective (Möller & Halinen, 2017; Ojala et al., 2018).

2.7 Conclusion

A strategy is a long-term set of actions to achieve long-term competitive goals. It consists of the vision, mission, plans and tactics that are developed with the aid of various models and concepts of strategy. The long-term nature of strategy does not, however, mean that the short term should be disregarded. Regular short-term analyses of the firm's position, the components of its strategy and how they relate to changed situations should be done to realign the long-term strategy, where necessary.

B2B strategy formulation, content and implementation benefit from the general concepts and practice of business strategy. However, the context of B2B emphasises positions in supply chains, networks, clusters and the business ecosystem. Thus, a B2B strategy must analyse and relate to the agglomerations discussed in the preceding sections. The research generally states that relationship management is a core strategy in B2B. The components of successful relationship management are integral parts of African culture. What is required for African B2B firms to succeed is to understand the processes and details of strategy as discussed in the preceding sections and apply them to their relevant supply chains, networks, clusters and ecosystems. However, the African business context impacts the current nature of strategy, and the ongoing changes in African markets are likely to lead to changes in the strategies of B2B organisations (DeBerry-Spence et al., 2008; Nwankwo, 2000).

In subsequent chapters, specific aspects of strategy introduced here will be discussed in more depth.

Case and Exercise: Unitrans – Getting Your Food to the Dining Table

Author: Dr Adele Berndt, Jönköping International Business School, Sweden.

When thinking about any retail operation, it is necessary to consider the delivery of products to the outlet. Deliveries of products are strategically significant for the retailer as, without these deliveries, the retailer will not have products to sell, which impacts profits and customer satisfaction.

PICK N PAY

Food retailing is a complex and challenging business, stocking a wide range of products to meet diverse customer needs and tastes. Products include dry groceries such as flour, sugar and tinned products but also fresh fruit, vegetables and pharmaceutical products. Expansion in product lines and changing customer needs means that stores have also started stocking liquor and clothing to be able to compete in a broader range of products.

A BRIEF HISTORY OF PNP

One leading grocery chain in South Africa is Pick n Pay (PnP). Started in 1967 by Raymond Ackerman in Cape Town, the chain has grown to 770 company-owned PnP stores and 305 franchised stores in South Africa.[3] The group employs 90,000 employees across all their retail brands which also include Boxer and TM Supermarkets in Zimbabwe.[4]

THE DISTRIBUTION MANAGEMENT IN PNP

With having so many stores selling both merchandised and private-label goods throughout South Africa, PnP uses a centralised warehousing system to distribute fresh products, grocery items, liquor and clothing. This means all items are delivered to 14 central warehouses. The two largest are

---

[3] Pick n Pay (2019). Unaudited condensed consolidated interim financial statements for the 26 weeks ended (accessed 1 September 2019).

[4] Pick n Pay at a glance (2019). https://www.picknpayinvestor.co.za/at-a-glance.php (accessed 19 November 2019).

Longmeadow outside Johannesburg and Philippi in the Western Cape.[5] Having grocery retailing as a core business, PnP made the decision that they would not be involved in the logistical distribution of products to stores, but rather build a partnership with Unitrans, a specialist supply chain organisation to manage this aspect of the business. The benefit that PnP get from using a centralised warehouse is that they can have lower inventory levels in the stores but also have a better supply of products on the shelves (which improves customer satisfaction). A further benefit is less congestion at the receiving centres at each store and lower transport costs for the supply chain. Deliveries from their warehouses are also done by Unitrans Supply Chain Holdings (Pty) Ltd. Their work at PnP involves distributing 1 million packages of groceries from Longmeadow and 400,000 packages from the Philippi warehouse to the stores. This is an important relationship for both parties, with PnP needing the goods in their stores and for Unitrans to operate their business profitably.

TRANSPORTATION DECISIONS – UNITRANS SUPPLY CHAIN HOLDINGS (PTY) LTD
WHO IS UNITRANS?

Unitrans is a diversified supply chain solution company that serves numerous sectors including the automotive industry and construction sector (e.g. cement) as well as the transportation of fast-moving consumer (FMCG) goods and refrigerated transport solutions.[6] One of their divisions is Unitrans Supply Chain Solutions (Pty) Ltd that focuses on supply chains, and how they contribute to strategic advantage for both partners.

Unitrans currently operates a fleet of 327 vehicles from PnP's Longmeadow distribution centre. The transport network services 455 PnP stores in Gauteng and areas as far afield as Botswana, Namibia, Swaziland and Lesotho.[7] "The Longmeadow operation is a world-class facility", says Theunis Nel, CEO of Unitrans. "We are happy to partner with PnP as it aims for greater efficiencies in its supply chain".[8] The transport operation employs 930 people, who work in several areas of the supply chain, including outbound deliveries to stores, reverse logistics and inter distribution centre trunking. The operation is further supported by the Unitrans control tower, which provides an essential comprehensive monitoring function.[9]

TRANSPORTATION ALTERNATIVES

As a transport company responsible for getting products to the various stores for PnP, trucks are foundational to their ability to meet the needs within the supply chain.

THE TRUCKS AS THE BACKBONE OF THE OPERATION

Any trucking organisation has their equipment, specifically trucks, as the backbone of their operation. When thinking about trucks, it is essential to remember that there are many components to consider. The first factor that needs to be considered is that any vehicle purchased must be fit for purpose. For example, when Unitrans is moving dry FMCG goods to PnP stores, it may not require any specific characteristics, but this would not apply when transporting cold goods which

---

[5] 2019 Integrated Annual Report Pick n Pay. www.picknpayinvestor.co.za › investor-centre › annual-report ›iar-2019 (accessed 8 November 2019).

[6] https://www.unitrans.co.za/.

[7] Anon (2018). Ano ns and Pick n Pay. *Focus on Transport and Logistics*, 19 April. http://www.focusontransport.co.za/another-decade-for-unitrans-and-pick-n-pay/.

[8] "Ibid.

[9] Ibid.

require refrigerated options. Vehicles needed to transport concrete, or heavy equipment would require additional features such as hoses or forklifts on the back of the vehicles.

THE OPERATIONAL COSTS ASSOCIATED WITH TRANSPORTATION

When deciding to acquire a new vehicle, the management has to decide whether to purchase the vehicle (i.e. pay for them) or whether to lease the vehicle. Not only is it the cost of the truck itself for which the company has to pay, but there are substantial costs associated with ensuring that the trucks are efficiently used. Fuel comprises a significant operating cost (approximately 40%–53% of these costs),[10] so negotiating a preferential price with a leading fuel company is one way to reduce operating expenses. These vehicles also need to be serviced regularly to ensure that they do not break down while goods and can operate at maximum efficiency. Once vehicles are purchased and fuelled, the driver is the next important key. Employing skilled drivers is vital due to the high levels of responsibility for getting the goods to the stores in an acceptable condition. Insurance costs are an additional cost. With increased accident rates and criminal attacks on vehicles in South Africa, this has raised insurance premiums for transport companies, impacting operating costs.

LOADING THE TRUCKS IN THE WAREHOUSE

As the trucks deliver the goods to the various stores, it is essential that they are loaded the correct products for delivery. This is the role of the warehouse management and the organisational (PnP) ordering system where the individual stores place their orders for items that are needed at the various stores.

RISKS ASSOCIATED WITH TRANSPORTING GOODS

There are numerous risks that Unitrans has to consider in its task of transporting goods to the PnP stores and managing their costs. Some of these include

- **The Risk of Accidents**: Goods are transported on roads which are maintained by the government and are used by many other vehicles. Road and vehicle conditions interact to impact the risks, and while Unitrans ensure that their vehicles are in a road-worthy condition, this does not remove these risks. For example, weather conditions such as heavy rain impact how promptly the driver can arrive at the delivery point. These are also conditions where the likelihood of accidents increases. Distances covered can be very long, and the roads can also be isolated, which increases the risks associated with an accident.
- **The Health and Safety of the Drivers**: This is also an important concern for the transport company. The health of drivers is a concern for transport companies due to the physical nature of their job, i.e. their eyesight and physical abilities to cope with driving conditions. Driving also impacts healthy eating (access to nutritious and healthy meals), which is associated with diabetes. HIV/AIDs is also a condition affecting transport companies. Not only is the organisation concerned with the physical risks but travelling on isolated roads at night increases the dangers to the driver of the driver being attacked or the vehicle being highjacked.
- **Routing Decisions**: The route that the vehicle takes to make the deliveries. This is a significant factor in customer satisfaction as should deliveries be late or the products do not arrive in optimal conditions, this impacts the relationship that has developed.[11]

---

[10] Braun, M. (2005). *Keys to better fleet management.* A Fleetwatch Publication, Johannesburg.
[11] Ibid.

- **Tyre Management**: A vehicle needs to have tyres that can safely transport the load which includes that they are correctly inflated (i.e. have the right amount of air or nitrogen) and not damaged by road conditions such as stones or potholes. This reinforces the importance of road maintenance for transport operations.
- **The Safety of the Load Being Transported**: There is an increased danger of trucks being attacked and the goods being stolen. In South Africa, the trucking industry has lost ZAR1.3 billion during 2019 (up until November 2019) as trucks have been looted and burnt by various criminal groups. While many of these vehicles that have been attacked are long-distance vehicles,[12] this remains a risk for all transport operators.

Not only are there costs associated with getting the products into the trucks and out to the PnP stores, but there are also office staff who provide essential jobs to facilitate the deliveries. Examples include route planners, schedulers, fleet managers and those responsible for loading the vehicle.

PnP AND UNITRANS: A LONG-TERM RELATIONSHIP

As any organisation wishes to satisfy customer needs efficiently, and Unitrans is an integral part of this. The relationship between PnP and Unitrans is viewed in a positive light by both parties, and the decision has recently been made that the contract will be extended for another 10 years. This relationship is described as a "valuable relationship" by PnP in their task of satisfying customer needs.

For Unitrans, this means they have been able to invest in improving their efficiency in the distribution centre through the purchase of equipment that can load the trucks more efficiently before they transport the goods to the various stores. Nevertheless, in the long term, they will need to continue providing value to PnP not only to keep the contract they have but also to ensure that both parties derive value from this partnership.

2.8 Questions

1. What benefits does a central warehousing system provide for a leading retailer like PnP?
2. How can PnP and Unitrans ensure that their partnership is extended into the foreseeable future?
3. What value does PnP derive from this relationship?
4. What value does Unitrans derive from this relationship?

References

Abor, J., & Hinson, R. (2005). Internationalising SME nontraditional exporters and their internet use idiosyncrasies. *Perspectives on Global Development and Technology,* 4(2), 229–244.

Adesida, O., Karuri-Sebina, G., & Resende-Santos, J. (2016). *Innovation Africa: Emerging hubs of excellence.* Emerald Group Publishing, Bingley, United Kingdom.

Adner, R. (2017). Ecosystem as structure: An actionable construct for strategy. *Journal of Management,* 43(1), 39–58.

---

[12]Naidoo, S. (2019). Concern as 1400 trucks burnt or looted since the start of 2019. IOL, 23 November. https://www.iol.co.za/weekend-argus/news/concern-as-1-400-trucks-burnt-or-looted-since-start-of-2019-37809420 (accessed 23 November 2019).

Adom, K., & Williams, C. C. (2014). Evaluating the explanations for the informal economy in third world cities: Some evidence from Koforidua in the eastern region of Ghana. *International Entrepreneurship and Management Journal*, 10(2), 427–445.

Asare-Kyire, L., Zheng, H., & Owusu, A. (2019). An empirical examination of the influencers of premature decline of African clusters: Evidence from textile clusters in Ghana. *South African Journal of Business Management*, 50(1), 1–13.

Barnard, H. (2020). The Africa we want and the Africa we see: How scholarship from Africa stands to enrich global scholarship. *Africa Journal of Management*, 6(1), 1–12.

Bengtsson, M., & Kock, S., (2000). Cooperate and compete simultaneously. *Industrial Marketing Management*, 29, 411–426.

Bengtsson, M., Wilson, T. L., Kinra, A., & Antai, I. (2010). Emerging logics of competition: Paradigm shift, fantasy, or reality check? *Competitiveness Review: An International Business Journal*, 20(2), 94–110.

Benjamin, N. C., & Mbaye, A. A. (2012). The informal sector, productivity, and enforcement in West Africa: A firm-level analysis. *Review of Development Economics*, 16(4), 664–680.

Berrou, J. P., & Combarnous, F. (2011). Testing Lin's social capital theory in an informal African urban economy. *Journal of Development Studies*, 47(8), 1216–1240.

Berrou, J. P., & Combarnous, F. (2012). The personal networks of entrepreneurs in an informal African urban economy: Does the 'strength of ties' matter? *Review of Social Economy*, 70(1), 1–30.

Bettis-Outland, H., Grönroos, C., & Helle, P. (2012). Return on relationships: Conceptual understanding and measurement of mutual gains from relational business engagements. *Journal of Business & Industrial Marketing*, 33(1), 145–152.

Bick, G., & Nicolaus, I. (2011). The role of internal marketing in engineering organisations in South Africa. *In Proceedings of International Conference on Enterprise Marketing and Globalization (EMG)*, (p. 36). Global Science and Technology Forum, Penang, Malaysia.

Boafo, C., & Dornberger, U. (2019, August 28-29). *The Internationalisation Degree of Urban Informal Enterprises in Ghana: An Extension of Internationalisation Theories* [Paper Presentation]. 23rd McGill International Entrepreneurship Conference, Southern Denmark University, Odense, Denmark.

Cantù, C., Corsaro, D., & Snehota, I. (2012). Roles of actors in combining resources into complex solutions. *Journal of Business Research*, 65(2), 139–150.

Carter, C. R., Rogers, D. S., & Choi, T. Y. (2015). Toward the theory of the supply chain. *Journal of Supply Chain Management*, 51(2), 89–97.

Christopher, M. (2011). *Logistics and supply chain management*. Pearson Education Limited, London.

Darley, W. K., & Blankson, C. (2020). Sub-Saharan African cultural belief system and entrepreneurial activities: A Ghanaian perspective. *Africa Journal of Management*, 6(12), 1–18.

DeBerry-Spence, B., Dadzie, K. Q., Darley, W. K., & Blankson, C. (2008). African culture and business markets: Implications for marketing practices. *Journal of Business and Industrial Marketing*, 23, 374–383.

Easmon, R. B., Kastner, A. N. A., Blankson, C., & Mahmoud, M. A. (2019). Social capital and export performance of SMEs in Ghana: The role of firm capabilities. *African Journal of Economic and Management Studies*, 10(3), 262–285.

Eisingerich, A. B., Bell, S. J., & Tracey, P. (2010). How can clusters sustain performance? The role of network strength, network openness, and environmental uncertainty. *Research Policy*, 39(2), 239–253.

Ellis, N. (2010). *Business to business marketing: Relationships, networks and strategies*. Oxford University Press, Oxford.

European Union (2015). User guide to the SME definition. Retrieved September 8, 2020, from file:///C:/Users/riowaa/Downloads/smedefinitionguide_en%20(1).pdf.

Federation of German Industries (BDI), Retrieved September 8, 2020, from Mittelstand: https://english.bdi.eu/topics/germany/the-mittelstand/.

Felzensztein, C., Stringer, C., Benson-Rea, M., & Freeman, S. (2014). International marketing strategies in industrial clusters: Insights from the Southern Hemisphere. *Journal of Business Research*, 67(5), 837–846.

Fu, X., Mohnen, P., & Zanello, G. (2018). Innovation and productivity in formal and informal firms in Ghana. *Technological Forecasting and Social Change*, 131, 315–325.

Galkina, T., & Lundgren-Henriksson, E. L. (2017). Coopetition as an entrepreneurial process: Interplay of causation and effectuation. *Industrial Marketing Management, 67*, 158–173.

Grant, R. M. (2016). *Contemporary strategy analysis: Text and cases edition.* John Wiley & Sons, New York.

Grönroos, C. (1994). Quo Vadis, marketing? Toward a relationship marketing paradigm. *Journal of Marketing Management, 10*(5), 347–360.

Grönroos, C. (2017). On value and value creation in service: A management perspective. *Journal of Creating Value, 3*(2), 125–141.

Hakansson, H., & Snehota, I. (2006). No business is an island: The network concept of business strategy. *Scandinavian Journal of Management, 22*(3), 256–270.

Hofstede, G. (1983). The cultural relativity of organisational practices and theories. *Journal of International Business Studies, 14*(2), 75–89.

Holm, D. B., Eriksson, K., & Johanson, J. (1999). Creating value through mutual commitment to business network relationships. *Strategic Management Journal, 20*(5), 467–486.

International Labour Organization. (2018). *Women and men in the informal economy: A statistical picture* (3rd ed.). ILO, Geneva, Switzerland.

Johanson, J., & Mattsson, L. G. (2011). Internationalisation in industrial systems–a network approach, strategies in global competition in banks. In N. Hood & J. Vahlne (Eds.), *The internationalisation of the firm: A reader* (pp. 303–22). Academic Press, London.

Johanson, J., & Vahlne, J. E. (2011). Markets as networks: Implications for strategy-making. *Journal of the Academy of Marketing Science, 39*(4), 484–491.

Karam, A. H. (2003). Marketing and architects in South Africa. *Engineering, Construction and Architectural Management, 10*(6), 402–412.

Keränen, J., & Liozu, S. (2020). Value champions in business markets: Four role configurations. *Industrial Marketing Management, 85*, 84–96.

Kothandaraman, P., & Wilson, D. T. (2001). The future of competition: Value-creating networks. *Industrial Marketing Management, 30*(4), 379–389.

Kotler, P., & Armstrong, G. (2010). *Principles of marketing.* Prentice Hall, Upper Saddle River NJ.

Kuada, J., & Mensah, E. (2020). Knowledge transfer in the emerging solar energy sector in Ghana. *Contemporary Social Science, 15*(1), 82–97.

La Porta, R., & Shleifer, A. (2014). Informality and development. *Journal of Economic Perspectives, 28*(3), 109–26.

Lenney, P., & Easton, G. (2009). Actors, resources, activities and commitments. *Industrial Marketing Management, 38*(5), 553–561.

Leuschner, R., Rogers, D. S., & Charvet, F. F. (2013). A meta-analysis of supply chain integration and firm performance. *Journal of Supply Chain Management, 49*(2), 34–57.

Mahmoud, M. A., Kastner, A., & Yeboah, J. (2010). Antecedents, environmental moderators and consequences of market orientation: A study of pharmaceutical firms in Ghana. *Journal of Medical Marketing, 10*(3), 231–244.

Mamman, A., Kamoche, K., & Zakaria, H. B. (2018). 5 Rethinking human capital development in Africa. *Africapitalism: Rethinking the Role of Business in Africa*, 99–136. doi: 10.1017/9781316675922.006.

Manhart, P., Summers, J. K., & Blackhurst, J. (2020). A meta-analytic review of supply chain risk management: Assessing buffering and bridging strategies and firm performance. *Journal of Supply Chain Management, 56*(3), 66–87.

Mbigi, L. (2005). *The spirit of African leadership, Johannesburg.* Knowledge Resources, Bryanston, South Africa.

Mena, C., Humphries, A., & Choi, T. Y. (2013). Toward a theory of multi-tier supply chain management. *Journal of Supply Chain Management, 49*(2), 58–77.

Mintzberg, H. (1987). The strategy concept II: Another look at why organisations need strategies. *California Management Review, 30*(1), 25–32.

Möller, K., & Halinen, A. (2017). Managing business and innovation networks: From strategic nets to business fields and ecosystems. *Industrial Marketing Management, 67*, 5–22.

Möller, K. (2013). Theory map of business marketing: Relationships and networks perspectives. *Industrial Marketing Management, 42*(3), 324–335.

Norden Machinery, Retrieved September 8, 2020, from https://www.nordenmachinery.com/en/about-us.

Nwankwo, S. (2000). Assessing the marketing environment in sub-Saharan Africa: Opportunities and threats analysis. *Marketing Intelligence and Planning*, 18(3), 144–153.

Ojala, A., Evers, N., & Rialp, A. (2018). Extending the international new venture phenomenon to digital platform providers: A longitudinal case study. *Journal of World Business,* 53(5), 725–739.

Owusu, R. A., & Habiyakare, E. (2011). Managing risk and turbulence in internationalisation of foreign companies to South Africa: Lessons from seven Finnish business-to-business firms. *Journal of African Business,* 12(2), 218–237.

Owusu, R. A., & Welch, C. (2007). The buying network in international project business: A comparative case study of development projects. *Industrial Marketing Management*, 36(2), 147–157.

Partanen, J., & Möller, K. (2012). How to build a strategic network: A practitioner-oriented process model for the ICT sector. *Industrial Marketing Management*, 41(3), 481–494.

Paul, J., Parthasarathy, S., & Gupta, P. (2017). Exporting challenges of SMEs: A review and future research agenda. *Journal of World Business,* 52(3), 327–342.

Porter, M. E. (1996). What is strategy? *Harvard Business Review,* 74(6), 61–78.

Porter, M. E. (1998). Clusters and the new economics of competition. *Harvard Business Review,* 76(6), pp. 77–90.

Porter, M. E. (2000). Location, competition, and economic development: Local clusters in a global economy. *Economic Development Quarterly*, 14(1), 15–34.

Porter, M. E. (2008). The five competitive forces that shape strategy. *Harvard Business Review*, 86(1), 25–40.

Rasmussen, E. S., & Petersen, N. H. (2017). Platforms for innovation and internationalisation. *Technology Innovation Management Review*, 7(5), 23–31.

Reeves, M., Levin, S., & Ueda, D. (2016). The biology of corporate survival: Natural ecosystems hold surprising lessons for business. *Harvard Business Review,* 94(1–2), 46–56.

Ribeiro-Soriano, D. (2017). Small business and entrepreneurship: Their role in economic and social development. *Small Business and Entrepreneurs*, 29(1), 1–3.

Rong, K., Hu, G., Lin, Y., Shi, Y., & Guo, L. (2015). Understanding the business ecosystem using a 6C framework in Internet-of-Things-based sectors. *International Journal of Production Economics,* 159, 41–55.

Sull, D., Homkes, R., & Sull, C. (2015). Why strategy execution unravels - and what to do about it. *Harvard Business Review*, 93(3), 57–66.

Williamson, P. J., & De Meyer, A. (2012). Ecosystem advantage: How to successfully harness the power of partners. *California Management Review*, 55(1), 24–46.

MARKETING AND PURCHASING IN THE BUSINESS-TO-BUSINESS MARKET

2

Introduction and Learning Goals

In Part 2, we will discuss the marketing and purchasing strategies of actors in the business-to-business (B2B) market. It consists of Chapters 3–5. Chapter 3 covers the marketing mix strategies for the B2B organisation. Chapter 4 focuses on selling strategies of the marketing organisation, and Chapter 5 deals with the buying strategies of the purchasing organisation. Each chapter ends with an African case study.

Chapter 3

The Marketing Mix in the Business-to-Business Market

At the end of the chapter, the reader will be able to:

- Understand the marketing mix within a business-to-business (B2B) relationship
- Understand the marketing mix as a strategy for business performance in B2B relationships in Africa
- Understand the use of product as a strategy in the business market
- Understand the use of pricing as a strategy in the business market
- Appreciate and identify promotional tools effective for B2B operations
- Identify distribution strategies and mechanism in B2B context
- Identify factors to consider when designing distribution channels in B2B relationships
- Identify the additional marketing mix and the applicability in a B2B context.

3.1 Introduction

The emergence of new markets and business models across the globe has strengthened the nature of B2B marketing relationships (Aykol et al., 2012; Leonidou & Hultman, 2019). The need to meet the demands of new markets swiftly by providing appropriate goods and services and timely delivery requires effective collaboration by businesses. With increased technological advancement, in addition to meeting these needs, a business must also put into consideration the changing process of delivering services and selling of goods. Consequently, the success of businesses lies in their ability to tap into opportunities in the global and local markets, which in most cases require a change in their internal operating systems (Wu et al., 2006). For example, goods and services can be purchased and sold online, and buyers pay at the point of e-purchase. This new dimension will require that businesses collaborate with financial organisations to provide quality service delivery (i.e. effective payment for products and services) to customers. Therefore, progress and development in every market will require more business-to-business collaborations.

Good knowledge of business purchasers' unique needs and segments enables organisations to recognise that no two purchasers are entirely the same. This non-uniformity in business purchasers' needs propels organisations to seek out a distinctive set of purchasers with uniform wants and expectations which, when integrated, represent possible market audience (Dibb et al., 1994). When the target market is appropriately defined, products and services can be effectively exchanged between parties. The exchange of goods and services between and among business organisations has been established as an integral aspect of market expansion and business development, with immense significance to firms and economies across the globe (LaPlaca, 2013; Leonidou & Hultman, 2019).

In the wake of increased globalisation, organisations operate beyond the domestic market to establish business relationships in international markets, thereby making B2B marketing gain more prominence (Samiee et al., 2015; Leonidou & Hultman, 2019). Despite enormous frontiers, which B2B marketing activities have covered, they still must operate within the scope of meeting the needs of the target market where they operate (Grönroos, 1989). The composition of a market notwithstanding, appropriate marketing of products and services demands that the business must know and understand the needs of the target audience. Maintaining good relationship becomes a critical factor in understanding the needs of the target audience. The changing definition of marketing reflects the importance of relationship marketing which is a key success factor in B2B relationships.

As stated in the introduction, the American Marketing Association (AMA) defines marketing as "the activity, set of institutions, and processes for creating, communicating, delivering, and exchanging offerings that have value for customers, clients, partners, and society at large" (American Marketing Association, 2017). The definition reflects the current focus of marketing on value exchange (Brodie et al., 1997; Griesienė, 2014). The new paradigm of marketing (i.e. value and relationship marketing) which has evolved over the years covers marketing from the perspective of service marketing (Gronroos, 1990; Brodie et al., 1997); inter-organisational exchange relationship (Håkansson, 1982; Ford, 1990; Hallen et al., 1991; Brodie et al., 1997); network relationship (Axelsson & Easton, 1992; Johanson & Mattsson, 1985; Brodie et al., 1997); relationship in value chains (Normann & Ramirez, 1993; Brodie et al., 1997); and information technology between and within organisations (Scott Morton, 1991; Brodie et al., 1997).

This chapter provides specific pathways on how the marketing mix can be utilised in the B2B relationship to create value for customers, given considerations to current market trends and new relationships demands.

3.2 The Marketing Mix and the Business-to-Business Market

As summarised in the Introduction and Chapter 1, the marketing mix has been influential in the development of marketing as a practice and academic discourse (Möller, 2006; Goi, 2009). The concept was propounded by McCarthy (1964), and it is traditionally represented with the 4Ps (product, price, promotion and place). However, as summarised in the Introduction, due to modifications and research work on the traditional 4Ps, there has emerged another 3Ps (people, processes and physical evidence) bringing the number of the marketing mix to 7Ps. These 7Ps of marketing represent a roadmap for translating marketing plans into practical realities that suit current market situations. The 7Ps are shown in Figure 3.1.

The new marketing mix helps organisations develop both long- and short-term marketing strategies to appeal to their target organisation (Palmer & Millier, 2004; Goi, 2009).

Figure 3.1   The 7Ps of the marketing mix.

Kent (1986) and Goi (2009, p. 2) described the marketing mix as "the holy quadruple of the marketing faith, written in tablets of stone" because of the foundations and pathways in the marketing practice (Möller, 2006). Figure 3.1 provides a graphical depiction of the marketing mix. Consequently, business organisation's marketing strategies have significantly been modified to accommodate rapidly changing factors. Furthermore, the scope of business operations must be aligned appropriately to fit into the B2B market. Therefore, it is expedient to have a holistic consideration of the 7Ps of marketing (product, promotion, price, place, people, processes and physical evidence) as it relates to a B2B organisation's marketing strategy. The next section examines the product, price, promotion, place, people, processes and physical evidence strategies of the marketing mix, within the context of B2B marketing in Africa.

3.3 Product Strategies and Mechanism in the Business Market

A product is a crucial element of the marketing mix; hence, B2B managers are always concerned about providing the right products or services (offerings) to the right target audience as this ultimately establishes the nature of the business relationship. According to Kotler and Armstrong (2010), a product refers to anything that can be offered to a market for attention, acquisition, consumption or use that satisfactorily meets the requirement of a need or want. The offerings of an organisation are considered from three basic features: the characteristics of the product and quality, the mix of services and quality and the price of the offering.

The product reflects the organisations' target market and likely key partners. In B2B, the product of the organisation serves as an offering of a firm to satisfy the need of customers (Zimmerman & Blythe, 2018). Stakeholders seek satisfaction in B2B, and the party occupying the role of the seller attracts the buying organisation as a result of the value created with the product offerings. The value created in the product and services is the source of relationship engagement and bonding among parties in the B2B relationship. What represents value must be mutually beneficial to the selling and buying organisations for the continuity of business relationship. For instance, in 2014, MTN

Nigeria and Ericsson signed major 5-year managed services agreements for the management, optimisation and field maintenance of 75% of the telecom company's network infrastructure in Nigeria (Ericsson, 2014). Under the terms of this contract, Ericsson will have full responsibility of the management, optimisation and field maintenance of MTN's network infrastructure in key locations of Lagos, Abuja, Enugu, Port Harcourt and Asaba, which represents 75% of the network. In this B2B relationship between MTN Nigeria and Ericsson, the latter must ensure that MTN is satisfied with the level of service delivery for the continuity of the business relationship. To create a product that will enhance and attract buyers–seller relationship for an organisation, the product must be strategically designed to meet the need of buyers or would-be sellers in a market (Zimmerman & Blythe, 2018). Hence, the organisation must have a product strategy that is related to quality, features and entire offering of a product (Zimmerman & Blythe, 2018).

The nature of the market will determine the product strategy to be utilised because there are differences that are important in the product strategy for B2B compared to B2C (business-to-consumers) markets. Consumer product focuses more on brand identity and emotional attachment, while the B2B product focuses more on tangible benefits, value creation, investment, availability and energy consumption (Schlipf et al., 2019). To strengthen the bond of the existing relationship between organisations and also attract more business relationship in B2B, firms provide augmented products to create value.

The product life cycle must be put into consideration to capture the implementation of the introduction, growth, maturity and decline stages as these can inform the purchasing decision of target customers, because marketing costs increase as products stay longer in the market (Schlipf et al., 2019). For a market like Africa, businesses must take into cognisance the dynamics of the operating business environment and its challenges in order to achieve their set goals. The product life cycle strategy is a critical element in the B2B marketing relationship, particularly for businesses in Africa, to understand the growth and decline stages of a product as it informs purchase decision in the product market.

B2B marketing managers must provide the parameters and standards for measuring the performance of their products. The product life cycle examination by marketing managers helps to determine the next action to take on the product. A product may need to be "retired" at the decline stage or be innovated. That is why product life cycle inspection is fundamental to ensuring that business buyers do not opt for another organisation in a bid to get a performing product that meets their needs. The essence of following up systems is to ensure a product evaluation process that will ascertain the problem relating to the use of the product and choose a strategy that can effectively resolve the issue.

3.4 Price Strategies and Mechanism in the Business Market

Price as a fundamental element represents one of the key strategic decision variables a marketing manager controls. Through its interaction with other elements of the marketing mix, it helps in the determination of the effectiveness of each variable of the marketing mix. Being a vehicle through which a firm attains its predetermined objectives, it is a key aspect in the B2B market, and it is the only activity in the marketing mix which generates revenues (Zimmerman & Blythe, 2018). Therefore, putting in place a good pricing strategy will enable a firm to yield more revenue, which invariably demonstrates an understanding of customers and the market. Hutt and Speh (2013) and Indounas (2019) agreed that price is a critical element in the B2B marketing strategy. Thus, a business organisation must understand the ability of customers to purchase their product and also set the price to align with the product value and competitive market environment. For example, an increase in price can lead to an increase in profit for the business if the rate of purchase does not decline, and production cost remains constant. However, an increase in price and a decrease in purchase may result in a financial loss for an organisation and more severe outcomes if the cost of production increases. The argument, therefore, is that the price strategy must take cognisance of the nature of the market, dynamic forces of supply–demand interaction and the target customers, particularly in the B2B environment.

The pricing strategy in B2B Africa context differs according to countries. For instance, advertising in South Africa, Nigeria and Kenya would cost more than advertising services in countries like Burkina Faso and Cameroun. A supplier organisation must be conscious of activities and interactions in the supply chain before fixing a price for its product/service. If a supplier fails in this regard, buyers might be forced to seek a good alternative, especially in a price-sensitive African market (Export Enterprises, 2019). Another factor that must be considered in fixing price is to have a well-organised pricing process. According to Zimmerman & Blythe (2018), there are certain conditions the price-sensitiveness must meet and are discussed as follows:

3.4.1 Set Appropriate Pricing Objective That Aligns with Corporate Objectives

A price objective can either be profit-oriented or sales-oriented. The former is targeted at getting returns on investment, while the latter is targeted at market penetration, thereby driving sales to increase market share. Within both frames of objectives, the price goal must still align with the corporate objectives. For example, when the South Africa MTN telecommunication firm penetrated Nigeria telecommunication industry, having invested heavily in installation of masts and other facilities, this was reflected in the prices of their products and services. At the time, there was only a second competitor, Econet (now Airtel). The two companies charged their subscribers a premium price to enjoy their services. However, in the wake of fierce competition, occasioned by new entrant, there was price reduction. However, MTN still maintains a premium appeal due to the pricing of its products, target market and service delivery.

3.4.2 Decide the Pricing Strategy

Deciding the price strategy entails examining socio-environmental factors that can influence the consumer purchase, based on price. A few of these factors are the environment (government laws and the economy), customers (value and perception towards product), competitors (price and cost), distribution channels (cost and capabilities) and firm (corporate objectives and marketing programme). These factors must be considered when deciding a price strategy in the African market.

3.4.3 Determine Demand – Customer Perception of Price and Cost

Determining demand entails evaluating a customer's perception of the product. This is because the customer will examine the cost and benefits in terms of the value obtained from the amount paid. Importantly, a business firm must ensure that the cost of acquiring a product or service which they render to another organisation must provide B2B benefits like reliability, trust and commitment of supplier and product/service benefits.

3.4.4 Review Offerings of the Competition

The firm must review competitive prices, including their prices and what the firm is offering. It is not recommended that a firm sets a higher price on its product than its competitors; however, this is dependent on the competitive nature of the market and the status of the business. Before fixing the price for product/service to be rendered to another organisation, the price offered by other competitors and the position of the business in the market are key and must be considered.

3.4.5 Select Pricing Method and Policy

Pricing policies and methods are formulated on the basis of pricing objectives and price settings (Avlonitis & Indounas, 2005). The pricing methods and policies guide and drive an organisation's pricing effort (Avlonitis & Indounas, 2005; Indounas, 2019). Pricing methods are the explicit steps a firm takes in making pricing decisions (Oxenfeldt, 1983; Avlonitis & Indounas, 2005). Two main pricing methods that an organisation can utilise are the cost-based and the demand-based pricing methods (Avlonitis & Indounas, 2005). Organisations must take cognisance of this in developing and determining the price of product/service.

3.4.6 Determine Price

Determining the price of a product is the last stage in the pricing process, and it requires a holistic analysis of the competitive and socio-economic factors surrounding the organisation. This is because the price of a product or service has a multiplier effect on the end-product user and can either attract the right customer or communicate the wrong message. An organisation must be both proactive and reactive to competitive market moves of price and must always ensure that the customer perceives more benefits in the consumption of a product.

Business operations in Africa where environmental factors have been responsible for the collapse of more than 70% of the micro, small and medium enterprises (SMMEs) (Bushe, 2019), and whose goal is to make a profit must, therefore, understand the dynamics of pricing to enhance their survival in a volatile B2B environment.

3.5 Promotion Strategies and Mechanism

Promotion in marketing is any form of business strategy targeted at communicating the products and services of an organisation in order to persuade the targeted audience and stimulate purchase. Promotion in marketing is carried out in both B2C and B2B. However, the strategy used in the B2C is different from the B2B because of the difference in the nature of the two markets (Murphy, 2007). Furman (2017) discussed promotion strategies for B2B as follows.

3.5.1 Trade Shows and Exhibitions

Trade shows refer to business expos, events and trade fairs that are collaboratively organised by multiple organisations in order to display services and products which they offer. Trade shows and exhibitions are the most lucrative places where companies can build a relationship with their partners and discuss the exploration of new markets. Some of the trade shows in Africa include but are not limited to

(1) Food East Africa – Kenya; (2) Invest Africa Expo – Morocco; (3) Sipal: Salon International Pour l'Alimentation – Senegal; (4) Morocco Food Expo – Morocco; (4) SARA (Salon International de l'Agriculture et des Ressources Animals) – Ivory Coast; (5) AgroFood Nigeria – Nigeria; (6) Aviana Nigeria – Nigeria; (7) East Africa International Trade Exhibition (EAITE) – Tanzania; (8) Food and Hospitality Africa – South Africa; and (9) Addis AgroFood – Ethiopia

3.5.2 Sample Product

The sample product is a promotion strategy that is important in the B2B market and can be used as ice breakers in business deals. It is a system whereby an organisation sends a product sample without charges to another business organisation for assessment or testing as a demonstration of the product quality. The sample product is usually used to convince the buyer of the quality of the product and thereby stimulate purchase. It also creates a system of integrity, trust and commitment from the selling organisation to the purchasing firm.

3.5.3 Trade-Ins

Trade-ins are promotion strategies whereby an organisation offers its new product at a discount or at an exchange for the older versions particularly to bring to the notice of the public the availability of the new product. In B2B markets, organisations make significant gains in sales and awareness when using product trade-ins as a promotional strategy for their new products.

3.5.4 Price Reduction

Price reduction is a strategy in product promotion in the B2B market that is used to attract potential buying organisations and boost sales of a product or service for a given period. This is mostly practised in the B2C market, but it is also used in the B2B market to sustain and enhance business partnerships. It is also a strategy that involves an organisation reducing the price of a product to compete with the price reduction offered by the other organisations.

3.5.5 Promotional Product

This is also a promotional strategy in the B2B market that involves an organisation branding its products such as t-shirts, pens and stationery which are given to the customers of the suppliers. It strengthens business relationships and creates a brand image with the supplier's customers and sends a message of a company's value. The product will most definitely have a symbol or logo of the organisation. The product promotion also entails an organisation offering the customers some of their new or old products for free for products awareness.

Marketing and sales promotion in the B2B context should have a strategic focus beyond price or revenue. Immediate product generation to building a strong partnership where more value is created, the business relationship developed, and profit enhanced should be the focus. Business in Africa must look beyond implementing strategies that can succeed and, more importantly, must focus on relationship building among their business stakeholders for better organisational performance.

Other promotional strategies include the following.

3.5.5.1 Personal Selling in B2B

The concept of personal selling is used to explain any form of B2B selling that facilitates, negotiates and secures sales by way of salespersons' proactive effort through visiting the customer or target firm to achieve sales. It can take the form of a personal presentation by the sales team of an organisation to build a customer relationship or make sales. The sales team reaches the customer either by

(1) In-person sales call/presentations; (2) telemarketing; (3) using digital platforms; or (4) effective selling, presentation and relationship management skills that are required traits of a good sales team.

3.5.5.2 Promotion Strategy in B2B Using Social Media

Promotion as a marketing mix can be enhanced using social media (Adeola et al., 2020). Organisations in the internet age must strive to understand the dynamics that form digital market operations and develop effective mechanisms that will help explore and exploit the benefits therein for business sustainability (Brennan & Croft, 2012). Social media promotion is a tool that can be effectively utilised to communicate the organisation's products and brands to its target audience through electronic technologies or network.

Social media marketing is, however, seen as a recent phenomenon, and the use of the media in the B2B context is still in its early stage, hence limited knowledge and academic research (Michaelidou et al., 2011; Brennan & Croft, 2012; Siamagka et al., 2015). Social media communications are remoulding the method organisations reach out to their audience. However, the strategic effectiveness of social communication has been challenging to determine, and there is little available evidence on the strategic reactions by B2B organisations to this new channel (Siamagka et al., 2015; Brennan & Croft, 2012; Michaelidou et al., 2011).

It is important to note that digital communication provides a platform for individuals and groups to establish, disseminate and publish content (Kietzmann et al., 2011; Kaplan & Haenlein, 2009). Generally, digital communication is gradually becoming an increasingly common channel for the development and control of online relationships with the target audience and visibility of product brands. As the relationships in B2B environment comprise large exchanges between and among actors which demand continuous management (Ford, 2011; Vargo & Akaka, 2009; Ford & Håkansson, 2006; Ford, 2011), social media can confer competitive edge, if effectively utilised. Social media can be used to continually promote the features and benefits of products and services, increase the visibility of a company by publishing and disseminating relevant content of interest to the target audience and establish the company as experts in a particular field.

3.5.5.3 Foreign Trade Missions – A Promotional Tool for B2B Marketing

In a bid to meet new sellers and buyers, executives of businesses do embark on international trips to missions organised by government or agencies of the regional or national government to take advantage of international business opportunities. During the trade mission, business executives or representatives are introduced to well-placed government officials and principal business contacts. Trade missions result from significant market research, which is aimed at establishing good international business relationships with prospective sales representatives, distributors or partners. Meeting one-on-one, particularly when facilitated by senior government officials, can create trust with foreign buyers (International Trade Administration, 2020).

Benefits of Foreign Trade Missions for B2B Managers

a. Foreign trade missions create the opportunity of meeting face-to-face with executives of foreign industries and officials of government whose business dealings are considered to fit the organisation's objectives be it for joint ventures in the local market, representation or direct sales.

b. Arrange events with business visitors from local industries encompassing business alliances and influential councils in the business environment.

c. Foreign trade missions present an environment that allows for visiting sites and facilities that organisations' technologies/services may be suited for.

d. During foreign trade missions, businesses can hold roundtable briefings with officials and business representatives on business opportunities and local practices.

e. Foreign trade missions also afford the organisation the benefit of gaining broader media coverage for visibility.

3.6 Place/Distribution Strategies and Mechanism in the Business Market

Generally, distribution is used to explain the place element of the marketing mix. Marketing managers in B2B must always think of the right place where their market offerings are made available at the right quantity and quality. As a key function of marketing, it entails the physical movement of goods and services from where they are produced to where they are needed and the transfer of ownership from seller organisation to buyer organisation in a B2B environment. The role of distribution is so important that no matter how good a product is, it remains meaningless until it gets to the user organisation.

An effective distribution network is strategic to building a strong competitive advantage by an organisation. It can be used as a tool to open and penetrate new markets. The failure of an organisation to recognise and supply its customers in B2B with the needed product or services might limit the scope of the market they can penetrate (Zimmerman & Blythe, 2018). According to Zimmerman & Blythe (2018), to achieve the desired business growth and penetrate the right market, there are conditions that the distribution channel must satisfy. These include adding value to the product, providing a link between the organisation and its market customers, and building appropriate channels.

Fast Moving Consumer Goods (FMCG) sector in Africa recognises the importance of having effective distribution channels and maintaining relationships with key distributors. MNCs, like Nestle, Unilever, Procter and Gamble, among others, have well-established distributor management framework and maintain relationships with these key accounts by having key account/distributor for the various channels. These managers have joint business plans (JBP) setting monthly, quarterly and annual business targets with the distributors whom they regard as business partners.

Thus, it is vital that businesses design robust and enabling business distribution channels that will provide all the needed factors to make a product excel in the business market (Zimmerman & Blythe, 2018). The nature and quality of the B2B distribution channel will determine whether product and services get to the buyers from the suppliers as at when due. An inappropriate or poorly organised distribution channel is most likely to affect the marketing success of a business organisation. There are some fundamental factors to consider when designing distribution channels.

3.6.1 Factors to Consider When Designing Distribution Channels

The following are basic factors that B2B marketing relationship must take into cognisance for an effective distribution/place channel.

3.6.1.1 Customers

Understanding the customer and segmenting appropriately are key factors in the success of B2B product distribution and sales. An organisation must recognise the key role segmentation plays in identifying buyer characteristics particularly, in making decisions. Also, customer orientation must be considered before choosing a particular distribution line.

3.6.1.2 Competitors/Culture

An organisation must also study competitors' trends by ensuring they are not using a similar pattern or repeating what the market has known the competitor as this might affect the business image. It is preferable for an organisation to create its own strategy to meet the need of its target market and collaborate with its business partners. Also, culture is another aspect that businesses must watch out for in the B2B market relationship. In a culturally sensitive market, business organisations must not be quick to change the process of the distributional channel used in such market as it may be difficult for other intending business partners to comprehend and adapt to the new process.

3.6.1.3 Company Objectives and Resources

The company's objectives also influence the choice of distribution channel. The particular goal a company wants to achieve with a particular business relationship or market should determine the kind of channel to be utilised. The distribution channel must be in line with the marketing strategy and corporate goal. If a distribution channel fails to meet the objectives of the business, it will lead to poor customer services, erode brand image and affect business relationships.

3.6.1.4 Distribution Strategy

A business distribution strategy is also important to the success of the product or service offered to partners. An organisation must decide the distribution strategy that aligns with the goal of the organisation, resources and the market. A choice must be made between intensive, selective and exclusive distribution strategies. Intensive distribution strategy deals with utilising different channels, selective strategy entails distribution through a purposive channel, while exclusive distribution deals with making use of one intermediary channel to market a product. The choice of the distribution channels will enable organisations to achieve business goals depending on the nature of the product and the market it operates.

3.6.1.5 Product Characteristics

The product characteristics determine the distribution strategy, and it is an important aspect to consider when designing a distribution channel. The characteristics of the product include terms of the price and targeted market, which will determine the channel to be utilised. If the product is liquid or of a delicate nature, the distribution channel should be selective or exclusive. Essentially, the characteristics of the product should determine and influence the choice and design of the distribution channel of a product. In the context of Africa, factors such as resources, culture, literacy level and security are factors to consider in designing a distribution channel. The African business environment though filled with opportunities is a peculiar market which must be understood before a channel of distribution is designed. Business relationships in Africa must take cognisance of environmental influence in determining and designing a distribution channel of products and services. The marketing mix is sacrosanct to the success of marketing goals all over the world; hence, B2B relationship in Africa must, therefore, utilise the benefits and opportunities identified in this chapter to enhance the achievement of their business goals, taking into consideration environmental factors prevalent in Africa.

3.7 People, Process and Physical Evidence Strategies and Mechanisms in the Business Market

There are unique features that differentiate the B2B market from the B2C market. The most essential of these features is the complexities of the products and the buying processes in the former, which results in high interdependence between sellers and buyers. Hence, Webster (1992) opines that the reason for industrial marketing is the buyer–seller relationship as each organisation depends on the other in pursuit of their organisational goals. The B2B market should focus not only on the products but also on the relationship that exists between the buyers and the sellers.

In this relationship, the moderating process should be regarded as a form of negotiation and not persuasion as intended by the traditional 4Ps of the marketing mix. In the 4Ps, the interaction approach of personal contacts is rarely present and when present, only in the context of salesperson–consumer interaction. In the B2B market, partners seek long-term relationships that deliver better results than achieving immediate sales whose product and brand loyalties do not last long. The traditional 4Ps did not consider the features of services since it was likely considered from the perceptive of manufacturing companies. The incorporation of the additional 3Ps to the marketing mix, making it a holistic 7Ps, should serve as a guide in planning marketing strategies, particularly for the service sector. These additional 3Ps are discussed in the context of B2B as follows.

3.7.1 People Strategy

The interest in B2B marketing is more on relationship building than on product features and brand loyalty. This relationship is built and maintained by representatives of the target organisations who initiate interactions in the hope of creating future business exchanges. Therefore, representatives of the selling organisation need to create a good impression as this will define the business relationship. Notably, the buying organisation can make decisions on the capabilities and technical know-how (products and services) of the intending partners through their representatives; hence, the need for training and development by organisations must be emphasised.

The B2B marketing strategy in Africa is interpreted from the perspective of exchange relationship with socio-economic benefits which integrates resources, activities and actors (Håkansson & Snehota, 1995). In this arrangement, a small number of individuals (employees) from the participating organisation, particularly from the selling and buying centres of each organisation, are involved in an interaction. The individuals representing each organisation must, therefore, be careful not to misrepresent the interest of the organisation they represent by creating false or wrong impression before their would-be customers/partners. Therefore, organisations must endeavour to develop strategic training programmes for employees whose functions are designed to suit the role.

Given that we are in the digital age, organisations must insist on employees with technological capabilities and interpersonal relationship skill at both agent and staff levels to undertake the task of formulating the policy of online conversation and ensure every participating individual stays on-message. Having understanding partners will equip organisations with the requisite knowledge to develop appropriate products and service. In a service industry where there is a high level of interpersonal conversation, it is important to apply the organisation's resources to meet customer needs effectively. Furthermore, the people representing the organisation in the fulfilment of this task must be readily available to deliver after-sales support to their partners without much marginal cost. After-sales support adds value to offerings and provides firms with a competitive edge over other firms to win trust and commitment of customers.

3.7.2 Process Strategy

The process strategy gives evidence of an organisation's capabilities, structure, ideas, concepts, creativity and coordination. When the right process is established, B2B programmes and activities can attract the right audience, which in turn results in long-term relationships. The satisfaction of customers in B2B arrangement is dependent on how an organisation handles the process of service delivery. Process takes care of the efficiency of business dealings, how fast the products or services are delivered, and the friendliness of the relationship and interaction between the businesses. It looks at the customer's entire journey and seeks to create value by simplifying the tasks the customer is required to perform when in contact with the company. When a good process is in place, organisations can improve service delivery and create value both in B2C and B2B relationships.

3.7.3 Physical Evidence

This simply refers to the environment where the service takes place, which influences the ability of the company to satisfy customer needs and wants. It includes the intangible experience of customers which is usually demonstrated through testimonials and reactions from customers. The ambience (buildings, physical layout, furnishings, noise level, colour, lighting, air conditioning, etc.) of the service environment has an impact on the customer's perception of service.

For example, a first glance at the orange colour of Guaranty Trust Bank (GTBank), Nigeria, portrays a picture of what their philosophy and corporate culture reflect. The setting (physical layout) of GTBank for some customers evokes a feeling of joy and warmth, which may elicit an intention of the business relationship in the minds of potential firms or customers to engage in business dealings with them.

According to Gan et al. (2011), physical evidence of banks affects customers' perception of the bank's overall quality of service delivery. The GTB orange colour environment has the capacity to evoke numerous stimuli which can potentially influence how customers act and buy their products and the extent to which they feel satisfied with their service quality.

3.8 Conclusion

The advent of new markets and businesses across the globe strengthened the nature of B2B relationship. Therefore, for businesses to work together to build a collaborative bond that meets the needs and desires of the customers for the satisfactory product and service delivery, organisations must swiftly meet the demand of new markets with the right product quantity and quality in the right place and at the right time. Consequently, marketing strategies in organisations have been modified to focus not only on B2C but also on B2B. The traditional marketing mix strategies commonly referred to as the 4Ps of the marketing mix, which includes the product, price, place and promotion can be applied to achieve marketing objectives of firms' tangible products. However, modifications of the 4Ps in the light of prevailing realities necessitated the addition of another 3Ps (people, process and physical evidence) to make 7Ps of the marketing mix which forms a strategic guide for developing and executing market plans and operations that will result in achieving marketing goals and objectives of the service industries and sectors where relationship management is a key, in this case, B2B.

Additionally, the AMA definition of marketing, which focuses on the creation, communication, delivering of value to stakeholders and the society, presents a framework upon which organisational marketing activities should be organised for effective results. Hence, the creation of value is fundamental to business success. For organisations to meet their marketing objectives, marketing managers must possess a good knowledge of the marketing mix and create value for the target customers, which are the bedrock of success in B2B relationships. Globally, the marketing mix is fundamental to the success of marketing goals; hence, B2B relationship in Africa must utilise the benefits and opportunities identified in this chapter to achieve business goals, taking into consideration the peculiarities of the African environment.

Case Study and Exercise

B2B RELATIONSHIP IN AN EMERGING MARKET: THE CASE OF OPUTA ENTERPRISE

Oputa Enterprise is owned by Mr Christopher Oputa, a businessman who deals in automobile spare parts and the construction of articulated motor vehicles in Nigeria. The business commenced operation in 1997 and has successfully grown into a well-known brand, attracting many customers with demands for the indigenous type of Lorries the company manufactures. The automobile parts are purchased from China as complete knock-down (CKD) parts and assembled locally into finished products. The importation of CKD parts enabled Oputa Enterprise as a local manufacturer to pay lower duties and take advantage of the Federal Government of Nigeria's localisation policy to support indigenous businesses.

In 2002, due to the success of his automobile business, Oputa decided to pursue a diversification strategy and expand his business into the telecommunication industry, a rapidly growing sector in Nigeria, given the successful introduction of the Global System for Mobile Communications (GSM). He incorporated a new company, L-Tell Limited, which became an Authorised Dealer of recharge cards of a GSM company, TMK-Mobile.

It had a successful business take-off after signing the Partnership Agreement with TMK-Mobile. Oputa invested huge funds in acquiring software, logistics, distributions channel, and putting in place the needed infrastructure. He expected a high turnover from the business but was disappointed with the first-year results. A look into the company's books showed that he needed to take drastic actions and reposition the business to become profitable.

The first challenge he observed was his relationship with the various retailers in his channel that serve as intermediaries for the purchase of recharge cards and other related services. It was quite challenging for him to build a good business relationship with these retailers over time, as he was not familiar with their mode of operation, which was different from what was obtainable in the automobile industry. In the automobile business, the buyers place orders and make outright purchases when satisfied with the vehicle's specifications. In the new business, the stakeholders in the value chain were always demanding constant face-to-face meetings to discuss volume and profit margins. They wanted to see him and not his sales team. The retailers were also unfamiliar with the mobile money payment platform Oputa introduced and preferred cash-and-carry arrangements or direct lodgement of proceeds to the banks.

Looking at his books, Oputa observed that most retailers were not making the expected returns or effecting payments under the Distribution and Retailer agreement. It appeared that they were cross-selling recharge cards of other network operators, contrary to the terms of the agreement. At a subsequent meeting with one of his key sub-resellers, AB Brothers Limited, Oputa was visibly angry. Anene Nnadi, the managing director of AB Brothers Limited, had informed him that the profit margin was low due to the high cost of the recharge cards, absence of competitive commission and the inconvenience of using the sophisticated payment portal. Additionally, he complained of a lack of marketing support from L-Tell to promote the sale of recharge cards.

Within the first 3 years of establishment, Oputa sold his unprofitable telecom business, L-Tell, together with the trademark, to another company and concentrated on the business of automobile spare part sale and assembly. Surprisingly, by the beginning of the second year of acquisition, L-Tell's new management expanded the business to other parts of the country. Oputa was puzzled. He made some enquires and found out what they did differently. They changed the marketing strategies, had great relationships with retailers, developed commercial propositions that enabled them to grow market share, and achieved the success that eluded L-Tell. They developed a joint business plan, agreed to, and signed by the retailers, which set out key objectives, goals, tactics and strategies, including product, pricing and distribution strategies. The promotion strategy included the modalities for the production of handbills and fliers containing relevant information on promos and discounts. Additionally, retailers that met set targets were given discounts on future purchases.

EXERCISE

1. What fundamental mistakes did Mr Oputa make in his business relationships with the retailers?
2. What did the new management team do differently to achieve business success? (Use identified aspects of the marketing mix to illustrate your answer.)
3. What are the key success factors in B2B customer relationship management?

References

Adeola, O., Hinson, R. E., & Evans, O. (2020). Social media in marketing communications: A synthesis of successful strategies for the digital generation. In B. George, & J. Paul (Eds.), *Digital transformation in business and society* (pp. 61–81). Palgrave Macmillan, Cham.

American Marketing Association (2017). Retrieved August 8, 2020, from https://www.ama.org/the-definition-of-marketing/.

Avlonitis, G. J., & Indounas, K. A. (2005). Pricing objectives and pricing methods in the services sector. *Journal of Services Marketing*, 19(1), pp. 47–57.

Axelsson, B., & Easton, G. (1992). *Network implications for business strategy. Industrial Networks-A.* Routledge, London.

Aykol, B., Leonidou, L. C., & Zeriti, A. (2012). Setting the theoretical foundations of importing research: Past evaluation and future perspectives. *Journal of International Marketing*, 20(2), 1–24.

Brennan, R., & Croft, R. (2012). The use of social media in B2B marketing and branding: An exploratory study. *Journal of Customer Behaviour*, 11(2), 101–115.

Brodie, R. J., Coviello, N. E., Brookes, R. W., & Little, V. (1997). Towards a paradigm shift in marketing? An examination of current marketing practices. *Journal of Marketing Management*, 13(5), 383–406.

Bushe, B. (2019). The causes and impact of business failure among small to micro and medium enterprises in South Africa. *Africa's Public Service Delivery and Performance Review*, 7(1), 1–26

Dibb, S., Simkin, L., Pride, W., & Ferrell, O.C. (1994). *Marketing: Concepts and strategies.* Cengage Learning EMEA, Andover.

Ericsson, S. (2014). Ambush marketing: Examining the development of an event organizer right of association. In N. Lee et al. (Ed.), *Intellectual property, unfair competition and publicity* (pp. 165–188). Edward Elgar Publishing, Cheltenham.

Export Enterprises (2019). Retrieved September 8, 2020, from https://www.nordeatrade.com/en/explore-new-market/nigeria/marketing.

Ford, D. (1990). *Understanding business markets: Interaction, relationships, and networks.* Academic Press, London.

Ford, D. (2011). IMP and service-dominant logic: Divergence, convergence and development. *Industrial Marketing Management*, 40(2), 231–239.

Ford, D., & Håkansson, H. (2006). IMP – some things achieved: Much more to do. *European Journal of Marketing,* 40(3/4), 248–258.

Furman, J. (2017, April 28). Selling to other businesses: 5 sales promotion methods for a B-TO-B market. Retrieved August 8, 2020, from https://www.business.com/articles/5-B-to-B-promotion-methods/.

Gan, C., Clemes, M., Wei, J. & Kao, B. (2011). An empirical analysis of New Zealand bank customers' satisfaction. *Banks and Bank Systems,* 6(3), 63–77.

Goi, C. L. (2009). A review of marketing mix: 4Ps or more? *International Journal of Marketing Studies*, 1(1), 2.

Griesienė, I. (2014). Business partnership development on the basis of internal and relationship marketing (Doctoral dissertation, Vilnius University).

Grönroos, C. (1989). Defining marketing: A market-oriented approach. *European Journal of Marketing*, 23(1), 52–60.

Gronroos, C. (1990). The marketing strategy continuum: Towards a marketing concept for the 1990s. *Management Decision*, 29(1), 9.

Håkansson, H. (Ed.) (1982). *International marketing and purchasing: An interaction approach.* Wiley, Chichester.

Håkansson, H., & Snehota, I. (Eds.) (1995). *Developing relationships in business networks* (Vol. 433). Routledge, London.

Hallen, L., Johanson, J., & Seyed-Mohamed, N. (1991). Interfirm adaptation in business relationships. *Journal of Marketing*, 55(2), 29–37.

Hutt, M. D., & Speh, T. W. (2013). *Business marketing management: B-TO-B, 11.* South Western Educational Publisher, Mason, OH.

Indounas, K. (2019). Market-based pricing in B-TO-B service industries. *Journal of Business & Industrial Marketing*, 34(5), 1030–1040.

International Trade Administration. (2020). Trade missions, United States. https://www.trade.gov/trade-missions.

Johanson, J., & Mattsson, L. G. (1985). Marketing investments and market investments in industrial networks. *International Journal of Research in Marketing,* 2(3), 185–195.

Kaplan, A.M., & Haenlen, M. (2009). Consumer use and business potentials of virtual worlds: The case of second life. *The International Journal of Media Management*, 11(3), 93–101.

Kent, R. A. (1986). Faith in four Ps: An alternative. *Journal of Marketing Management,* 2(2), 145–154.

Kietzmann, J. H., Hermkens, K., McCarthy, I. P., & Silvestre, B. S. (2011). Social media? Get serious! Understanding the functional building blocks of social media. *Business Horizons*, 54(3), 241–251.

Kotler, P., & Armstrong, G. (2010). *Principles of marketing*. Pearson Education, London.

LaPlaca, P. J. (2013). Research priorities for B2B marketing researchers. *Revista Española de Investigación de Marketing ESIC*, 17(2), 135–150.

Leonidou, C. N., & Hultman, M. (2019). Global marketing in business-to-business contexts: Challenges, developments, and opportunities. *Industrial Marketing Management*, 78, 102–107.

McCarthy, E. J. (1964). *Basic marketing*. Richard D. Irwin, Homewood, IL.

Michaelidou, N., Siamagka, N. T., & Christodoulides, G. (2011). Usage, barriers and measurement of social media marketing: An exploratory investigation of small and medium B-TO-B brands. *Industrial Marketing Management*, 40(7), 1153–1159.

Möller, K. (2006). The marketing mix revisited: Towards the 21st century marketing by E. Constantinides. *Journal of Marketing Management*, 22(3), 439–450.

Murphy, D. (2007, April 6). B-TO-B vs B2C marketing: Similar but different. Retrieved from https://masterful-marketing.com/marketing-B-to-B-vs-b2c/.

Normann, R., & Ramirez, R. (1993). From value chain to value constellation: Designing interactive strategy. *Harvard Business Review*, 71(4), 65.

Oxenfeldt, A. R. (1983). Pricing decisions: How they are made and how they are influenced. *Management Review*, 72(11), 23–25.

Palmer, R. A., & Millier, P. (2004). Segmentation: Identification, intuition, and implementation. *Industrial Marketing Management*, 33(8), 779–785.

Samiee, S., Chabowski, B. R., & Hult, G. T. M. (2015). International relationship marketing: Intellectual foundations and avenues for further research. *Journal of International Marketing*, 23(4), 1–21.

Schlipf, M., Keller, C., Lutzenberger, F., Pfosser, S., & Rathgeber, A. (2019). Measuring life cycle costs for complex B-to-B products. *Journal of Quality in Maintenance Engineering*, 25(2), 355–375.

Scott Morton, M. S. (1991). *The corporation of the 1990s: Information technology and organizational transformation*. Sloan School of Management, Oxford University Press, New York.

Siamagka, N. T., Christodoulides, G., Michaelidou, N., & Valvi, A. (2015). Determinants of social media adoption by B2B organizations. *Industrial Marketing Management*, 51, 89–99.

Vargo, S. L., & Akaka, M. A. (2009). Service-dominant logic as a foundation for service science: Clarifications. *Service Science*, 1(1), 32–41.

Webster Jr, F. E. (1992). The changing role of marketing in the corporation. *Journal of Marketing*, 56(4), 1–17.

Wu, F., Yeniyurt, S., Kim, D., & Cavusgil, S. T. (2006). The impact of information technology on supply chain capabilities and firm performance: A resource-based view. *Industrial Marketing Management*, 35(4), 493–504.

Zimmerman, A., & Blythe, J. (2018). *Business to business marketing management: A global perspective*. Routledge, New York.

Chapter 4

Selling to Business Buyers

After reading the chapter, the reader will be able to:

1. Identify and explain who business buyers are in a business-to-business (B2B) transaction
2. Discuss the B2B buying situations and stages in the B2B decision-making process
3. Enumerate the factors that influence the buying behaviour of B2B buyers
4. Discuss effective B2B buying and selling strategies.

4.1 B2B Buyers

According to Grewal et al. (2015), global business-to-business (B2B) transactions are growing rapidly and accounted for nearly 42% of US total revenue in 2015. Similarly, the B2B transactions dominate the business landscape in Africa and other emerging markets (Ndubisi & Nataraajan, 2016; Verster et al., 2019; Swani et al., 2019). It is therefore crucial for organisations that sell in the B2B marketplace, particularly in emerging markets, to have a comprehensive understanding of B2B buyers, their buying behaviours, decision-making processes and strategies. This is because B2B buying behaviours differ substantially from consumer buying behaviours. In B2B buying, organisations buy goods and services to meet the needs and wants of other organisations (Grewal et al., 2015). A B2B buyer, therefore, is a business customer. The B2B buyer buys on behalf of an organisation, not for personal use, and the organisation is the purchaser of goods and services (Zimmerman & Blythe, 2018). B2B buyers' organisations include manufacturers, resellers, government and institutional organisations.

4.1.1 Manufacturer B2B Buyers

Zimmerman and Blythe (2018) explained that manufacturer organisations purchase foundation (core) and facilitating products for making other products. Goods and services usually purchased by these organisations range from equipment (including parts) through raw materials to service products (including legal, cleaning, maintenance and building services). Manufacturer organisations base their purchasing decisions on established specifications and are very particular about the quality of the products or services they buy.

4.1.2 Reseller B2B Buyers

Not all buying organisations in B2B transactions are manufacturers. Distributing organisations also engage in B2B transactions by selling manufactured products (Munif, 2018). Popularly, organisations that engage in the resale or distribution of manufactured goods are referred to as intermediaries. The reseller organisations negotiate with suppliers; carry out promotional activities such as advertising and sales promotion; perform warehousing functions such as storage and product handling; undertake shipments; undertake inventory control functions; and perform marketing research such as the collection of price, competitor and market information. Reseller organisations do not necessarily need to have technical knowledge about the products they resell (Zimmerman & Blythe, 2018). However, they need to be certain about the demand for the products. Demand for the products is what motivates reseller organisations.

4.1.3 Governmental B2B Buyers

In Africa, government entities are the largest buying firms of almost all goods and services. Zimmerman and Blythe (2018) affirm that governments (local and central) constitute the largest market in the world. The buying decisions of government organisations are characterised by the tendering system. Firms bid for contracts. Nevertheless, the highest bidder does not always win the contract. In sub-Saharan African countries, even though regulations on procurement are to guide the buying activities of governments, many government officials in most cases circumvent the procurement procedures, resulting in a high incidence of corruption allegations (Nandonde & Kuada, 2016). It must be noted, however, that the tendering system of the government is not applicable in all instances, particularly in situations where the production of goods and services in question (e.g. military hardware such as guns) are not available to the public. (See more about the marketing activities of government agencies in Chapter 9.)

4.1.4 Institutional B2B Buyers

Institutions such as charities, universities, hospitals, schools, churches and non-profit organisations engage in institutional buying. These organisations operate with funded budgets which are almost always very tight. Zimmerman and Blythe (2018) indicate that institutional organisations have very substantial aggregate spending power in practice. Institutional organisations rely on public generosity to raise funds to support the purchase of needed products and services (Calitz et al., 2018). In some instances, some suppliers contribute to the charity works of these institutional organisations in cash or kind and help them to raise money to buy their goods and services (See more about the marketing activities of institutions in Chapter 9.)

4.2 Participants in the B2B Buying Decision-Making

Inconsistency characterises B2B buying decision-making, and several groups are involved in B2B buying decisions. Webster and Wind (1972) developed the buying behaviour model, which has been important to understand the organisation of buying by the purchaser (see also Donthu et al., 2005; Wind & Webster, 1972; Vincent et al., 2017). The buying behaviour model analyses the different actors, their roles and powers in the buying process, and how sellers can understand and influence them. Together, they are called the buying centre (also called the decision-making unit (DMU) by

Kotler (2009) (see Chapter 11)). Thus, members of the buying centre have different backgrounds, experiences and motives. Participants who engage in B2B buying decisions are as follows:

Initiators: These actors request for goods and services to be purchased by the organisation.

Users: These members of the organisation have a need for the products to be bought and usually initiate the buying process by indicating what they want.

Influencers: These experts provide specifications and information for assessing alternative products. As a result, they are important influencers.

Deciders: Deciders make the decision regarding which specifications to buy and from which suppliers.

Approvers: Approvers give authorisation to the proposed actions of deciders or the buyers.

Buyers: Buyers, usually top-level management, select the supplier and negotiate the terms of purchase.

Gatekeepers: Gatekeepers (receptionists and secretaries) control the flow of information. The nature of gatekeepers has changed with time. In the days when salespeople mainly called or visited potential purchasers, gatekeepers could direct them to the right members of the buying centre. With the advent of digital communications, websites and social media, the gatekeeper's role has changed as communication mode increasingly moves online, and sellers have more direct access to companies.

4.3 B2B Buying Situations

Different organisations face different buying situations and thus, must employ varying buying techniques. Some of such buying situations that B2B buyers may commonly encounter include straight re-buy, modified re-buy and/or new task situations (Gomes et al., 2016).

4.3.1 Straight Re-buy Situation

There are instances where B2B buyers have a need for repeat purchase. Hence, they do not require any new information, as they do not assess any new alternatives. All these instances require routine decision-making processes instead. In the routine decision-making process, the B2B buyer uses already-developed and time-tested rubrics for selection. The application of already-developed rubrics for making purchase decisions is described as a straight re-buy situation. Beckman (2019) defined straight re-buy as buying the same goods and services from the same sources in the same quantities. Straight re-buy situation occurs automatically and regularly, limits human involvement, requires no/minimal information and does not consider alternative sources of supply.

4.3.2 Modified Re-buy Situation

B2B buyers may encounter situations that warrant re-evaluation of the way they made purchases in the past. The re-evaluation, in most instances, is necessitated by changes in component specification, supply source and required quantity. Several factors ignite the modified re-buy situation. Introspectively, a firm scans its operations and discovers new methods, new requirements and new sources. Additionally, the intensity of competition from suppliers puts firms under intense pressure to switch supply sources. Changes in demand, as observed by Siluk et al. (2017), are a trigger of modified re-buy situation. In contrast to the straight re-buy situation where the B2B buyer engages in cause purchasing which is automatic and does not require new information, in a modified re-buy situation, the B2B buyer may well require potential suppliers to bid against each other for the business based on new information and some level of re-evaluation (Beckman, 2019).

4.3.3 New Task Situation

According to Zimmerman and Blythe (2013), a new task buying situation arises when the B2B buyer is being faced with entirely new purchasing decisions. Difficulty in evaluating options, uncertainty in dealing with suppliers and technical complexity of some products are some factors that trigger a new task situation. The B2B buying decision-making process in a new task situation is relatively complex. The B2B buyers are not guided by previous experience, and the present suppliers may not be able to meet the new need (Sivhabu, 2018). The features of a new task situation include the involvement of several decision-makers, the depth of information required, the difficulty associated with alternative evaluation and the length of time required. Comparatively, new task buying is the most difficult, complex and risky situation. The new task situations could be judgmental and/or strategic (Zimmerman & Blythe, 2013). Judgmental new task situations are masked in the technical complexities of the product, complicated evaluation of alternatives and negotiation with new suppliers (Mubango, 2017). Strategic new task situations, on the other hand, is characterised by long-term planning and involvement of top-level management, emphasising its strategic importance to the firm (Juntunen et al., 2019).

4.4 Modes of B2B Buying

B2B buying requires close relationships with relevant stakeholders. Several internal and external stakeholders influence the buying decisions of the B2B buyer. Consequently, the degree of interaction between the network of individuals and the relationship thereof with the supplier is impacted. Grewal et al. (2015) describe the degree of the relationship between the B2B buyer and the B2B seller as *modes of B2B buying* and identify three B2B buying modes.

4.4.1 Routinised Exchange Relationships Mode

A routinised exchange relationship is created when the purchased products are consistent with the predictions. This mode of B2B buying involves repetitive buying activities and routine interactions between authorised entities. The routinised exchange relationship is characterised by the enactment of standard procedures by the implementers to guide the ordering, receiving and replenishment of goods and services. The standard procedures are usually within the laid down parameters. As a result, the domain of authorised buying activities is delineated. Grewal et al. (2015) argue that routine buying activities in the routinised exchange relationship mode are conducted by automated systems. Increasingly, routinised exchange relationships are prevalent in a high interdependency relationship that includes systems integration.

4.4.2 Organic Buying Relationships Mode

Organic buying relationships require continuous human involvement and interpersonal interactions, as well as adjustments between buyer and seller firms (Grewal et al., 2015). The organic B2B buying relationship requires integrated solutions such as co-development and key account relationships. In the organic buying relationship mode, the B2B buying contexts are not acqui-escent to routinisation. The buying decision and implementation could be centralised or decen-tralised and require continuous interaction between the B2B buyer and seller. The strength of an organic buying relationship lies in its capabilities to ensure operational integration, which grants the B2B buyers access to customised goods, enhanced services, supply that is more consistent and cost savings.

4.4.3 Transactional Buying Operations Mode

There are several instances where B2B buying is carried out through ad hoc buyer–seller inter-actions such as spot markets, auctions and bids for specified goods or services. These buying options are usually one-time agreements. They impose no obligations or any expectations on the buyer and seller to engage in a future business relationship. B2B buying of this nature is described as a transactional buying operation (Grewal et al., 2015). Transactional buying operations are characterised by unpredictable demand and quick buying decisions. As a result, the buyer–seller interdependence is low. Usually, the goods and services that are transacted through transactional buying operations mode are relatively unimportant and not complicated. Therefore, in transactional buying operations, the B2B buying activities could be carried out by following acceptable standards. Periodically, however, a supervisor may reassess and confirm the activities of the B2B buyer.

4.5 B2B Buying Decision-Making Process

The B2B buying decision-making process, which describes a comprehensive series of phases, goes through concurrent decision-making processes (Grewal et al., 2015). Hence, far-reaching nego-tiations characterise the B2B buying process. This, perhaps, may be due to the high volume of products ordered. The differences in perspectives of different stakeholders involved in the B2B buying decision do not only heighten the level of bargaining but also elongate the time required in b-to-b-decision-making process (Grewal et al., 2015). Therefore, there are complexities associated with the decision-making process in B2B transactions. To navigate the buying decision process effectively, several procedures and steps have been outlined to be followed in the B2B decision-making process. While Grewal et al. (2015) condensed the states into implementation, evaluation, reassessment and confirmation, Kemp et al. (2018) expanded the stages into (1) need recognition, (2) the definition of product type, (3) development of detail specification, (4) search for supplier, (5) acquisition and analysis of proposal, (6) evaluation and selection of supplier, (7) placing and receiving of order and (8) evaluation of performance. Several other scholars used the five-stage model which focuses on the identification of needs, establishment of specification, request for pro-posal, evaluation of the proposal, and order and review process (Boström, 2015; Diba et al., 2019).

4.5.1 Need Recognition

The B2B buying process, according to Kemp et al. (2018), starts when an organisation identi-fies the need for a purchase. This need recognition originates from the users and/or initiators and sometimes from the selling organisations through their promotion campaigns. The need for organisations varies and may include replacing existing machinery or items, replenishing depleting stocks, or purchasing a new product or service that is accessible in the market.

4.5.2 Specification and Research

After the purchasing is recognised, the purchasing team specifies the quantities, performance and technical requirements for the products or services required. The purchasing team will then use these specifications to source for potential suppliers. They may utilise the web in finding products or firms whose products and services match their specification.

4.5.3 Request for Proposals

The next stage after specification and research is request for proposal. The purchasing team requests the suppliers to submit a quotation or make a presentation of what they have to offer in relation to specified specifications. This is done usually through the issuance of a formal document known as a request for a proposal.

4.5.4 Evaluation of Proposals

Proposal evaluation is an assessment of the proposals submitted by the suppliers. The assessment focuses on the product and the supplier. Specifically, the product is assessed on price, performance and value for money. The supplier, on the other hand, is evaluated in terms of the reputation of the company, financial stability, technical reputation and reliability. Selling organisations can influence this stage by providing purchaser decision-maker's information, case studies, and independent audit and review reports on their company and its products.

4.5.5 Order and Review

The order and review as a stage in B2B buying decision-making encompass the contractual agreement reached between the buyer and the seller. Price negotiations, terms and modes of payment, and delivery date and mode precede the order placement. The purchasing team then places an order with the chosen supplier. The contract is executed when the order is completed and delivered. The next activity after delivery is the review of the contract in terms of the performance of both the product and the supplier. The idea is to assess the extent to which the agreed specifications are met by both parties, the buyer and the supplier.

4.6 Determinants of B2B Buying Behaviour

As indicated earlier, several individuals with different backgrounds and incentives are involved in the buying process (Vincent et al., 2017; Webster & Wind, 1972). Collectively, the dispositions of these individuals define the buying behaviour of the organisation. Some factors, internal and external, shape and influence the collective buying behaviour of the firm. The determinants of B2B buying behaviour of firms include physical, technological, economic, political and legal, and cultural influences (Zimmerman & Blythe, 2013).

4.6.1 Physical Influences

The physical factors describe the location of suppliers and indicate whether products are sourced locally or internationally. The physical location of the supplier is thus a critical consideration for the purchasing firm when making purchasing decisions. In sub-Saharan Africa, for example, many private firms prefer to source supplies locally, except when the local sources are rare (Farole & Winkler, 2014). On the contrary, governmental organisations prefer to source most of their items from the international markets, even if such goods and services exist locally (Zimmerman & Blythe, 2018), leading to the dollarisation of many economies in Africa (Asongu et al., 2018).

4.6.2 Technological Influences

Another consideration of influence on the buying behaviour of B2B firms is technological advancement. The technological development of the supplier influences what the buyer can obtain and how they can obtain it. It is recommended, therefore, that the purchasing firm ensures technological compatibility with the supplier. The challenge, however, is premised on the argument that African countries have not succeeded in harmonising technical standards across the continent, leaving the continent replete with fragmented technical standards (Czubala et al., 2009) and heavy reliance on their former colonial master for technical standards (Zimmerman & Blythe, 2018).

4.6.3 Economic Influences

Macroeconomic indicators greatly influence the behaviour of B2B buyers. The inflation rate, which defines the level of prices of goods, affects the choices B2B buyers make. Exchange rate, a delicate component of macroeconomic factor, indicates the relative stability of a country's local currency and impacts the buying behaviour of purchasing firms. The general outlook of the economy in terms of growth measured in GDP, income level, unemployment level and standard of living of the population affects not only the buying decisions of firms but also their operations. As a result, macroeconomic factors are a major consideration for firms when making purchasing decisions.

4.6.4 Political and Legal Influences

Businesses, including B2B buyers, operate with the confines of local and international regulatory frameworks. The passage and administration of the regulations rest with state or government agencies. Primarily, the state agencies, as part of their mandate in enforcing the regulation, perform regulatory, promotional and facilitatory functions. It is essential, therefore, that B2B buyers incorporate these regulatory frameworks in their buying decisions. Resultantly, the legal regime of a country affects the purchasing behaviour of B2B buyers (see Chapter 9). The stability and policy direction of the government of the day significantly determines how firms behave, what they buy, what they invest in and how they generally operate. Therefore, political and legal influences are key considerations that shape the buying behaviour of the purchasing firms.

4.6.5 Cultural and Ethical Influence

Cultural and ethical issues are major considerations of firms in their buying decisions. Culture, defined as the values, language, attitudes, custom, social behaviour, religion and art of a given group of people, could be internal, national or organisational. Organisations need to consider all three set of cultures -the international culture, the national culture and the organisational culture in their purchasing decisions. In Africa, at a meeting to negotiate a contract for the purchase of goods and services, it might be customary to serve tea or coffee, and even food. In contrast, in another jurisdiction, it might be considered unacceptable. Beyond the national culture is the corporate culture, which encompasses the strategic vision of the organisation, its ethical stance and its attitudes towards suppliers, among other things. Additionally, many businesspeople act by their professional, ethical standards as well. Cultural and ethical values and beliefs, therefore, affect the way B2B buying is carried out.

4.7 B2B Buying Techniques

It is vital that B2B buying is made effective. This requires the application of some critical techniques by the purchasing firm in purchasing decision-making and implementation. Value analysis, supplier capability evaluation and supplier performance assessment are commonly used techniques to ensure the effectiveness of B2B buying.

4.7.1 Value Analysis

Value relates to benefits derived from the use of a particular product or service. Value analysis is thus an evaluation of the benefits associated with products purchased. Value analysis focuses on components, raw materials and even manufacturing processes to determine ways of cutting costs or improving finished products. Different products have different economic values. Kijewski and Yoon (1990) refer to this as value-in-use, which they define as a product's economic value to the user relative to a specific alternative. It is the outcome of the cost-benefit analysis of the product and/or a supplier.

4.7.2 Evaluating Supplier Capability

Not all suppliers have the capacity to meet the requirements of B2B buyers. Impliedly, B2B buyers need to satisfy themselves with the capacity of potential suppliers to meet the specifications. Technical expertise, reliability, financial stability, production capacity and quality assurance processes are usually the critical areas of assessment when undertaking supplier capability evaluation. Supplier capability evaluation enables B2B buyers to assess the suitability of potential suppliers in meeting specifications.

4.7.3 Evaluating Supplier Performance

Most B2B buying processes are continuous. It is important, therefore, that the purchasing company reviews the supplier's performance periodically, even after the contract is awarded. This review is necessary, particularly when the circumstances of the buying organisation have changed considerably in the course of what will be a lengthy relationship. Also, the review of the performance of the supplier serves as a check on suppliers, barring them from relaxing once the contract has been awarded.

4.8 B2B Selling Strategies

B2B selling can be incredibly challenging. Long sales cycles, tough lead generation and fierce competition imply that to survive, businesses must continuously adapt to the changing buyer–seller relationship. The landscape of selling is changing, maybe due to an expanded focus on services as well as the extensive amount of information accessible to customers during their purchasing process. This has made B2B selling a volatile, uncertain and complex phenomenon. It is observed that customers are willing to collaborate with fewer partners and save costs by developing longer-term relationships with strategic partner companies (Andersen & Kumar, 2006; Boyd & Spekman, 2004). The B2B market involves increasingly complex dealings, environmental uncertainty and lengthier buying processes, e.g. with systems and project purchasing (see Chapter 8). Therefore, getting new business customers is more difficult than before, and the traditional product-oriented sales strategies may soon become ineffective. An aggressive selling strategy is thus required.

A selling strategy is an accumulation procedure that organisations use in selling their products and services. In today's highly competitive business environment, businesses are keen on how to develop effective selling strategies to increase their sales performance, which can contribute to the creation of strong, and long-lasting positive relationships with business customers. Developing the best products and services available to a market is not enough; it has to be accepted by the market as the best in its product category. If firms are to survive, they must give great attention to their selling strategy as well as the training and development of their sales force. Conventionally, the principal strategy for prospering in B2B markets is to focus on establishing B2B customers' product needs, offering high-quality products to meet these needs, and selling the products at competitive prices. The following strategies are mostly used as B2B selling strategies.

4.8.1 Adaptive Selling Strategy

Spiro and Weitz (1990) assert that meeting the needs of the B2B buyer depends largely on information about the selling situation. When a sales representative gathers information on the selling situation and uses same to design sales presentations that meet the buying requirements of the B2B buyer, the sales representative is said to have used an adaptive selling strategy. In using the strategy, the sales representative changes sales behaviour when interacting with the potential buyer (Weitz et al., 1986). In other words, adaptive selling alters the selling approach from one customer to another, altering the sales style from one pitching situation to the next. The ability to adapt the personal selling process depends on the salesperson's effectiveness in gathering information about the sales interaction, and effectively designing and transmitting the sales message appropriate for the targeted market or customer, and then gathering feedback from the buyer to determine if the sales message has been effective. Therefore, high-level communication skills are essential if an adaptive selling strategy is to be used effectively. A salesperson's listening skills are crucial in assessing a customer's needs or acquiring information concerning the selling environment (Morgan & Stoltman, 1990).

4.8.2 Customer-Oriented Selling Strategy

The customer-oriented selling strategy emerges from promoting customer-focused selling within the selling organisation. The organisational philosophy, in this case, strives to satisfy the needs of the B2B buying firm through a well-planned and well-coordinated set of activities. A customer-oriented selling strategy is generally perceived as an essential element in a B2B selling strategy (Flaherty et al., 1999; Keillor et al., 2000). To achieve successful execution of a customer-oriented idea in an organisation, the sales force must be equipped with the needed knowledge and skills to collect B2B information and understand the needs of the buying firm.

4.8.3 Relational Selling Strategy

Before or soon after a need for industrial buying is triggered, the B2B buyers instantly have some potential suppliers in mind, perhaps, as a result of the existing relationship between them. This suggests that B2B sellers need to establish intimate relationships with their B2B customers, leading to the adoption of a relational selling strategy. A relational selling strategy is a strategic approach a B2B supplier uses to establish a mutually beneficial long-term relationship with its B2B customers. Primarily, the strategy depends on supplier–customer interdependence, exchange of important information and trust between the partners (Slater & Olson, 2000). The strategy is usually applied to key (or strategic) high-volume accounts due to the high cost and risk involved. The intimacy of the relationship determines whether or not the B2B buyers will have a repeat purchase from the same supplier. However, building strong intimate relationships with B2B customers entail a great deal of effort. Through pre-sales interactions, B2B customer service, account-based marketing, niche marketing, articulation of unique value proposition, knowing and understanding the B2B buyer, and the use of an extended line of credit, B2B suppliers build long-lasting and profitable relationships with their B2B buyers. The success of the relational selling strategy is strongly linked to its capacity to generate interpersonal bonds between the B2B seller and buyer (Narayandas & Rangan, 2004).

4.9 Conclusion

B2B buying, described as the purchasing of goods, services, systems and projects by one organisation (manufacturing, reselling, government or institutional) from another organisation, differs significantly from consumer buying. Extensive bargaining, substantial negotiation time, a high volume of products, involvement of several stakeholders (initiators, users, influencers, deciders, approvers, buyers and gatekeepers) and high-level technicality characterise the nature of B2B buying. As a result, it goes through very complex but contemporaneous decision-making processes which include needs recognition, specification and research, request for an evaluation of the proposal, order placing and review of performance. Different B2B techniques such as value analysis, supplier capability and performance evaluation are commonly employed, depending on the buying situation (straight re-buy, modified re-buy and new task) and the buying relationship (routinised exchange, organic buying and transactional buying) facing the organisation. Physical, technological, economic, political, legal, cultural and ethical environments also influence B2B buying. Strategically, adaptive, customer-oriented and relational selling strategies are adopted to sell to B2B buyers successfully.

Case and Exercise

THE LAND OF MILK AND BUSINESS BUYING

"How could you! Of what value is this to my business…? We are not in this business to cut corners but to provide the end-user with a great experience. Quality is our hallmark…" Kojo Banks, CEO of Kasepan Limited.

He banged his fist on the boardroom table and angrily paced out of the room. With this action, Kojo Banks, the CEO of Kasepan Limited had unofficially just cancelled its business partner's contract.

Kasepan Limited is a manufacturing company, headquartered within the Central Business District of Accra in Ghana. The company deals in the production and redistribution of fast-moving consumer goods (mostly milk-based products), and has been in existence for over 3 years. Kasepan Limited is famous for its quality products since its existence. During one of their daily operational reviews, Matilda, a member of the production team, had reported that the most important ingredient – Milk – had run out. Questions as to why there was no alternative suddenly became the chorus at the meeting. Feeling pressured, Matilda burst out and indicated that their supplier, Konolf 2, had been verbally informed some weeks ago about replenishing the supply, but it seems he had long forgotten.

Their supplier, Konolf 2, a multinational located in Cameroun, had just begun operations some months back in Ghana and was still acclimatising to the new terrain. Besides dealing with the language barrier, it was clear that conducting business with other African countries was not as easy as within their homeland – Cameroun. One of their top executives had high-lighted in a press interview that port authorities and government officials have been experiencing difficulty in procuring the right resources for doing business in West Africa, which has posed a challenge. However, in the Konolf 2 website, the mission was stated as providing other business entities with different grades of milk, which reads "in bulk quantities, delighting our stakeholders with on-time, quality product delivery, aiding other businesses to achieve expected demand within the value chain". After reading this on their website, the sourcing team at Kasepan did not hesitate to contract Konolf 2 as the vendor of preference and sole supplier of the most important ingredient used in manufacturing. Unfortunately, it ended up being the biggest mistake in their partnership with suppliers to date. That morning, Kojo Banks was throwing a fit in the boardroom, infuriated, not only because the procurement head at Konolf 2 had proposed a lower grade of milk to address the issue of low supply, but also because September 2014 was the month Kasepan was expected to double their production capacity and rake in 50% more revenue than they had ever done in 3 years. This was due to the projection of increased milk consumption among the populace. A leadership team meeting was quickly scheduled to discuss: (1) operations in September 2014 – shut down or continue production and (2) source for a new supplier.

More critical to Kasepan was the possibility of meeting their December target with new raw materials, especially as December was another month where they stood to rake in millions of cedis. As expected, the "operations in September" subject was put on hold to thoroughly discuss sourcing and buying from a new supplier considering what was at stake. Kojo Banks had moved the motion for a change in supplier and managed to get all leadership team on the same side.

The message was communicated to Matilda James by her boss, Amy Whitehead, the Head of Supply Chain of Kasepan Limited. Matilda had been singled out as the Single Point of Contact (SPOC) for the project set up to recruit a new supplier. Matilda had just assumed the role 2 months prior after completing a year of National Service and 2 years as a management trainee. Her desire and willingness to win, as well as attention to detail, stood out as qualities that excited everyone within the business. She exhibited the values of Kasepan.

During the session where Konolf 2 was let go, it came to light that they were operating in Cameroun on behalf of the French Government. The Department of Animal Husbandry had embarked on a national programme to supply some of the nation's rich resources to developing countries, mostly colonies and other African countries, at a subsidy. With such a great initiative, it required the services of a willing and cooperative agency to execute this agenda. During the period where Kasepan patronised Konolf 2, it was clear their structure was not set up to accommodate the depth of business. On average, they needed nothing short of 200 tonnes worth of milk just to meet the average demand monthly. With this background of the issue leading to the collapse of the partnership, which had started as a flourishing one, Matilda was more than equipped to begin the process of identifying a new supplier for her company and assemble a project team. At her initial kick-off meeting of the team, the agenda was a very simple one: "Vision: Know Ourselves. Get the Right Supplier and Milk the Gold Mine to our Future. Weird…?" Well yes, in her mind, she had managed to create a thematic agenda to the kick-off. Project team members were expected to know each other, bringing to the fore their background, expectations and views on how to proceed as a team eliminating the mess already created.

After all employees had shared their views which was premised on getting a local supplier, the most controversial employee as generally perceived in the company, Mukesh, was given the opportunity to speak. Matilda had included Mukesh Ambani on the team because he was deeply knowledgeable and had an opinion about everything, was an expert in working with cross-functional teams, and was very direct, never beating about the bush. Mukesh insisted that if they were to engage a local supplier, there must be laid down procedures which would require the provision of supporting details. The supporting details would include the number of employees, capacity (minimum and maximum), average delivery period, values, vision, quality certification and source of material. Thus, he had advised that the modus operandi of their next supplier was very critical in the run-up to selection. Mukesh convinced five out of the seven-team members who valued his inputs and unanimously confirmed it was the right approach. Matilda lent her support too. By the third team meeting, Matilda and her team had managed to evaluate four possible suppliers Kasepan could buy from. A thorough evaluation that included a supplier site audit led to a shortlist of two companies – Mayak and K12–9.

In order to have the opportunity to evaluate them, the project team succeeded in convincing management to sign both companies for 3 months for the purchase of very minimal materials that Kasepan currently was sourcing elsewhere. These materials did not impact the outcome or quality of final products sold to the end consumer. After obtaining the approval, Mayak and K12–9 were set up as suppliers in the system and purchasing from them begun. Mayak is an institution located in Ghana that resells raw materials to corporate bodies after buying from other suppliers. They have been in existence for 12 years, and their speciality lies in offering their customers value for money, even though they act as intermediaries. K12–9, on the other hand, is a very traditional organisation that has been around for decades. With their experience in working locally with all the leading production houses, their plan now is to acquire the rights to begin exporting raw materials to big corporations outside the shores of Ghana. Following a 3-month evaluation process and confirmation from other businesses they have sold to, Matilda and her team had settled to work with and purchase the supply of milk from K12–9. The team considered over ten parameters before settling on a decision. The primary criteria for the decision to engage K12–9 were the final quality assessment carried out on the specs of milk supplied as well as on the finished goods. Not only did the samples exceed the target set for them, Faukyewa Thomas and Christian Anderson in the management team of K12–9 had shared a contingency plan on the buying process if their multi-million-dollar factory shuts down. They also outlined their plan on growing their farm to increase its size by 25% within the next 5 years. This was very much appreciated and welcomed by Kasepan. They had put in very modern place structures, and employees were technologically inclined, mainly because the world is rapidly swaying towards automation. In addition to this, K12–9 had a very structured organisation that ensured that decision-making process would not be compromised in any way.

After an initial 4-week process of selecting qualified suppliers and an additional 3 months to evaluate processes of final candidates, Kasepan was ready to resume normal operations. On January 15, 2015, the contract was finally signed between both companies, and bulk purchasing had begun in earnest once again. Just before the business picked up again after the holidays, Kojo, the CEO of Kasepan, had met Faukyewaa and Christian at a fundraising programme for a "save our green world" campaign where participants from major organisations across Africa had met to sell the concept and benefits of organic materials. The presentation of K12–9 on the day filled Kojo with so much delight that he commended Matilda and her team for the stellar work done. "Today I celebrate our very own colleagues." "We are in for a great year!" exclaimed Matilda after listening to Kojo's speech. She quickly reached out to her Demand Planning and Brand Manager to share all the documents, volumes and any additional information on the project before the next call in a week. September was one month the leadership team of Kasepan would strive to forget after missing huge revenue targets the previous year. The organisation vowed to do everything possible to ensure production will not fail and avoid reoccurrence. Among the most critical was keeping a positive relationship between both businesses. If the conduct of K12–9 was anything to go by, at least after their first few quarters, then yes! "September will be great", Mr Yves, the Finance Head of Kasepan echoed. Although K12–9 was not comfortable with the payment terms of receiving money 45 days after the invoice was issued when Matilda communicated it to them, as a supplier, they valued and understood the long-term value of this business relationship and thus worked to accommodate the arrangement.

For the next 5 years, the processes concerning procuring raw materials had improved drastically. The involvement of K12–9 in the business operations led to the expansion of the business of both parties. On the one hand, K12–9 had now increased the size of the farm to ensure constant supply and also meet the growing demand following the renovation project to introduce a powdered milk brand to suit the "on-the-go" consumer. They had also diversified into new marketing and were now selling other materials to the organisation.

Buying had now taken a new turn at Kasepan. Procurement was now central in all its business buying operations. The relevance of this ensured cost-efficient means was always considered concerning buying. The size of the team had now increased from 5 to 25, including operational buyers who managed the day-to-day purchases on behalf of the organisation as well as the strategic buyers considered for the high-risk-related options. Due to their knowledge of the job and the trusted partnership that had been built since January 15, 2015, they were now "official partners". They played roles that included advisory services on specific raw materials or ingredients and training of new employees of Kasepan. The small traditional startup had managed to overcome competitive business types and become the main supplier of an emerging manufacturing firm. The strategy of buying mostly from governmental agencies was no more the practice; focusing solely on producers who had industry knowledge for more effective service and continuous training of employees were the keys to success.

4.10 Discussion Questions

1. "Unfortunately, it ended up being the biggest mistake within their short existence to date". Discuss this statement in the context of Kasepan Ltd contracting Konolf 2 as its raw material supplier.
2. Compare and contrast, highlighting the possible benefits and challenges of the procedures followed in the selection of Konolf 2 and K12–9, the raw material suppliers to Kasepan Ltd.

References

Andersen, P. H., & Kumar, R. (2006). Emotions, trust and relationship development in business relationships: A conceptual model for buyer–seller dyads. *Industrial Marketing Management*, 35(4), 522–535.

Asongu, S., Raheem, I., & Tchamyou, V. (2018). Information asymmetry and financial dollarization in sub-Saharan Africa. *Research in International Business and Finance,* 9(2), 231–249.

Beckman, M. (2019). Green brand equity in industrial B2B markets: A cross-sectional study of Sandvik Coromant's customers.

Boström, G. (2015). Social media's significance on the need recognition and information search, in B2B investment decisions of 3D printers.

Boyd, D. E., & Spekman, R. E. (2004). Internet usage within B2B relationships and its impact on value creation: A conceptual model and research propositions. *Journal of Business to Business Marketing,* 11(1–2), 9–34.

Calitz, A., Bosire, S., & Cullen, M. (2018). The role of business intelligence in sustainability reporting for South African higher education institutions. *International Journal of Sustainability in Higher Education*, 19(7), 1185–1203.

Czubala, W., Shepherd, B., & Wilson, J. S. (2009). Help or hindrance? The impact of harmonised standards on African exports. *Journal of African Economies*, 18(5), 711–744.

Diba, H., Vella, J. M., & Abratt, R. (2019). Social media influence on the B-TO-B buying process. *Journal of Business & Industrial Marketing,* 34(7), 1482–1496.

Donthu, N., Hershberger, E. K., & Osmonbekov, T. (2005). Benchmarking marketing productivity using data envelopment analysis. *Journal of Business Research,* 58(11), 1474–1482.

Farole, T., & Winkler, D. (Eds.) (2014). *Making foreign direct investment work for Sub-Saharan Africa: Local spillovers and competitiveness in global value chains.* The World Bank, Washington, DC.

Flaherty, T. B., Dahlstrom, R., & Skinner, S. J. (1999). Organizational values and role stress as determinants of customer-oriented selling performance. *Journal of Personal Selling and Sales Management*, 19(2), 1–18.

Gomes, M., Fernandes, T., & Brandão, A. (2016). Determinants of brand relevance in a B2B service purchasing context. *Journal of Business & Industrial Marketing*, 31(2), 193–204.

Grewal, R., Lilien, G. L., Bharadwaj, S., Jindal, P., Kayande, U., Lusch, R. F., … & Spekman, R. (2015). Business-to-business buying: Challenges and opportunities. *Customer Needs and Solutions*, 2(3), 193–208.

Juntunen, M., Ismagilova, E., & Oikarinen, E. L. (2019). B2B brands on Twitter: Engaging users with a varying combination of social media content objectives, strategies, and tactics. *Industrial Marketing Management*, 89, 630–641.

Keillor, B. D., Parker, R. S., & Pettijohn, C. E. (2000). Relationship-oriented characteristics and individual salesperson performance. *Journal of Business and Industrial Marketing*, 15(1), 7–22.

Kemp, E. A., Borders, A. L., Anaza, N. A., & Johnston, W. J. (2018). The heart in organizational buying: Marketers' understanding of emotions and decision-making of buyers. *Journal of Business and Industrial Marketing*, 33(1), 10.

Kijewski, V., & Yoon, E. (1990). Market-based pricing: Beyond price-performance curves. *Industrial Marketing Management*, 19(1), 11–19.

Kotler, P. (2009). *Marketing management.* Pearson Education, London.

Mubango, P. (2015). Business to business dimensions of relationship marketing in the South African cement manufacturing industry (Doctoral dissertation). University of Kwazulu-Natal.

Morgan, F. W., & Stoltman, J. J. (1990). Adaptive selling: Insights from social cognition. *Journal of Personal Selling and Sales Management*, 10(4), 43–54.

Munif, F. (2018). The role of social media in building value for the reseller in B2B marketing (Doctoral dissertation, Auckland University of Technology).

Nandonde, F. A., & Kuada, J. (2016). Modern food retailing buying behaviour in Africa: The case of Tanzania. *British Food Journal*, 118(5), 1163–1178.

Narayandas, D., & Rangan, V. K. (2004). Building and sustaining buyer–seller relationships in mature industrial markets. *Journal of Marketing*, 68(3), 63–77.

Ndubisi, N. O., & Nataraajan, R. (2016). Marketing relationships in the new millennium B-TO-B sector. *Psychology and Marketing, 33*(4), 227–231.

Siluk, J. C. M., Kipper, L. M., Nara, E. O. B., Neuenfeldt Junior, A. L., Dal Forno, A. J., Soliman, M., & Chaves, D. M. D. S. (2017). A performance measurement decision support system method applied for technology-based firms' suppliers. *Journal of Decision Systems, 26*(1), 93–109.

Sivhabu, K. A. (2018). An investigation of buying behaviour of explosives by mines in South Africa (Doctoral dissertation, North-West University).

Slater, S. F., & Olson, E. M. (2000). Strategy type and performance: The influence of sales force management. *Strategic Management Journal, 21*(8), 813–829.

Spiro, R. L., & Weitz, B. A. (1990). Adaptive selling: Conceptualization, measurement, and nomological validity. *Journal of Marketing Research, 27*(1), 61–69.

Swani, K., Brown, B. P., & Mudambi, S. M. (2019). The untapped potential of B2B advertising: A literature review and future agenda. *Industrial Marketing Management, 89*, 581–593.

Verster, A., Petzer, D. J., & Cunningham, N. (2019). Using brand identity to build brand equity: A comparison between the South African and Dutch business-to-business architectural industry. *South African Journal of Business Management, 50*(1), 1–12.

Vincent, O. R., Makinde, A. S., & Akinwale, A. T. (2017). A cognitive buying decision-making process in B2B e-commerce using Analytic-MLP. *Electronic Commerce Research and Applications, 25*, 59–69.

Webster Jr, F. E., & Wind, Y. (1972). A general model for understanding organizational buying behavior. *Journal of Marketing, 36*(2), 12–19.

Weitz, B. A., Sujan, H., & Sujan, M. (1986). Knowledge, motivation, and adaptive behavior: A framework for improving selling effectiveness. *Journal of Marketing, 50*(4), 174–191.

Wind, Y. & Webster, F. E. (1972). On the study of industrial buying behavior: Current practices and future trends. *Industrial Marketing Management, 1*(4), 411–416.

Zimmerman, A., & Blythe, J. (2013). *Business to business marketing management: A global perspective.* Routledge, Abingdon.

Zimmerman, A., & Blythe, J. (2018). The future of business marketing. In *Business to business marketing management: A global perspective* (pp. 393–409). Routledge, Abingdon.

Chapter 5

Buying from Business Sellers

By the end of the chapter, you will be able to:

1. Explain the nature of business-to-business (B2B) selling
2. Identify and explain who business sellers are in B2B transactions
3. Discuss the stages in the B2B selling process
4. Explain the principles and techniques for effective B2B selling.

5.1 Nature of Business-to-Business (B2B) Selling

B2B buying does not take place in isolation. It takes at least two companies to engage in B2B exchanges. Therefore, B2B transactions may take any of these two forms: a firm buying from another firm (B2B buying) or a firm selling to another firm (B2B selling). While the former was discussed in Chapter 4, the latter is discussed in this chapter. Connick (2019) defines B2B selling as sales of a firm's products and services to other organisations, not individual customers. B2B selling, therefore, describes a situation where an organisation sells its products to another organisation (Aten, 2019).

B2B selling involves dealing with professional buyers, high-level executives and/or gatekeepers. Most companies prefer to use professional buyers in their B2B transactions. Professional buyers receive extensive training and are knowledgeable about how B2B selling works. They are packed with and employ tricks and tactics that allow them to wrangle better prices and even manipulate sales force and processes. B2B selling also requires knowledge about high-level executives such as Chief Executive Officers (CEOs), Managing Directors (MDs), Chief Financial Controllers (CFCs), and other Managers and Directors. These high-level executives are the decision-makers who are extremely busy people who do not appreciate others wasting their valuable time, and they can be very intimidating. B2B selling also requires knowledge about key gatekeepers such as receptionists and assistants. The gatekeepers are the "password" to accessing high-level executives who have the ultimate authority to commit to the sale. An in-depth understanding of the tricks and tactics of professional buyers, how to get past the gatekeepers and how to penetrate the heart of high-level executives to commit to the sale is fundamental to the success of B2B selling (Connick, 2019).

Generally, the B2B selling process is complex. It is complicated because it highly depends on personal interaction with experts who usually operate in complicated domains. In explaining the level of complexity associated with B2B selling, Weitz and Bradford (1999) argue that multiple actors from both the selling firm and the buying firm are involved in the process. Another reason that explains the complexity of B2B selling is the inclusion of the service element. According to Neu and Brown (2005), the service element varies greatly and is difficult to specify. Owing to the high-level interactions between the B2B seller and the B2B buyer, it is suggested that the parties establish collaborative relationships to enable them to gradually develop a common solution. The development of the good and collaborative relationship between the B2B seller and buyer will enable the selling organisation to build better relationships with buying firms (Hunter & Perreault, 2007; Keillor et al., 2000).

B2B selling requires a more complex and nuanced approach. The B2B selling process is relational and consultative, and involves a longer sales cycle (Aten, 2019). As a result, it entails building and managing relationships with different professional service companies. To navigate the complex B2B selling processes and successfully build B2B selling relationships, companies rely on the use of active B2B sales teams and strong sales support teams. In a B2B selling, a combination of products and services that companies use in their systems and processes are sold. Additionally, B2B sellers engage in complex negotiations and contracts, resulting in higher overall costs and pricing. Nevertheless, the nature of B2B selling differs from an organisation to organisation. To some extent, the type of organisation engaged in B2B selling determines the nature of B2B selling.

5.2 B2B Sellers

B2B sellers are companies who sell products chiefly to other companies. They do not sell to individual consumers. It is important that the categories of businesses engaged in B2B selling are identified, and their operations understood. Connick (2019) classifies B2B sellers into manufacturing, merchandising, service and hybrid B2B sellers.

5.2.1 Manufacturing B2B Sellers

A manufacturing B2B seller manufactures products that it sells to B2B customers. Manufacturing B2B companies, therefore, sell products they have produced themselves to other businesses. They usually sell materials and other parts to meet the manufacturing need of other businesses. They also engage in selling products such as office supplies and computer equipment that meet the consumption needs of other businesses. Manufacturing B2B sellers only sell products they have transformed from raw materials or other products. Many such sellers package their goods, services and technologies into systems or sometimes projects that include turnkey construction (see Chapter 8).

5.2.2 Merchandising B2B Sellers

Merchandising B2B sellers buy goods at low (wholesale) prices and retail them to other firms at a profit. They are generally known as *buying and selling* businesses. Dominant merchandising B2B sellers are wholesalers. In a typical distribution supply chain, wholesalers are B2B firms that sell products to retailers. Unlike manufacturing B2B sellers, merchandising B2B sellers sell their products without changing their form. Merchandising B2B sellers sell products that are produced by other firms.

5.2.3 Service B2B Sellers

Some B2B firms render service rather than sell a physical product to their B2B customers. That is, a service B2B seller is the one that renders services to other business organisations. There are several service B2B sellers. For instance, accounting firms provide audit services to companies, while law firms provide legal services to companies. Service B2B sellers mostly offer professional skills, expertise and advice.

5.2.4 Hybrid B2B Sellers

Some companies engage in multiple or combined forms of B2B selling. They sell products they manufactured themselves, resell products they purchased from other manufacturers or wholesalers, and render professional services to their B2B customers. These hybrid B2B sellers lend themselves to more than one type of B2B selling. A restaurant is a typical example of hybrid B2B seller. This is because the restaurant prepares meals for other companies (manufacturing B2B selling), sells drinks to other companies (merchandising B2B selling) and fills customer orders (service B2B selling). A type of hybrid B2B seller is the system or project marketer that includes other companies in a network or supply chain (see Chapter 8).

From the above discussions, B2B sellers are either product-based, service-based or hybrid. While product-based B2B sellers, such as Kingdom Bookshop and Samatex Timber Company Limited in Ghana, concentrate on selling physical and tangible goods, service-based B2B sellers engage in services such as call answering services, marketing (advertising) agency services, legal services, security services, insurance services, accounting and auditing services, and catering services. Hybrid B2B sellers, on the other hand, are both product-based and service-oriented.

5.3 Principles of B2B Selling

The B2B selling process aims at building relationships with business prospects and converting them into new business customers. The practices that businesses use in converting business prospects into business customers are described as principles of B2B selling and are described below.

5.3.1 Relational Sales Process

In a relational sales process, the B2B sales teams are focused on discovering the needs of their business customers through a relationship-based dialogue. The B2B sales teams in this process address specific problems they identify during the interactions with their B2B customers (Castillo & George, 2018). Aten (2019) describes the relational sales process as *consultative selling* because it is based on consulting with the prospects, discovering their needs and selling them exactly what they need. This affirms the assertion of Grove et al. (2018) that "what a B-TO-B customer buys and considers value is never a product. It is always utility, that is, what a product or service does for the firm" (p. 55). The key responsibility of the B2B sales team in a consultative B2B selling process is to understand the specification their B2B prospects need. Consultative B2B selling, according to Aten (2019), results in a happier and longer-term relationship with B2B customers. It is crucial, therefore, that in B2B selling, B2B sellers become outcome-oriented, which involves collaboration with B2B customers to understand their needs and create products that meet those needs.

5.3.2 B2B Sales Pipeline

The B2B sales pipelines are the specific steps through which the B2B seller moves sales opportunities during the B2B selling process. It involves clearly defining the stages in the B2B sales pipeline. Some stages involved in the B2B sales pipeline include, but are not limited to, consultations, qualified leads, proposals and negotiations. The B2B sales pipeline is usually long for complicated products and services. B2B sales pipeline management makes it easy for a B2B seller to drag deals through the B2B selling process and measure the effectiveness of its B2B sales strategies.

5.3.3 B2B Customer Account Management

B2B selling, as elaborated earlier, entails building and maintaining a relationship with B2B buyers. To achieve this, B2B sellers dedicate sales teams to manage the sales transactions of key B2B customers. The B2B customer account management is not limited to the initial selling process. It extends to maintaining a close relationship with B2B customers. It leads to the discovery of new sales opportunities within the accounts of the existing B2B buyers.

5.4 B2B Selling Process

B2B selling, like any other selling, goes through a series of stages. In the B2B selling process, new B2B prospects are discovered and converted into customers (Aten, 2019). Therefore, the B2B selling process, as noted by Åge (2011), seeks to qualify, assess and win sales opportunities. Comprehensively, the steps involved in the B2B selling process include finding prospects, qualifying the prospects, setting up meetings, delivering a pitch, delivering cost proposal, negotiating price and closing the sale (Åge, 2011; Aten, 2019).

5.4.1 Finding Prospects

The B2B selling process begins with B2B prospect finding. The B2B prospect finding is the process leading to the discovery of who an organisation's B2B customers are. B2B prospecting is a continual process and depends on the ability of B2B sales teams to constantly identify and understand the needs of the prospects, and also source new opportunities (Forrest, 2017). Several approaches exist for B2B prospecting. These include upleading, customer profiling, researching prospects and cultivating referrals. Upleading allows B2B sellers to search for B2B prospects by industry, role and geographic location. The intention is to identify the contact information of decision-makers in the potential target companies. B2B sales force are encouraged to create a B2B database of existing and potential business customer profile which helps them identify the right prospects or target market. The B2B customer profiling entails a summary of the ideal B2B customer's demographics, like how long the company has been in business, the industry the firm operates in and its location (Lim, 2019). Having identified new prospects, the B2B sales force, using professional networks, gathers strategic information such as former roles, education and goals of the representatives of the prospect companies. This act of researching each prospect helps qualify the individual lead as well as providing information about touchpoints necessary for profitable conversation and smooth take-off of the B2B selling process. Cultivating referrals involves asking existing B2B customers to recommend other B2B customers who could also benefit from the products and services being offered in the B2B selling process (Toth et al., 2017). Prospects acquired from existing customers' recommendations have a higher propensity of becoming B2B customers.

5.4.2 Qualifying Prospects

The second stage of the B2B selling process is qualifying prospects. Qualifying prospects is the process of ensuring that the prospects are a good fit. It is the process of understanding the need of the potential B2B customers and their ability to pay for the products and services of the company (Meire et al., 2017). Qualifying prospects helps eliminate prospects that are not a good fit, that are not interested, and that would not be profitable B2B customers. Qualified B2B customers are thus decision-makers with authority to make a purchase. They have a need for the organisation's products and have a budget that can support their purchase desire.

5.4.3 Setting up Meetings

Setting up a meeting with a qualified lead is a crucial part of the B2B selling process. After the prospects are qualified, the B2B sales team arranges meetings with qualified prospects to gain appointments with them. A meeting with the qualified lead allows the B2B sales team to initiate a conversation around the needs of the potential B2B customer (Biggins, 2018). During the process, the B2B sales team creates needs dialogue, which is a compilation of the needs of the would-be B2B customer. The needs dialogue helps in determining the specific needs gaps the prospects have, how best those needs can be satisfied and with what products and services. This initial meeting with the prospects assists in evaluating the various products and services on offer and developing customised solutions that meet both the needs and budgets of the potential B2B customers. It is important, therefore, that during this initial cold calling, the focus of the B2B seller is not on selling the products and services, but on gaining an appointment (Das et al., 2018). If this is successfully done, the rest of the process of B2B selling would be less complicated.

5.4.4 Delivering a Pitch

Das et al. (2018) assert that sales pitch delivery is a stage that follows gaining appointments to meet with qualified prospects. B2B sales pitching is making presentations about the products and services of the B2B seller to qualified B2B prospects (Pandey & Shinde, 2019). It involves the introduction of the B2B sales team and telling the story of the products and services of the B2B seller. The product story in the pitch is centred on the value proposition and its benefits to the qualified prospects (Anaza et al., 2019). That is, generally, in a sit-down meeting, the proposed or customised solution is presented to the prospective B2B customers, and all their questions are clarified and addressed, and proposed solutions modified where necessary. The sales pitch delivery process must end with a summary of key messages, which help confirm the prospects' understanding and commitment to make a purchase. The sales pitch could be done relying on in-person presentations, video conference presentations, phone presentation or a combination of such presentations. Whatever the case, B2B sales pitch delivery should be preceded by adequate preparations: getting the script/slides ready, rehearsing thoroughly and managing time appropriately.

5.4.5 Delivering a Cost Proposal

The fifth stage in the B2B selling process is delivering a cost proposal. Once a B2B seller had met with potential B2B customers, discerned their needs and offered a solution through a sales pitch, the B2B seller prepares and presents cost proposal to the prospects. The cost proposal performs several functions. It comprehensively embraces the needs of the B2B customers, specifies the proposed solutions, indicates the associated costs and finally highlights the benefits for B2B customers

(Russo et al., 2017). Cost proposal delivery is an important step in the B2B selling process. It communicates to and assures the B2B customers that the firm understands their needs fully. Besides, it provides an opportunity for the B2B sellers to check and be sure that they are on the same page with the B2B customers. A cost proposal also concretely establishes expectations which might culminate into the sales of the products to the B2B customer (Aten, 2019).

5.4.6 Negotiating Price

Price negotiation is a major step in the B2B selling process. Price negotiation is initiated after the B2B sales pitch is completed. Usually, price negotiation is preceded by objection handling where all objections likely to derail the closure of sales are handled. Negotiating price, as part of the B2B selling process, allows the B2B sellers to understand what the B2B customers want and how important the products and services are to them (Niemi & Hirvonen, 2019). During price negotiation, Aten (2019) advises that B2B sellers should be honest and open to building trust, be mindful of setting precedent, switch off their ego, negotiate face-to-face and negotiate only after the selling is completed, but not closed.

5.4.7 Closing the Sale

The final stage in the B2B selling process is closing the sale. Closing the sales, according to Aten (2019), is a process of asking closing questions that formalise and finalise the solutions that have been agreed upon to meet the needs of the B2B customers. That is, once the terms of the B2B sales are agreed on, a purchase agreement or contract is signed to finalise the agreement. Closing B2B sales involve an intentional commitment of the B2B sales teams to the B2B selling sales process. Closing the sales is a logical conclusion reached if B2B sales teams adopt a consultative sales approach, giving the B2B customers precisely what they want and need (Diba et al., 2019). Moore et al. (2015) contend that effective closing of sales requires adequate preparation where the B2B sales teams are armed with all the relevant items and information needed to close a sale. It also rests predominantly on an assumption of B2B customers' readiness to buy. This reduces the level of anxiety and uncertainty of the B2B sales teams and makes them confident in their expertise and in what they are selling. Asking B2B customers multiple-choice questions such as "Do you prefer paying with cheque, cash or credit card" is also an effective way of closing B2B sales. Receiving the signed purchase agreement or contract is evidence that the B2B sale is complete.

5.5 B2B Selling Techniques

Åge (2018) recommended business manoeuvring as a set of techniques that ensure success in B2B selling (and buying). The author defined business manoeuvring as a social process that captures the dynamic nature of contemporary B2B sales and describes how B2B sellers and buyers resolve their selling and purchasing concerns. Based on business manoeuvring, B2B selling techniques cover several strategies. The strategies include business standardisation, business fraternisation, business personalisation and probationary business rationalisation. The B2B sellers and buyers should manage the strategies with dexterity and skill.

5.5.1 Business Standardisation

Business standardisation refers to the formality of organisational practices. Different business standardisations exist. These include purchasing, selling and service standardisations. Åge (2018) describes purchasing standardisation as standardised procedures buyers follow when purchasing. The major drawback of purchasing standardisation is the hindrance it imposes on a close collaborative and interactive relationship between the B2B buyer and seller. Knowledge of the purchasing standardisation of a B2B customer is a plus to the B2B seller in strategising approaches that conform to such standards. The procedure B2B seller adopts to sell their products to B2B buyers can also be standardised. The formalisation of the selling process or procedure by the B2B seller is termed selling standardisation. Selling standardisation covers such activities as determining the deals to pursue and negotiating prices. Like purchasing and selling, services can also be formalised. Service formalisation, which entails specification of service procedures to adhere to, is known as service standardisation. It must be noted, however, that the degree of standardisation differs from one firm to another and impacts organisations differently (Peleg & Lee, 2015).

5.5.2 Business Fraternisation

Another recommended technique for making B2B selling effective is business fraternisation. Business fraternisation, according to Graça et al. (2016), is how B2B sellers and buyers collaborate to develop and maintain relationships. The establishment of business fraternisation is usually based on mutual understanding and respect. In business fraternisation, different units work together towards a common goal. Different components of business fraternisation can be identified: distance reduction, operational trust, fraternisation competence and the learning process (Åge, 2018). Distance reduction ensures physical closeness in establishing close collaborative relationships. Operational trust defines the level of confidence the B2B buyer has in the ability of the B2B seller to deliver what it promises. Fraternisation competence refers to the knowledge of the B2B seller about the B2B buyers and the challenges they face. During business interactions, B2B sellers and buyers learn from each other about their business processes and operations. These learning opportunities are described as the business process (Claro et al., 2020).

5.5.3 Personalisation

Personalisation, as a technique of B2B selling, describes the attitudes of individuals engaged in B2B selling and buying (Åge, 2018). The B2B seller faces the challenge of changing the perception of the B2B buyers about its offerings in general. This type of challenge is referred to as a pedagogic challenge. Whenever a B2B buyer purchases a service from another firm, there are a bundle of benefits associated with the services, albeit intangible. The attempt by the B2B seller to make the B2B buyer aware of the value associated with the service function is known in personalisation as service awareness (Järvinen & Taiminen, 2016). B2B buyers hold certain expectations about the products of B2B sellers. These expectations could be realistic and unrealistic. The B2B seller has the arduous tasks of managing these expectations of the B2B buyers, hence the changing expectations. Another component of the personalisation is behavioural trust. The behavioural trust is a summary description of the behaviour of the B2B seller, particularly towards the B2B buyer (Alves et al., 2017).

5.5.4 Probationary Business Rationalisation

Another B2B selling technique proposed by Åge (2018) is probationary business rationalisation, which he defined as the B2B sellers' and buyers' concern for costs and risks associated with the B2B selling process. Åge (2011) argued that focusing only on the price is not a guarantee for a long-term successful business project. There is, therefore, the need not only to reduce the cost for both parties but also to reduce both financial and operational risks (Chatterjee, 2018). This is because economic concerns regarding risks and costs are always present in B2B projects and are being calculated continuously.

Effective management of the B2B selling process requires not only the business manoeuvring techniques but also strategies and tactics (Ahola et al., 2019). That is, in addition to the four basic business manoeuvring B2B selling techniques, the following strategies and tactics are also helpful in enhancing B2B sales.

5.5.5 Adopt a Focused Approach

B2B marketers need to adopt an extremely focused approach to make their B2B selling effective and beneficial (Altounian et al., 2016). B2B sellers should be intentional in dealing with their B2B customers. This requires that the B2B sellers prepare a list of their target B2B customers (Järvinen & Taiminen, 2016). As they prepare the focus list of potential customers, they should bear in mind the products and services being offered and how such products and services would be useful to their customers.

5.5.6 Choose the Right Mode of Communication

B2B sellers need to choose the right mode of communication. Communication plays a critical role in the success or otherwise of B2B sales (Hänninen & Karjaluoto, 2017). It is important, therefore, that the B2B sellers try to fix up a meeting with the representative of the B2B buying organisation. During the conversation, the B2B sales team should be very polite and confident. Anders et al. (2020) advised that if the conversation is via phone, the B2B sellers should not receive phone calls at a noisy place and that they should keep a pen and paper handy to jot down important requirements or points the potential B2B buyers may make. Also, the B2B sales teams should politely introduce themselves and their organisation and be good and patient listeners. If they must meet with the buyers, they should request for a convenient time for the meeting.

5.5.7 Always Be on Time for Business Meetings

When appointments are booked with potential B2B buyers, B2B sellers should endeavour never to be late to any meeting with the customer. B2B marketing professionals should always dress formally. Very importantly too, B2B sales teams should not forget to carry their business cards which contain all the necessary information about them and their organisation, and all other essential documents such as the company's brochures and demo kits (Kaski et al., 2017).

5.5.8 Be Very Confident and Professional While Interacting with B2B Customers

B2B buyers and professionals can quickly relate the quality of a firm's products and services to the professionalism and confidence of the B2B sales teams (Kaski et al., 2018). Therefore, B2B sales teams need to be knowledgeable and believe in the organisation's brand and also be prepared to answer any questions posed by B2B buyers. The role of B2B sales teams is to convince B2B buyers to purchase the organisation's products or services (Madhavaram & Hunt, 2017). However, the persuasion should be done tactfully. The customers should be allowed to make their own purchasing decisions and should never be forced or deceived into buying the products or services.

5.5.9 Follow-Up Is Essential

B2B buyers are usually business executives and managers who are very busy people. There is, therefore, a high tendency that they may forget about purchasing intentions expressed. It is important, therefore, that the B2B sales teams send regular reminders to the potential buyers and follow-up on them. However, this should also be done cautiously because excessive reminders and follow-up can irritate buyers and even spoil the entire purchasing deal. Regular follow-up is essential (Järvinen & Taiminen, 2016), but that does not mean that the B2B sales team should be overly aggressive in pursuing a customer (Wang et al., 2016).

5.6 Conclusion

Generally, the B2B selling process is a complex process that is dependent on personal interaction with experts within a company. This requires high-level interactions between the B2B seller and the B2B buyer and, therefore, establishing a collaborative relationship is key to success. Building relationships with key stakeholder will enable the seller to create value. Selling techniques highlighted in the chapter include B2B selling strategies which include business standardisation, business fraternisation, business personalisation and probationary business rationalisation. Hence, B2B sellers should put into consideration these strategies in their dealings. A team approach to B2B selling is advocated to navigate the complex selling processes and successfully build B2B selling relationships. Hence, companies should rely on the use of active B2B sales teams and strong sales support teams.

Case Study: The Great Ghana Bank (GGB)

THE ROLE OF AN EFFICIENT BUSINESS SELLER IN SERVICE DELIVERY OF A BANK

BACKGROUND INFORMATION: THE GREAT GHANA BANK (GGB)

The Great Ghana Bank (GGB) is a financial institution in Ghana. It is one of the most respected traditional or government banks in Ghana. It has been in existence for 40 years and has contributed a lot in long-term financing of many businesses in Ghana. It has won many awards in the past for long-term finance. The bank was established principally to promote and strengthen rapid industrialisation in all sectors of the Ghanaian economy. GGB became involved in the set-up of major joint ventures in the country as Ghanaian manufacturers or the private sector did not have the required funding for startups. In this case, GGB either lends to enterprises or puts in the needed equity. Overall, GGB was able to set up over 250 joint enterprises. The bank remained committed to its core mandate of providing development finance for industries. However, the bank transitioned to commercial banking to complement its development banking services as a result of the problems associated with raising long-term capital. Under the development banking services, it provides short-term loans, long-term loans, and working capital loans to businesses. It lends to manufacturing, building and construction, and agro-processing sectors as well as the service industry. The GGB headquarters is located in Accra, the capital city of Ghana, with about 40 branches in all the regional capitals of Ghana.

Due to stiff competition in the Banking Industry in Ghana, the traditional bank which usually focuses on development banking services only is now offering universal banking services which include development banking services and commercial banking services. It has, therefore, engaged the services of a software business seller, Fase 5 Support Service Limited, to provide Mastercard services to the Banks' clients. Fase 5 Support Services Limited has a 24-hour service which runs a shift system with expert and experienced staff. Fraud is monitored 24 hours and has a highly secured network. As a result, the card can be used on all websites and all social media platforms for any transaction within the limit of the card. Fase 5 Support Service provides and programmes each client's card as and when requested by the GGB e-Banking Department. The firm charges the bank per each card issued out. The banking industry in Ghana has become competitive over the years.

THE CASE

Naa Shidaa Fearon, the CEO of NSF Kloset, opened a business current account with the Windy Win Bank (WWB), at the Airport City Branch of the bank in June 2016 on the referral of one of her childhood friends. The Branch Manager, Mr Manan Bugase had been given a high deposit mobilisation target and was working hard to achieve it. He believed in personal selling and word-of-mouth communications and had informed his family and friends to help him get big business customers as he also goes about his duty of introducing his bank to businesses and individuals in his catchment area. Naa has a successful clothing line business in South Africa, where she resides with her husband. She was born and raised in South Africa. Her husband, a diplomat, had been transferred to Ghana for the next 10 years, and relocated with his family. Looking at the clothing industry in Ghana, she realised that it was a huge untapped market as most people shopped for cheap substandard clothes from Tamata Market in Accra. Most working-class people had busy lifestyles and found it extremely difficult to find time to shop at Tamata. Some resorted to sewing locally. She, therefore, registered her business in Ghana and informed her childhood friend to recommend a good bank for her. Her friend immediately introduced Naa to his brother, the Branch Manager of WWB. After a successful meeting with the Branch Manager at the Airport Branch of WWB, she opened the account.

After 2 months, she opened a trust dollar account for her twin sons. Upon her recommendations, her husband also opened a dollar account as well as some of her new family friends in Ghana. The Bank sent a bulk text message after 6 months of her opening the account of its introduction of WWB Mastercard that can be used for all online purchases and an introduction of its mobile app that can be used for interbank transfers, an account to wallet transfers, and vice versa. This was great news for Naa as it will be of great help to her business.

The Airport area where the Branch was located is an affluent residential community and a commercial zone for prestigious businesses. Almost all banks and non-banking financial institutions and big businesses are represented in this area. Competition is, therefore, overwhelmingly keen in the vicinity. There were consistent and constant bashing on the doors of businesses and homes of individuals by bank officials. This is one of the main reasons why Naa wanted the recommendation from a known person before committing herself to open an account in Accra. She was particularly interested in a bank's mobile banking applications given the nature of her business.

WWB primarily uses WWB Mastercard and Mobile App Service, two products sold to the bank by RHE Technologies. Additionally, another company, DNH Technologies also sells its

Mastercard and Mobile App Service to WWB. Customers recently began to complain about RHE Technologies' two products as the company was experiencing internal challenges managing the Mastercard and Mobile App Services. They lacked the financial muscle and technical expertise to manage these two services successfully. Unfortunately for WWB, RHE Technologies entered into the contract with the bank mainly through its connections with the CEO of WWB. The CEO of WWB used his influence on the top executives of the bank and misled the board of directors into awarding the contract to RHE Technologies.

Among the many customers who complained about the WWB Mastercard and Mobile App Service services was Naa. Her business involved the importation of her clothes from South Africa, Turkey, the UK, and the USA. Most of her purchases were made online, from business suppliers. She placed her orders online with her WWB Mastercard, and when her suppliers tried debiting her accounts on many occasions, the process was unsuccessful. Her suppliers already had good faith in her because of her successful dealings with them in the past and were confident of her decision to use WWB Mastercard when she moved to Ghana.

Although Naa's company, NSF Kloset had only been operational in Ghana for 1 year, it already had a database of customers from aggressive personal selling and had secured many orders. Naa had shipped a lot of her clothing from South Africa when she relocated with her family to Accra and had almost finished selling all the clothes. She was running out of stock and, therefore, needed to replenish her stock with new trendy, high-quality, and unique styles from her numerous suppliers. She complained bitterly through the various complaint channels of the Bank, including by telephone and by filling complaints forms. She even went to the extent of detailing her frustrations to the Customer Service Department at their Head Office in Accra, but to no avail. The Airport Branch Manager, Mr Bugase, however, kept on telling her to give the Bank some time as it was a technical issue. However, in business, time wasted is revenue lost. Unknown to her, the MD of the bank had been forced to resign by the board of directors, and a new person had been appointed. The Bank also engaged the services of two new Support Service Sellers to provide them with improved Mastercard and Mobile App services, but it would take about a year to fix the technical challenges.

It was amidst this frustration that Maame Serwaah Amuzu, a Relationship Manager in the Airport City Branch of a competing bank, the Great Ghana Bank (GGB), in her usual aggressive personal selling mode, paid a visit to NSF Kloset. She had heard of the business prospects of this new firm which operated an online as well as a brick-and-mortar business in Accra. She initiated her conversation by ordering for two corporate dresses. She was not interested in any of the physical stock and showed business owner, Naa, two dresses she had seen advertised on NSF online website. She went ahead and told Naa she was a Relationship Manager at the GGB and would love for her to open an account with them as she also chooses her business as her clothing line shop amidst smiles. The woman told her of her frustration of doing business with the Banks in Ghana. Maame assured her that her Bank also has a MasterCard Service and that their big customers have never been dissatisfied with their service.

Maame also assured her that she would personally manage her account if she decides to open a business account with her Branch. Naa was elated, as she did not have a personal relationship banker though she had big-dollar accounts for herself, her twins and her husband. Maame informed her that she will personally open the account for her at her convenience at her office and that she does not need to drive to the Branch to do so. She was surprised at such a service. Maame ordered her dress and told her all the requirements for the account opening. Naa told Maame to come the next day at 10:30 am to open the account for her. Maame exchanged pleasantries with her and left for other places for personal selling. Naa was dumbfounded at their level of service as the following day her account was opened, which was March 20, 2017. Within 24 hours after the account was opened, she was given her GGB Mastercard delivered to her office personally by the Relationship Manager, Maame Serwaah Amuzu.

Naa happily informed her suppliers that she has a new Mastercard from another Bank and they asked her to re-order with the new Mastercard. Her frustrations finally ended as her suppliers did not have any problem debiting her card with the payments. NSF Kloset did not close its account with WWB, but gradually withdrew all its money in the account and moved to the business account at GGB, Airport Branch by June 2017. She went ahead and took all her dollars from her twins' trust account amounting to US$400,000.00. Her husband, who needed no convincing of the excellent service of GGB due to how they had handled his wife's account, withdrew all his savings from WWB and opened new accounts at GGB through the Relationship Manager, Maame, at Airport City Branch.

It has been just 2 years of operating the business account at GGB, and NSF Kloset is trending as the No. 1 Retail Clothing Line in Ghana. It won an award from the Ghana Business Awards in June 2019. Naa's revenue channelled through its GGB account at Airport City is around GH¢17M annually, making her one of the top five customers of GGB Bank. The secret to GGB's success is in its Mastercard Service provided by Fase 5 Support Service Limited. The company was chosen by the Bank following due processes and after careful market research on companies operating in the industry. Fase 5 always operates efficiently as it keeps up with changes in technology due to its huge investment in Research and Development and high expertise of staff. Although it was expensive for GGB to do business with them, its value proposition was worth it. The Relationship Manager, Maame, was recognised by the Bank after its mid-year review and awarded with a paid trip to Paris, promoted to the rank of Senior Manager and subsequently given a new Branch to handle given her success in poaching a high-value customer from their competitor. She is also on the verge of poaching another big business prospect, Treasure Limited, on referral by NSF Kloset.

Windy Way Bank's new MD, on seeing their former customer in the media winning the Ghana Business Awards, Best Retail Shop in Ghana, directed the Branch Manager of its Airport City Branch to try and win NSF Kloset account back to the Bank. NSF Kloset, which formerly was not a big business when it opened its account with WWB, is now a well sought-after business account among all the banks in the country.

All the names of the companies used in this case are for instructional purposes only and do not necessarily represent the true state of affairs in any of the companies used as illustrations or the Ghanaian banking industry, in general.

5.7 Discussion Questions

1. Discuss the prospects and constraints the bank manager of Windy Way Bank (WWB) faced in meeting his deposit mobilisation target?
2. Where did WWB go wrong, and what are the key learning points?
3. What should the Branch Manager, Mr Manan Bugase, do to win NSF Kloset back to the Bank?
4. How important is effective service delivery in the banking sector and what role do business sellers/suppliers play?

References

Åge, L. J. (2011). Business manoeuvring: A model of B2B selling processes. *Management Decision*, 49(9), 1574–1591.

Åge, L. J. (2018). Business maneuvering: A dynamic view of B2B selling processes. In P. Andersson, B. Axelsson, & C. Rosenqvist (Eds.), *Organizing marketing and sales* (pp. 113–123). Emerald Publishing Limited, Bingley.

Ahola, T., Aaltonen, K., Artto, K., & Lehtinen, J. (2019). Making room to manoeuvre: How firms increase their influence with others in business networks. *Industrial Marketing Management*. DOI: 10.1016/j.indmarman.2019.08.010.

Altounian, D., Wiley, R., Woo, V., & Roberts, S. (2016). From customer engagement to the customer journey: Understanding the drivers of engagement in B2C and B2B environments. In *Let's get engaged! Crossing the threshold of marketing's engagement era* (pp. 611–614). Springer, Cham. DOI: 10.1007/978-3-319-11815-4_184.

Alves, V., Campos, P., & Felício, M. (2017). Analysis of trust in B2B relationships: The case of automatic storage and retrieval systems. *International Journal of Marketing, Communication and New Media*, 5(8), 52–83.

Anaza, N. A., Kemp, E., Briggs, E., & Borders, A. L. (2019). Tell me a story: The role of narrative transportation and the C-suite in B-TO-B advertising. *Industrial Marketing Management*. DOI: 10.1016/j.indmarman.2019.02.002.

Anders, A. D., Coleman, J. T., & Castleberry, S. B. (2020). Communication preferences of business-to-business buyers for receiving initial sales messages: A comparison of media channel selection theories. *International Journal of Business Communication*, 57(3), 370–400. DOI: 10.1177/2329488417702476, First Published April 11, 2017.

Aten, J. (2019, September 4). B-TO-B sales: The ultimate guide to business-to-business selling. Retrieved January 20, 2020, from https://fitsmallbusiness.com/b-to-b-sales-business-selling/.

Biggins, D. (2018). How to write a B2B social media strategy that will impress your CEO. *Journal of Brand Strategy*, 7(3), 214–224.

Castillo, J., & George, B. (2018). Customer empowerment and satisfaction through the consultative selling process in the retail industry. *International Journal of Customer Relationship Marketing and Management (IJCRMM)*, 9(3), 34–49.

Chatterjee, S. (2018, May 30). Salespeople's experiences on international B-TO-B sales process: A qualitative case study. Retrieved October 31, 2019, from http://epublications.uef.fi/pub/urn_nbn_fi_uef-20181105/urn_nbn_fi_uef-20181105.pdf.

Claro, D. P., Ramos, C., Gonzalez, G. R., & Palmatier, R. W. (2020). Dynamic effects of newcomer salespersons' peer relational exchanges and structures on performance. *International Journal of Research in Marketing*, 37(1), 74–92. DOI: 10.1016/j.ijresmar.2019.07.006.

Connick, W. (2019, November 22). The difference between B2B sales and B2C sales and how they work. Retrieved December 15, 2019, from https://www.thebalancecareers.com/what-is-b-to-b-sales-2917368.

Das, S., Deshpande, S., Salvi, S., Goyal, S., & Bhirud, N. S. (2018, August). RATAN: A smart business to business (B2B) communicator. *In 2018 Fourth International Conference on Computing Communication Control and Automation (ICCUBEA)* (pp. 1–5). IEEE. DOI: 10.1109/iccubea.2018.8697704.

Diba, H., Vella, J. M., & Abratt, R. (2019). Social media influence on the B2B buying process. *Journal of Business & Industrial Marketing*, 34(7), 1482–1496.

Forrest, R. (2017). *The ultimate guide to B2B sales prospecting: Four steps to unlock your hidden market*. BookBaby, Portand, OR.

Graça, S. S., Barry, J. M., & Doney, P. M. (2016). B2B commitment building in emerging markets: The case of Brazil. *Journal of Personal Selling & Sales Management*, 36(2), 105–125.

Grove, H., Sellers, K., Ettenson, R., & Knowles, J. (2018). Selling solutions isn't enough. *MIT Sloan Management Review*, 60(1), 55–59.

Hänninen, N., & Karjaluoto, H. (2017). The effect of marketing communication on business relationship loyalty. *Marketing Intelligence & Planning*, 35(4), 458–472.

Hunter, G. K., & Perreault Jr, W. D. (2007). Making sales technology effective. *Journal of Marketing*, 71(1), 16–34.

Järvinen, J., & Taiminen, H. (2016). Harnessing marketing automation for B-TO-B content marketing. *Industrial Marketing Management*, 54, 164–175.

Kaski, T. A., Hautamaki, P., Pullins, E. B., & Kock, H. (2017). Buyer versus salesperson expectations for an initial B-TO-B sales meeting. *Journal of Business and Industrial Marketing*, 32(1), 46–56.

Kaski, T., Niemi, J., & Pullins, E. (2018). Rapport building in authentic B-TO-B sales interaction. *Industrial Marketing Management*, 69, 235–252.

Keillor, B. D., Stephen Parker, R., & Pettijohn, C. E. (2000). Relationship-oriented characteristics and individual salesperson performance. *Journal of Business & Industrial Marketing*, 15(1), 7–22.

Lim, W. M. (2019). How can challenger marketers target the right customer organization? The ACOW customer organization profiling matrix for challenger marketing. *Journal of Business & Industrial Marketing*, 34(2), 338–346.

Madhavaram, S., & Hunt, S. D. (2017). Customizing business-to-business (B-TO-B) professional services: The role of intellectual capital and internal social capital. *Journal of Business Research*, 74, 38–46.

Meire, M., Ballings, M., & Van den Poel, D. (2017). The added value of social media data in B-TO-B customer acquisition systems: A real-life experiment. *Decision Support Systems*, 104, 26–37.

Moore, J. N., Raymond, M. A., & Hopkins, C. D. (2015). Social selling: A comparison of social media usage across process stage, markets, and sales job functions. *Journal of Marketing Theory and Practice*, 23(1), 1–20.

Neu, W. A., & Brown, S. W. (2005). Forming successful business-to-business services in goods-dominant firms. *Journal of Service Research*, 8(1), 3–17.

Niemi, J., & Hirvonen, L. (2019). Money talks: Customer-initiated price negotiation in business-to-business sales interaction. *Discourse and Communication*, 13(1), 95–118.

Pandey, N., & Shinde, S. (2019). V-Xpress: B-TO-B marketing in the logistics industry. *Emerald Emerging Markets Case Studies*, 9(1), 1–23.

Peleg, B., & Lee, H. L. (2015). Impact of standardization on business-to-business collaboration. In M. J. Shaw (Ed.), *E-commerce and the digital economy* (pp. 43–61). Routledge, New York.

Russo, I., Confente, I., Gligor, D. M., & Cobelli, N. (2017). The combined effect of product returns experience and switching costs on B-TO-B customer re-purchase intent. *Journal of Business & Industrial Marketing*, 32(5), 664–676.

Toth, Z., Nieroda, M. E., & Koles, B. (2017, May). Business mating online: How online referrals influence supplier selection? An abstract. In *Academy of marketing science annual conference* (pp. 351–352). Springer, Cham.

Wang, W. Y., Pauleen, D. J., & Zhang, T. (2016). How social media applications affect B-TO-B communication and improve business performance in SMEs. *Industrial Marketing Management*, 54, 4–14.

Weitz, B. A., & Bradford, K. D. (1999). Personal selling and sales management: A relationship marketing perspective. *Journal of the Academy of Marketing Science*, 27(2), 241.

COMPETITIVE ASPECTS OF THE BUSINESS-TO-BUSINESS MARKET

3

Introduction and Learning Goals

In Part 3, we will discuss current and strategic aspects of the business market that enable B2B companies to position themselves towards segments, niches, products, and services, and how to build their competitiveness in those areas. This part takes up: business services; sourcing and outsourcing; systems and project business; and managing business relations with institutions, governments, and non-business actors.

Chapter 6

Business-to-Business Service Delivery

After reading the chapter, the reader should be able to:

- Explain the concept of business-to-business (B2B) service
- Discuss the major categories of B2B services
- Identify the challenges that characterise B2B service delivery
- Assess B2B service quality.

6.1 B2B Service Concept

B2B firms do not only engage in the production and exchange of tangible goods but also rendering of business services. B2B service refers to a set of activities a business firm delivers to another business firm or series of activities an organisation purchases from another organisation. While the organisation that renders the B2B service is the B2B service provider/producer, the firm to which the services are rendered is the B2B service consumer/user. B2B services usually take place as interactions between the B2B service customers and the B2B service providers. B2B services are provided as solutions to business problems. Pelli et al. (2017) provide three perspectives of B2B services: services as a set of economic activities, services as outputs of a company's offerings and service as a strategic consideration. The three perspectives are summarised as production-focused, product-focused and process-focused B2B services.

6.1.1 Production-Focused B2B Services

Pelli et al. (2017) see B2B service as production-focused and define it as a set of activities that support the transformation of raw materials. Additionally, production-focused services can be standalone businesses, leading to the creation of the services sector or industry. Production-focused B2B services are knowledge-intensive and include legal services, finance and accounting services, IT services and R&D services. These set of services support production across extractive, manufacturing and service industries.

6.1.2 Product-Focused B2B Services

B2B services are also looked at from the perspective of services outputs (product-focused), which is defined as an offering by a B2B service provider to a B2B service customer (Pelli et al., 2017). Services outputs can be produced in all sectors. In the manufacturing sector, for example, the concept of servitisation is gaining ground. In servitisation, products are augmented with services (Vandermerwe & Rada, 1988). Largely, companies are becoming service-oriented (Oliva & Kallenberg, 2003), resulting in a combination of tangible products and intangible services. This combination of tangibles and intangibles is described as "product and service bundles" (Cohen & Whang 1997), "product-service systems" (Mont, 2002), "integrated solutions" (Brady et al., 2005) or "hybrid offerings" (Ulaga & Reinartz, 2011). The central theme of the servitisation, therefore, is to support physical products with services for enhanced customer satisfaction (Neely et al., 2011; Stehrer et al., 2014). The product-focused B2B services are defined based on their characteristics of B2B services being distinct from physical products (see B2B service characteristics).

6.1.3 Process-Focused B2B Services

The third perspective of B2B services, according to Pelli et al. (2017), is process-oriented. The process-oriented concept argues that B2B partners strategically fuse their business models. To this end, the B2B service provider cannot create value alone but co-produce it with the B2B service consumer (Prahalad & Ramaswamy, 2004). Under this perspective, service quality is assessed based on B2B service customer's perceptions, not based on the standards defined by the B2B service provider. The process-oriented B2B service applies to all categories of organisations (Grönroos, 1990). The process-focused B2B services view value creation as a process of interactions and resource integration. It rejects the notion that value creation is a linear process of value-addition in successive stages (Bitner & Brown, 2008). The integrative process of process-oriented B2B services is evident in the interaction among B2B networks (Maglio & Spohrer, 2008).

6.2 B2B Service Industry

B2B service industry refers to various categories of standalone business firms that primarily render services to other businesses (Wirtz & Lovelock, 2016). Pelli et al. (2017) classify the B2B service industry into two major categories: market services industry and non-market services industry.

6.2.1 Market Services

Usually, private companies render market services with little public regulations (Bryson & Daniels, 2007). Market services include wholesale and retail services, transportation and storage services, accommodation and food services, financial and insurance services, information technology and communication services and other various business services (Pelli et al., 2017).

6.2.2 Non-Market Services

Non-market services, in contrast to market services which are provided for a fee, are rendered for free (Fialová et al., 2018). If there is any fee charged at all for the provision of non-market services, the fees are economically insignificant (OECD, 1996). The prices charged for non-market services will not significantly affect the amounts that service producers are willing to supply or the amounts that service purchasers wish to pay. Governments and public institutions mostly provide non-market services (Bryson & Daniels, 2007). According to Pelli et al. (2017), public administration services, education services, health and social work services, arts and entertainment services are some examples of non-market services.

6.3 Characteristics of B2B Services

B2B services have several characteristics that imply important consequences (Bryson & Daniels, 2007). The fundamental characteristics of many B2B services include intangibility, heterogeneity, simultaneity and perishability, making their provision, purchase and consumption complex (Geigenmüller & Bettis-Outland, 2012).

6.3.1 Intangibility of B2B Services

Intangibility is one of the distinctive characteristics of B2B services (Santos, 2002) and a major determinant of a B2B offering is a product or a service (Bebko, 2000). B2B services, in general, are physically intangible, which dominate their value creation (Wirtz & Lovelock, 2016). That is, B2B service does not have physical existence and appearance (attributes) and does not appeal to the sensory organs. This means that B2B services cannot be touched, felt, smelled, tasted, seen or heard. Instead, they are deeds, processes, performances or actions (Hinson et al., 2019). Moeller (2010) sees the intangibility of B2B services as a transformation process that is dependent on the integration of the resources of both B2B service producers and consumers.

Specifically, the attribute of intangibility is related neither to the facilities, which include the providers' resources, nor to the customers' resources acting as input and as an outcome of the transformation. Rather, we perceive the change or transformation of the customers' resources and not the resources themselves as intangible (p. 363).

McDougall and Snetsinger (1990) argue that many B2B services do not exist before they are bought (and, in some cases, virtually non-existent after they are bought). As a result, B2B customers can hardly evaluate B2B services before a purchase. The intangibility of B2B services makes it difficult for B2B marketers to describe the exact nature of B2B services. The intangibility of services also makes it challenging to formulate standards to guide service delivery (Bebko, 2000). Several difficulties arise from B2B service intangibility. The challenges of quality control cannot go unnoticed. A distinction is made between the degree of intangibility of the service outcome and the degree of intangibility of how services are rendered. The intangibility of B2B services increases the perceived risks of the B2B service consumer, as seen in the pre-purchase dilemma. Bebko (2000) argues that B2B service intangibility accounts for variability, inseparability and perishability of services.

6.3.2 Heterogeneity of B2B Services

B2B service delivery defers from time to time and from provider to provider. This means that different B2B service providers will provide similar B2B services differently and that B2B service cannot always be provided in the same manner by the same organisation. Each interaction a B2B service provider has with a B2B service consumer is unique. Affirming this, Hinson et al. (2019) indicate that every service delivered is diverse in character or content, and different. Therefore, no two-service provisions are exactly alike. Two B2B services are never the same. Consequently, difficulties arise when comparing the productivity and quality of B2B services over time. Focusing on professional firms, Malhotra and Morris (2009) argue that differences in organisational structures, resources, policies and practices largely account for the degree of variability of services across different professions.

The B2B service heterogeneity is not limited only to the production of B2B service. B2B service consumption and experience differ from one interaction to another and from one customer to another. No two B2B service customers are, therefore, the same. B2B service customers have unique B2B services experiences anytime B2B service is delivered, even by the same B2B service provider. The high level of heterogeneity in B2B service delivery and experience makes standardisation of B2B service extremely difficult. According to Gremler and Brown (1996, p. 171), "even if the B-TO-B service provider does satisfactorily meet the B-TO-B service customer's needs during one encounter, ensuring that the identical service will be provided in the next interaction may be very difficult". B2B services are varied at each time of delivery and consumption.

6.3.3 Simultaneity of B2B Services

B2B service production and consumption occur simultaneously. The simultaneous production and consumption of B2B services mean that both the B2B service provider and consumer are physically present when the service production and consumption are taking place. This requires a relationship between the B2B service producer and consumer (Bryson & Daniels, 2007). B2B service production is thus not separated from B2B service consumption. Therefore, both the consumption and the production of B2B services are inseparable. In furtherance of this argument, Hinson et al. (2019) explain that the B2B services providers are inextricably woven with the services they provide. It also implies that the B2B service consumers are equally inextricably woven in the services they consume. In this regard, an argument is advanced in favour of the co-production of B2B services (Bryson & Daniels, 2007).

The more the B2B service has the character of co-production, the higher the involvement of the B2B service user as well as the B2B service producer in deciding and agreeing on the use of certain methods to reduce the level of uncertainty that characterised B2B services.

6.3.4 Perishability of B2B Services

Perishability of B2B services indicates that services perish in the very instant of their performance (Moeller, 2010). According to Hinson et al. (2019), B2B services cannot be inventoried for any period. This means that B2B services are perishable because any unsold B2B service is lost for good. That is because B2B services cannot be inventoried; they are perishable. However, Gummesson (2000) debunks the assertion and states, "The claim that services cannot be stored is nonsense. Services are stored in systems, buildings, machines, knowledge, and people" (p. 124). Even though Hill (1977, p. 319) argues that "the fact that services cannot be put into stock has nothing to do with their physical durability". Service consumption is a transformation process.

All that remains after the transformation process is the perceived utility of the service, not the transformation itself. Similarly, unlike tangible items where the manufacturers rely solely on their resources, B2B service providers depend on the resources of B2B service customers. As soon as the service transformation process ends, the capacity represented in the resources of the B2B service consumers is also not available, making B2B services perishable.

Aside from the four major characteristics – heterogeneity, intangibility, perishability and simultaneity of B2B services, Bryson and Daniels (2007) identify very important features worth noting. According to them, the quality of productivity and consumption of B2B services, unlike physical goods, are challenging to measure. This notwithstanding, there are suggested models for assessing the quality of B2B services. Below is a discussion of some of the service quality models.

6.4 B2B Service Quality Models

The characteristics of B2B services, as discussed above, have implications for B2B service quality. Perceived B2B service quality is fundamental for satisfactory B2B service experience. However, B2B service quality is an overly complex phenomenon and difficult to understand the concept. Service quality is described as "…the relationship between planned services (objectives); services provided (outcomes); and the customers' perceived performance based on their expectations" (Soteriades, 2011, p. 5). B2B service is said to be of quality if the service provider consistently meets the expectations of the B2B services customers. Service quality is, therefore, a B2B consumer's judgement about the superiority of the services provided (Kang & James, 2004). This means that consistently delivering B2B services to conform to B2B customer expectations amounts to high-quality B2B service. When assessing B2B service quality, B2B service consumers compare their service expectations with the perceived quality of the services they receive from B2B service providers. B2B service consumers use a number of variables to judge the quality of B2B service. This leads to the development of several service quality models (Braimah, 2014). Below is a description of some service quality models.

6.4.1 Grönroos' (1984) Service Quality Model

Grönroos (1984) proposes a model for assessing the quality of services. He models service along three quality dimensions, technical quality, functional quality and corporate image. The technical quality refers to the actual outcome of the service encounter, which can be measured subjectively. Functional quality defines the quality of subjectively perceived interaction between the B2B service provider and the consumer. Corporate image is how the firm is generally perceived in relation to service delivery. The corporate image, as a service quality dimension, is a function of price, external communication, appearance, competence and employee behaviour of the B2B service firm.

6.4.2 Haywood-Farmer's (1988) Service Quality Model

Haywood-Farmer developed the attribute service quality model in 1988. The attribute service quality identifies physical facilities and processes, people's behaviour and professional judgement as to the basic features that determine the quality of services. Using the Haywood-Farmer (1988) service quality model, attention is paid to facilities used in the service delivery, the processes followed in the service delivery, the behaviours encountered during the service delivery process and the professionalism with which services are judged.

6.4.3 Lehtinen and Lehtinen's (1992) Service Quality Model

Another three-dimensional model for measuring the quality of service is the one developed by Lehtinen and Lehtinen (1992). Their model is anchored on physical quality, corporate quality and interactive quality. Physical quality, according to the authors, refers to the adequacy and condition of the items used to deliver services. Corporate quality explains the organisation's image and profile in relation to service delivery. It is a presumption that a firm that is experienced in the provision of a particular service will provide quality service. Interactive quality, similar to functional quality in Grönroos (1984) model, refers to the interaction between the B2B service provider and customer.

6.4.4 IT Alignment Model

The IT alignment model is a service quality model designed by Berkley and Gupta (1994). The authors argue that it is important for B2B service firms to align and coordinate their strategies for information system and service quality. IT alignment relies on the use of IT to improve service quality. The model relies on reliability, responsiveness, competence, access, communication, security and understanding of the customer to measure the quality of B2B service.

6.4.5 Perceived Service Quality and Satisfaction Model

Spreng and Mackoy (1996) are the brains behind the perceived service quality and satisfaction model. The model attempts to establish a link between the perceived service quality and the level of satisfaction derived by the service consumer. The indicators used in this model include the impact of expectations and perceived performance, on overall service quality and customer satisfaction.

6.4.6 Philip and Hazlett's (1997) Service Quality Model

Philip and Hazlett's (1997) model has three dimensions of service quality. Its dimensions are pivotal attributes, core attributes and peripheral attributes. The outputs of the service encounter are the pivotal attributes. The pivotal attributes are expressed in what a B2B service customer wishes to derive from the service encounter. Every service is delivered through structure, processes and resources. The set of structures, processes and resources used in service delivery explain the core attributes of this service quality model. The peripheral attributes refer to the "extras" that are added to a B2B service encounter that gives the B2B service customer a delightful experience. The model, however, lacks empirical validation.

6.4.7 Integrative Service Quality Model

The integrative service quality model is developed by Oh (1999). The model uses perception, service quality, consumer satisfaction, price, customer value and repurchase intentions as key indicators for evaluating service quality. The model establishes a relationship between customer value and customer satisfaction.

6.4.8 Antecedents, Consequences and Mediators Model

Dabholkar et al. (2000) developed "antecedents, consequences and mediators" service quality model. The model investigates the connection between antecedents such as reliability, personal attention and comfort and consequences such as customer satisfaction and customer behavioural intentions.

6.4.9 The GAPs Model

The "GAPs model" is developed by Parasuraman et al. (1985), based on different gaps: listening gap (Zeithaml et al., 2009), management perception-service quality specification gap (Parasuraman et al., 1988), performance gap (Seth et al., 2005), service delivery-external communications gap (Parasuraman et al., 1988) and expected service-perceived service gap (Parasuraman et al., 1985). These gaps undermine the quality of service delivery.

The listening gap (Gap 1) explains the situation where there is a difference between B2B service consumers' expectations and perception of management of B2B service providers of those expectations. The listening gap is also known as the expectation-management perception gap. The management perception-service quality specification gap (Gap 2) captures the difference between management perceptions of consumer's expectations and the translation of those perceptions into service quality specifications. Gap 2 is also known as the service design and standard gap (Zeithaml et al., 2009). The performance gap (Gap 3) is an illustration of the difference between the service delivered and service quality specifications. This gap is referred to as the service quality specifications-service delivery gap. The service delivery-external communications gap (Gap 4) is an evaluation of whether or not B2B service delivered matches the B2B service promised (Seth et al., 2005). The expected service-perceived service gap (Gap 5) is the difference between B2B service consumer's expectations and perceived service. Parasuraman et al. (1985) assert that gaps 1–4 in the GAPs model relate to the B2B service provider (marketer), while Gap 5 relates to the B2B service consumer. This is because gap 5 is dependent on the size, scale and direction of the first four gaps.

6.4.10 SERVQUAL

The SERVQUAL is a multi-item scale framework developed by Parasuraman et al. (1985) for measuring how customers perceive service quality (Braimah, 2014). Originally, SERVQUAL has ten indicators for measuring service quality. These indicators include reliability, responsiveness, tangibility, competence, courtesy, credibility, security, access, communication and understanding/knowing your customer. It must be noted, however, that Parasuraman et al. (1988) collapsed their original ten items in the SERVQUAL into five main service quality dimensions. The authors believe that reliability, responsiveness, assurance, empathy and tangibility are the best measures of service quality. Reliability, responsiveness and tangibility are part of the original ten determinants. Attributes such as communication, competence, credibility, courtesy and security were collapsed into assurance, while access and understanding/knowing the customers were classified as empathy. The extent to which what is promised is delivered, is measured by reliability. Responsiveness, as a measure of service quality, measures how quickly and effectively the service provider responses to complaints.

Although the SERVQUAL is extensively used to measure service quality, it is replete with several weaknesses. First, scholars condemn constant modification and revalidation of the model in every situation to make it usable (Carman, 1990; Cronin & Taylor, 1992; Getty & Getty, 2003). It is, therefore, not a generic model with a wide spectrum of application. Second, the SERVQUAL ignores the outcome of the service encounter and focuses only on the service delivery process (Grönroos, 1990; Sureshchandar et al., 2002). As a result, it lacks comprehensiveness. Third, the SERVQUAL instrument lacks a strong theoretical underpinning (Braimah, 2014).

6.4.11 SERVPERF

SERVPERF is developed to address the weaknesses inherent in the use of SERVQUAL (Cronin & Taylor, 1992). The SERVPERF focuses on performance as the key determinant of service quality (Ali et al., 2010). The performance measures of SERVPERF comprise tangibles, reliability, responsiveness, assurance and empathy (Akdere et al., 2018).

6.5 The Relevance of B2B Service Quality Improvement

Braimah (2014) argues that firms whose B2B services are perceived to be of high-quality benefit from a large market share and a higher return on investment. This suggests an association between service quality on one hand and business performance, costs, customer satisfaction, customer loyalty and profitability on the other hand (Zeithaml et al., 2009). Braimah (2014) summarises that B2B service quality determines not only the competitiveness of B2B service provider but also its long-term profitability, survival and customer satisfaction and retention. Improvement in service quality is thus critical to the competitiveness and performance of the service firm.

6.6 Conclusion

Service quality is an essential element of B2B marketing and crucial to its success. The SERVQUAL framework highlighted in the chapter can be used to measure service quality using the five main service quality dimensions of reliability, responsiveness, assurance, empathy and tangibility. Responsiveness is very critical, given the nature of B2B transactions. Service quality improvement plans should be put in place, particularly where gaps are observed as this would enhance relationship and competitiveness and improve the performance of the service firm.

Case Study: Delighting the B2B Service Recipient – The Value of the Basics

Tildex is a global pharmaceutical organisation with well-established subsidiaries located within the continent of Africa. Emanating from its global vision, they seek to be a leader in health and wellness driven mainly through innovation and renovation as well as a reference in delivering value not only to consumers and investors, but also to employees. Based on corporate policies and some local legislation, employees at Tildex are regarded as progressive with very attractive compensation and benefits entitlements earned during their tenure as employees of the organisation compared to other competitors.

Red Spice, an African catering franchise well known in the African continent, won the rights to cater during lunch hours at Tildex's Ghana Office, which also doubles as the Headquarters for its Central and West African businesses. Besides catering at the inauguration service of three different Presidents in Africa, their model of "Only One Africa" seeks to promote solely African meals, not only to individual consumers but also to corporate entities.

Tildex had failed in attaining the various corporate goals of the entire region for five consecutive years and as such, year ending activities which usually induced excitement were never held.

On the contrary, at the Eastern and Southern African hub, merrymaking during year-end resulted in a delighted workforce at Red Spice. The Management believed that this excitement was as a result of the quality of catering service rendered that yielded a happy and healthy workforce at Tildex throughout the year.

During the third quarter staff meeting, the Head of Compensation and Benefits – Joanna Anderson, communicated that she had received an anonymous complaint about Red Spice on service delivery and entreated other employees to share details of their displeasure or otherwise regarding the service provider since "they make Tildex". To her surprise, within an hour of communicating this directive, she had received 19 different subpar reports. This was an issue that required discussion and possible resolution with the management of Red Spice, considering Tildex's mandate to deliver value and provide quality service across all levels to its employees.

A sample of one letter that struck Joanna the most, read:

Dear Madam,
Our Health and Wellness at Work also Matters
I write to you today following your challenge about our unwillingness to speak up about the very divergent norms with our values we are encountering. I am baffled as to why Red Spice still renders service as a supplier. The expectation in the least is that they understand and subscribe to our safety and health pledge by offering suitable meal options that complement this drive. They have failed over five years to exhibit any knowledge of who their stakeholder is. Perhaps, their own success stories from the past still inundate their minds, thus affecting their expected delivery. Because they had in the past catered for different presidents and still have significant service contracts with other organisations, their management is, perhaps, of the view that they are meeting all standards.

They have exhibited no level of anticipation of options to offer which will cater to the beliefs, background, and religion of employees. In addition, Red Spice has failed in comprehending consumer trends regarding weight and fitness. Their meals are heavily soaked in oil and serve a plethora of carbohydrates and starchy foods.

Unfortunately for Red Spice, their representation on-site (At Tildex) throws me off all the more. Courtesy is not that expensive, is it? When representatives from the organisation serve food with their left hand, and without food serving gloves or hairnets, I cringe! Wondering if it is really Tildex, I am working at.

After reading the last paragraph, Joanna winced and signalled Mr Boris, the procurement head to meet with her in her office immediately. She said angrily: "I am echoing the voice of our Union leader who has also vowed to write to you and the management officially to register the union's displeasure. How do you explain why we still use the same cutlery and plates from 3 years ago? It is physically not appealing! Contour lines, cracks in plates and rusting cutlery. Very appalling! We expect to feed between 12 pm and 2 pm each day as stipulated in the employee handbook; however, it seems our favourite service providers are not aware of this, as they have consistently set up after 12:50 pm on numerous occasions".

Joanna decided to schedule a meeting with the Tildex leadership team, including the Union President two days after the staff meeting with an agenda to audit the services of Red Spice as well as arrange for an official meeting with their leadership to fully comprehend the present situation. Present at the internal Tildex meeting to discuss abysmal service rendered by the supplier was Finance Head, HR Head, Procurement Head, President of the Union, and the Head of Compensation and Benefits.

Ringbone Sharp, the Finance Director, who was not present at the staff meeting, queried if the value received from the supplier was tantamount to the money paid out. Chris Boris, the former Procurement Lead had insisted on this preferred supplier because Red Spice worked in other Tildex markets as the ideal supplier and customer survey reports reflected positive feedback from all employees and leadership team members from the Eastern African Hub. He was the team leader of the committee set up to select a reputable supplier for the company about 3 years earlier. The mood within the decision-making unit was one that signalled sheer discontent across all team members. In making the decision, Chris Boris, however, had acted in isolation and appended his signature without the knowledge of the other team members, granting Red Spice the license to operate. He shivered as Ringbone analysed the project. He acted contrary to the code of ethics which specifically streamlined the power and activities of the team leads who served on specific committees. His act of signing the contract without further consultation with the decision-making body or any other supply chain or procurement specialist had cost Tildex about 100,000 Ghana cedis per quarter – 24% more than the actual cost.

As the final decision maker, Mrs Ayesha Amadu, Tildex's Head of Human Resources was perplexed about how the decision to roll out relied on a "preferred supplier". Based on information available to her, she was contemplating changing the supplier, but not until after the meeting with the management of Red Spice.

Back at the Red Spice office, words had filtered out to the management about Tildex's displeasure with service rendered. Charlotte Kankam, the Head of Operations, was just about to leave the office, but could not until she responded to "allegations" of a massive failure on site of their second-biggest customer following the phone conversation between Mr Kwesi Atta, the owner of Red Spice, and Mrs Amadu.

As Mr Kwesi Atta, the owner of Red Spice, summoned her into his office, Charlotte's first words were somewhat indicative of the fact that she was aware of the state of affairs. She sheepishly disclosed, "Sir, delivering consistently across service-oriented organisations is difficult since human personnel operate it". By this, she indicated that the operations at the Eastern hub receive a consistent delivery of great service mainly due to the efficiency of the service providers on the ground. Beneficiaries of operations run in Ghana, however, are not fortunate enough to be on the receiving end of such excellent service daily due to the different skill set and expertise of employees who represent the company.

As much as Mr Atta valued the very honest and transparent work evaluation session with Charlotte, he was still wondering how he will convince Tildex to retain them as their supplier during their meeting scheduled within the next few days. Part of the work evaluation session included the submission of a strategic plan by Charlotte on how to improve their service delivery to Tildex and sustain their leadership position. A re-orientation of their purpose for existence was paramount, should they be granted the opportunity to still render services to Tildex. "Only One Africa" model will not suffice, especially when the world and Tildex also, are adopting and accepting the notion of a "Global Culture", Charlotte stressed. Diversification in their menu to suit the varied cultures will be widely accepted, she insisted. Interestingly, surveys conducted in the Eastern hub indicated that the success of the operations of Red Spice hinged on diversity.

Charlotte, in her submission, highlighted "one of the major parameters on which Tildex will express their displeasure is time to serve". Digitising employee registration over writing names in books and reducing the service encounter time from 240 to 120 s possibly will possibly lead to a change in heart by Tildex.

Back at Tildex, for the very first time in 3 years, the Compensation and Benefits team had managed to put together a survey seeking feedback on the services rendered by Red Spice just in time for the meeting. The recommendations following the meeting suggested that the contract under which both parties operated undergoes some form of reconciliation or review, mainly because there was little or no involvement from the supply chain counterparts on both sides.

Tildex had tendered in as evidence the feedback from the survey, which declared an appalling satisfactory level of 45%. The CEO of Red Spice was particularly surprised at this low score, and as expected, he challenged this and raised issues about the possibility of addressing the identified gaps if Tildex had shared results of the survey much earlier and frequently.

At this stage of the meeting, the representatives of Tildex in unison had their minds made up about terminating the contract; however, doing so meant they would have to deal with the uncertainty of selecting a new vendor. The morale of employees had already hit rock bottom, and there was no need in making matters worse by cancelling the contract with Red Spice when there was no alternative.

Before the meeting ended, Charlotte, the operations manager of Red Spice had asked for the opportunity for her team to share their two-point strategy with which they sought to address the change expected at Tildex in service delivery. They presented a strategy that communicated diversification across their entire business: a complete overhaul in personnel at Tildex – a much older staff, experienced and in possession of soft skills, a few attributes they shared.

Charlotte, on behalf of the team also asked that sharing of reports and customer feedback becomes a regular monthly task to enable them to react to any challenge identified by Tildex rapidly. In the meantime, she communicated to the leadership team their desire to introduce a new and improved menu that cuts across all cultures represented at Tildex and meals that catered to various menu preferences such as vegan and ketogenic, among others. Besides, they opted to redesign the canteen to give it a cosier look and feel and change all utensils and cutlery used in service to depict the status of Tildex as the leading Health and Wellness business within West Africa.

To address the issue of long queues, they had proposed introducing another service point within the canteen and expanding it to accommodate the consistently growing number of visitors and employees at Tildex. There was an innovative proposal to digitise employee registration to track the total number of employees served daily. This was also the answer to reducing the wait time (inline) for food drastically by 50%. Tildex team agreed to the terms and stated that they would keep a close watch on service delivery of Red Spice. By the year end, HR team of Tildex used the last session to discuss updates on the services rendered by Red Spice since the third quarter staff meeting. The organisation had committed to regular communication with the staff to obtain feedback for improvement purposes.

As Joanna mounted the podium to deliver her speech, there was loud applause following the appearance of a female employee of Red Spice in a branded outfit in their corporate colours of white, blue, and red.

Interestingly, the regular melancholic demeanour that characterised their brand was missing. She was new to the site and beaming heavily with smiles. Not long after, three other females and one male also appeared, pleasantly dressed in their corporate colours. The HR lead had announced at this stage that Red Spice was ready with finger food and drinks, and will be walking around to serve during the meeting. The staff of Tildex were very happy at the very last employee engagement compared to previous ones.

The leadership team of Tildex had decided against sourcing for a new supplier and accepted the proposal shared by Red Spice, communicating change, but more importantly, improved service delivery. The year started after the holidays, and employees had already subscribed 23% higher than in the same period last year and 44% higher compared to the previous month to the canteen service. Various departments had reported an increase in employee relationships within the team, and Tildex, by the end of quarter one, had recorded a growth of 4%, a feat heavily celebrated by all including Red Spice.

6.7 Discussion Questions

1. "Only One Africa" is a business model used by Red Spice. Discuss the prospects and constraints of this model in the service delivery of Red Spice and particularly to Tildex.
2. Identify and explain the major service quality challenges that threatened the business continuity of Red Spice with Tildex, and proffer some solutions to address the issues raised.

References

Akdere, M., Top, M., & Tekingündüz, S. (2018). Examining patient perceptions of service quality in Turkish hospitals: The SERVPERF model. *Total Quality Management and Business Excellence*, 31(3–4), 342–352.

Ali, M. H., Ali, N. A., & Radam, A. (2010). Validating SERVPERF model in government agencies. *The Journal of Human Resource and Adult Learning*, 6(1), 84–93.

Bebko, C. P. (2000). Service intangibility and its impact on consumer expectations of service quality. *Journal of Services Marketing*, 14(1), 9–26.

Berkley, B. J., & Gupta, A. (1994). Improving service quality with information technology. *International Journal of Information Management*, 14(2), 109–121.

Bitner, M. J., & Brown, S. W. (2008). The service imperative. *Business Horizons*, 51(1), 39–46.

Brady, T., Davies, A., & Gann, D. (2005). Can integrated solutions business models work in construction? *Building Research & Information*, 33(6), 571–579.

Braimah, M. M. (2014). Service quality in small hotels in Ghana: A comprehensive framework (Doctoral dissertation, University of Ghana).

Bryson, J. R., & Daniels, P. W. (Eds.) (2007). *The handbook of service industries*. Edward Elgar Publishing, Cheltenham.

Carman, J. M. (1990). Consumer perceptions of service quality: An assessment of T. *Journal of Retailing*, 66(1), 33.

Cohen, M. A., & Whang, S. (1997). Competing in product and service: A product life-cycle model. *Management Science*, 43(4), 535–545.

Cronin Jr, J. J., & Taylor, S. A. (1992). Measuring service quality: A re-examination and extension. *Journal of Marketing*, 56(3), 55–68.

Dabholkar, P. A., Shepherd, C. D., & Thorpe, D. I. (2000). A comprehensive framework for service quality: An investigation of critical conceptual and measurement issues through a longitudinal study. *Journal of Retailing*, 76(2), 139–173.

Fialová, H., Adamcová, L. & Ambrozo, A. (2018). Non-market services as quaternary sector of the economy. *Proceedings of International Academic Conferences, International Institute of Social and Economic Sciences*, Prague, Czech Republic, 7809648.

Geigenmüller, A., & Bettis-Outland, H. (2012). Brand equity in B-TO-B services and consequences for the trade show industry. *Journal of Business & Industrial Marketing*, 27(6), 428–435.

Getty, J. M., & Getty, R. L. (2003). Lodging quality index (LQI): Assessing customers' perceptions of quality delivery. *International Journal of Contemporary Hospitality Management*, 15(2), 94–104.

Gremler, D. D., & Brown, S. W. (1996). Service loyalty: Its nature, importance, and implications. *Advancing Service Quality: A Global Perspective*, 5(1), 171–181.

Grönroos, C. (1984). A service quality model and its marketing implications. *European Journal of Marketing*, 18(4), 36–44.

Grönroos, C. (1990). Service management: A management focus for service competition. *International Journal of Service Industry Management*, 1(1), 6–14.

Gummesson, E. (2000). Services marketing self-portraits: Introspections, reflections, and glimpses from the experts. In R. P. Fisk, S. J. Grove, & J. Joby (Eds.), *Services marketing: Introspections, reflections, and glimpses from the experts* (pp. 109–132). American Marketing Association, Chicago.

Haywood-Farmer, J. (1988). A conceptual model of service quality. *International Journal of Operations & Production Management*, 8(6), 19–29.

Hill, T. P. (1977). On goods and services. *Review of Income and Wealth*, 23(4), 315–338.

Hinson, R. E., Adeola, O., Nkrumah, K. O., Agyinasare, C., Adom, K., & Amartey, A. F. O. (2019). *Customer service essentials: Lessons for Africa and beyond*. IAP, Mumbai.

Kang, G. D., & James, J. (2004). Service quality dimensions: An examination of Grönroos's service quality model. *Managing Service Quality: An International Journal*, 14(4), 266–277.

Lehtinen, U. & Lehtinen, J. R. (1992). Service quality: A study of quality dimensions. Working Paper. Service Management Institute, Helsinki.

Maglio, P. P., & Spohrer, J. (2008). Fundamentals of service science. *Journal of the Academy of Marketing Science*, 36(1), 18–20.

Malhotra, N., & Morris, T. (2009). Heterogeneity in professional service firms. *Journal of Management Studies*, 46(6), 895–922.

McDougall, G. H. G., & Snetsinger, D. W. (1990). The intangibility of services: Measurement and competitive perspectives. *Journal of Services Marketing*, 4(4), 27–40.

Moeller, S. (2010). Characteristics of services–a new approach uncovers their value. *Journal of Services Marketing*, 24(5), 359–368.

Mont, O. (2002). Drivers and barriers for shifting towards more service-oriented businesses: Analysis of the PSS field and contributions from Sweden. *The Journal of Sustainable Product Design*, 2(3–4), 89–103.

Neely, A., Benedettini, O., & Visnjic, I. (2011, July). The servitization of manufacturing: Further evidence. *In 18th European Operations Management Association Conference* (Vol. 1). Cambridge, England.

OECD (1996). Productivity measurement for non-market services. http://www.oecd.org/sdd/na/2666071.pdf.

Oh, H. (1999). Service quality, customer satisfaction, and customer value: A holistic perspective. *International Journal of Hospitality Management*, 18(1), 67–82.

Oliva, R., & Kallenberg, R. (2003). Managing the transition from products to services. *International Journal of Service Industry Management*, 14(2), 160–172.

Parasuraman, A., Zeithaml, V. A., & Berry, L. L. (1985). A conceptual model of service quality and its implications for future research. *Journal of Marketing*, 49(4), 41–50.

Parasuraman, A., Zeithaml, V. A., & Berry, L. L. (1988). Servqual: A multiple-item scale for measuring consumer perc. *Journal of Retailing*, 64(1), 12.

Pelli, P., Haapala, A., & Pykäläinen, J. (2017). Services in the forest-based bioeconomy–analysis of European strategies. *Scandinavian Journal of Forest Research*, 32(7), 559–567.

Philip, G., & Hazlett, S. A. (1997). The measurement of service quality: A new PCP attributes model. *International Journal of Quality & Reliability Management*, 14(3), 260–286.

Prahalad, C. K., & Ramaswamy, V. (2004). Co-creating unique value with customers. *Strategy & Leadership*, 32(3), 4–9.

Santos, J. (2002). From intangibility to tangibility on service quality perceptions: A comparison study between consumers and service providers in four service industries. *Managing Service Quality: An International Journal*, 12(5), 292–302.

Seth, N., Deshmukh, S. G., & Vrat, P. (2005). Service quality models: A review. *International Journal of Quality & Reliability Management*, 22(9), 913–949.

Soteriades, M. (2011). *Service quality in the hotel industry: Issues and challenges: Crucial role and contribution of human resources* (p. 63). Lambert Academic Publishing, Germany.

Spreng, R. A., & Mackoy, R. D. (1996). An empirical examination of a model of perceived service quality and satisfaction. *Journal of Retailing*, 72(2), 201–214.

Stehrer, R., Baker, P., Foster-McGregor, N., Koenen, J., Leitner, S. (2014). Study on the relation between industry and services in terms of productivity and value creation. (Final report). Directorate General Enterprise and Industry (ENTR/90/PP2011/FC), Vienna.

Sureshchandar, G. S., Rajendran, C., & Anantharaman, R. N. (2002). Determinants of customer-perceived service quality: A confirmatory factor analysis approach. *Journal of Services Marketing*, 16(1), 9–34.

Ulaga, W., & Reinartz, W. J. (2011). Hybrid offerings: How manufacturing firms combine goods and services successfully. *Journal of Marketing*, 75(6), 5–23.

Vandermerwe, S., & Rada, J. (1988). Servitization of business: Adding value by adding services. *European Management Journal*, 6(4), 314–324.

Wirtz, J., & Lovelock, C. (2016). *Services marketing: People, technology*. World Scientific Publishing Company, Singapore.

Zeithaml, V., Bitner, M., & Gremler, D. (2009). *Service marketing* (5th ed.). McGraw-Hill, New York.

Chapter 7

Business-to-Business Sourcing and Outsourcing

By the end of the chapter, the reader should be able to:

1. Distinguish between business-to-business (B2B) sourcing and outsourcing
2. Trace the evolution of global outsourcing
3. Identify and discuss the determinants of B2B outsourcing
4. Evaluate outsourcing challenges in Africa.

7.1 Introduction

Modern businesses are inundated with enormous business activities and processes, some of which are core and/or auxiliary. Increasingly, it is becoming difficult for businesses to be able to carry out all these business activities and processes effectively. While some firms do well in some selected activities, others perform poorly in some business functions. Many businesses are also faced with inadequate resources and competencies required for the effective execution of the entire spectrum of business functions. Consequently, businesses, in recent times, have resorted to contracting out some of their functions to other firms (vendors), giving birth to the concept of outsourcing. Outsourcing, in this chapter, can be regarded as a form of business-to-business relationship focused on firm B handling key activities of firm A. Outsourcing has increased tremendously in recent times (Ndubisi, 2011; Oshri et al., 2009; Willcocks et al., 2006), creating the need for scholarly work on the concept, particularly from emerging markets' perspective. This chapter is dedicated to explaining and discussing why businesses source and outsource, the evolution of global outsourcing, determinants of outsourcing, outsourcing challenges in Africa and effective outsourcing strategies and techniques.

7.2 Why Source and Outsource?

A critical question or dilemma for many business firms is whether to buy or to make. Whatever the decision, there is a need for the firm to source its resources, activities and processes, whether from within the organisation (insourcing) or from outside the firm (outsourcing). As defined by Oshri et al. (2009), "Sourcing is the act through which work is contracted or delegated to an external or internal entity that could be physically located anywhere" (p. 2). Sourcing is a common practice of every firm. However, sourcing arrangements differ from firm to firm, depending on the peculiar needs of the sourcing firm.

Sourcing encapsulates back-end and front-end concerns of supply chain activities. While front-end considerations include distribution, consumer services and customer relationship management, back-end concerns concentrate on identifying and selecting appropriate source, controlling suppliers, designing sourcing mechanisms and managing supplier relationship. Sourcing thus entails the integration of the flow of information and goods and services along the value chain. As indicated by Seshadri (2005), sourcing activities affect the buyer–seller relationship aspect of supply chain activities. Sourcing has evolved over the years and moved from a mere function of purchase to functional and strategic sourcing. Functional and strategic sourcing requires new and company-wide policies and strategies.

7.2.1 Functional Sourcing

Functional sourcing is basically the purchasing management approach based on system theory (input, process and output). Functional sourcing designs a system to perform a given function better (Seshadri, 2005). Additionally, functional sourcing aims at serving the factory timely, lowering costs, coordinating purchasing, integrating cross-functional purchasing and implementing supply processes. The major activities undertaken in functional sourcing are identifying vendors, creating a profile of vendors and offerings, receiving, reporting and managing orders. However, functional sourcing is changing with the introduction of electronic and automated platforms. This requires that the sourcing needs of the firms are strategic, hence strategic sourcing.

7.2.2 Strategic Sourcing

Functional sourcing has short-term application focus, an inherent weakness. Strategic sourcing seeks to overcome this weakness from two perspectives: long-term focus and risk-benefit analysis. Strategic sourcing recognises conflict management in purchasing and is, therefore, based on decision theory and game theory (both important in understanding agents' choices and decisions). Entering into and exiting product markets, building and managing supply-based capacity, selecting and maintaining vendors and controlling long-term cost and price discovering processes are the key activities in strategic sourcing (Seshadri, 2005). Strategic sourcing seeks to, among other things, influence the behaviour of sellers, develop supply base and build competitive advantage from sourcing efficiencies (reduce costs and increase profits). Unlike functional sourcing jobs, the roles of strategic sourcing remain unchanged.

7.3 The Scope of Sourcing

Sourcing could be done in-house and/or through an external arrangement known as outsourcing. The discussion in this chapter focuses on outsourcing.

7.3.1 Outsourcing

Outsourcing occurs when a company contracts another company to perform some of its peripheral functions for a specified length of time and cost (Oguji & Owusu, 2014; Oshri et al., 2009). Predominantly, outsourcing is becoming a cost reduction strategic decision for several companies.

Ndubisi (2011) indicates that when companies outsource, they purchase a supplier or appoint an agent to represent it. That is, in outsourcing, external vendors are allowed to perform part of or an entire activity for an organisation (Seshadri, 2005). The scope and degree of outsourcing have grown in recent times and continue to grow.

7.3.2 Global Outsourcing Evolution

The nature and scope of outsourcing across the globe are evolving and continue to grow. Historically, outsourcing originated from manufacturing industries (Vining & Globerman, 2017), where companies concentrated on core business functions of production and outsourced other auxiliary business functions. That is, the choice between external acquisition and an internally developed solution made outsourcing a make-or-buy decision (Lee et al., 2000). The "buy" component of the make-or-buy decision represents the outsourced functions. The role of the vendor in the outsourced function depends on the type and size of the contract. The nature of the outsourcing relationship in this era was a contractual-based relationship.

Outsourcing has grown in momentum and has become a cross-national and global phenomenon, commonly described as offshoring. In offshoring, organisational functions are performed by a wholly owned subsidiary or by an independent vendor located in another country (Oshri et al., 2009). The offshoring, as a strategy, is done to reduce costs. IT services, engineering services, finance and accounting services are among the most frequently offshored functions. Irrespective of the business function that is offshored, the offshoring could take the captive model, outsourcing model or nearshoring model of service delivery. The captive model of service delivery is an offshoring model where functions of an organisation are offshored to a centre that is located in another country but owned by the same organisation. The outsourcing model is an offshoring model where the functions of a company are assigned to an independent vendor located in another country. Nearshoring is an offshoring model which sees functions of a company completely relocated to a neighbouring country. For example, Ghanaian companies can nearshore by relocating their functions to neighbouring countries such as Togo.

Even though claims exist in the literature that companies outsourced in order to reduce costs (Lee et al., 2000), a counter argument exists that outsourcing has become a strategic choice for companies. The discussion in extant literature regarding outsourcing is that outsourcing has emerged as a prominent issue for business survival (Vining & Globerman, 2017) in the competitive business environment.

It is also argued that only small and medium-sized firms outsourced in the past. In recent times, however, outsourcing has become a normal business practice of large companies, including conglomerates and multinational companies. In this regard, Grover et al. (1996) asserted that outsourcing has evolved in such a manner that larger companies are now outsourcing. Larger companies, although they have access to certain services internally, have also resorted to outsourcing to concentrate their efforts and resources on core business functions to produce high value-added products and services. Outsourcing is, thus, no longer a preserve of smaller companies.

It was indicated earlier that the role of service suppliers in outsourcing in the past was limited. This is not the case in recent times. Almost every business function can be outsourced (Grover et al., 1996). Affirming this, Liu et al. (2014) state that the provision of outsourcing services has shown a rapid increase. Functions that are contracted out in outsourcing contracts include, but are not limited to, human resource functions (Morley et al., 2006), logistics services (Chen et al., 2011), supply chain services (Zhang et al., 2006), research and development services (Brook & Plugge, 2010), information technology (Lacity et al., 2010), distribution and advertising functions

(Seshadri, 2005), and accounting systems (Vining & Globerman, 2017). Lee et al. (2000) highlighted that there is more functional outsourcing now than before. Grover et al. (1996) explained that outsourcing is no longer a restricted choice between in-house function and external acquisition as in the past. Rather, firms chose the functions they wish to outsource. This is based on the justification that the choice between in-house function and outsourcing no longer captures the complexities associated with outsourcing. According to Vining and Globerman (2017), both primary inbound and outbound logistics and secondary value chain activities are being extensively outsourced. Therefore, for strategic reasons and competitive advantage, firms outsource functions which, when outsourced, produce more benefits than when performed internally. This suggests that almost every business activity and service is outsourceable in the future. Observably, there has been an evolution of management responsibilities and risks acceptance of the parties in outsourcing contracts.

It could be safe to argue that outsourcees are accepting management responsibilities and there are risks in outsourcing contracts now more than in the past, due to the speed of global business development. In the past, the role of service providers was limited. Presently, however, several outsourcees are taking on management responsibilities and risks willingly. In some cases, when executing outsourced contracts, vendors incur significant risks such as unclear requirements from clients.

Therefore, the nature of the relationship the outsourcing company has with the service provider is changing rapidly. Taking the argument further, Lee et al. (2000) elaborated that the contractual-based outsourcing relationship in the 1990s has evolved into a partnership-based outsourcing relationship in recent times. They identified five steps in outsourcing partnership-based relationships as motivation, scope, performance, partnership and contracts.

The critical issues of concern under outsourcing partnership motivation include the nature of, the reasons for, and the benefits and risks associated with outsourcing partnerships. Regarding the scope of an outsourcing partnership, Lee et al. (2000) state that it clarifies the magnitude of outsourcing (selective or total), its duration (short term or long term), number of vendors involved (single or multiple) and its types (service or asset). They are concerned about what strategies of outsourcing partnerships will work for both the client and the service providers. The third stage, the outsourcing partnership performance stage, is characterised by improvement in outsourcing partnership, mutually beneficial strategic outsourcing partnership, determinants of a successful outsourcing partnership, and evaluation and verification of the performance of the outsourcing partnership. The next step in the outsourcing partnership relationship centred on circumstances suitable for outsourcing partnerships, decision-making frameworks for outsourcing partnerships, criteria for determining the need for outsourcing partnerships and contingent factors that influence the introduction of outsourcing partnerships. The final step in the outsourcing partnership-based relationship, as explained by Lee et al. (2000), is the partnership contract. Partnership contract addresses process and management issues of an outsourcing partnership, negotiated issues in the outsourcing partnership and factors that make outsourcing engagements in partnership-based contracts. It is envisaged, therefore, that in the future, outsourcing decisions and activities of firms will be based more on collaborative partnership engagements than on dyadic relationships between a vendor and a client. Thus, the evolution of outsourcing is a journey from make-or-buy decisions to a collaborative partnership.

Commenting on the drivers of outsourcing evolution, Lee et al. (2000) stated that the changing phase of outsourcing is as a result of strategic alliance and environmental factors. The acceptance of strategic alliances also drives the current trend of the outsourcing agenda in that it allows companies to bring on board partners who can complement their skills and operations. The benefits of the strategic alliance can be seen in the lesser time and resources the outsourcing companies spend building internal infrastructure. Changing environment is another factor that drives outsourcing evolution. Competition and technology are some key elements of the changing environment and play critical roles in the evolution of outsourcing.

The evolution history of outsourcing illustrated above clearly indicates that companies regard outsourcing as a competitive and dynamic strategy. This is reflected in the transformative nature of the outsourcing relationship from vendor–customer relationship to partnership relationship. Lee et al. (2000) describe the outsourcing relationship as an inter-firm relationship aimed at achieving shared goals. Outsourcing benefits are thus realised through partnerships.

7.4 The Future of Global Outsourcing

The growth of outsourcing is on the ascendency in the business landscape. Oshri et al. (2009) projected that revenue from outsourcing would be more than US$ 450 billion in 2009 and would grow thereafter at an annual rate of 20%. Willcocks et al. (2006) speculated that the future of global sourcing markets would be characterised by the following features.

7.4.1 Spending Will Continue to Rise in All Global Sourcing Markets

Irrespective of some major back-sourcing ventures, Willcocks et al. (2006) assert that global outsourcing will continue to witness unprecedented growth. Specifically, they indicated that the most prevalent course of action at the end of a contract will continue to be contract renewal with the incumbent supplier, with only a quarter of contracts to be re-tendered and awarded to new suppliers and a tenth, back-sourced.

7.4.2 Developing Countries Will Become Important Players in the Global Outsourcing Market

Developing countries and emerging markets are building and gaining expertise and experiences that the global outsourcing market requires (Oguji & Owusu, 2014; Oshri et al., 2009). As a result, they will become important players in the global outsourcing market.

7.4.3 Business Process Outsourcing Will Overshadow IT Outsourcing

Increasingly, back-office administrative functions such as procurement, legal services, finance and accounting and human resources management are secondary to many companies. Consequently, such functions will drive the expected increase in global outsourcing. It is estimated that outsourcing in these activities will rise by 10% annually (Willcocks et al., 2006). Suppliers who build competencies in those back-office administrative functions will have an advantage in the global outsourcing market.

7.4.4 Outsourcing Will Continue to Grow but with New Value Propositions from the Market

Oshri et al. (2009) propose that the consolidation of networks will emerge as one of the new and innovative value propositions in the global outsourcing market. The consolidation of networks is preferred because private networks are very expensive to manage by companies (Willcocks et al., 2006).

7.4.5 Selective Sourcing with Multiple Suppliers Will Remain the Dominant Trend

Selective sourcing with different suppliers is speculated to dominate the outsourcing trend in the future. Willcocks et al. (2006) report that offshoring, information technology and business process are the major selective functions that will be outsourced, mostly by companies in developed countries to multiple suppliers.

7.4.6 Clients Will Control Driving and Designing Deals

Outsourcing deals in the past were designed and controlled by suppliers. The trend has changed. The outlook of global outsourcing will see clients dominating the design and management of outsourcing deals. Oshri et al. (2009) observe that over 80% of outsourcing contracts are now being designed by the client. However, effective design and control of outsourcing deals require an in-depth understanding of the conditions under which the outsourcing contracts are discharged.

7.4.7 Clients Will Invest Much More in Contract Management

It is the responsibility of the clients to invest in the management of outsourcing contracts. As the burden of designing and controlling contract deals has shifted from the supplier to the client, the client should invest in the management of outsourcing contracts. Willcocks et al. (2006) explain that the clients' investment in outsourcing contract relates to the cost of getting the contract and its ongoing management costs, such as cost of capacity building. They hinted that the ongoing management costs range between 12% and 15% of the contract value.

7.4.8 Outsourcing Will Help in Insourcing

Insourcing is the practice whereby a firm sources its work, activities, resources and processes from within. The techniques being used in insourcing are similar to those used in outsourcing. Outsourcing thus provides the framework to guide insourcing. For example, a Service Level Agreement (SLA) is an outsourcing principle but is being used extensively in insourcing (Oshri et al., 2009). As a contractual agreement, SLA provides a definition and description of the services to be provided. It also stipulates the metrics to be used as benchmarks for evaluating the level and quality of services provided. The SLA provides a framework for reporting and governance of service provision. It is a common practice, therefore, for companies to guide their in-house operations with outsourcing techniques.

7.4.9 Outsourcing Failures and Disappointments Will Continue

Outsourcing is not without challenges. Despite the numerous benefits associated with outsourcing, it is a risky enterprise, particularly for the very many inexperienced firms. Estimating the future risk level of global outsourcing, Willcocks et al. (2006) argue that only 50% of outsourcing deals eventually achieve the desired outcome. This is particularly the case of B2B service outsourcing where, for instance, a bank gets less than satisfactory service quality of tellers after outsourcing that function to an external agency. Admitting the risky nature of outsourcing, Oshri et al. (2009) revealed that outsourcing will continue to carry high amounts of risk.

7.4.10 Clients Will Move from "Hype and Fear" into Maturity

The practice of outsourcing is a learning curve. The more a company engages in outsourcing, the better it gets at it. Willcocks et al. (2006) identify four stages along the outsourcing learning curve. The stages are awareness and excitement, engagement and cost reduction, operational strategy and competitive strategy. At the awareness and excitement stage, firms become aware of an outsourcing market through marketing "hype" or irrational propaganda. At the engagement and cost reduction stage, firms initially engage in outsourcing to seek lower costs. From the initial cost reduction focus, firms begin to see outsourcing as an operational strategy which aims at improving the quality of operations at the same time reducing the cost of operation. At the fourth stage, the focus of firms moves from viewing outsourcing as an operational strategy to a corporate-level competitive strategy. At this stage, firms use outsourcing to increase business agility, access and create new markets and outperform competitors. On this basis, Oshri et al. (2009) suggest that outsourcing has become an integral component of budgets and organisational management. This enhances the experience of organisations in the management of outsourcing ventures.

7.5 Why Do Businesses Outsource?

Several factors account for the growth of outsourcing. These include the following.

7.5.1 Cost Minimisation

The primary aim of outsourcing is to reduce the cost of doing business (Lacity et al., 2012). Seshadri (2005) also affirms that the objective of outsourcing is to minimise cost. This requires classification of costs and a comparative analysis of which costs are traded off when business processes are outsourced. It is argued that in-house work requires a high degree of asset specificity, which dictates the degree of in-house production. Incentives and other operational and recurrent costs are difficult to maintain internally. When companies outsource, they utilise the unique expert knowledge of the outsourcees. As a result, the companies are able to achieve significant cost advantages through economies of scale. Therefore, outsourcing, when undertaken carefully, allows the risks of high transaction costs to be minimised. However, outsourcing may lead to cost escalation. It is asserted that outsourcing escalates operational cost through vendor selection and contract management (Liu et al., 2014). It is argued further that the cost relating to outsourcing may exceed those relating to in-house projects, thereby defeating cost minimisation objectives of outsourcing. Firms should, therefore, assess the projected cost of outsourcing before embarking upon it.

7.5.2 Access to Capabilities and Competencies

The set of value chain activities and business processes embedded in the production of goods and services are many and cannot be competently handled by a single firm. As a result, firms outsource those competencies they are not experts in to vendors they consider more competent. This is guided by the principle that the most capable firm should undertake the business activity. As argued by Plugge and Bouwman (2013), firms outsource in order to acquire the competencies of suppliers. Usually, the expertise firms acquire through outsourcing is either not available internally or too expensive to acquire and use internally (Quinn & Hilmer, 1994). Therefore, outsourcing enables firms to use capabilities of service providers which may be costly or impossible for the company to develop in-house.

7.5.3 Concentration on Core Business Activities

As firms outsource competencies which they lack the expertise, to vendors they consider more competent, it accords them the opportunity to concentrate on the core activities that are critical to the attainment of the strategic objectives of the firm. When firms outsource peripheral activities and focus on core functions, they achieve economies of specialisation. Specialisation, as argued by Lee et al. (2000), leads to standardisation of output, thereby reducing diversity in the final product.

7.5.4 Sourcing Capability

Outsourcing requires transferring competence to firms that are good at it. Put differently, not all firms can outsource successfully. The ability to outsource profitably has been a major push for firms to embark upon outsourcing. Lee et al. (2000) state that the sourcing capability of the organisation is particularly important in successful outsourcing. "Sourcing capability refers to an assembly of skills, techniques, and know-how developed over time which enables an organisation to acquire, deploy, and leverage investment in pursuit of business strategies" (Plugge & Bouwman, 2013, p. 377). Therefore, a company that is endowed with the competencies and skills of sourcing is intrinsically motivated to outsource whenever it is feasible and profitable to do so.

7.5.5 Risk Mitigation

Value creating and delivery through business and outsourcing processes are characterised by various categories of risks, such as selection risk, incentive risks, relationship risks, unsuitable vendors, inadequate or incomplete contracts, lack of vendor commitment, unclear requirements and lack of experience. To provide buffers for business functions, firms outsource high-risk business activities. Buffering from outsourcing helps in the ability to spread business risks. Even though some organisations consider outsourcing to be a risk mitigation approach, outsourcing involves undesirable outcomes such as cost escalation (Bahli & Rivard, 2013), negative outcomes (Lacity et al., 2012) and unnecessary project delay (Qi & Chau, 2012).

7.6 Why Has Africa Not Succeeded in Becoming an Outsourcing Hub?

Outsourcing has been touted to provide opportunities for organisations and countries to become competitive. Location plays a critical role in outsourcing decisions. That is, a decision to outsource to a particular location depends on how attractive the location is (Oshri et al., 2009). In this regard, how has Africa positioned herself as an attractive destination in global outsourcing deliberations? Waema et al. (2009) report, "It emerged that no African country featured in the top ten preferred outsourcing destinations in the USA and in the UK" (p. 2). Oguji and Owusu

(2014) surveyed the research on outsourcing in Africa and found that very few African countries had been outsourcing destinations over the years. The following have been identified as the major impediments to African countries becoming global outsourcing and offshoring hubs.

7.6.1 High Outsourcing Costs across African Countries

Companies, in their outsourcing considerations, pay particular attention to outsourcing costs of potential outsourcing destinations. It is observed that Africa is unable to attract outsourcers because of high outsourcing costs. The types of costs most African countries are disadvantaged in include infrastructure costs and corporate taxes. Even though labour costs across Africa are competitively low to attract the attention of offshore outsourcers, the quality of the labour in many African countries leaves much to be desired. Outsourcing costs are, therefore, a major impediment for Africa on its bit to become an outsourcing hub.

7.6.2 Unavailability of Requisite Skills across Africa

The availability of the requisite skill set in Africa is a major determinant of whether Africa will be the ultimate destination for outsourcing decisions. Oshri et al. (2009) hinted that outsourcers' decision to outsource to a particular location is influenced by delivery, transformation and relational competencies. Delivery competency relates to the ability of the potential outsourcee to respond to or meet the outsourcing needs of the outsourcer. Transformation competency explains the outsourcee's ability to improve the quality and cost of service delivery of the outsourcer. Relational competency assesses the readiness of the outsourcee to realign its business model to be in tandem with the core values and goals of the outsourcer. Unfortunately, the skill pool and vendor landscape in outsourcing contracts from Africa is low. This is hampering the ability of African countries to attract offshoring contracts. Therefore, the inability of African countries to attract offshoring clients can be explained by the unavailability of the requisite skill set.

7.6.3 Unfriendly Outsourcing Environment across Africa

Relatively, the general outsourcing environment in Africa is unattractive to global outsourcing clients, making Africa miss its quest to be a hub of outsourcing. As highlighted by Oshri et al. (2009) and Oguji and Owusu (2014), outsourcing clients, especially from offshore countries, consider a number of environmental factors before making their outsourcing decision. The general business environment, living conditions, accessibility and government support are the environmental factors that are critical to outsourcing clients, especially from offshore countries. Comparatively, African countries are disadvantaged in all these sets of outsourcing environments. This affects the selection of any African country as an offshoring destination of foreign outsourcing clients.

7.6.4 Poor and Inadequate Infrastructure across Africa

"Africa in general is viewed as a continent with challenged infrastructure" (Waema et al., 2009, p. 3). Availability of quality infrastructure occupies a strategic position in outsourcing destination considerations. Unfortunately, Africa is replete with the inadequacy of infrastructure. The few available infrastructural frameworks tend to be of poor quality. The required infrastructure to support and qualify Africa for outsourcing and offshoring destination is thus lacking. Oshri et al. (2009) itemised telecommunication and IT, real estate, transportation and power as the most critical infrastructure needs of outsourcing and offshoring clients. The poor road network, unstable power supply, poor internet connectivity, decent accommodation challenges and limited telecommunication services are some infrastructural challenges that off-scaled Africa as a preferred destination for outsourcing needs.

7.6.5 High-Risk Profile across Africa

The high-risk profile of African countries is a major threat to Africa becoming a hub of outsourcing and offshoring destination. Many outsourcing and offshoring clients are concerned about the risk profile of their outsourcing and offshoring destinations. They are particular about security risk, risk due to the possibility of disruptive events, regulatory risks, macroeconomic risks and intellectual property risk (Oshri et al., 2009). For example, the outbreak of diseases, looming terrorist attacks on the continent and the high rate of cyber fraud create a perception that African countries are unsafe to live in and visit (Oshri et al., 2009). This is a major barrier to Africa being considered as a hub of outsourcing and offshoring destination (see also Oguji & Owusu, 2014).

7.6.6 Weak Market Potential of African Countries

A key consideration in the selection of outsourcing destination is market potential in the preferred destination. The market potential of a sourcing destination is assessed based on the attractiveness of the local market and access to nearby (Oshri, et al., 2009). Many African countries report perennial low GDP growth rate, an indication of a weak potential market to support outsourcing services. Besides, African countries are less attractive as outsourcing and offshoring destinations because of perceived language and cultural incompatibility (Oshri et al., 2009).

In 2007, among the top 50 emerging global outsourcing destinations, only three African countries (Egypt – 13th, Ghana – 27th and South Africa – 31st) featured on the list (Kearney, 2007; Oshri et al., 2009). Again, in 2013, Again, in 2011, only four African countries were ranked in a list of "top 50 potential global sourcing destinations" – Ghana (26th), South Africa (30th), Kenya (32nd) and Senegal (33rd) (Oguji & Owusu, 2014). There is an assertion that Africa is not an attractive destination for outsourcing (Waema et al., 2009). Kuada and Hinson (2015) lamented that

> African countries have not been considered attractive candidates for offshore outsourcing largely due to the sluggish growth of their manufacturing sectors combined with a high cost of operation, lower average educational level of the labour force, and less technological and organizational skills (p. 49).

7.7 Conclusion

Despite the myriads of problems identified in the chapter, there is hope for Africa to become the hub of global outsourcing and offshoring destinations if only African counties can show commitment to addressing the critical issues relating to outsourcing. The problems that need to be addressed include (1) outsourcing costs, such as infrastructure cost, corporate tax issues and labour cost; (2) outsourcing environment, including governance support, business environment, living environment and accessibility; and (3) availability of labour resources such as delivery competence, transformational competence and relational competence. Others are infra-structure challenges such as telecommunication and IT, real estate, power and transportation; and outsourcing risks such as security issues, disruptive events, macroeconomic risks and intel-lectual property risks; and market potential. The commitment of African countries to this call will signal that indeed, the continent is building and gaining expertise and experiences the global outsourcing market requires.

Case Study

CALL CENTRE OUTSOURCING AT SFS

BACKGROUND INFORMATION

The Société de Financement Solidaire (SFS) is a French financial institution with strong presence across Africa. It was founded in 1987 by Jean-Patrice Lemar, a former military officer and son of immigrant Ivoirian parents who had resettled in France. Jean-Patrice was severely injured in a war at the age of 34, cutting short his predominantly West African-based military career and creating a need to re-strategise his future. He invested his severance package in what is now SFS, leveraging his experiences with locals in war-torn zones during his military days. SFS started by providing African immigrants in France, mostly residing in the country illegally who wanted to send money back to their families in Africa, a formal remittance channel. The business model was in two folds; one aspect was to help this target market save money, and the other was to facilitate their remittances back home.

Today, SFS has over 12 operations in African countries with a focus in West Africa and cur-rently exploring an entry into Asia. Jean-Patrice is not just the founder, but currently the Group Chairman. The target market of this institution includes small-scale businesses and individuals in the informal sector who are mostly illiterate to semi-literate. The company is passionate about this category of people and aims to give them financial liberation through their products which essentially focus on micro-loans as well as current and saving accounts. This is borne out of the founders' observation of poverty and poor financial decisions among the target market during his military days. The company's vision is to be the household name for financial services among its target market. This it has done quite well as it currently is the market leader in micro-financial services in West Africa through acceptable customer management practices.

Over the years, the operating countries of SFS have attained a semi-autonomous status; they have their structures and local operations but take strategic direction from the parent company in Lyon – France. SFS Senegal is the shining star in the group with a double-digit growth rate year-on-year since 2012. It is the de facto Headquarters for the African operations and the model coun-try for other operations. It is the highest single contributor (41%) to the business's global revenue. Last year, profit from Senegal was used to cushion the organisation's Beninois Operations from an imminent collapse. A key differentiator in SFS' operations in line with the parent company's vision of being exceptional at customer service is a great, reliable, responsive and well-resourced call centre for customer queries and complaints which operate 24/7.

THE CASE

It's 9 a.m. on a relatively sunny Wednesday morning in Dakar, Senegal. Didi Camara, the Head of Supply Chain Management (SCM) at SFS, is pacing in the board room while rehearsing his submissions ahead of a call with the board of directors in their Lyon-based Headquarters. On this call, a key decision on the call centre operation faces him. Being Head of SCM of SFS Africa, reporting to the CEO of the Africa Region with a dotted reporting line to the Group CEO, his input, arguments and justification on whether or not to outsource the business's highly acclaimed call centre will be critical. The success or otherwise of this decision will impact his bonus and his desperate bid to move ahead as Group Head of Supply Chain. The Call Centre, though not the organisation's core business, is the one aspect of SFS's business that provides the key differentiator between the company and its two closest competitors; La Compagnie Financier d'Alliance Strategique (CFAS) and Banque d'Agriculture. The facility runs 24/7 and provides real-time assistance to the financial needs of clients. The introduction of this call centre, its reliability and the comfort it gives the target market, has been one of the driving factors to becoming the market leader in the micro-finance industry in Senegal. The other has been the payment terms of the micro-loans, which seem favourable to the relatively financially unstable clientele.

On the call will be the entire board of the parent company and the CEO of SFS Senegal Operation. In the last 6 months, average daily calls had increased significantly since the launch of a new well-patronised financial product targeted at clientele in agriculture. Agents who attend to customer complaints are overwhelmed as their workload has doubled in a short time. Waiting time per customer has increased from the average 30 s to 3 min, and customers are losing patience. Besides, the call centre that used to be toll-free is no longer free to customers. This decision was made as a short-term measure to manage the costs of running the facility. Two weeks earlier, a popular customer, a retiree who is known for his influence among other retirees, had accosted the Head of Marketing at the entrance to their Dakar Head Office complaining bitterly about how the company used to treat them well but is now treating them with sheer disdain because the company has become a market leader. SFS even threatened to get the retirees off the micro-finance's services, leaving them to patronise CFAS, a major competitor. To add to the growing challenges, there was an increasing customer base from the ethnic groups in the hinterlands which had brought an additional burden to recruit their dialect-specific local language agents. Costs for running the call centre were ballooning, and something needed to be done urgently. The call centre that offered a differentiator was now too expensive to run, and projections indicate SFS may miss their net income target for the year.

Beyond all these, there is a sentimental factor with the call centre operations; two out of every four agents are physically challenged. It was a deliberate decision by the company to absorb this marginalised group. SFS prides itself in this regard and has won several human resource awards locally and internationally for this feat. To use physically challenged personnel to deliver top-notch quality is a further reiteration that disability is not inability.

The call centre handles complaints, queries and customer education on financial services. Given the clientele and the type of industry this organisation is situated in, clarity on finances as promptly as possible as well as timely complaint resolution on "money matters" was critical for trust and needed to be managed with all the tact it deserved. This is another reason why the many issues plaguing the call centre in recent times have become a key area of concern for the business.

The operations of the call centre can be described as support services. Before new products, offers, changes to existing products, etc. are made, call centre agents are engaged well in advance and trained on managing customer queries. They help to explain new products to customers, check outstanding loans for customers and reverse wrong transactions expeditiously, among others. Engagements with customers are in both local languages and French depending on customer's preferences. The agents are trained to be patient with customers and take them through relevant procedures for complaint resolution.

Being a very democratic organisation, an earlier Senior Management meeting to discuss the issue was organised to gather views from key personnel. The Chief Information Officer,

Pierre DeMont – a French expatriate and a childhood friend of Jean-Patrice – indicated his indifference on whether to outsource the call centre services or not. His only position, however, was that if a third party were to manage the call centre, the third-party company would have limited access to the SFS's core banking applications and systems. This limited integration was to reduce the risk of information security breaches and potential hacking. It was a non-negotiable Information Systems Policy of the organisation.

The Marketing Director, Michel Diallo, opposed this position, stating that the relevance of a call centre was to have empowered frontline personnel who could resolve queries and complaints at the first attempt. Limited access would mean delayed complaint resolution. For this reason, the call centre ought to remain as it is, and other business sector costs managed to accommodate the increasing costs. Asked whether he would sacrifice a portion of his publicity costs to cater for these costs, Michel responded in the negative and reiterated the limited budget he was already working with.

The newly appointed Finance Director, Kofi Asare, argued that based on all three proposals received by agencies looking to get the outsourcing bid, outsourcing was a preferred option. The company with the best expertise interestingly has the most affordable rate. "It's a no brainer", he maintained. Regardless of anything, the organisations that bid for the project gave him comfort, the call centre business would be in safer and more experienced hands.

Maria Cisse, the Human Resources Director, disagrees with outsourcing. She has concerns about people, job losses and the backlash on their much-touted Diversity & Inclusion policies which included disability empowerment. Based on experience with other outsourced services, promises of the new company employing existing staff have not happened as expected. Remuneration to the outsourced staff is woefully inadequate, she indicated. She added that training is said to be done by the contracted organisation, but service delivery always confirmed that training, if any, was inadequate. To aggravate the situation, attrition always increased when services were outsourced, another factor that had affected her ratings in prior experiences.

Louisa Von Hesse, the Head of Legal & Corporate Services, had promised to ensure that if the organisation opted to outsource, the new contract would ensure expectations are spelt out clearly with no room for ambiguities. Maria insisted on this assurance measure asserting that they had the same hopes when outsourcing media operations to Continental Media 3 years ago, but the fiasco it turned out to be was evident for all.

In the Lyon Headquarters, however, they had not explicitly expressed their preference. To Jean-Patrice, whatever decision the Senegal Operations arrived at should not affect shareholder value. However, Didi knows one thing the founder of the organisation is passionate about, the ethos and essence of the organisation as one which stands with the less privileged in society by providing them with the much-needed financial support at a margin will not be compromised.

Among the three bids received from potential companies, the front runner most likely and most preferred to get the contract is Messrs Cante Ltd (MCL), well known for their expertise in customer service delivery. It is a high performing organisation reputed for its autocratic leadership style, top multinational clients and sophisticated technological tools for service delivery. Their quoted cost is unusually reasonable and within budget, given their impeccable brand. This is possibly as a result of their predicament in the last 10 months. It has been embroiled in two major scandals and has suffered bad publicity and loss of major deals and contracts. The first scandal was a tax evasion scandal for which they were fined huge sums and a possible 1-year prison term for their former CFO who is still in court. The second is a sex scandal involving the former Chief Operations Officer who has resigned after glaring evidence on sexual harassment against him was provided by one of the contract staff as well as three other employees had also accused him without evidence. These issues have sunk MCL into rough times.

The other two companies, according to Didi Camara's unofficial sources within the industry, may not have the financial muscle to take on a call centre the size of SFS. They are hoping that this big contract will be their breakthrough into large businesses and corporations. While one has an existing call centre management contract with a financial services provider, the company is one-third the size of SFS. The other had no experience in financial services.

The Lyon headquarters is convinced that even without a firm decision on whether to outsource or not, a good reputation is non-negotiable for any partner company. The SFS Senegal directors who are pro-outsourcing, however, feel that customers do not need to know about an outsourced service so this should not be a matter of concern. Besides, the people involved in MCL's scandals are out of the company. The board, however, is not convinced and will need more assurance should the final decision be to outsource the call centre which has won numerous customer service awards.

7.8 Discussion Questions

1. What arguments would you advance in favour of SFS Senegal outsourcing its call centre services, and to which company?
2. Discuss the threats the outsourcing of the call centre services of SFS Senegal poses to the current operation of SFS Senegal in particular, and to SFS Lyon in general.

References

Bahli, B., & Rivard, S. (2013). Outsourcing information technology services: A moderated mediation analysis. *Decision Support Systems*, 57(4), 37–47.

Brook, J. W., & Plugge, A. (2010). Strategic sourcing of R&D: The determinants of success. In *International workshop on global sourcing of information technology and business processes* (pp. 26–42). Springer, Berlin, Heidelberg.

Chen, Y., Dubey, P., & Sen, D. (2011). Outsourcing induced by strategic competition. *International Journal of Industrial Organization*, 29(4), 484–492.

Grover, V., Cheon, M. J., & Teng, J. T. (1996). The effect of service quality and partnership on the outsourcing of information systems functions. *Journal of Management Information Systems*, 12(4), 89–116.

Kearney, A. T. (2007). Growth opportunities for global retailers. The AT Kearney 2007 Global Retail Development Index. AT KEARNEY Inc.

Kuada, J., & Hinson, E. (2015). Outsourcing in Ghana: An integrated perspective. *African Journal of Business and Economic Research*, 10(2–3), 47–86.

Lacity, M. C., Khan, S., Yan, A., & Willcocks, L. P. (2010). A review of the IT outsourcing empirical literature and future research directions. *Journal of Information Technology*, 25(4), 395–433.

Lacity, M. C., Willcocks, L. P., & Solomon, S. (2012). Robust practices from two decades of ITO and BPO research. In Mary C. (Eds.), *Advanced outsourcing practice* (pp. 1–24). Palgrave Macmillan, London.

Lee, J. N., Huynh, M. Q., Chi-Wai, K. R., & Pi, S. M. (2000, January). The evolution of outsourcing research: What is the next issue? In *Proceedings of the 33rd Annual Hawaii International Conference on System Sciences* (p. 10). IEEE, Maui, Hawaii.

Liu, J. Y. C., Yuliani, A. R., & Wu, C. L. (2014, June). Adaptive weighted-function models for time series prediction. *In Proceeding of the 11th World Congress on Intelligent Control and Automation* (pp. 4871–4874). IEEE, Shenyang, China

Morley, M., Kosnik, T., Wong-MingJi, D. J., & Hoover, K. (2006). Outsourcing vs insourcing in the human resource supply chain: A comparison of five generic models. *Personnel Review*, 35(6), 671–683.

Ndubisi, N. O. (2011). Conflict handling, trust and commitment in outsourcing relationship: A Chinese and Indian study. *Industrial Marketing Management*, 40(1), 109–117.

Oguji, N., & Owusu, R. (2014). Africa as a source location: Literature review and implications. *International Journal of Emerging Markets*, 9(3), 424–438.

Oshri, I., Kotlarsky, J., & Willcocks, L. P. (2009). Overview of the global sourcing marketplace. In *The handbook of global outsourcing and offshoring* (pp. 4–14). Palgrave Macmillan, London.

Plugge, A., & Bouwman, H. (2013). Fit between sourcing capabilities and organisational structure on IT outsourcing performance. *Production Planning & Control*, 24(4–5), 375–387.

Qi, C., & Chau, P. Y. (2012). Relationship, contract and IT outsourcing success: Evidence from two descriptive case studies. *Decision Support Systems*, 53(4), 859–869.

Quinn, J. B., & Hilmer, F. G. (1994). Strategic outsourcing. *MIT Sloan Management Review*, 35(4), 43.

Seshadri, S. (2005). *Sourcing strategy* (pp. 5–12). Springer Science & Business Media, New York.

Vining, A. R., & Globerman, S. (2017). The outsourcing decision: A strategic framework. In R. Gervais (Ed.), *Global Outsourcing Strategies* (pp. 27–40). Routledge, Abingdon.

Waema, T. M., Odera, G., Adeya-Weya, C. N., Were, P., Masinde, E. M., Chepken, C., … & Kenduiywo, P. (2009). Development of a business process outsourcing industry in Kenya: Critical success factors. Policy brief submitted to the International Development Research Centre, Ottawa IDRC Grant (104488-001).

Willcocks, L. P., Lacity, M. C., & Cullen, S. (2006). Information technology sourcing: Fifteen years of learning. In C. Avgerou, R. Mansell, D. Quah, & R. Silverstone (Eds.), *The Oxford handbook of information and communication technologies* (pp. 244–272). Oxford University Press, New York.

Zhang, L. J., Chao, T. J., Sayah, J. Y., Chang, H. Y. H., Chung, J. Y., & Zhou, Q. (2006). System and method of dynamic service composition for business process outsourcing. U.S. Patent No. 7,114,146. Washington, DC: U.S. Patent and Trademark Office.

Chapter 8

Systems and Project Business

INTRODUCTION AND OBJECTIVES

In this chapter, we will discuss systems and project business. Both are significant parts of business-to-business (B2B) that some companies concentrate on as their strategic niche and others do besides individual products/services business. Their importance will continue to increase in African B2B markets, as they grow and become more competitive. It is, therefore, necessary to provide a thorough review of the strategies, which are seldom discussed or adequately understood in most B2B textbooks.

At the end of this chapter, the reader will understand and be able to plan strategies for:

- Systems and project business
- The nature and role of relationships and networks in systems and project business
- The relationship between project management and project business
- Risks and success factors for systems and project business in Africa.

8.1 What Are Systems and Project Business?

8.1.1 Systems Business

A B2B system is a combination of products, services, technologies and consulting supplied in a package to meet the needs of a purchaser (Bonaccorsi et al., 1996; Davies & Mackenzie, 2014; Owusu et al., 2007). A system is most often not ready-made and available. However, it has to be developed from the supplier's existing products, services, technologies, innovation, as well as using its other business relationships with its suppliers, some original equipment manufacturers (OEMs) and consultants to develop, adapt and tailor the system to the requirement of the purchaser. Thus, a successful system business often involves an intensive period of information sharing, negotiation and relationship building between the involved parties that may lead to the maintenance of contacts and new deals going forward (Hadjikhani, 1996; Owusu & Welch, 2007; Paliwoda & Bonaccorsi, 1993).

Daikin Company, a leading international air conditioning system manufacturer and supplier, produces and supplies a range of air conditioning systems and products, and has operations internationally and in Africa. The company has ambitions to become a leading supplier and partner for air conditioning systems all across Africa (https://www.daikinafrica.com/en_us/customers.html/). As it manufactures various types of air conditioning systems and qualities and has the capabilities to develop tailored solutions, its products are not necessarily waiting on the shelves to be picked up by an African company that needs steel products for its building project, unlike B2C customers going to a grocery shop and picking up the groceries they need. When Uganda's Mutoni Construction Company is going to put in a bid to construct a housing complex, it plans its offer, including the types and quality of air condition systems to be included. Mutoni Construction states that it provides "broad-based civil engineering and construction solutions". To do this, it has to put in the best quality bids that are innovative and meet the real needs of the client or buyer. Mutoni has operations in many African countries, and like Daikin, it wants to expand further and become a trustworthy Pan-African Construction Company. Thus, Mutoni may enter bids in several African countries and bid for projects that are competitive and challenging, and require innovative and value-creating solutions. Companies like Mutoni adopt the advisable strategy of concentrating on their core competencies, which are design, installation and construction of buildings (http://mutoni.co/). As air conditioning systems are a vital component of its innovative and value-creating office construction solutions, Mutoni needs to work with a company like Daikin to supply it the right type of air conditioning products, services, technologies and consulting to compete successfully.

Whenever a buyer like Mutoni contacts Daikin, it is never the same as a consumer going to the grocery shop to buy a brand of sugar. While the grocery shop will have several already priced brands of sugar on the shelves for which the consumers will choose their preferred product, the specific types and qualities of air conditioning systems that Mutoni would need for the housing complex project bid will not be waiting on the shelves to be picked up immediately. Additionally, as Mutoni is bidding for a competitive, lucrative project, the prices, qualities and quantities of steel it needs have to be negotiated. Mutoni would, thus, be buying air conditioning systems from Daikin that is a combination of products, services, technologies and consulting that will go into its bid. While Mutoni is the expert in the construction, Daikin is the expert in air conditioning.

A B2B systems buying process thus involves a considerable period of information sharing and negotiation between the parties. The negotiating parties can include technical/business consultants of the primary marketer and purchaser. Information is provided by the purchaser (Mutoni) about their needs, plans, the bid they intend to go for with the system they are buying, their experiences, their requirements, etc., to the marketer (Daikin) which weighs the information against their existing products, innovation and competencies. Research has shown that many times, the exact products, services and technologies the purchaser needs have to be developed based on existing products, services, technologies and innovation (Bonacorsi et al., 1996; Davies & Mackenzie, 2014; Owusu & Welch, 2007). For example, while Daikin has already designed many air conditioning systems, it has to consider the design of the buildings, the site of the buildings (e.g. a moist tropical forest area in the Congo or a dry part of the Kalahari Desert in Botswana), in offering systems to the purchaser. The parties have to discuss and negotiate the solution of products, services and technologies that Daikin will provide Mutoni. Mutoni needs to include the required systems to be supplied by Daikin in its bid. Thus, the nature of the deal that develops between the two companies becomes one of the critical components for the success of Mutoni's bid. Research has emphasised that strategic and competitive B2B marketers should ensure that they meet the real needs of the purchaser, that the systems they supply are made to fit, and that they provide the purchaser with appropriate pricing to enable the latter's bid to be competitive in quality, technology, price, etc. (Owusu & Welch, 2007; Paliwoda & Bonaccorsi, 1993). To meet Mutoni's need, Scaw may have to develop new products, services and technologies, and may have to employ new staff. Over time, the initial contact can grow into a business relationship (Owusu et al., 2007). The two companies commit resources and undertake activities over some time until the supply deal is completed. Often a guarantee period follows during which the supplier has to be available to deal with any problems that arise. All companies involved might establish key account management to ensure that the partner is taken care of well.

While pricing and profitability are essential for B2B firms, the length of time and intensity of contact required over a period may make the relationship building and management aspects equally crucial to the success of the deal. Where other actors than just the marketer and purchaser are involved (e.g. marketer's suppliers may be brought in to ensure that the supplier can keep its part of the deal, as well as consultants of both sides), a business network is created. For this specific deal, the network will be temporary, but it may develop long-term characteristics based on previous relationships as well as future sales that build on the current one (Owusu & Welch, 2007; Skaates et al., 2002).

Consulting companies and systems integrators are an essential part of systems business (SB). Take, for example, the company Tenece, which is fast developing into an African multinational company (MNC). The company describes itself as a "…multi-competency enterprise, transformation and technology consultancy firm" and a "first-class systems integrator" (https://www.tenece.com/). The company has had business in many African countries, representing, consulting and servicing the systems and products of many top global and African industrial companies. Its clients range from companies in oil and gas, financial services, manufacturing, the public sector and education. Such a company has broad and deep expertise in its business areas, and either markets its systems or consults for systems deals as described in the preceding. While the company has some own products and services, it sometimes depends on its suppliers (OEM companies it represents), to supply its systems. Thus, the company's SB establishes relationships with B2B buyers as well as suppliers. Similarly, in the study by Kauda and Mensah (2020), 5 out of the 12 solar firms interviewed asserted that they collaborate to jointly design systems that are adaptive to the local market and consumers' preferences. One of the leading solar firms, DC Solar, designs their systems and contracts their Chinese partners to manufacture them, which is more cost-effective than when produced locally in Ghana (Kuada & Mensah, 2020).

8.1.2 Project Business

A project is defined as a set of temporary marketing and management activities and relationships to achieve specified goals (Artto & Wikström, 2005; PMBoK Guide, 2017). Projects as organisational arrangements are used by companies when they want to define who, what, how and when specific organisational goals are achieved. Resources, activities and personnel are specifically designated for a project – often a project team with a Project Manager. The resources, activities and personnel will be the relevant competencies and may come from several levels and parts of a company (Artto & Wikström, 2005; PMBoK Guide, 2017; Tikkanen et al., 2007).

Systems supplied by Tenece may be going to a project in the oil and gas industry. In one of the new gas exploration and production concessions granted by the Government of Mozambique, many systems suppliers will be supplying and installing their systems that together form the exploration and production of gas by one of the concession holders. The major companies like

ExxonMobil that are taking the concessions usually have strong relationships with suppliers from previous projects but may also want to use some local or African suppliers in order to strengthen their ties to African companies like Tenece. Others like Tullow Oil and Gas (which states that "Africa is the heartland of Tullow" and is active in many African countries) and Kosmos Energy (active in many African countries) are smaller players in the industry but have invested in their Africa business, and are trying to build their local content by using African system suppliers. Mozambique's prospects to bring in much-needed revenue to the country from its gas reserves are enormous, and the companies that have received the exploration concessions want their projects to succeed, as the projects involve large investments (https://africanbusinessmagazine.com/sectors/energy/mozambique-set-to-become-gas-exporting-giant/). Thus, only the best system suppliers are contracted by companies undertaking projects.

Thus, Tenece's system supply to the oil and gas industry may be defined as a project within the company. Tenece will create a specific project team with leadership given the specific goal of ensuring that it builds and manages strong relationships with the prospective client, wins the deal, supplies and provides value to the client, makes the client satisfied and raises the possibility of a re-buy as well as gains good references for new projects with other clients. In this sense, the system and the project are two sides of the same coin for Tenece. Tenece would be marketing its system or project to the gas exploration company and is, thus, a systems or project marketer. The gas explorer undertaking its project, as stated earlier, combines many systems so that its project consists of many systems that are purchased from several suppliers. From the perspective of projects like a housing complex that Mutoni wants to win, it will be marketing its project to the City Council of Kampala that wants to build new housing estates. As explained earlier, Mutoni's project has backward linkages to projects with system suppliers and forward linkages to the project purchaser, the Kampala City Council. Project marketing is, thus, the marketing of a package of products, services, technologies and consulting to satisfy the requirements and needs of the purchaser. Project purchasing is the purchasing of a package of products, services, technologies and consulting to meet the needs and requirements of the purchaser. Combining the two, project business is the marketing and purchasing of a package of products, services, technologies and consulting to satisfy the requirements and needs of the marketer and purchaser.

The liberalisation and growth of African economies have expanded the private sector. Governments have sold and privatised former state corporations in countries all across Africa like Tanzania, Zambia, Algeria and Zambia. Thus, private industry project purchases have increased. Projects are purchased by both local African companies and foreign investors. For example, the liberalisation of higher education has led to the purchase of projects for new university campuses like Central University and Valley View University in Ghana. Vastly increased intake of students has required the building of new hostel villages all over African university campuses like Strathmore University that have provided project purchases from local and foreign project marketers. Apart from business and industrial projects purchased by businesses and organisations, major public construction and infrastructure are often purchased as projects. The reason is that they are large and complex; involve new ideas, technologies, innovation and significant financing needs; and, thus, demand even more intensive and longer-term information sharing and relationships than with systems.

Infrastructure projects often start with vague and ambitious ideas and hope for the development of communities, nations and politicians. In African countries, the lack of infrastructure is massive and a significant bottleneck to economic and human development. Inadequate and poor quality of electricity, water, roads, housing and schools is getting more critical as Africa's population has doubled in the last 40 years and could double again in the next 40 years. While the level and quality of infrastructure have been improved over the last 50 years, even in countries where improvements have kept pace with population growth, the inherited legacy from colonial times was so low that much more should have been done to bring it to adequacy (see the case study of this chapter below). Additionally, the new generations have even higher ambitions and demands than their parents. They expect and have a right to dependable infrastructure, quality water in homes, quality housing, etc. As a result, calculations of Africa's infrastructure project needs are immense, and a combination of local and foreign project marketers and financiers are expected to continue to take part in African business and infrastructure projects (see the case study below and Chapter 9).

In the preceding section, we mentioned that projects are, basically, a mode of organising business activities in which firms want to be efficient by dedicating specific resources and planning activities to achieve specific goals within a specified time. This mode is used when selling or buying systems or infrastructure by both the marketer and purchaser. In that case, the project exists both internally in each company and between them after they get into contact, share information, evaluate and negotiate needs and requirements, the deal is awarded and the contract signed. Thus, a B2B inter-organisational project is created for supplying, installing and constructing a package of products, services, technologies and consulting to satisfy the requirements and needs of the purchaser, to ensure that value is provided to the purchaser and both sides are satisfied.

8.1.2.1 Types of Project Business

Terminologies are used in the industry and research to differentiate between different combinations of systems and project business. Owusu et al. (2007) summarise them as follows:

Systems Business (SB): SB involves information sharing, negotiation, delivery and installation of the system as described previously. The system might be a whole package deal in itself and, thus, constitute a project for the system marketer and purchaser. Systems are also parts of a turnkey project or EPC as described below.

Turnkey Project: In a turnkey project, the project marketer takes full responsibility for completion and handing over of agreed facilities after contract signature. The marketer will deliver a functioning set of approved facilities for which the purchaser can just "turn the key" and be able to use it. The turnkey project combines systems and usually involves construction or installation of agreed facilities in which the systems are integrated.

Turnkey-Plus Project: The marketer continues to manage the completed facilities for an agreed period after the turnkey project is completed. The marketer will train the staff of the purchaser to use the project and help them to run it for an agreed period. This is done because projects usually involve new systems that the purchaser is not used to. Besides, the marketer is sometimes required to prove that the facilities will function and provide value to the purchaser as agreed in the contract.

Engineering, Procurement and Construction (EPC): This terminology used in the industry is similar to a turnkey project. The parties share information, negotiate and sign the deal, and the marketer procures systems, constructs and delivers the turnkey project.

8.1.2.2 Characteristics of Project Business

The "D-U-C" features have been used to summarise some of the main characteristics of project business. They are discontinuity, uniqueness and complexity (Jalkala et al., 2010; Mandják & Veres, 1997). A project is temporary as the parties agree on a specific end date when the contracted systems or constructed facilities should have been supplied. Thus, even though a project marketer and purchaser may have had several projects previously, each project is completed and accounted for separately. Besides, large business and infrastructure projects are unlikely to be purchased continuously by any buyer as they involve large investments. While governments buy road projects every year, they usually portion them out into different lengths, qualities and parts of the country, to negotiate, award and account for each project separately. Each project is unique on the bases of providing targeted value, the dynamics of the need and requirements of a single purchaser or different purchasers, as well as the complexity of marketing, management and technical elements of projects. While GE Electric would have built previous power stations in other African countries, a new power station in Rwanda cannot just be negotiated, designed and built on the exact blueprint of a previous project in Liberia. The two power projects are different because of the various governments, needs and requirements of the purchaser, economic, technical and negotiation competencies of each party, the business ecosystems, geographical terrain and climate, etc. The period of construction and delivery are unique periods. As described in Owusu (2002), even though IVO International had extensive experience of projects in many African and similar Asian countries, the Ashanti Electrification Project (AEP) presented many unique opportunities and challenges for them. This was partly due to the nature of the negotiations, the geography, needs and requirements, and business ecosystem of the AEP (see the case study below). The previous aspects create the complexity of projects. The complexity of projects is, thus, generated by the marketing, management and technical uniqueness of each project. In projects, pre-project modelling of technical functions does not provide 100% certainty that the systems that are combined and integrated will perform as expected. In many cases, such models and plans can be implemented only after the projected deal has been secured, and sometimes after testing when construction or installation is completed (Bonaccorsi et al., 1996; Cova et al., 1993; Lemaire, 1996) (see Section 8.4). Also, another characteristic is said to be a relatively high level of financial investments. This is particular to large projects.

In most cases, the purchaser needs long-term funding, as the project takes time to be completed, and the purchaser needs time to generate revenue from the project. Therefore, marketers sometimes need to support purchasers to get funding for the projects (see Section 8.4 and the case study below). Projects necessarily create temporary business relationships and networks. The purchasing process and period of information sharing, negotiation, installation, construction and post-project guarantee or turnkey-plus period require the participation of many parties. They intensively interact, and their activities and resources are jointly responsible for the success of the project (see Section 8.2).

8.2 The Nature and Role of Relationships and Networks in Systems and Project Business

As systems and projects most often require three or more B2B parties to complete, a business network, albeit temporary, is created. An example is the network for the AEP. The project marketer brings in its network of system suppliers, sub-contractors, financiers and consultants, just as the project purchaser brings in its network of financiers, consultants, and even suppliers and sub-contractors (Owusu & Welch, 2007; Skaates et al., 2002; see the case study of this chapter below).

The Project Management Institute (PMBoK Guide, 2017) strongly suggests the inclusion of a neutral consultant in the project. Thus, several consultants may be involved by providing specific

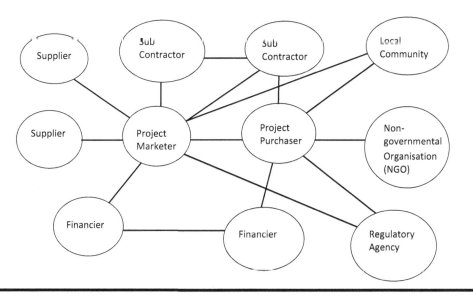

Figure 8.1   A project network.

competencies in the technical, financial or management aspects as well as in the network of the marketer and purchaser. As Figure 8.1 shows, financiers, sub-contractors, suppliers, different levels of institutional actors and non-governmental organisations (NGOs) may be involved in the project.

Each of these B2B parties brings their resources and capabilities to support the project marketer or purchaser. Some are business actors such as the suppliers, sub-contractors and financiers who join the business network due to their hopes of making a profit. Others are non-business actors like the local community that has an interest in the project and hosts the project, e.g. an electric power extension project as in the AEP (see the case study of this chapter below). They can also be environmental NGOs that follow the project to ensure that it meets their objectives of protecting the natural environment. Government regulatory agencies whose task is to supervise the standards of the infrastructure or public utility are always involved.

The project network is temporary because it formally works together during the project, and the contracted relationships end at the completion and hand-over of the project. However, some of the parties have a history of previous relationships and have, therefore, long-term relationships. Project marketers like Mutoni Co. usually work with the same suppliers when they are satisfied with the relationships as it assures them of the future quality of the relationships and systems they receive. Depending on where the project is situated, they may also negotiate with new suppliers, for example, those in the country of the project for cost or relational reasons. Similarly, some sub-contractors are old relationships. In every new country, they believe it is advantageous to work with local sub-contractors, who may thus be new. Also, local content regulations often demand the use of a minimum value of local suppliers and sub-contractors. That has to, however, meet the demands of the creditor, as foreign government aid and concessional funding often requires a minimum level of purchases from the creditor's country (Owusu & Vaaland, 2016; Owusu & Welch, 2007; see the case study of this chapter below). Some of the new relationships will be carried over to forthcoming projects, thus providing the opportunity for longer-term relationships that transcend single projects into multi-project relationships and networks.

8.3 B2B Opportunities for Suppliers, Sub-Contractors, Consultants and Financiers

While the project marketer/Turnkey contractor/EPC contractor takes on the full financial and legal responsibility to deliver the complete project, almost all project marketers employ sub-contractors and suppliers, and work with some consultants for project success. Thus, many small- and medium-sized enterprises have opportunities for projects. They may follow project marketers that they have worked with before, or they may use their project scanning and marketing processes to identify suitable projects that will give them dependable deals. In many public infrastructure project purchases, institutional buyers demand the use of some level of local suppliers and sub-contractors, which limits the competition for local suppliers (see the case study of this chapter below). Thus, the opportunities for project business exist for many B2B companies.

8.4 The Project Business Process

International project marketing companies undertake market scanning by following project announcements in national and international media. Companies and governments advertise their project needs in industry journals, in published government gazettes and online. The sites and publications of multilateral institutions and organisations such as the World Bank, United States Agency for International Development (USAID), European Union (EU) and Swedish International Development Agency (SIDA) are used for these calls for bids for projects. International funding agencies publish information about projects that they finance in their outlets and other international outlets. Sometimes, projects are negotiated on sole tender agreements with previous marketers who provided a successful project and built good relationships. Calls for bids are often competitive, but good relationships may offer advantages in terms of information and knowledge of needs and requirements. Some project marketers have agents or relationship facilitators at regional centres to inform them of prospective projects. Project scanning is also based on an evaluation of economic growth and needs of various countries (see the case study of this chapter below).

When project marketers see a good call for bids, they get to work developing an offer. The development of the offer is based on their strategies and resources. Also, they contact their prospective suppliers, sub-contractors and financiers to negotiate the inclusion of the latter's systems into the project. A strategy of including suppliers and sub-contractors from the project purchasing country is useful, as they can have critical local relationships and knowledge. Previous relationships are most promising due to contacts, experience and references to build on. After the deadline, the project purchaser shortlists the bidders and invites them to submit further bids/clarifications/specifications and/or negotiations. Based on the knowledge of the project purchaser, the marketer might include proposals for funding the project from its network. This might be funders that have financed its previous projects like national export funding agencies, or bilateral and multilateral international development agencies. The funding possibilities and challenges are among the areas of competitive advantage in some cases (see the case study below) and, in other cases, present obstacles that sometimes put a brake on the project. The purchaser makes further shortlisting, negotiations and selection of the final project marketer (or contractor). The World Bank and many international multilateral agencies demand competitive bidding with a transparent and fair selection of project marketers, while individual governments (e.g. concessional credit funds) demand a minimum (80%) purchases from their country. Notably, the Chinese government loan/grant-funded projects require 100% purchase from China.

8.4.1 Phases of Project Business

In analysing projects, researchers, managers and consultants distinguish between four distinct phases: pre-project, project negotiation, project implementation and post-project phases. These phases are different in the level of marketing, managerial, technical and relationship contents. Pre-project consists mainly of pure marketing components: marketing scanning; contacts; relationship building and maintenance; market, business ecosystem and network evaluation; building good references, etc. Project negotiation adds technical and technological components to the marketing components. Project implementation intensifies the two previous phases. With resources and activities on the ground, logistics, network management, relationships with local actors, NGOs, cultural challenges, etc. are the critical factors. When the project construction is completed, test-running, hand-over, turnkey-plus training of the staff of the purchaser and post-project guarantee period management are vital components. Many researchers have added the maintenance of "sleeping relationships" to the post-project phase. This means that the marketer keeps useful contacts with the network partners in order to be well placed to implement future projects (Cova & Salle, 2000; Hadjikhani, 1996).

8.5 The Relationship between Project Management and Project Business

We defined project business as the marketing and purchasing of a package of products, services, technologies and consulting to provide value to the purchaser and marketer. We stated that this B2B process usually takes several years from project scanning/problem recognition through information sharing, negotiation, contract signature, project installation/construction and completion to the post-project phase. To manage this complex business process and the relationships and networks that develop, the whole deal is designed as a project to define clear timelines, goals, follow-up, payments and certifications (see Figure 8.2 and the case study below). Each of the companies and organisations involved establishes its project management system. They develop project teams consisting of the relevant staff, resources and competences. They use project management knowledge, strategies and methodologies to ensure a successful project internally and in the relationships

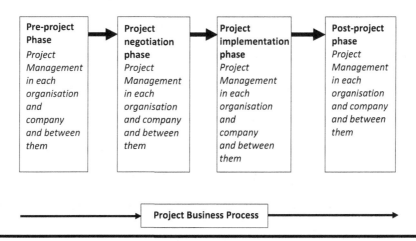

Figure 8.2   The relationship between project management and project business.

with the other parties (Dahlgren & Söderlund, 2001; Owusu et al., 2007; PMBoK Guide, 2017). A successful project will provide value to each party, and leave them with good references and relationships for future project success. As in the AEP case (see the case study below), regular meetings of the "AEP Project Management Committee" were attended by the Project Managers of IVO International, the Electricity Company of Ghana (ECG), the Volta River Authority (VRA), consultants and other relevant parties.

Project management is thus the knowledge, strategies and methodologies that project managers use to ensure the success of phases of project business. According to the PMBoK Guide (2017, p. 10): "Project management is accomplished through the appropriate application and integration of the project management processes identified for the project. Project management enables organisations to execute projects effectively and efficiently". As Cova and Salle (2008) emphasise, it is thus a component of the project business process, closely intertwined with all phases and aspects of the process and, therefore, critical for the success of the process, as illustrated in Figure 8.2.

As Figure 8.2 shows, we see project business as encompassing the whole process of a project deal. Project management ensures that specific activities are managed with concepts, principles and practices of project management. However, another set of overarching processes and activities are purchasing and marketing. The project marketer/turnkey or EPC contractor, suppliers, sub-contractors and consultants are selling/marketing their products, services and technologies, and the project recipient is purchasing them. Thus, from a B2B point of view, we defined project business in Section 8.1.2 from project marketing and project purchasing perspectives.

8.6 Risks and Project Business Strategy

It is a truism that entrepreneurship and business innately involve the ability to strategise against and manage risks. The B2B services company, like Tenece Company, that employs staff and markets projects, takes the risk of losing money if it does not win those projects. However, the risk is significantly increased in the case of large business construction and infrastructural projects for both the marketer and purchaser. When the marketer like IVO International decided to go for the AEP, it had to invest money in developing and marketing its project solution (see the case study below). As soon as IVO International won the project, it had to start to employ or retain the relevant staff, order supplies, use sub-contractors and establish a project management office as well as move staff and equipment to the project sites. Both IVO International and the Ghanaian project purchasers should have worked out their risk management strategies, as these are different for the purchaser and marketer, particularly in infrastructure and development projects (Parihar et al., 2015; Al Khattab et al., 2007; Sudirman & Hardjomuljadi, 2011; Thamhain, 2013; see the case study below).

In the case of the AEP, IVO International had its risks reduced largely by the concessional credit/loan (CC) funding from which it was paid directly by the creditor in Finland. However, during the project construction on the ground in Ghana, the company had to meet the turnkey conditions and assume some risks with ensuring that all the project plans were executed in the challenging project context of the large geographical area in which the electric infrastructure had to be constructed as well as the moderately unstable Ghanaian business and social environment at that time. Apart from the payment arrangements, the project management arrangement pre-empted and dealt with risks that arose (see the case study below).

Development projects and business projects in Africa have been shown in research to be different from pure business projects in other parts of the world due to the objectives of development, the African political, social and, economic context, political, social and economic instability, and the role of local actors and NGOs (Bayiley & Teklu, 2016; Famiyeh et al., 2015; Al Khattab et al., 2007; Zhang & Wei, 2012; Paribar et al., 2015). However, several studies have shown that good interactions and relationship management help to pre-empt and manage risks (Krane et al., 2012; Skaates et al., 2002; Owusu, 2002). In the final analysis, overcoming the risk factors is related to achieving the success of the project.

8.7 Success Factors for Systems and Project Business in Africa

Project business success is a complex, multi-faceted concept. Success can be analysed within a firm or from a single firm perspective, or from the perspective of all or many stakeholders (marketer, purchaser, supervising agency, local community, NGOs, other network members). It can also be analysed based on technical achievement, economic value over the lifetime of the project, relationship management, or residual relationships post-project and how they impact new project business opportunities. Also, the quality of references gained from a project, financial profit from the marketer perspective or value for money from the purchaser perspective can be the bases of analysing success (Jitpaiboon et al., 2019; Jugdev & Müller, 2005; Landoni & Corti, 2011; Pinto & Slevin, 1988a,b; Skaates et al., 2002; Yu et al., 2019). The type of project and the context of the project do significantly impact success according to the studies mentioned above. In the African context, among other factors, nature and strength of institutions; levels of corruption; competences of local consultants, staff, sub-contractors and suppliers; strength of economy; the spirit of collaboration from local stakeholders; and nature of funding do strongly impact the success of different types of projects from the various perspectives described earlier (Ahadzie et al., 2008; Damoah et al., 2018; Muriithi & Crawford, 2003). The study by Asiedu and Adaku (2019) shows that the failures to keep to planned cost calculations of government projects were due mainly to bad planning and supervision; a weak institutional and economic environment; and ineffective coordination among the project actors. The primary reason, by far was "poor contract planning and supervision" (p. 78). The study by Lundin et al. (2015) of state housing projects in Ghana found similar reasons. Thus, infrastructure projects involve institutional, political and non-business actors and add complex spices of their own (Bayiley & Teklu, 2016; Ikejemba et al., 2017a,b). For example, development projects financed through soft loans and some development aid are expected to be approached differently by all stakeholders (Owusu & Welch, 2007).

In the midst of all the foregoing factors, competing interests, and research analysing different perspectives, the majority of research emphasises achieving the goals set for the project. In that case, all network actors and stakeholders work towards achieving the purposes of the project. These are stated in the project documents, which detail responsibilities of the purchaser vis-à-vis the marketer, that is turnkey or turnkey-plus, project management and evaluation regulations, post-project phase activities, etc. Therefore, the views and concepts suggested in the preceding studies must be applied regarding the type and context of the project in order to decide the success or otherwise of project business.

8.8 Conclusion

In developed economies with established industry and manufacturing, systems and project business constitute at least half of the B2B market (Artto, 1998; Jalkala et al., 2010). It has become clear recently that project business has become a competitive B2B strategy in the international business of developed countries like Sweden that have high salaries and other costs against rising emerging market industries and the "factory of the world" (China) that can compete with lower prices. To compete better despite their high costs and thus higher pricing, B2B firms from developed countries use systems and project business strategies to create total solutions for clients, as well as try to get the commitment of the buyer through relationships, rather than transactions (Brady et al., 2005; Jalkala et al., 2010; Owusu et al., 2007; Skaates et al., 2002). This follows the general evolution of B2B marketing to be more competitive through greater servitisation, that is adding more service components to create projects and solutions that compete better through emphasising value, co-creation, etc. (Cova & Salle, 2008a,b; Grönroos, 2017). Therefore, African B2B companies should improve their understanding and formulate strategies for systems and project business that include increased servitisation. On the one hand, they can strategise better as project buyers (Owusu & Welch, 2007), and as suppliers, sub-contractors and consultants for projects to compete in local and foreign systems and projects opportunities (Owusu et al., 2007).

On the other hand, as African economies grow and industrialise, wages and costs will rise, and systems and project business will provide better competitive opportunities. While currently, African exports tend to be lower value raw materials and upstream products, revenues to the local economy can be increased as they integrate into systems, projects, solutions and servitisation, and thus move their participation in the value chain downstream, which is usually more profitable. Currently, African companies are not participating adequately in the large and technologically complex projects on the continent. Foreign companies from the rich Western countries and more developed emerging markets like Brazil, India, Russia, China and South Africa win the bulk of those projects.

Finally, the strategies of systems and project business espoused above share similarity with the concept of value to the B2B purchaser that we have mentioned previously in this and other chapters. Furthermore, they reflect an understanding of the marketing philosophies (see Chapter 1) and improved servitisation of B2B offerings that will enhance the competitiveness of African B2B firms.

Case and Exercise

IMATRAN VOIMA INTERNATIONAL AND GHANA'S NATIONAL ELECTRIFICATION SCHEME (NES)

The case that follows is provided as an illustration of an infrastructure project purchase and the marketing activities of a project marketer.[1]

GHANA'S ELECTRIC POWER PRODUCTION AND DISTRIBUTION AFTER INDEPENDENCE IN 1957

Ghana, the first sub-Saharan African country to gain independence from formal colonial rule in 1957, had at that time a trade surplus and moderate foreign exchange reserves as a result of the good world prices for its raw materials as North America, Europe and Asia rebuilt after the Second World War. However, infrastructure was non-existent in most parts of the country. Most of the population of nearly 6 million had no access to electricity. Diesel-powered generating stations existed only in the national and regional capitals and the mining towns. They produced small amounts of power that were connected only to the "Government Quarters" – initially the location

---

[1] Analyses, in this case, are based on the author's perspectives. Case information is based on interviews, documents provided by the interviewees and public documents available in Finland and Ghana.

of the homes of the colonial District Commissioner and civil servants – areas that also housed the hospitals, clinics and, in some towns, the Waterworks stations. Even in those towns, the majority of the native population did not have electricity. Therefore, building and connecting electric power were among the main plans of the post-independence government. Successful negotiation led to the completion of the Akosombo hydro-electric power project in 1965 with financing mainly from the United States, the United Kingdom and the World Bank. The Kpong Dam followed this project in 1977. The two dams and newer diesel-powered generating stations extended electricity to more towns and provided power for industry.

THE NATIONAL ELECTRIFICATION SCHEME (NES): PROJECT BUSINESS PHASES

PRE-PROJECT PHASE

Despite the new power generation facilities built in the first two decades after independence, with a fast-growing population, by 1988 only 33%[2] of the population had access to electricity.[3] The National Electrification Scheme (NES) was drawn up to provide electricity to all parts of the country within 30 years from 1990 to 2020. The programme grew out of the Economic Recovery Programme (supported and financed mainly by the World Bank and Western countries) which had resulted in improved economic conditions and further heightened the need for dependable and widespread electricity access.

The NES was planned in six 5-year phases from 1990 to 2020. Phase 1 consisted of the electrification of all district assembly capitals as well as all communities lying along the route of the extension lines that will take power to these towns.[4] Other communities that had earlier started their attempts at electrification (own funding through local contributions) were added to this phase. According to the plan, the aim of Phase 1 was to electrify the selected areas without regard to economic cost, but under a belief that as political and economic centres of the districts, their electrification could speed up economic development there. Phases 2–6 would first electrify those areas with a lower unit cost of service to maximise the economic benefits of the programme. Phase 1 was scheduled to cost US$99.2 million, and the total cost of the six phases was estimated at US$729 million in 1990. Demand for electricity was projected to rise from 826 to 1394 MW within the period of the scheme. At that time, the total installed generating capacity was around about 1060 MW, so the programme included the construction of new generating capacity of about 600 MW. This was projected to consist of combinations of gas turbines and oil-fired steam plants. Additionally, a third hydro-electric dam at Bui was planned.

Much of the financing of the NES was expected to come from foreign loans. The National Electrification Board (NEB) under the Ministry of Power was established to oversee the programme. NEB planned to prepare project specification packages about 5 years in advance of every project commissioning date. The package would include, among others, technical and geographical details of each project in the programme and preliminary cost. It will then be announced to prospective project marketers and presented to possible funding agencies for consideration.

The Government of Ghana (GoG) expressed its intention to encourage and help develop Ghanaian companies to participate in and benefit from the NES. Examples were mentioned as the timber industry for poles, aluminium and steelworks for cross-arms and transmission towers, and the ceramics industry for insulators. It also expressed its intention to help Ghanaian contractors to

---

[2] This was, however, an increase from the level of about 5% of the population at independence.

[3] See National Electrification Planning Study. Executive Summary, March 1991, 11.

[4] At the start of the scheme, 41 out of 110 district capitals were not connected to the national grid, and most did not have electricity.

participate in the implementation as sub-contractors or turnkey project marketers. Furthermore, GoG demanded effective programmes for the training of the staff of the NEB, the Volta River Authority (VRA, the parastatal company that operates the power production dams and stations) and Electricity Company of Ghana (ECG, the parastatal company that operates the supply of power to consumers), as part of each project package. Project marketers were, thus, required to transfer technology to the Ghanaian partners, both public and private that would participate in their project network.

In this case illustration, we focus on one of over ten main projects in Phase 1: the Ashanti Electrification Project.

IVO INTERNATIONAL AND ITS ROLE IN PHASE 1 OF THE NES

IVO International was a subsidiary of the Finnish company Imatran Voima Ltd (IVO); Finland's largest electric power company IVO was a parastatal that controlled about half of Finland's electric power market. The company had broad expertise in power production and distribution. Its power plants included hydro, nuclear, thermal and gas turbine units. Its plants generated about 6500 MW (six times Ghana's total generating capacity at that time), and the value of its power system was about US$6000 million (IVO International, Power Transmission and Distribution, 1993). IVO International was established in 1981 to internationalise IVO. It had since sold projects in over 50 countries, including Kenya, Tanzania, Egypt, Sudan and Ethiopia as well as Middle Eastern and South-East Asian countries. The company had an average turnover of about US$288.5 million and employed 1300 workers. Among the expertise, it offered its customers were feasibility studies; planning and engineering services; project management and supervision; construction management; operation and maintenance training; testing and commissioning services; and R&D and laboratory services. The company could sell turnkey, turnkey-plus, EPC or systems projects. At the time Ghana planned the NES, the Project Manager IVO International regarded his company as knowing Africa well. Through their project scanning activities, they had been looking at Ghana, after its successful Economic Recovery Programme (ERP) and relative stability. Thus, when the NEB completed the specification of Phase 1 of the NES and announced a call for bids in early 1990, the company was ready to go for it.

As part of its internationalisation strategy, IVO bought the Swedish company Trans-Electric (TE) in 1990 but left the management of TE intact to continue to internationalise on its own, and as a separate profit-making subsidiary. Both IVO International and TE were active in projects in Africa, among other developing areas of the world. While planning its strategy to sell its project to the NES, IVO International decided that it did not have enough relationship expertise of the Ghanaian project purchasing ecosystem. Fortunately, TE had already strategised for projects in Ghana. TE had already made visits to Ghana and gained some knowledge and experience of Ghana. Thus, the two companies decided to share knowledge of the Ghana project. They chose not to compete, but sell projects for different sections of the NES and to cooperate and share information. The two companies, however, negotiated their project marketing separately, as they were separate profit centres, each with its management in the IVO Corporation. As Table 8.1 shows, IVO International staff made two visits to Ghana before the final arrival of their staff to start project construction in 1993.

PROJECT NEGOTIATION PHASE

As TE, IVO's Swedish subsidiary had already started its project marketing activities in Ghana and made five visits, IVO International's first visit in 1991 had the advantage of information and contacts from TE. After their first visit to Ghana, IVO International invited representatives

Table 8.1   Visits of Ghanaian and Finnish Delegations to Finland and Ghana

Visits by IVO International Staff to Ghana		
Date	*Delegation*	*Reason for Visit*
Five visits before December 1991	Trans-Electric staff	To get to know the Ghanaian project purchasing ecosystem and negotiate for a project within the NES
December 1991	IVO International staff	To negotiate on AEP and to meet Ghanaian parties
March 1993	IVO International Project Manager	To complete arrangements for the start of work on AEP
August 1993	IVO International Project Manager and two other staff	To start construction and training
Visits of Ghanaian Delegations to Finland		
Date	*Members of Delegation*	*Reason for Visit*
Late 1991	Including Project Manager of NES	To meet Finnish parties (including funders) and present NES and AEP
July 1992	Delegation led by Minister for Power and including a Principal Secretary at MOP	To meet Finnish parties (including funders)
December 1992	A joint delegation of MOP and MOF	To finalise a loan agreement with FEC and final contract prices with IVO International

Source: Summary based on the interviews.

The name of the ministry was changed in 1993 from Ministry of Power (MOP) to Ministry for Mines and Energy (MOE).

of the Ghanaian project purchasers to visit their company in Helsinki, to aid the due diligence analysis of the Ghanaians,[5] and also to learn more about the financing opportunities from IVO's Finnish financing network. The Ghanaian official delegations included the Minister for Power, the Principal Secretary of the MOP and representatives from the MOF.

FUNDING THE PROJECT

The GoG and MOP stated that they expected the majority of financing for the NES to come from loans and aid from abroad. It was hoped that the World Bank and wealthy countries would provide CC/loans and donations. Considering Ghana's economic status at that time, concessional credit was allowed by the Organisation for Cooperation and Development (OECD). This meant that the wealthy OECD members (the USA, Canada, Western Europe, Japan, etc.) could provide funding that required at least 80% to be used for purchases from their companies.

---

[5] This is common practice with large projects. The purchaser visits the marketer's offices/factories to assure itself of the quality of work and management of the marketer, as part of the due diligence process.

In previous project marketing, IVO International had worked with the Finnish project and export financing network. Thus, during their first visit, they informed the Ghanaians of the possibility of funding from Finland. Thus, the three separate visits of Ghanaian delegations to Finland were mainly to discuss financing opportunities from the Finnish network of IVO International. The initial contract between the MOP and IVO International in December 1991 was to lay the bases for completing the financing negotiations. After the visit of the Ghanaian delegation for meetings with the Finnish financing network, a positive feasibility study and analyses were conducted in Ghana by a delegation of the Finns.

The CC) agreement was signed between Ghana's Ministry of Finance (MOF) on behalf of the Ghanaian purchaser and GoG, and the Finnish Export Credit Co. (FEC) in March 1993. FEC agreed to loan an amount of US$10.790 million or 85% of the contract price, to the MOF/GoG under the terms of the credit agreement to enable the MOP to pay part of the contract price. Additionally, the agreement mentioned that the Government of Finland through the Finnish International Development Agency (FINNIDA) had agreed to provide an interest subsidy to the FEC to cover the legal interest on the loan. Furthermore, the Finnish Guarantee Board (FGB) provided credit insurance to on behalf of MOF/GoG for the agreement. It was also mentioned that the MOF/GoG would cover the remaining 15% of the contract price. The credit agreement stated that the non-Finnish equipment, tools and components used in the contract must not exceed 20% of the contract price.

Furthermore, the MOF/GoG would pay a commitment fee of 1/2% p/a on the non-disbursed balance of the credit at any point in time from the date of the agreement. The GoG would also pay an arrangement fee of 3/8% flat of the credit payable 30 days from the date of issue of the credit. Furthermore, the MOF/GoG was to pay all taxes and documentary taxes, costs, charges or expenses incurred outside Finland in connection with the agreement as well as charges and fees related to the agent and the process agent. Besides, the borrower would pay to the lender all reasonable costs, charges and expenses arising out of the credit insurance which the lender incurs. The loan itself was to be repaid in 17 equal instalments every half-year starting April 15, 1995. The loan amounts were to be paid directly to the IVO International by the lender. Each payment was to be made after the delivery of a Certificate of Drawdown and a Promissory Note to the lender by the borrower.

In summary, the GoG did not have to pay any legal interest on the loan as it was covered by a development aid grant given through FINNIDA by the Government of Finland. Eighty-five percent of the cost of the project was covered by the loan, and 15% would be provided by the GoG. This amount would actually be paid in local Ghanaian currency and used by IVO International for its expenses in Ghana. At least 80% of the loan had to be used for purchasing the project of IVO International, that is Finnish products, technology and services. As the loan amount would be paid directly from FEC to IVO International, the company did not risk default from the GoG. In the final analysis, the various costs that the GoG could incur on servicing the loan amounted to about 1% interest rate (GoG's expenses that were not covered by the FINNIDA aid grant). IVO International was to be regularly paid a portion of the project price after the certification by the purchaser's consultant, Aikins Consulting of the half-yearly project report and the final payment after all parties accept the project completion report authored by Aikins Consulting.

THE ASHANTI ELECTRIFICATION PROJECT (AEP)

With a population of over 2.1 million, the Ashanti Region was the most populous and geographically third largest of the ten administrative regions of Ghana at that time. Apart from Accra, the country's capital city region, the Ashanti Region had always been economically, politically and socially most important in Ghana, producing cocoa, minerals, timber and food crops, and maintaining its rich old culture and traditions. The area of the AEP stretched out from the Ashanti Region into a part of the adjoining Brong Ahafo region. The total area of the project has a population (estimated in 1992) of about 101,000 and a population growth rate of 4.58% pa.

THE PROJECT CONTRACT

The initial contract for the AEP was signed between IVO International and the Ministry of Power (MOP), which was the supervising ministry for the NES on December 19, 1991. Amendments were later made to it on June 10, 1992 and on September 24, 1992. The total value of the project was US$11.8 million. About US$10.790 million was the CC loan from Finland, and the rest was the GoG part (see Table 8.2). The contract price consisted of a "Basic Scope" and a "Contingency" part. The MOP was the purchaser; however, the ECG was the "receiver", "owner" and "engineer" of the project. The signatory of the loan agreement was the MOF on behalf of the GoG. The contract was a turnkey. It consisted of the building of 178 km of 33 kV lines and 116 km of 0.4 kV lines. Also, 69 pieces of 33/0.4 kV distribution transformers and 2000 service connections were to be installed. The 33 kV lines were to be built using bare overhead lines and the 0.4 kV lines using ABC-AMKA (which was a new cable technology for Ghana). There were five main connection lines in all, as follows: Bechem – Tepa, Barekese – Mankranso, Kumasi – Manso Nkwanta, Obuasi – New Edubiase and Nkoranza – Sekyedumase. The project would thus electrify four district capitals, one major population centre and over 40 towns along the route of supply.

The responsibility of IVO International was a) design, installation and construction, material delivery as well as staff training: line survey for the 33 and 0.4 kV lines; detailed design of the 33 and 0.4 kV networks; material specifications, procurement and deliveries; complete construction and installation of the 33 and 0.4 kV networks including the lines, distribution transformers, service connections and connection points to the existing system; delivery of line tools and vehicles; and training of staff of the Ghanaian purchasers on the new technologies included in the project.

Table 8.2 Contract Price for AEP

Basic Scope	
Total US$	9.63 million
Total cedis	482.11 million
Total in US$	10.314 million
Contingency	
Total US$	1.44 million
Total cedis	556.84 million
Total in US$	1.554 million
Grand total: US$	11.86 million

Source: Ministry of Power Project Documents.

Around the same time, TE got a similar project, the Eastern Electrification Project, which covered parts of the Eastern region.

It was thus a turnkey contract. The contract required IVO International to perform the works stated under the supervision of a consultant engineer, the Ghanaian consulting firm Aikins Co, appointed by the MOP. The consultant engineer was to represent the interests of the purchaser, to supervise the observance of the contract and the quality of delivery, and to act as a contact person between the purchaser and IVO International. The agreement stated that IVO International would perform "all other things which may be reasonably implied and inferred from it", even if this was not explicitly stated in the contract documents.

PROJECT IMPLEMENTATION AND CONSTRUCTION PHASE

The nature of the project implied a big responsibility placed on IVO for its successful completion. In summary, there would be almost 300 km of different types of high to low tension lines; five separate lines that extended over mainly rural communities and tropical forests in an area where most of the land was owned by many families, clans, traditional chiefs and royals. The area was also in the most densely populated region of Ghana with valuable cash crops and timber reserves. Due to the firmly maintained traditional culture of the area, land encroachment was a tricky task because the government did not own the land nor did it have the right to nationalise or expropriate any lands without compensation. As an electric power extension project, access to the whole length of the land and adjoining areas was necessary to design, install and build the lines, transformer stations, individual transformers at different locations and extensions to homes in the communities earmarked to benefit from the project.

In reality, the initial contract signed in December 1991 was for a "Commitment, Memorandum of Understanding, and Non-Disclosure Agreement" to lay the groundwork for the loan agreement to be negotiated. After the loan agreement was signed in March 1993, detailed project negotiations continued. It was now that the technical and economic details of the project could be finalised. Talks on specific project technical, technological and management issues were undertaken until project construction was started in October 1993 and scheduled for 2 years. These included the mapping and delineation of the exact paths of the transmission lines, positioning of transformer stations, individual transformers, cable and connection components to consumers, agreements with Ghanaian sub-contractors and suppliers and the formation of the AEP Project Management Team (AEP PMT). Among others, IVO International surveyed the whole length of the lines, and with the help of the MOP, ECG, regional and district administrations, and local communities designed the extension of power to private and business customers in the communities. The assumptions and plans agreed to in the final contract did not, in several cases, hold during project construction. The consultant, Aikins Co., was present during the construction, followed and inspected the quality of materials and construction on behalf of the purchaser.

The AEP PMT consisted of representatives from IVO International, MOP, ECG, VRA and the Regional Administration. They met every month to discuss the progress of the work. The AEP PMT was critical for IVO to deal with land access problems and misunderstandings with Ghanaian parties. They were several problems with land access and even a few non-violent confrontations with landowners, farmers and property owners. In one case, a private educational institution whose land would be infringed upon by the line of the project initially refused to allow access to IVO International staff. All these problems were successfully dealt with through the intervention of the Ghanaian members/authorities of the AEP PMT. In several instances, they went directly after the meeting to the site of problems to meet aggrieved parties to provide the right-of-way and opportunity to IVO International to continue its work as soon as possible. Throughout the 2 years, such issues were speedily and successfully solved. Another advantage, in this case, was that the receiving communities were optimistic about the project, and both traditional and governmental conflict resolutions were used to deal with disagreements speedily, for example payment of compensation to landowners and traditional conflict resolution using community members and elders.

Monthly meetings of the PMT were officially minuted, mentioning problems and apportioning responsibilities for dealing them. Together with the half-yearly reports, they provide an excellent description of the implementation process.

Project construction was completed 2 weeks ahead of schedule in October 1995. The turn-key project was handed over after the certification that all constructed facilities were working. The lines were energised, and electrical power flowed to consumers. The consultant authored the Project Completion Report, Aikins Company, which was accepted by all parties, and the project construction phase was legally completed. This opened the way for payment of the final project prices to IVO International.

POST-PROJECT PHASE

A 1-year guarantee period was provided under the contract. During this period, IVO International had to be available to deal with any problems that arose and meet its guarantee obligations. A few minor issues came up and were dealt with successfully according to both sides.

POSTSCRIPT: FURTHER PROJECT BUSINESS OF IVO INTERNATIONAL IN AFRICA

Due to restructuring and privatisation in Finland, IVO was sold to Fortum Co., which then became Finland's new energy giant. Fortum Co. continued international project marketing in African countries. New electrification projects were sold to Ghana, Tanzania and Ethiopia, among others. Fortum later sold part of its foreign electrification division including the African part to El Tel Networks. El Tel Networks has added mobile telecommunication networks to its project portfolio, using a network of Finnish and Swedish suppliers and collaborators in mobile telecommunication technologies including Nokia Corporation and Ericsson Corporation, two of the world's leading mobile telecommunication B2B companies.

POSTSCRIPT: THE NES, ELECTRIFICATION AND ELECTRIC POWER INFRASTRUCTURE IN GHANA IN 2020

At the beginning of the NES, only 33% of Ghana's population had electricity from the national grid. Installed power production capacity has since quadrupled. The most recent analysis is summarised in Table 8.3. It shows that while Ghana's population more than doubled, the percentage connected to electricity rose to 83% (that is two and half times), which is among the better electrified African countries, as the sub-Saharan Africa average is below 50%. However, with a 10%–15% rate of growth due to economic and population growth, power production will have to double in the next 10 years to meet increased demand. The infrastructure also has to be continuously rehabilitated. In fact, due to the lack of rehabilitation and other problems, dependable capacity is lower than installed capacity. Severe power cuts were faced during 2014–2016 (the "Dumsor" period), which reduced the country's economic growth rate by half. While the situation has improved very much since 2016, planned and unplanned power cuts still occur.

Table 8.3   Ghana's Electric Power Infrastructure

Population in 1990	14.77 million
Population in 2019	30.41 million (that is, doubled in 30 years)
Electric power demand (2019)	Over 5000 MW
Total installed capacity (2019)	4399 MW (increased four times)
Dependable capacity	3842 MW
% of the population connected to the national grid	83% (has increased two and a half times) (the sub-Saharan African average is under 50%)
% increase in demand per annum	10%–15% (this means that demand will double in about 8 years)
% of renewables	Under 1%

8.9 Questions and Analysis

1. Who are the two main parties to the AEP? Explain why.
2. Draw the network for the AEP, showing all the parties on the Finnish and Ghanaian sides. The network figure should illustrate the nature of relationships between each party to the main parties
3. What are the reasons for the completion and hand-over of the turnkey project 2 weeks ahead of schedule? Do you think the AEP has successful? Why?
4. Describe and discuss the sole procurement decision for the AEP. Do you agree with the decision to accept the CC and its conditions from Finland? Do you think the project could have been purchased through a more advantageous contract for Ghana? Discuss your reasons.
5. What other optimal project business strategies could have been used for this project and why?
6. As a Ghanaian sub-contractor/supplier, describe a strategy for selling your own projects within the NES.
7. Considering the simultaneous vast improvements co-existing with lack of quality electrical power to some Ghanaians, what are your suggestions for raising both installed and dependable capacity to over 100% to eliminate power cuts and shortages?
8. Discuss the preceding questions similarly to other African countries.

References (Main Text)

Ahadzie, D. K., Proverbs, D. G., & Olomolaiye, P. O. (2008). Critical success criteria for mass house building projects in developing countries. *International Journal of Project Management*, 26(6), 675–687.

Al Khattab, A., Anchor, J., & Davies, E. (2007). Managerial perceptions of political risk in international projects. *International Journal of Project Management*, 25(7), 734–743.

Artto, K. A. (1998). Management of finances and profitability in project companies. *Project Management*, 4(1), 62–69.

Artto, K. A., & Wikström, K. (2005). What is project business? *International Journal of Project Management*, 23(5), 343–353.

Asiedu, R.O., & Adaku, E. (2019). Cost overruns of public sector construction projects: A developing country perspective. *International Journal of Managing Projects in Business*, 13(1), 66–84.

Bayiley, Y. T., & Teklu, G. K. (2016). Success factors and criteria in the management of international development projects. *International Journal of Managing Projects in Business*. DOI: 10.1108/IJMPB-06-2015-0046.

Bonaccorsi, A., Pammolli, F., & Tani, S. (1996). The changing boundaries of system companies. *International Business Review*, 5(6), 539–560.

Brady, T., Davies, A., & Gann, D. M. (2005). Creating value by delivering integrated solutions. *International Journal of Project Management*, 23(5), 360–365.

Cova, B., & Salle, R. (2000). Rituals in managing extra business relationships in international project business: A conceptual framework. *International Business Review*, 9(6), 669–685.

Cova B., & Salle, R. (2008a). Six key points to merge project marketing into project management. *International Journal of Project Management*, 23 (2005), 354–359.

Cova, B., & Salle, R. (2008b). Marketing solutions in accordance with the SD logic: Co-creating value with customer network actors. *Industrial Marketing Management*, 37(3), 270–277.

Cova, B., Mazet, F., & Salle, R. (1993). Towards flexible anticipation: The challenge of project marketing. *Perspectives on Marketing Management*, 3, 375–400.

Dahlgren, J., & Söderlund, J. (2001). Managing inter-firm industrial projects: On pacing and matching hierarchies. *International Business Review*, 10, 305–322.

Damoah, I. S., Akwei, C. A., Amoako, I. O., & Botchie, D. (2018). Corruption as a source of government project failure in developing countries: Evidence from Ghana. *Project Management Journal*, 49(3), 17–33.

Davies, A., & Mackenzie, I. (2014). Project complexity and systems integration: Constructing the London 2012 Olympics and Paralympics Games. *International Journal of Project Management*, 32(5), 773–790.

Famiyeh, S., Adaku, E., Kissi-Mensah, L., & Amoatey, C. T. (2015). Risk management for a tailings re-mining project in Ghana. *International Journal of Managing Projects in Business*, 8(2), 241–255.

Grönroos, C. (2017). On value and value creation in service: A management perspective. *Journal of Creating Value*, 3(2), 125–141.

Hadjikhani, A. (1996). Project marketing and the management of discontinuity. *International Business Review*, 5(3), 319–336.

Ikejemba, E. C., Mpuan, P. B., Schuur, P. C., & Van Hillegersberg, J. (2017a). The empirical reality and sustainable management failures of renewable energy projects in sub-Saharan. *Africa Renewable Energy*, 102, 234–240.

Ikejemba, E. C., Schuur, P. C., Van Hillegersberg, J., & Mpuan, P. B. (2017b). Failures and generic recommendations towards the sustainable management of renewable energy projects in Sub-Saharan Africa. *Renewable Energy*, 113, 639–647.

Jalkala, A., Cova, B., Salle, R., & Salminen, R. T. (2010). Changing project business orientations: Towards a new logic of project marketing. *European Management Journal*, 28, 124–138.

Jitpaiboon, T., Smith, S. M., & Gu, Q. (2019). Critical success factors affecting project performance: An analysis of tools, practices, and managerial support. *Project Management Journal*, 50(3), 271–287.

Jugdev, K., & Müller, R. (2005). A retrospective look at our evolving understanding of project success. *Project Management Journal*, 36(4), 19–31. DOI: 10.1177/875697280503600403.

Krane, H. P., Olsson, N. O., & Rolstadås, A. (2012). How project manager–project owner interaction can work within and influence project risk management. *Project Management Journal*, 43(2), 54–67.

Kuada, J., & Mensah, E. (2020). Knowledge transfer in the emerging solar energy sector in Ghana. *Contemporary Social Science*, 15(1), 82–97. DOI: 10.1080/21582041.2018.1510132.

Landoni, P., & Corti, B. (2011). The management of international development projects: Moving toward a standard approach or differentiation? *Project Management Journal*, 42(3), 45–61.

Lemaire, J. P. (1996). International projects' changing patterns: Sales engineers' changing roles. *International Business Review*, 5(6), 603–629.

Lundin, R. A., Tryggestad, K., Amoatey, C. T., Ameyaw, Y. A., Adaku, E., & Famiyeh, S. (2015). Analysing delay causes and effects in Ghanaian state housing construction projects. *International Journal of Managing Projects in Business*, 8(1), 198–214.

Mandják, T., & Veres, Z. (1998, January). The DUC model and the stages of the project marketing process. *In 14th IMP Annual Conference Proceedings* (Vol. 3, pp. 471–90). Turku School of Economics and Business Administration, Turku.

Muriithi, N., & Crawford, L. (2003). Approaches to project management in Africa: implications for international development projects. *International Journal of Project Management*, 21(5), 309–319.

Owusu, R. A. (2002). Project marketing to Africa: Lessons from the case of IVO Transmission Engineering and Ghana's national electrification scheme. *Journal of Business and Industrial Marketing*, 17(6), 523–537.

Owusu, R. A., & Vaaland, T. I. (2016). A business network perspective on local content in emerging African petroleum nations. *International Journal of Energy Sector Management*, 10(4), 594–616.

Owusu, R. A., & Welch, C. (2007). The buying network in international project business: A comparative case study of development projects. *Industrial Marketing Management*, 36(2), 147–157.

Owusu, R. A., Sandhu, M., & Kock, S. (2007). Project business: A distinct mode of internationalisation. *International Marketing Review*, 24, 695–714.

Paliwoda, S. J., & Bonaccorsi, A. J. (1993). Systems selling in the aircraft industry. *Industrial Marketing Management*, 22(2), 155–160.

Parihar, S., Bhar, C., & Srivastava, N. K. (2015). A project risk management methodology based on probabilistic and non-probabilistic approach: A study on transmission line installation projects. *Jindal Journal of Business Research*, 4(1–2), 27–45.

Pinto, J. K., & Slevin, D. P. (1988a). Project success: Definitions and measurements techniques. *Project Management Journal*, 19(1), 67–72.

Pinto, J. K., & Slevin, D. P. (1988b). 20 Critical success factors in effective project implementation. *Project Management Handbook*, 479, 167–190.

Project Management Institute (2017). *A guide to the project management body of knowledge (PMBOK Guide)* (6th ed.). Project Management Institute, Newtown Square, PA.

Skaates, M. A., Tikkanen, H., & Lindblom, J. (2002). Relationships and project marketing success. *Journal of Business & Industrial Marketing*, 17, 389–406.

Sudirman, W. B., & Hardjomuljadi, S. (2011). Project risk management in hydropower plant projects: A case study from the state-owned electricity company of Indonesia. *Journal of Infrastructure Development*, 3(2), 171–186.

Thamhain, H. (2013). Managing risks in complex projects. *Project Management Journal*, 44(2), 20–35.

Tikkanen, H., Kujala, J., & Artto, K. (2007). The marketing strategy of a project-based firm: The four portfolios framework. *Industrial Marketing Management*, 36(2), 194–205.

Yu, J. H., Yoo, S. E., Kim, J. I., & Kim, T. W. (2019). Exploring the factor-performance relationship of integrated project delivery projects: A qualitative comparative analysis. *Project Management Journal*, 50(3), 335–345.

Zhang, J., & Wei, W. X. (2012). Managing political risks of Chinese contracted projects in Libya. *Project Management Journal*, 43(4), 42–51.

References (Case)

Finnish International Development Agency (FINNIDA) (1993a). FINNIDA News 2(93), Helsinki, Finland.

Finnish International Development Agency (FINNIDA) (1993b). Finnish Development Assistance, Helsinki, Finland.

Finnish Guarantee Board (1993). Annual Report, Helsinki, Finland.

Finnish Export Credit (1993). Annual Report Helsinki Finland.

IVO International (1993a). Power is our strength. Helsinki, Finland.

IVO International (1993b). Annual Report, Helsinki, Finland.

IVO International (1993c). IVO International Review, Issue 2, Helsinki, Finland.

IVO International (1994). IVO International OY:n Toiminta Kehitysmaissa, Helsinki, Finland.

IVO International (1993). Power Transmission and Distribution.

Ministry of Fuel and Power (1991). *National electrification planning study, executive summary*. Accra, Ghana.

Interviews

Over 30 interviews with IVO staff, staff of Ghanaian Ministries and relevant agencies and parastatals between 1993 and 2001.

Chapter 9

Managing Business with Governments, Institutions and Non-business Actors

INTRODUCTION AND OBJECTIVES

As introduced in Chapter 1, governments, institutions and non-business actors are active in various ways in the business market. B2B companies have to do business not only with other profit-making B2B companies, but also non-profit institutions, government agencies, non-governmental organisations (NGOs) and even organisations that are hostile to their business. Governments, institutions and non-business actors have the power to create and change the business environment and make it enabling or disabling for business. At the same time, they are also buyers and sellers of products and services. Therefore, in this chapter, we will discuss the characteristics of these parties and how to do business with them.

At the end of this chapter, the reader will understand and be able to plan strategies for:

- The characteristics and roles of governments, institutions and non-business actors in the B2B market
- The modus operandi of governments, institutions and non-business actors in the B2B market
- The characteristics, roles and modus operandi of international institutions and non-business actors in the B2B market.
- How B2B actors should deal with the different faces of governments, institutions and non-business actors

9.1 What Are Institutions?

As defined in Chapter 1, many institutional actors (or political actors) are related to the role of governments at all levels from national to local. Others emanate from other established structures or pillars of society. As stated earlier, the definition of institutions ranges from narrow (formal only) to broad (both formal and informal). Formal institutions are legal governmental or societal institutions, while informal institutions are those that are not necessarily registered or legalised but that are legitimate and accepted by the whole or a portion of society, for example ethnic, cultural and religious institutions (Jansson et al., 2020; North, 1990, 1995; Scott, 1995; Williamson, 2000). Here, we will consider institutions as active parties in the B2B market. Therefore, we are focusing on institutions as organisations and agencies of government and other formal or established structures of society (Hadjikhani & Thilenius, 2005; Korsakienė et al., 2015; Meyer & Peng, 2005, 2016; Peng, 2002; see the case study below).

9.1.1 Roles of Institutions in the African Business-to-Business Market

Institutional actors have the following functions in business-to-business (B2B) market:

1. Creating and managing the B2B environment: Governments have the power to make and implement laws that form the business environment. Governments operate through many levels and agencies. In federal republics like Nigeria, state governments duplicate all the central/federal institutions. Still, the state governments supervise the local administrations, while the central/federal government institutions oversee all the states. In unitary states like Senegal, the central government appoints regional and local leaders. In the diffusion of power, some African unitary states like Kenya provide for local administrations elected by residents. In Ghana, the Local/Municipal/City Councils consist of both elected officials (to represent the democratic will of the people) and some appointed by the central government to provide the expertise of civil servants. These levels of institutions have the power to make and implement laws and regulations that impact businesses. Nwankwo (2000) emphasised the changes taking place in African markets and the role of government and institutional actors in determining the nature of the business environment.

2. Implementing government policy and regulating businesses: The level of political control versus autonomy of regulatory agencies in African countries varies. Some regulatory agencies are kept under political oversight to maintain the continued political control of areas of the economy that are considered crucial and that requires public management. Others are given broad autonomy in the constitutions of some African countries. The reason is to prevent political interference and allow them to make and implement regulations without political influence, to ensure the application of rational administrative and social principles. Regulatory agencies like the National Oil Companies in many African countries (Vaaland et al., 2012; Owusu & Vaaland, 2016) regulate the oil and gas industries. They can make some new regulations and propose others to the Legislature, Executive or other relevant higher arms of government. They supervise industries such as oil and gas, mining, and food and drugs.

3. In Chapter 1, we briefly discussed the position of government-owned companies as institutions. Whether they are institutions/political actors or parastatal companies depends on their statutes and modus operandi. In the last two decades of democratisation and privatisation in most African countries, governments have reduced their level of ownership in the economy. They have allowed some parastatal companies to pursue profit objectives and also

privatised some previously public services (Bayliss, 2003; Egan & Agyeman, 2019; Etieyibo, 2013; Mothusi & Dipholo, 2008). In many cases, the statutes nowadays require that the parastatal companies and even some central public institutions should financially break even through the use of some marketing and business principles. For example, passport and visa sections of the Ministry of Foreign Affairs in many African countries charge high enough processing fees to break even. Many parastatal companies have been given the mandate to make profits, thus to operate under business principles, while being partly or wholly owned by the government and, therefore, having powers and a position in the B2B market that private companies do not have. Such parastatals would make efforts to transform with business principles, which means that they should negotiate, purchase projects, and purchase and market goods and services with business principles.

We will continue to discuss institutions in two areas: (1) non-profit/idealistic/administrative/social objectives, and (2) marketing and management interactions and relationships.

9.1.2 Non-profit/Idealistic/Administrative/Social Objectives

Governmental institutions have mostly non-profit/idealistic, administrative or political objectives. Ministries and agencies of government are most often established for the sake of law-making, implementation, adjudication or citizen welfare. Such institutions, like the various levels of national and local administration, the judicial system, regulatory agencies, medical and educational services, exist primarily to ensure the proper functioning of the government and citizen welfare. They are funded mainly with government revenues in the form of taxes. The management and staff representing them are often trained in administrative or technical careers, and would not all be expected to have a business management or entrepreneurial approach. Their objectives/statutes are often written in the constitution/decisions of Parliament or Government Decrees. Thus, their administrative/political objectives are backed by the powers of the government.

9.1.3 How Should B2B Companies Manage the Idealistic/Administrative/Social Objectives of Institutions?

Managing the idealistic component of formal institutions is a complex managerial task for a B2B company. Every B2B company must at least break even to be able to pay interest on its credits and pay back its credits and loans. In the long term, a B2B company must pay dividends or profits to its owners or risk losing investments or share value. As the idealistic component of institutions is backed by government power and resources and meant to highlight the political/social interest, the B2B company should do the following:

1. Develop a strategy for managing relationships with institutions. The components of a good strategy should take cognisance of the business context of the company. In what industry is the company working? What are the institutions that legislate and supervise the industry? What are the current laws regulating the industry and what are the potential changes – considering the political and social dynamics going on in the country? How are other firms within the industry relating to the relevant institutions?
2. What are the legal lobbying channels, and how can they be used to improve the position of the company/industry? Lobbying, including contributions to political groups, is legal in most countries. However, in this regard, the individual company should be careful not to

politicise itself and risk being on the wrong side of political changes. Companies commonly complain in many African countries that changes of government or even Ministers within the same government can lead to drastic changes in policies that affect them negatively. If they are considered supporters of the opposition party, they may lose support and not get supply contracts. As a result, companies should instead join industry associations or groups to lobby and relate to institutions with the strength of numbers rather than individually. The nature of legal lobbying is affected by democratic conditions. In some African countries, an adequate level of democracy and the rule of law is maintained, while some are still controlled by "strongmen" or dictatorial Presidents or parties. In the former case, companies have been able to seek redress in the courts, while in the latter, being on the wrong side of the dictatorial President can put a company under severe negative pressure. Overall, the ability to effectively manage government relations is vital for a B2B company, particularly when expanding business activities abroad to countries or sub-regions characterised by political volatility and complexities (Boso et al., 2019; Parente et al., 2019).

3. Strategy components should also include strong corporate social responsibility (CSR) to the local community and nationally. The correct details of CSR will vary depending on the industry/local context. The first step is to be a good corporate citizen that is obeying the law and the regulations. The next step is showing responsibility by going beyond the demands of the law and contributing to social good through a commitment to the staff and the community (Kuada & Hinson, 2012).

4. Strategy components should include relationship marketing and management, as discussed in Chapter 2 and Part 4 of this book. The general principles of relationship management with institutions are the same as businesses. However, the B2B company should be careful with some of the purely business relationship management tactics, as some tactics that are accepted in business may be seen as unethical or corrupt concerning public officials. Well-run countries have codes of conduct for public officials that must also be observed by companies as "bribery", or unethical dealings are judged as perpetrated by both the giver and receiver (Sutherland, 2018; see the case study of this chapter below).

5. In the final analysis, an essential overarching strategy when dealing with institutions regarding their idealistic/administrative/social objectives is to combine business objectives with social goals. The B2B company should endeavour to achieve a balance between the two as the stability of the state and well-being of the society are foundations for the positive development of the business environment, which benefits all companies.

9.1.4 Marketing and Management Interactions and Relationships with Institutions

The core function of the government and its core institutions is to create an enabling environment for business. B2B is the backbone of all economies. It is at the level of B2B that business and entrepreneurial relationships and networks, ecosystems and clusters develop technologies, innovate, produce, transport, consult and deliver products to the consumer market. Therefore, an excellent B2B market environment is a critical link in economic development. Creating the environment for responsible and accessible banking and credit, entrepreneurial and innovative companies, free-flowing logistic infrastructure, and local and foreign investment is all about the B2B level. African institutions have recently changed and understood their roles as enablers rather than as sole providers of core infrastructure. Contrary to the immediate post-independent "socialist" dispensations and, for example, even the anti-business "revolutions" in many African countries, current

African governments and institutions have recently taken a more business-oriented approach and actively enabled business (Hansen & Collins, 1980; Nwankwo, 2000). This new attitude implies potentially active and mutually beneficial contacts between public institutions like the investment promotion centres, ministries responsible for trade/industry, export promotion organisations, industry associations, companies, and local and foreign investors.

In recent times, some level of the current administration and even business principles have been brought into state institutions to generate revenue to enable the state to continue to finance them. In the enthusiasm of independence, many of Africa's independence leaders announced "free" services to serve "the people". Policies of free health, free education, etc. were pushed by leaders like Julius Nyerere, Jomo Kenyatta, Kenneth Kaunda and Kwame Nkrumah. With mostly informal economies and fast-growing populations, most of these services and governments were going bankrupt in the 1970s and 1980s. Changes were forced even on the coup makers who also promised free services to the people, like the Provisional National Defence Council (PNDC) government in Ghana and Nigeria's military leaders (Hansen & Collins, 1980). In the new dispensation, many services such as education, health and administrative services have been allowed to charge break-even fees or have even been privatised. Former parastatals have been wholly or partly privatised. In Nigeria, the privatisation of the electric power function is still ongoing (Duruji & Okachikwu, 2017; Nigeria Electricity System Operator (NSONG), 2017). The National Electric Power Authority (NEPA) had a notorious reputation of incompetence, leading to a reformulation of its acronym[1] by the public and, finally, the desire of the government to improve power supply (Onuoha, 2010). As government institutions and former parastatals have been given business mandates, they are hiring business educated career management and adopting entrepreneurial approaches to their activities.

In their new break-even or business functions, government institutions are looking at improved ways of bringing in revenue to finance their services. They are strategising to charge competitive but socially oriented prices for their services. In many African countries, private companies are being allowed to compete to provide public goods and services like education and health, or public infrastructure like electric power and private road networks. (Egan & Agyeman, 2019; Etieyibo, 2013; Mothusi & Dipholo, 2008). Therefore, these institutions are having to deal with B2B companies with partly business principles while still having to fulfil their social/administrative/idealistic statutes or objectives. Thus, some institutions have become competitors with private companies. In many African countries, private educational institutions exist at all levels in competition with government educational institutions (Banya, 2008; Benbow & Thornton, 2013; Olaleye et al., 2020). Yet the government educational institutions are financed from the public purse. The government educational institutions have to promote and brand themselves and undertake marketing and management activities to compete, albeit they usually have an advantage due to tradition and government-supported facilities (Mogaji et al., 2020). In so doing, they might do business with B2B companies regarding various marketing and promotion activities around branding, advertising, improving services marketing, etc.

Institutions often have large budgets. Government institutions are responsible for purchasing large amounts for their use – supplies to the health system, education system, administration, etc. Institutions are large buyers of recurrent supplies such as stationery, vehicles, repairs and refurbishing of equipment services (see the case study below).

Governments and institutions are major buyers of infrastructure systems and projects (see Chapter 8). In so doing, they may use a business approach to the purchasing process itself and may

---

[1] Nigerians dubbed the National Electric Power Authority (NEPA) as "never expect power always".

employ consultants to help them. The prevailing regulations for purchase or procurement will still be an essential backdrop that companies should study (Owusu & Welch, 2007).

As African institutions are becoming more business and services marketing-oriented, and facing competition, some are understanding the importance of good services quality to customers, as well as branding. The old one-sided power of institutions towards the private sector is giving way to a more citizen/customer-oriented approach, and they are training their staff to become business and services marketing-oriented. This promises better interactions with B2B companies. In collaboration with marketing consulting companies, some institutions are running promotion and branding campaigns coupled with customer surveys.

Legislative and supervisory institutions are demanding more from B2B companies, particularly the big foreign and local investors that benefit from natural resources. Apart from stricter environmental and corporate responsibility rules, local content requirements are being imposed to ensure that these businesses are linked with and contribute to the local economy (Vaaland et al., 2012; Owusu & Vaaland, 2016). Local content is being considered in the purchase of projects, shortlisting bids and the total "value for money" calculations. The natural resource and other industries are being required to localise their value chains in Africa to benefit the local economy more.

9.1.5 How Should B2B Companies Manage Marketing and Management Interactions and Relationships with Institutions?

The project business case in Chapter 8 and the case illustrated at the end of this chapter show the massive potentials of the institutional market. At the same time, the changes, administrative /social objectives and sometimes corruption make it difficult for companies to do business with institutions (Sutherland, 2018). The case study presented at the end of this chapter shows that, in some cases, the honest, law-abiding company with the best supply or project bid may not necessarily win it. The question of when a bidder/project marketer should be "totally legal" or "join the bribery game" is tricky for companies that want to sell projects/supplies to these institutions.

In selling systems/projects to institutional actors, local content requirements are nowadays a vital part of the competitiveness of the bid. Thus, foreign project marketers should look for local partners to succeed (Owusu & Welch, 2007; Owusu, 2002; Vaaland et al., 2012). As discussed in Chapter 8, these local partners can be essential conduits to other valuable relationships and value chains.

Additionally, the new approach of institutional actors towards a more business and service orientation opens up markets for management consulting and marketing companies.

To manage the marketing and management interactions and relationships, B2B companies should:

1. Develop a strategy for dealing with institutional actors that takes cognisance of their different characteristics. Like every good strategy (as discussed in Chapter 2), it should integrate visions and missions, tactics and dynamics of the national institutional context. It should be able to follow and prepare for the changes that inevitably come with changes in power and control of formal institutions.

2. A component of the strategy should be to achieve a reputation for supporting the efforts of the institutional actors to improve the business climate and engender economic and social development. African institutional actors are developing massive and expensive

plans for infrastructural development, but lacking their funding. B2B companies can support these efforts in various ways financially, technically and socially and thus gain good reputations.

3. The strategy component of relationship marketing and management, as discussed in Chapter 2 and Part 4 of this book, should be adjusted here in the form of buying NGO products and services as part of a donation strategy, thus contributing to the good works of NGOs.

9.2 International Institutions and Non-business Actors in African Business-to-Business Markets

International institutions and NGOs have been very influential actors globally in the development of African B2B markets (Egan & Agyeman, 2019; Nwankwo & Richards, 2001; Teegen et al., 2004). There are two main reasons for this. First, African countries came out of colonialism poor, with very low literacy and lacking infrastructure. Therefore, foreign aid was from the beginning critical for development. As a result, institutions of donors such as the United States Agency for International Development (USAID) and the US Government; the Department for International Development (DFID) and the UK Government; the Federal Ministry for Economic Cooperation and Development and the German Government; and the Chinese Government donate and finance projects and are influential in the design, purchase and implementation of projects. Additionally, multilateral agencies like the World Bank, the United Nations (UN) with its many organs like United Nations Conference on Trade and Development (UNCTAD), and the African Development Bank, etc. have been important players in the development of African B2B markets.

Foreign development or crisis-oriented NGOs have been very active in African countries. The larger ones include the Red Cross/Red Crescent, Action Aid, Christian Aid, CARE International, Islamic Relief Worldwide, Oxfam, Doctors without Borders and Plan International. Others are pressure groups with narrower aims like Greenpeace and the Environmental Investigations Agency (EIA). They have the potential to wage campaigns against specific companies or nations (see Section 9.3 below on NGOs).

The national (bilateral), and international (multilateral) development agencies have over the years supported specific infrastructure and development projects such as roads, power stations, ports and schools in African countries. According to the OECD (2016), total development aid to Africa by the ten largest donors (the largest being the USA) in 2014 was US$ 54,193 million. They have given large sums for development and crisis-solving projects either directly to African governments or indirectly through NGOs involved in Africa. For example, Kujala and Owusu report the role of the US Government agencies in the African Growth and Opportunities Act (AGOA) and its consequent support for the internationalisation of African textile exports. Owusu and Welch (2007) analyse the role of Finnish and Australian concessional credits and aid for the implementation of infrastructure projects in Tanzania and Ghana. Also, Frimpong (2020) reports on the role of the German government aid in the establishment of a Volkswagen assembly plant in Ghana, which is part of the Ghanaian government's plans to support the growth of a motor vehicle industry in the country. The crisis-oriented NGOs often provide aid to the needy (individuals in crisis areas) and thereby contribute to the maintenance of economies. With big budgets for purchasing goods and services, they also become B2B parties (see below). The jury is still out on the impact of foreign aid on the development of African countries. Some research has found positive effects (Cai et al., 2018; Loxley & Sackey, 2008), while others find that the effects depend on the quality of African institutions, stability or how the aid funds are managed or implemented (Killick & Foster, 2007; Ouedraogo et al., 2020). Some other research claims that foreign aid has had negative impacts (Moyo, 2009).

The strategies with which African B2B companies should relate to and benefit from foreign aid are similar to those discussed in the preceding sections and subsequent sections for dealing with institutions and NGOs. However, our research has shown that African B2B companies have not succeeded very much in participating in projects funded by international agencies. One reason is that much foreign aid (donations and "concessional credits", that is low-interest loans in which the interest is covered by an aid/donated part from the foreign government) is tied to purchases from the donor's/creditor's country (Owusu & Welch, 2007; Owusu, 2002; see the case study in Chapter 8).

9.3 Non-governmental Organisations (NGOs)

NGOs are citizen organisations established to achieve idealistic, policy or societal objectives (Martens, 2002). The opportunity and "last straw" that wakes up many citizens to establish and support these organisations is the realisation of problems in society that have not been dealt with by state authorities. Local interest NGOs abound in Africa, from small, local socio-economic development-oriented groups like the Apire Town Development Committee (Apire TDC) to national and international pressure groups like Greenpeace (https://www.greenpeace.org/africa/en/). The former was established by the residents of Apire, in 1990 to achieve economic and social development of the suburb. On its part, the main objective of Greenpeace is to work towards a "green and just world".

9.3.1 Non-profit/Idealistic Objectives

The non-profit characteristic is a result of idealistic, policy or societal objectives of organisations. Some NGOs, for example, both Apire TDC and Greenpeace (https://www.greenpeace.org/africa/en/), may have been established by citizens or individuals specifically to interact with B2B companies in various ways.

Apire TDC is registered as a non-profit local citizens' development organisation whose aim is to bring socio-economic development to the suburb. Located as the last suburb on one of the minor roads leading out of Ghana's second-largest city Kumasi, Apire was not connected to the city's electricity or water supply at that time. Natives who made some money moved out of their ancestral homes to build in other suburbs that had electricity and water connections. After years of neglect by the City Council, the citizens decided to establish the TDC to collect and save contributions from citizens, lobby and negotiate for the provision of socio-economic infrastructure, including running water, electricity, schools and an industry that would provide jobs to the youth of the area. To achieve these objectives, Apire TDC stated that it wanted to interact with other organisations, companies, institutions, etc. In this endeavour, Apire TDC contacted government agencies, institutions, and other NGOs locally and abroad to collaborate, solicit donations and support from them, and to encourage companies to establish offices, factories or industries in the area to provide jobs for the inhabitants. Apire TDC offered free land and local support to companies that would want to establish in the area. Through its promotion activities, Apire TDC came in contact with a potential donor, the Finnish-Ghanaian Friendship

Association (FIGFA), which became a major sponsor that provided funding for extending water and electricity to the suburb.[2]

The idealistic goals of Apire TDC are positively oriented to companies and other B2B actors. Still, some other B2B actors like government agencies and the Kumasi City Council may experience the lobbying and pressure differently, as the modus operandi of Apire TDC is to negotiate, lobby and pressure them to provide resources that Apire TDC feels that the suburb deserves from these agencies and institutions.

The main objective of Greenpeace is to police the activities of companies to ensure that their actions do not contradict the organisation's definition of a "green and just world". This includes pressuring and, when necessary, confronting companies to stop them from undertaking activities that Greenpeace deems to impact the achievement of its objectives negatively. Besides, they lobby decision-makers (governments, government agencies and institutions) to make and implement "green" policies and to supervise them. Therefore, they impact the activities of B2B companies on this idealistic track both directly and indirectly. Indirectly through lobbying for policy and its implementation, their effect on the strongly profit-oriented company may be constraining, even though this should not necessarily be the case for all companies in the long term.

One can argue that the idealistic goals of non-business actors should, in the long term, create a more sustainable world, with sustainable resources that provide raw materials to businesses for a long time. Sustainability is to the benefit of all companies and society as a whole, and it can create a positive enabling environment for socially responsible companies. For example, the activities of Greenpeace and similar NGOs including the EIA in policing and confronting both legal and illegal harvesters of timber in Congo and Gabon, as well as lobbying and pressuring the governments both nationally and internationally, led to the decision by the Gabonese government to take steps to regulate the industry more actively in 2019. In the short term, this will reduce the available timber resources and negatively affect the whole timber value chain in Gabon. In the long run, it is likely to make the industry more sustainable and provide the impetus for the development of forest-related sectors as tourism and wildlife management (see Chapter 1).

9.3.2 How Should B2B Companies Manage the Idealistic Component of Non-governmental Organisations?

The idealistic component of NGOs often impacts the business environment overall, as NGOs lobby and pressure governments and institutions to make and implement regulations that set clear boundaries for business activities in their areas of interest (Navarro-Flores, 2011; Teegen et al., 2004). In some cases, specific companies may be targeted, thus negatively affecting their activities and exposing them to negative publicity and negative brand image. Greenpeace has been active in "naming and shaming" specific companies for activities that go against its objectives. In some cases, activists of Greenpeace have undertaken direct actions to stop business activities or make them more difficult.

Individually, B2B companies should study the NGOs that can impact them, understand their strategies and pre-empt being unexpectedly targeted. Some examples have shown that it is not

---

[2] FIGFA was formed by a group of Finnish students who wanted to support socio-economic development in Africa and five Ghanaian students in Finland including one native of Apire. Between 1994 and 1997, FIGFA raised support from the Finnish International Development Agency as well as through other fund-raising activities like selling Ghanaian food and products throughout the country. All in all, FIGFA provided ca. US$100,000 in support to Apire TDC.

enough to follow the laws and regulations as the company interprets them because NGOs like Greenpeace often interpret the existing laws to fit in with their objectives. While the B2B company may deem the offensive actions of Greenpeace as illegal, they would still be detrimental to the company's competitiveness in terms of wasting its time and resources, negatively affecting its image and creating legal costs. Apart from Greenpeace, other community NGOs have undertaken offensive actions against natural resources extraction companies in Africa, the most famous being the NGO actions in South-Eastern Nigeria against Royal-Dutch Shell, after years of environmental degradation caused by the company's activities and perceived lack of benefits to the local communities, in spite of many years of oil extraction and profits by Royal-Dutch Shell (Taylor, 2019).

On the assumption that B2B companies follow the law and regulations in their industry, they need to manage relationships with NGOs. Some suggested ways to pre-empt and deal with problems are listed below:

1. Develop a strategy for relationships with NGOs. The components of a good strategy should take strong cognisance of the business context of the company. What industry is the company working in? How sensitive is the sector concerning existing and potential ideals of NGOs? A company in natural resource extraction is often a particularly sensitive industry that should have a clear strategy and be dynamic in reformulating components of the strategy to meet new needs and challenges.
2. Strategy components should include strong CSR to the local community and nationally (Kuada & Hinson, 2012). The correct details of CSR will vary depending on the industry/local context. An essential element of CSR that has recently become evident from the case of Royal-Dutch Shell and others is towards the local community where the business is located. It should be surprising to the researcher or observers that Royal-Dutch Shell continued to exploit onshore oil reserves in Eastern Nigeria for over 40 years without significant benefit to the local community and caused environmental damage through oil spillage into streams and the creeks that the local people depended on for fishing. Moreover, the company continued to flare gas for over 30 years, which caused acid rain and is accused of engaging in corruption (Payne & Falush, 2015). This example shows that it is vital to consider the interests and needs of the host community, apart from the company's profits, obeying national laws and trying to achieve national level CSR.
3. Strategy components should include relationship marketing and management, as discussed in Chapter 2 and Part 4 of this book.

9.3.3 Marketing and Management Interactions and Activities of Non-governmental Organisations

As NGOs undertake activities to achieve their objectives, they undertake many traditional marketing tasks (Seu et al., 2015). As non-profit organisations, they were not established to sell products/services for profit. However, they sell to raise funds for their activities. As we are focusing on B2B in this book, we are interested in the products and services they sell to other B2B actors. Other B2B parties are an important market in this situation as they are potentially large buyers. NGO products/services are of many kinds. For example, Apire TDC got traditional artefacts and handicrafts from citizens to raise money to achieve its objectives. Companies, institutions and other organisations were approached to buy these artefacts at "donation rates", that is to pay very high prices, much of which were donations to Apire TDC. Similarly, the Finnish-Ghanaian Friendship Association had to raise "counterpart funding" (20% of the value of the project), to get foreign aid support from FINNIDA to support Apire TDC. Counterpart funding was generated partly through the sale of Ghanaian cultural artefacts to B2B actors (among others) at donation prices in Finland. This development/marketing-oriented approach of NGOs is similar to the case described in the study of Navarro-Flores (2011) and conceptualised by Seu et al. (2015).

Promotion activities (information, personal selling, advertising, branding, etc.) are a significant marketing activity undertaken by NGOs. The B2B aspect is to build and manage relations with likeminded NGOs, companies, governments and institutions, to inform and to develop a positive brand image. These are necessary to attract funding from companies, institutions, governments (foreign aid), etc. (Venable et al., 2005; Vestergaard, 2008; Voeth & Herbst, 2008). Owusu-Frimpong and Mmieh (2007) indicated in a study carried out in the Eastern Region of Ghana that some NGOs help Rural Community Banks (RCB) to improve their service delivery to the smallholders in the rural communities. Such NGOs gather the smallholder groups and organise educational campaigns to educate the rural folk on how they can access the services of the banks in their locality. They partner the banks to monitor how the loans given them are being used to avoid diversification of funds. The NGOs are given donations by the banks to support their activities. In turn, the NGOs promote the banks to the rural people to patronise the services of the banks. This is aimed at assisting the rural populace to improve their lives as well as the banks to achieve their business objectives (Owusu-Frimpong & Mmieh, 2007).

NGOs undertake the purchasing of products/services needed for their own internal and external activities. NGOs like the Red Cross/Red Crescent and doctors without borders have large purchasing needs when they go out to address crises. The Red Cross purchases goods and services to the tune of over USD 2000 million yearly (ICRC, 2019). There is ample scope for a large number of African companies to supply the Red Cross products/services it needs to deal with the many crises that arise on the continent. In addition to products/services purchased, transportation and other logistical services are critical for the success of the Red Cross, and these are often purchased locally in Africa.

9.3.4 How Should B2B Companies Manage the Marketing and Management Interactions and Relationships with Non-governmental Organisations?

From the above, B2B companies interact with NGOs on several marketing and management fronts, and these should be dealt with in the following ways for competitive success:

1. Develop a strategy for marketing to NGOs. A good number of B2B managers do not realise the size of the NGO purchasing market. The US$2000 million budget of the International Committee of the Red Cross (ICRC, 2019) does not take into account all the national and local purchases done for the Red Cross/Red Crescent around the world. Non-business parties often have a different purchasing process and skills than business actors. It is likely that they may not have an equally hard-bargaining and professional approach as business actors, and this can be taken into account in the strategy. The quantity of their buying cannot often be planned as many of their purchases are targeted to crises that suddenly arise. It is, therefore, more likely for them to return to established suppliers and purchase from them as that will shorten the process.

2. Additionally, due to logistical challenges, they would instead buy from as near the place of the crisis as possible. Therefore, while an old supply relationship and the need for speed are

likely to work to the advantage of old suppliers or established relationships, the need for speed and of delivery could simultaneously benefit of local African suppliers. While the B2B marketer cannot predict crises, there are often signs or warnings of emergencies like hurricanes, floods or civil wars. These can be used to position the marketer in terms of production, logistics and relationship management to continue to be the preferred supplier.

3. Local NGOs like Apire TDC can be more easily targeted by African project marketers as their purchases will be planned in relation to their socio-economic development objectives and the funding they receive for that. However, they may also sometimes be in the situation of buying to deal with crises as in the case of the Red Cross discussed previously. Over the years, Apire TDC purchased projects with the funds received from FIGFA and other sources to the tune of about US$150,000. Apire TDC purchased electricity, running water and other socio-economic infrastructure as projects from local project marketers.

4. It was mentioned previously that the contents of strategy should include strong CSR to the local community and the host nation. This could be part of a strategic element of the right brand image that many NGOs consider when purchasing from companies. Idealistic NGOs like the Red Cross and Greenpeace follow established certifications of companies as "responsible" or not. Individual NGOs may have their own standards that a marketer should consider when relevant. However, there are established ISO and other international standards of responsible corporate practice that a company can use to position itself universally as a responsible actor.

5. The relationship marketing and management aspects of strategy, as discussed in Chapter 2 and Part 4 of this book, should be targeted to buying NGO products and services as part of a strategy of donating to support the social development objectives of NGOs.

9.4 Conclusion

While they are not founded as for-profit actors, governments, government agencies, institutions and NGOs play essential roles in the B2B market. Governments, their agencies and institutions have the power to create the enabling environment for business and therefore also the "power to create a disabling environment" from the perspective of a business. As the B2B market is the primary market that develops, produces and distributes goods and services that provide value to both B2B and B2C markets, the power of the non-business actors is critical for all business actors. Besides, governments, government agencies, institutions and NGOs undertake marketing activities in the form of marketing and purchasing goods and services. In these activities, they are increasingly learning to use marketing and management strategies that have been developed by for-profit firms to break even, meet revenue goals, and provide value and service quality to their publics. They are also increasingly undertaking promotion activities like branding, advertising and public relations to establish good brand images among their publics. Parastatals are being asked to justify their existence by breaking even, making profits and competing against private firms. Increasing privatisation in many areas of the economy that was previously reserved for the government like education, water, electricity and roads is creating direct competition between private B2B firms and the parastatals, government agencies, institutions and NGOs. The budgets of these actors for purchasing goods and services are big. Governments, their institutions and agencies buy most of the infrastructure of African countries. They also buy large quantities of capital and recurrent needs such as office equipment, furniture and supplies to offices, hospitals, educational institutions, etc. They are, thus, a potentially lucrative market for many B2B firms.

However, each of these actors is different in their characteristics, capabilities and processes. Thus, B2B firms dealing with them should analyse each of them, analyse the context of interactions with them and plan appropriate strategies for marketing, purchasing, negotiating, lobbying, collaborating and coopeting.

Case and Exercise: How to Improve Public Purchasing and Save Money for the Government? The Case of Ghana's National Procurement Policy

INTRODUCTION

Through the Public Financial Reform Programme (PUFMARP), the Government of Ghana (GoG) identified problems in public procurement. These included (1) unclear public procurement policy, (2) lack of a comprehensive law for the public procurement system, (3) absence of an integrated governmental institution with the expertise to supervise public procurement, (4) lack of transparency and competition in the award process and perceived corruption in the award of contracts, (5) absence of an independent appeals process with the power to address complaints from aggrieved bidders and provide corrective remedies, (6) lack of rules and authority to dispose of public assets, and (7) absence of clearly defined roles and responsibilities of individual procurement entities (Government of Ghana, 2003a; World Bank, 2000).

To eliminate these problems, the government decided to enact a comprehensive public procurement law. The Public Procurement Act 2003 (Act 663) was passed in 2003 (Government of Ghana, 2003a). The Act required the government to take appropriate administrative and institutional arrangements with an oversight body to superintend the public procurement system. The new rules were expected to promote the use of public procurement as a tool for national development. They would harmonise the application of procurement-related rules with international conventions and treaties. They were also expected to foster competition, efficiency, transparency and accountability in the public procurement process. They would be equal access for any local company to participate in the public procurement process (Osafo-Marfo, 2003; PPA Manual, 2020).

ESTABLISHMENT OF THE GHANA PUBLIC PROCUREMENT AUTHORITY (PPA)

The Act established the Public Procurement Authority (PPA) with the following objectives:

- To streamline and integrate public procurement
- To advise government agencies on procurement
- To centralise some procurement processes, to negotiate and purchase to the benefit of government entities and save money.

According to Addai-Donkor (2014) and PPA Manuals (2020) since its inception, the Act has made significant impacts on the public procurement practice in Ghana. Notable among these achievements are said to be

(1) The professionalisation of procurement practice with the establishment of the procurement class in the public service, (2) visibility of the procurement function in government agencies, (3) establishment of procurement structures, (4) increased competition and transparency in the contracting process, (5) established appeals procedures, (6) opportunities for continuous professional education through PPA facilitated capacity building activities, (7) an informed private

sector through yearly interactions with government agencies, and (8) improved records management in public procurement. In summary, the public procurement processes have been streamlined, thus engendering a high level of sanity in the procurement process (Addai-Donkor, 2014; PPA Manuals, 2020).

The PPA has faced various challenges since its establishment. Preparation and submission of procurement plans by public institutions to the PPA is a requirement per Section 21 of the PP Act 2003. Most government institutions have not been meeting this legal requirement. Thus, the budget releases have been erratic and inadequate, making the implementation of the plans difficult. Many institutions have been unable to honour their payment obligations under contracts; thus, they have faced threats of lawsuits leading to a lack of trust and confidence in the public procurement system. The resultant effect is that suppliers, contractors and project marketers incorporate in their prices the cost of capital that eventually compromises on the principle of efficiency and value for money (Addai-Donkor, 2014). Additionally, Addai-Donkor (2014) stated that some heads of government institutions do not allow procurement officers to make procurement decisions based on expertise and procurement principles. Closely related to the above is the lack of procurement practitioners in public institutions with the requisite knowledge and experience to handle procurement issues.

Several studies have shown that interferences in the procurement process from politicians, public officials and the general public is common. This puts pressure on procurement practitioners and limits their ability to run fair, transparent and competitive tendering. From advertisement through evaluation and award, politicians, technocrats and other members of the public, demand or offer bribes that challenge the transparency, competitiveness and overall sanctity of the procurement process (Addai-Donkor, 2014; Aning & Edu-Afful, 1992; Thai, 2008). Procurement corruption within public institutions is dominant at the procurement planning and final account preparation stage, thus making the process prone to manipulation and fraudulent deals (Ameyaw et al., 2013). According to Appiah (2014), like all other government institutions, the PPA has suffered its own logistical and other financial challenges. Thus after 10 years, it had yet to establish offices as required across the country to monitor public procurement activities. Another major challenge that confronts the PPA, regarding the effective implementation of Act 663 is ensuring that the planned procurement activities of government institutions are linked to budget releases for effective fiscal discipline. Additionally, the PPA lacks funds to undertake its task of training procurement officers in government agencies.

SUPPLIER/PROJECT MARKET PERSPECTIVE

The Public Procurement Act (663 of 2003) states that in furtherance of its objectives, the Authority shall assist the local business community in becoming competitive and efficient suppliers to the public sector. This provision places an obligation not only on the Authority but also on other government institutions to ensure that their conduct encourage Ghanaian suppliers and project marketers to succeed in the public procurement process.

Baffour (2014) lists the following as some of the challenges that confront Ghanaian suppliers and project marketers in the public procurement process:

(1) Obscure publication of tender invitations by government institutions and agencies; (2) procurement entities of government institutions intentionally create shortages of tender documents, thus preventing some prospective suppliers from being part of the procurement process. It is believed that this is done to give advantages to other suppliers, thus implying corruption of the process; (3) inappropriate procurement packages, that is unclear descriptions of the goods, services and projects to be purchased, which may be due to lack of professionalism or attempts to favour

some suppliers who might be provided more details privately; (4) undue delays of the procurement process; (5) refusal to notify suppliers of the outcome of a tender process, in contravention of section (29) (5) of the Act, which reduces their ability to make appeals or take legal action; (6) non-opening of tenders at the originally publicised date and time, which may be due to lack of professionalism or attempts to reduce public scrutiny of the process; and (7) delays in payment for accepted goods and executed jobs.

The fact that ACT 663 permits sole sourcing has raised concerns in various circles over the selection and approval of suppliers when it is used. The perception has been that these sole sourcing decisions are often skewed to benefit some favoured suppliers without necessarily considering the value for money of the deal. Sole sourcing from a supplier without competition is subject to a specific approval being granted by the Public Procurement Board. Single-source procurement may be appropriate when (1) the purchase is for urgently needed products, provided this is restricted to the minimum quantity to meet the urgent need until purchase by other methods can be fulfilled; (2) the requirement can only be supplied by one source for physical, technical or policy reasons; for example, the required equipment is proprietary and obtainable only from one source; and (3) when national security (non-economical) considerations are paramount (PPA Manuals, 2020). For infrastructure project purchases, single-source procurement may be appropriate when (1) the purchase is for urgently needed remedial works, provided this is restricted to the minimum requirement to meet the urgent need until a procurement by other methods can be fulfilled; and (2) the works can only be provided by one source for physical, technical or policy reasons, e.g. requiring the use of proprietary techniques that are obtainable only from one source (PPA Manuals, 2020).

As implied by the PP Act 663, the collective and collaborative effort of both the procurement and supplying entities, working under the supervision of the board, in satisfying the needs of each other will be to the mutual benefit of all stakeholders.

RECENT PROCUREMENT-RELATED SCANDALS

Despite the promulgation of the Public Procurement Act 2003 (Act 663), there are still reported procurement infractions resulting in considerable losses to the country and loss of public confidence in the procurement system and government institutions generally.

- The "Contract for Sale" documentary made by Investigative Journalist Manasseh Azure Awuni featured the then Chief Executive Officer (CEO) of the PPA allegedly reselling government contracts through his own private company, "Talent Discovery Limited (TDL)", and thus indirectly profiting from contracts awarded by his own PPA, and taking bribes for the award of public contracts (https://www.youtube.com/watch?v=TFhYPuRdg8s). The CEO was subsequently sacked by the President of Ghana (Business and Financial Times, 2019; Africafeeds.com, 2019). The criminal indictment is still going through the courts at the time of this manuscript. Based on reports provided by the CEO and the PPA, he had been earlier cited for "excellence" and received various national and international awards at the same time that he had allegedly planned and executed corrupt practices (https://www.youtube.com/watch?v=TFhYPuRdg8s). A year earlier, the CEO had received an award for "Outstanding Contribution to Public Procurement" and "Top 50 Africa Public Sector Leader" at the "African Network of Experts in Public Procurement" (PPA, 2018). He was specifically named and praised by the President of Ghana in a speech, and by the Minister for Finance in a budget statement to Parliament for "high achievements and saving money for Ghana" (https://www.youtube.com/watch?v=TFhYPuRdg8s).

- The Auditor General of Ghana stated in an interview for the documentary that procurement-related corruption was the most common item of corruption usually reported by his office and caused massive losses to the taxpayers every year (https://www.youtube.com/watch?v=TFhYPuRdg8s).
- The former Electoral Commissioner (Head of Ghana's election administration body), and two of her Deputies were impeached and removed from office in 2018 due to allegations of improper procurement procedures leading to losses to the Government of Ghana (Frimpong, 2018). The sacking was challenged but declared legal by the Supreme Court of Ghana (Ghanaweb.com, 2019a,b).
- A former Director-General of the National Communications Authority (NCA), the former Board Chairman of the Authority, and a former National Security representative have been charged and sentenced for stealing, using public office for personal gains, and wilfully causing financial loss to the state in respect of the purchase of equipment worth US$4 million to, among others, assist in the fight against terrorism. This scandal resulted in a US$4 million financial loss to the state (Ghana Legal Information Institute, 2020).
- The former Director-General of the Social Security and National Insurance Trust (SSNIT) (which manages the pensions of government workers and other companies) and four others are in court over the award of $72 million Operating Business Suite (OBS) contract for the development of the software to help SSNIT in its dealings with pensioners (Ghanaweb.com, 2019a,b; GBC, 2019). They have been charged with conspiracy to wilfully cause financial loss to the state, in contravention of Public Procurement Act; possession of forged documents; and authoring forged documents, among others. The defendants state that they are innocent, but the Supreme Court of Ghana dismissed their application challenging an earlier decision of a High Court that went against them. The case was still in court at the end of August 2020.
- A forensic audit alleged that the former Executive Director of the Ghana Standards Authority (GSA), took a US$1.2 million kickback from a construction company, the firm that he awarded a contract to build a new training school and hostel facility for the GSA. The report further indicted the former GSA boss for misappropriating US$820,000 and has recommended that he should be made to account for them. The Head of Procurement at GSA, was also cited for procurement irregularities at the cost of US$1.5 million. The forensic audit report also cited former heads of six other state-owned agencies, for corruption and causing losses to the state (Ghanaweb.com, 2018).
- The management of the Ghana Cocoa Board (COCOBOD) is accusing the previous management of the board of awarding contracts for "ghost" "cocoa roads" in the country. It said an interim audit on the contracts for the roads conducted by technical consultants had revealed that many of the roads for which contracts were awarded and paid were non-existent or the contract prices were inflated (Business Ghana, 2017).
- The Government of Ghana has ordered a probe into an alleged €5 million bribes paid to a close relative of a top government official (acting as Agent) by Airbus to sell planes to Ghana. The European planemaker Airbus settled with European and US regulators to discontinue legal measures against it concerning alleged bribes paid to a close relative of "a top Ghana government official" (acting as Agent) to sell its aircraft to Ghana. Ghana is one of several developing countries where bribes were allegedly paid between 2009 and 2015 (Reuters, 2020). Holmey (2020) states that this "top government official" is a former President of Ghana.

CONCLUSION

The Government of Ghana (2003a,b) has formally passed the necessary laws and amendments to stop corruption in public purchasing and created the PPA to oversee this. The Public Procurement Law 2003 Act 663 states clear structures and processes that, if followed with integrity, should streamline public purchasing, remove corruption and save money for the country. It is, however, challenging to achieve the lofty aims of the Public Procurement Law 2003 (Act 663) when top government officials including a former President, CEO of the PPA itself, and Chairperson of the Electoral Commission are accused of blatant corruption, flouting the law and causing massive losses to a country where public infrastructure is lacking or inadequate to large portions of its 30 million population. Based on the above, one can argue that the passage of the Public Procurement Law and its implementation has not made any impact in curbing corruption in public procurement in Ghana (Ameyaw et al., 2012).

Overall, according to the Corruption Perceptions Index (CPI) report by Transparency International, Ghana's corruption perceptions score (at 41 in 2019) is above the sub-Saharan African average of 32 (which is thereby perceived by its citizens as the most corrupt region in the world). In other words, Ghana is quite corrupt by world standards, but among the less corrupt African countries (Transparency International, 2019).

From a regional perspective, Africa is the most corrupt part of the world. Considering the corruption scandals proved and alleged in the foregoing section, the fact that Ghana is among the less corrupt African countries is indeed a sad commentary on the quality of African public institutions, business environment and society.

CASE DISCUSSION

1. List and discuss the role of different formal and informal institutions in your country. How important do you think are the informal institutions in the business environment of your country?
2. How would you characterise the role of formal institutions in supporting or hindering B2B companies in your country? How can their contributions be improved?
3. How active are your local NGOs in relation to B2B companies?
4. How active are international NGOs in your country in relation to B2B companies?
5. What kinds of business opportunities do government institutions, parastatals and NGOs provide to B2B companies in your country?
6. Describe the organisation of government purchasing in your country. Is it well organised? How does it compare to the case of Ghana described above?

References (Chapter)

Banya, K. (2008). Globalisation, knowledge economy and the emergence of private universities in sub-Saharan Africa. *Research and Praxis*, 6(1), 231–259.

Bayliss, K. (2003). Utility privatisation in Sub-Saharan Africa: A case study of water. *Journal of Modern African Studies*, 41, 507–531.

Benbow, T., & Thornton, R. (Eds.). (2013). *Dimensions of counter-insurgency: Applying experience to practice.* Routledge, Abingdon.

Boso, N., Adeleye, I., Ibeh, K., & Chizema, A. (2019). The internationalisation of African firms: Opportunities, challenges, and risks. *Thunderbird International Business Review*, 61(1), 5–12.

Cai, J., Zheng, Z., Hu, R., Pray, C. E., & Shao, Q. (2018). Has international aid promoted economic growth in Africa? *African Development Review*, 30(3), 239–251.

Duruji, M. M., & Okachikwu, D. (2017). Privatisation of the National Electric Power Authority (NEPA) and the reform of the electricity sector in Nigeria. *Handbook of administrative reform theory and practice in Nigeria*. Parakletos Immunis Drive, Enugu. ISBN: 978-978-956-7935.

Egan, M., & Agyemang, G. (2019). Progress towards sustainable urban water management in Ghana. *Sustainability Accounting, Management and Policy Journal*, 10(2), 235–259.

Etieyibo, E., (2013). Preliminary reflections on the privatisation policy in Nigeria. *African Journal of Economic and Management Studies*, 4(1), 144–152.

Frimpong, E. D. (2020, August 3). Akufo-Addo unveils first VW vehicles assembled in Ghana. Retrieved May 8, 2020, from https://www.graphic.com.gh/news/general-news/akufo-addo-unveils-first-vw-vehicles-assembled-in-ghana.html.

Greenpeace Africa. (2020, August). Retrieved August 8, 2020, from https://www.greenpeace.org/africa/en/.

Hadjikhani, A., & Thilenius, P. (2005). *Non-business actors in a business network: A comparative case on firms actions in developing and developed countries*. Elsevier, Amsterdam, New York etc.

Hansen, E., & Collins, P. (1980). The army, the state, and the 'Rawlings Revolution' in Ghana. *African Affairs*, 79(314), 3–23.

International Committee of the Red Cross (ICRC). (2019). Finance and administration. The financial year 2018, 547–609.

Jansson, A. H., Savikko, N., Kautiainen, H., Roitto, H. M., & Pitkälä, K. H. (2020). Changes in prevalence of loneliness over time in institutional settings, and associated factors. *Archives of Gerontology and Geriatrics*, 89(5), 104043.

Killick, T., & Foster, M. (2007). The macroeconomics of doubling aid to Africa and the centrality of the supply side. *Development Policy Review, 25*(2), 167–192.

Korsakienė, R., Diskienė, D., & Smaliukienė, R. (2015). Institutional theory perspective and internationalisation of firms: How institutional context influences internationalisation of SMES. *Entrepreneurship and Sustainability Issues*, 2(3), 142–143.

Kuada, J., & Hinson, R. E. (2012). Corporate social responsibility (CSR) practices of foreign and local companies in Ghana. *Thunderbird International Business Review*, 54(4), 521–536.

Loxley, J., & Sackey, H. A. (2008). Aid effectiveness in Africa. *African Development Review*, 20(2), 163–199.

Martens, K. (2002). Mission impossible? Defining non-governmental organisations. *International Journal of Voluntary and Nonprofit Organisations,* 13(3), 271–285.

Meyer, K. E., & Peng, M. W. (2005). Probing theoretically into Central and Eastern Europe: Transactions, resources, and institutions. *Journal of International Business Studies*, 36(6), 600–621.

Meyer, K. E., & Peng, M. W. (2016). Theoretical foundations of emerging economy business research. *Journal of International Business Studies*, 47(1), 3–22.

Mogaji, E., Maringe, F., & Hinson, R. E. (2020). Emerging challenges, opportunities, and agenda for research, practice, and policy on marketing and brand communications of higher education institutions in Africa. In *Strategic marketing of higher education in Africa* (pp. 238–249). Routledge, Abingdon.

Mothusi, B., & Dipholo, K. B. (2008). Privatisation in Botswana: The demise of a developmental state? Public Administration and Development. *The International Journal of Management Research and Practice,* 28(3), 239–249.

Moyo, D. (2009). *Dead aid: Why aid is not working and how there is a better way for Africa*. Macmillan, New York.

Navarro-Flores, O. (2011). Organising by projects: A strategy for local development: The case of NGOs in a developing country. *Project Management Journal*, 42(6), 48–59.

Nigeria Electricity System Operator (NSONG) (2017). Retrieved August 8, 2020, from https://nsong.org/AboutUs/History.

North, D. C. (1990). *Institutions, institutional change and economic performance*. Cambridge University Press, Cambridge.

North, D. C. (1995). The new institutional economics and third world development. *The New Institutional Economics and Third World Development*, 21, 31–40.

Nwankwo, S. (2000). Assessing the marketing environment in sub-Saharan Africa: Opportunities and threats analysis. *Marketing Intelligence & Planning*, 18(3), 144–153.

Nwankwo, S., & Richards, D. C. (2001). Privatisation-The myth of free market orthodoxy in sub-Saharan Africa. *International Journal of Public Sector Management*, 14(2), 165–180.

Olaleye, S., Ukpadi, D., & Mogaji, E. (2020). Public vs private universities in Nigeria: Market dynamics perspective. In E. Mogaji, F. Maringe, & R. Ebo Hinson (Eds.), *Understanding the higher education market in Africa* (pp. 19–36), Routledge Studies in Marketing, 12. Routledge, Abingdon.

Onuoha, K. C. (2010). The electricity industry in Nigeria: What are the challenges and options available to improve the sector? Available at SSRN 1664788.

Organisation for Economic Cooperation and Development (OECD) (2016). Development aid at a glance (Africa), Retrieved December, 15, 2019, from https://www.oecd.org/dac/stats/documentupload/2%20Africa%20-%20Development%20Aid%20at%20a%20Glance%202016..pdf.

Ouedraogo, R., Sourouema, W. S., & Sawadogo, H. (2020). Aid, growth, and institutions in sub-Saharan Africa: New insights using a multiple growth regime approach. *The World Economy*, 44, 107–142. DOI: 10.1111/twec.12968.

Owusu, R. A. (2002). Project marketing to Africa: Lessons from the case of IVO transmission engineering and Ghana's national electrification scheme. *Journal of Business & Industrial Marketing*, 17(6), 523–537.

Owusu, R. A., & Vaaland, T. I. (2016). A business network perspective on local content in emerging African petroleum nations. *International Journal of Energy Sector Management*, 10(4), 594–616.

Owusu, R. A., & Welch, C. (2007). The buying network in international project business: A comparative case study of development projects. *Industrial Marketing Management*, 36(2), 147–157.

Owusu-Frimpong, N., & Mmieh, F. (2007). An evaluation of the perceptions and marketing practices of nontraditional exporters in Ghana. *Thunderbird International Business Review*, 49(1), 57–76.

Parente, R., Rong, K., Geleilate, J. M. G., & Misati, E. (2019). Adapting and sustaining operations in weak institutional environments: A business ecosystem assessment of a Chinese MNE in Central Africa. *Journal of International Business Studies*, 50(2), 275–291.

Payne, J., & Falush, S. (2015, January 7). Shell to pay out $83 million to settle Nigeria oil spill claims. Retrieved May 8, 2020, from https://www.reuters.com/article/us-shell-nigeria-spill/shell-to-pay-out-83-million-to-settle-nigeria-oil-spill-claims-idUSKBN0KG00920150107.

Peng, M. W. (2002). Towards an institution-based view of business strategy. *Asia Pacific Journal of Management*, 19(2–3), 251–267.

Scott, W.R. (1995) *Institutions and organisations*. SAGE Publications, Thousand Oaks.

Seu, I. B., Flanagan, F., & Orgad, S. (2015). The good Samaritan and the marketer: Public perceptions of humanitarian and international development NGOs. *International Journal of Nonprofit and Voluntary Sector Marketing*, 20(3), 211–225.

Sutherland, E. (2018). Bribery and corruption in telecommunications: The case of Nigeria. *Digital Policy and Governance*, 20(3), pp. 244–272.

Taylor, C. (2019, March 1). Shell facing multiple charges over corruption, emissions, and an explosion. Retrieved August 8, 2020, from https://www.cnbc.com/2019/03/01/shell-to-be-prosecuted-with-criminal-charges-over-nigerian-oil-deal.html#:~:text=Shell%20will%20be%20prosecuted%20for,chemical%20emissions%20and%20an%20explosion.

Teegen, H., Doh, J. P., & Vachani, S. (2004). The importance of non-governmental organisations (NGOs) in global governance and value creation: An international business research agenda. *Journal of International Business Studies*, 35(6), 463–483.

Vaaland, T. I., Soneye, A. S., & Owusu, R. A. (2012). Local content and struggling suppliers: A network analysis of Nigerian oil and gas industry. *African Journal of Business Management*, 6(15), 5399–5413.

Venable, B. T., Rose, G. M., Bush, V. D., & Gilbert, F. W. (2005). The role of brand personality in charitable giving: An assessment and validation. *Journal of the Academy of Marketing Science*, 33(3), 295–312.

Vestergaard, A. (2008). Humanitarian branding and the media: The case of Amnesty International. *Journal of Language and Politics*, 7(3), 471–493.

Voeth, M., & Herbst, U. (2008). The concept of brand personality as an instrument for advanced non-profit branding–an empirical analysis. *Journal of Nonprofit & Public Sector Marketing*, 19(1), 71–97.

Williamson, O. E. (2000). Economic institutions and development: A view from the bottom. In S. Kahkonen, & M. Olson (Eds.), *A new institutional approach to economic development*. Oxford Scholarship Online, pp. 92–118. DOI: 10.1093/0198294905.001.0001.

References (Case)

Addai-Donkor, K. A. (2014). The challenges of implementation of act 663 over the last decade-perspective of the public sector. *Public Procurement Authority: E-Bulletin*, 5(3), 5–7.

Africafeeds.com (2019, August 22). Retrieved July 17, 2020, from https://africafeeds.com/2019/08/22/ghanas-president-suspends-top-official-for-selling-contracts/.

Ameyaw, C., Mensah, S., & Osei-Tutu, E. (2012). Public procurement in Ghana: the implementation challenges to the public procurement law 2003 (Act 663). *International Journal of Construction Supply Chain Management*, 2(2), 55–65.

Ameyaw, C., Mensah, S., & Osei-Tutu, E. (2013). Curbing corruption in the public procurement process in Ghana. *Public Policy and Administration Research*, 3(5), 44–53.

Aning, K., & Edu-Afful, F. (1992). *Legal and policy frameworks regulating the behavior of politicians and political parties in Ghana: Interrogating institutional me*chanisms (Vol. 7). International IDEA, Stockholm.

Appiah, R. (2014). The challenges of implementation of act 663 over the last decade -perspective of the public procurement authority. *Public Procurement Authority: E-Bulletin*, 5(3), 1–4. Retrieved August 5, 2020, from http://ppaghana.org/documents/Bulletins/PPAE-BulletinMayJun2014Final.pdf.

Baffour, T. N. (2014). The challengees of implementation of act 663 over the last decade-perspective of the private sector. *Public Procurement Authority: E-Bulletin*, 5(3), 8–11.

Business and Financial Times (2019). President suspends PPA boss, https://thebftonline.com/2019/business/president-suspends-ppa-boss/.

Business Ghana (2017, November 2). Retrieved August 8, 2020, from https://www.businessghana.com/site/news/general/154796/COCOBOD-uncovers-ghost-cocoa-roads-awarded-under-NDC-government-Aidoo.

Frimpong, E. D. (2018, June 28). Charlotte Osei and two EC deputies sacked. Retrieved August 8, 2020, from https://www.graphic.com.gh/news/general-news/charlotte-osei-and-two-ec-deputies-removed.html.

Ghana Broadcasting Corporation (GBC) (2019, October 16). Retrieved August 6, 2020, from, https://www.gbcghanaonline.com/general/supreme-court-dismisses-ex-ssnit-boss-stay-of-proceedings-application/2019/.

Ghana Legal Institute (2020, May). R v Bonnie and Others (Suit No. CR/904/2017) GHAHCCrimD. Retrieved August 5, 2020, from https://ghalii.org/gh/judgment/high-court-criminal/2020/1.

Ghanaweb.com (2018, September 18). Retrieved August 8, 2020, from https://www.ghanaweb.com/GhanaHomePage/NewsArchive/EX-Ghana-Standards-Authority-boss-hot-over-1-2m-kickback-687321.

Ghanaweb.com (2019a, February 6). Retrieved August 8, 2020, from https://www.ghanaweb.com/GhanaHomePage/NewsArchive/Supreme-Court-affirms-Charlotte-Osei-s-sacking-721211.

Ghanaweb.com (2019b, October 19). Retrieved August 8, 2020, from https://www.ghanaweb.com/GhanaHomePage/NewsArchive/Supreme-Court-bounces-ex-SSNIT-boss-789673.

Government of Ghana (2003a). Public procurement act, 2003 (Act 663). Retrieved August5, 2020, from https://www.ppaghana.org/documents/Public%20Procurement%20Act%202003%20Act%20663.pdf.

Government of Ghana (2003b). Budget Statement (2003). Retrieved August 5, 2020, from https://www.mofep.gov.gh/sites/default/files/budget-statements/Budget2003.pdf.

Holmey, O (2020, May 11). Ghana: John Mahama splashed by Airbus corruption affair. Retrieved August 5, 2020, from https://www.theafricareport.com/27714/ghana-john-mahama-splashed-by-airbus-corruption-affair/.

Osafo-Marfo, Y. (2003). *Improving efficiency and transparency in public procurement*. Accra, Ghana.

PPA (2018, October 30). Retrieved July 17, 2020, from https://ppaghana.wordpress.com/tag/mr-a-b-adjei/.

PPA Manuals (2020). Retrieved August 5, 2020, from https://ppa.gov.gh/online-documents/manuals/#1546943956828-6360611b-50a3.

Reuters (2020, February 3). Ghana to probe bribery accusations in Airbus deal. Retrieved August 8, 2020, from https://www.reuters.com/article/airbus-probe-ghana/ghana-to-probe-bribery-accusations-in-airbus-deal-idUSL8N2A32H3.

Thai, K. V. (Ed.) (2008). Public procurement reforms in Africa: International public procurement: Concepts and practices. In *International handbook of public procurement*, (pp. 1–24). CRC Press, Boca Raton, FL.

Transparency International (2019). Corruption perceptions index, 2019. Retrieved August 6, 2020, from https://images.transparencycdn.org/images/2019_CPI_Report_EN_200331_141425.pdf.

World Bank (2000, September 29). Ghana-public financial management reform project II. Report No. PID9535. Retrieved from http://documents1.worldbank.org/curated/en/909541468771587604/pdf/multi0page.pdf.

STRATEGIC ALLIANCES AND COLLABORATIVE RELATIONSHIPS MANAGEMENT IN THE BUSINESS-TO-BUSINESS MARKET

4

In Part 4, we will discuss strategies for building and managing relationships, strategic alliances, brand image and loyalty in the business-to-business (B2B) market. In Chapter 10, we will focus on strategic equity-based alliances such as joint ventures and partial acquisitions and discuss how to select suitable partners, the governance structures and mechanisms as well as factors that affect the performance of equity-based alliances. Chapter 11 will discuss non-equity alliances such as supplier relationship, partnerships in R&D, manufacturing, licensing, marketing and supply chain relationships. Chapter 12 will discuss how to build brand and customer loyalty in the B2B market.

Chapter 10

Strategic Alliance Relationships and Performance in the Business-to-Business Market

INTRODUCTION AND OBJECTIVES

In Chapter 1, we discussed how business-to-business (B2B) marketing involves marketing activities between two or more organisations. These organisations often have professional buyers and sellers, and there are close and intense interactions and relationships between the buyer and seller. The buyer organisation usually prefers project buying, that is, to buy a combination of products, services, technologies, infrastructures and training, i.e. systems, or including construction, i.e. projects (see Chapter 8). The business interactions between B2B organisations involve contracts and relationships that can last for a relatively long time. As a result of these complexities, the selling organisations are developing organisational structures such as joint ventures and partial acquisitions that allow them to jointly and effectively develop customer solutions and share the economic rents that accrue from it with other business organisations.

At the end of this chapter, the reader will understand and be able to plan strategies regarding

- Joint ventures and partial acquisitions as strategic relationship model
- Partner selection for joint ventures and partial acquisitions
- Key success factors for joint ventures and partial acquisition.

10.1 Joint Ventures and Partial Acquisitions as Strategic Relationship Model

Joint ventures (JVs) and partial acquisitions are two forms of equity-based collaborative strategy that B2B organisations leverage to secure necessary resources (materials, customers, information) from upstream supply chain and co-create solutions for customer organisations (see Figure 10.1). The greenfield entry is a new incorporation a company establish when entering a foreign market (Dadzie & Owusu, 2015; Demibag et al., 2008). Partial acquisition is an acquisition in which the parent firm acquires part of the equity of a local firm in the form of a direct investment involving some level of control (Oguji & Owusu, 2017). JVs are partially owned greenfield organisation or a new organisational entity where ownership stake is shared with another partner to exercise ownership and control over the JV (Chen, 2008). These two forms of equity-based collaborative strategies are somewhat different. For instance, JVs are greenfield market entries, and they require the setting up of a new venture which adds additional capacity into the industry. In contrast, partial acquisitions do not add additional capacity into the industry (Chari & Chang, 2009). While control in JVs is achieved through negotiated management placements and seats on the JV board, control in partial acquisitions is exercised primarily through board seats in the local target firm (Chari & Chang, 2009).

We discussed in Chapter 13 that organisations transition to customer-centric organisations to enhance innovation, competitiveness and co-create value for customers. To achieve this, they need to align, integrate and collaborate with supply chain partners. JVs and partial acquisitions are organisational forms they can utilise for collaboration to enhance knowledge creation and supply chain integration.

JVs receive resources and support from its partners (such as advanced technology, managerial expertise and connections to local government, local business and labour unions) to operate effectively (Chen et al., 2014). Through JVs, supply organisations can develop new technologies and new designs for new product or services. The B2B literature has documented several instances of value co-creation for end customers via JVs (see, e.g., Rod et al., 2014). In some cases, these JVs involve a foreign firm and a local partner firm (i.e. international JVs). They could be used not only

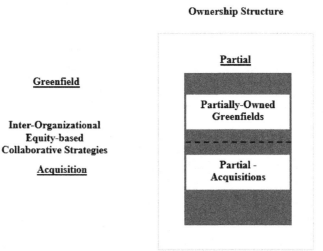

Figure 10.1 Inter-organisational equity-based collaborative strategies.

for value creation for customer solutions but also as an alternative to partial acquisitions when there are no suitable targets to acquire partially. It is also used to navigate institutional barriers such as local content legislation (Vaaland et al., 2012) and host government suasion (Bartels et al., 2002). For example, if local laws restrict the exports of a foreign firm into an African country, the foreign firm could decide to enter into a JV with a local firm to produce solutions to serve the local business customers. This way, the foreign firms will navigate the institutional barriers through the setting up of an International Joint Venture (IJV) to ensure the continual development of products and services for its local customers. It is also one of the prevalent strategies used by foreign firms to gain market entry into Africa and for securing access to raw materials and critical resources used for co-production with suppliers (Bartels et al., 2002).

Like JVs, partial acquisitions can be used to achieve similar motives (López-Duarte & García-Canal, 2004). For example, supply organisations could acquire part of upstream suppliers to secure and ensure corporate control over sources of their raw materials. The B2B literature has emphasised this type of partial acquisitions in the form of intra-firm sourcing aimed at securing sources of critical components and acquiring know-how in sales, marketing, strategy, management and technologies (Kotabe & Murray, 2004; Sven, 2019). Furthermore, partial acquisitions could be sought for because the potential partners for JVs are performing poorly. As a result, organisations could acquire partial equity from the company as a way to significantly restructure the target firms, which, in turn, improves the overall future capabilities of the partially acquired organisation.

To be able to leverage the synergy potential from partial acquisitions and JVs, the firm must select the right partner with complementarity and compatibility of objectives and must ensure the proper management of the venture to achieve success. In the below section, we discuss how to select partners for JVs and partial acquisitions in Africa.

10.2 Partner Selection for Joint Ventures and Partial Acquisitions

When firms enter into JVs or partial acquisitions, one of the most critical decisions is the selection of suitable partners for the formation of the JV as well as suitable targets for partial acquisitions (Table 10.1).

The selection of relevant partners and targets has been shown to influence the performance of the JV (e.g. Salavrakos & Stewart, 2006; Dong & Glaister, 2006) and partial acquisitions. In Figure 10.2, we show a modified framework for partner selection based on Roy and Oliver (2009), mainly developed for JVs but could also be applied to partial acquisitions.

When selecting a suitable partner for JVs or selecting a suitable target for partial acquisitions, B2B organisations seek out for partners and targets with institutional capability, that is, targets and partners that can negotiate with the government, possess institutional knowledge and access to government and regulatory permits. They also seek for partners and targets with marketing and distributional capabilities as well as those with suitable technological competence. Furthermore, the potential partner ability for alliance relationships, their partnering intent, market power, image and reputation are vital criteria considered when selecting suitable partners and targets for JV and partial acquisitions.

Organisations do not place an equal amount of weights on these selection criteria. The importance placed on these criteria could depend on the degree of the property-based resources (e.g. degree of product diversification, parent firm size) and knowledge-based resources (e.g. partner-specific experience, host country experience, international experiences) possessed by the organisation.

Table 10.1   Partner Selection Criteria in JVs and Partial Acquisitions

Task-related criteria	Partner-related criteria

• Partner-institutional capability
  • Institutional knowledge
  • Institutional ties and the ability to negotiate with the government
  • Access to regulatory permit
• Partner-marketing and distribution capabilities
  • Market knowledge
  • Distribution channel knowledge
  • Established marketing and distribution system
  • Links with major buyers and brands
  • Access to the product, services, raw materials and natural resources
• Partner technological competences
  • Experience in technology applications
  • Access to technology
  • Partner learning ability
  • Knowledge of production processes
  • Access to skills and labour
	• Character
	  • Image/reputation (local, industry and/or international) and legal compliance
	  • Trustworthiness
	  • Transparency of the firm and/or ethical values/beliefs
	• Market power
	  • Financial capabilities (assets, ability to raise financing)
	  • Partner company size
	  • Market share or industry position
	• Partnering intent
	  • Goals, objectives, aspirations or synergy potential
	  • Commitment, seriousness and/or enthusiasm for the partnership
	• Partnering ability
	  • International experience/successful partnering record with other firms
	  • Favourable past association with your firm or mutual acquaintances

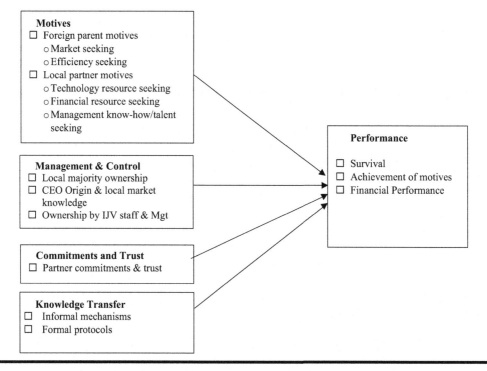

Figure 10.2   Performance of joint ventures and partial acquisitions in Africa.

10.3 Key Success Factors for Joint Ventures and Partial Acquisition

As discussed in Section 10.1, firms invest in JVs and partial acquisition for knowledge co-creation. To achieve knowledge co-creation, complementary and compatible capabilities are critically important because while partners' compatibility is positively related to knowledge co-creation, complementarity has a curvilinear relationship with knowledge co-creation (Jeanine et al., 2019). Partner complementarity refers to the degree to which the partners' resources, technological capabilities, managerial experiences and expertise complement each other. Partner compatibility refers to the degree in which the partners' corporate culture, management styles and operating strategies are compatible with each other (Jeanine et al., 2019). As a consequence, when selecting JV partners and acquisition targets in Africa, care must be taken to select partners with compatible corporate cultures and management styles because they are the foundation for collaboration and they promote the exchange of ideas and resources and encourage joint problem-solving. Also, selecting a partner with complementary capability has a double-edged effect, in the sense that partners with complementary capabilities will positively influence knowledge co-creation initially, but this will diminish over time at a certain threshold and becomes negative. Thus, there is need for the organisation to evaluate and compare their strength with their potential partners' advantage and offer only a sufficient base of related knowledge, technological capability, and managerial expertise that drives motivation to communicate and learn from the other. Otherwise, if they offer unrelated knowledge, unrelated technological capability and managerial expertise, it will hinder intra-firm learning because too much difference limits partners' common understanding and reduces the efficiency of the integration and creation processes (Jeanine et al., 2019).

In addition to the partners' unique expertise and capabilities, researchers (Oguji et al., 2020; Oguji, 2018; Oguji & Owusu, 2017) have also explored JVs and partial acquisitions in Africa with foreign parents and have shown that the partner's motives, the management and ownership structure, knowledge transfer, commitment and trust impacts the performance of the venture (see Figure 10.2). Most of the JVs in Africa are undertaken in key resource industries, and foreign firms use such ventures as vehicles for mitigating institutional complexities as African economies undergo economic and institutional changes. Similarly, partial acquisitions studied so far, even though sought in other manufacturing industries than traditional extraction industries, are used as a foothold strategy to enter the market while mitigating institutional complexities (see Oguji & Owusu, 2017).

In these JVs, while foreign firms provide strategic assets such as technologies and finances as well as management know-how. Local African firms offer market access and distribution and supply networks. Knowledge transfer is an essential vehicle for achieving the strategic objective of the venture. In Africa, firms are utilising both informal channels (ties, communication, networking, cultural sharing, trust) and formal knowledge transfer mechanism to gain knowledge from foreign partners (see Ado et al., 2017). Partially acquiring a target in Africa has been suggested as a strategy to enhance effective knowledge transfer and ease integration challenges in Africa. This is because it provides a slower-paced and more adaptive process for knowledge sharing considering the low absorptive capacity and inadequate corporate governance mechanisms in the continent (Kimberly et al., 2015). In general, knowledge sharing among employees, the use of the local firm's capabilities, and how capabilities are shared creates the social integration and combination necessary for exploitative and explorative innovative outcomes in the JVs and partially acquired firms in Africa.

Commitment and trust between both partners are essential for the survival and achievement of the strategic motives of setting up the venture. While trust and commitment have been widely researched in JVs, in partial acquisitions, the organisational structure in itself creates an opportunity for trust-building and gaining experience working with the partner (Oguji & Owusu, 2017). Nevertheless, most of the executives in Africa have noted that trust and justice expectations are still relatively low in business in Africa (Kimberly et al., 2015).

Finally, the management and control of the JV have been shown to have a positive effect on the performance of the JVs. A significant body of IJV literature has demonstrated that dominant managerial control exercised by foreign parents has a positive influence on IJV performance (e.g. Ding, 1997). In the context of Africa, empirical evidence suggests that the appointment of a CEO who hails from the host country of the IJV or a CEO who understands the local market has a positive influence on the performance of the IJV (Gómez-Miranda et al., 2015). Similar studies show that local managerial control is positively linked to the success of IJVs in Africa (Hearn, 2015).

Case Study A

50:50 JOINT VENTURE BETWEEN VIVO ENERGY PLC (VIVO ENERGY) AND KUKU FOODS EAST AFRICA HOLDINGS

Vivo Energy plc (Vivo Energy) is the pan-African retailer and distributor of Shell and Engen branded fuels and lubricants as well as the provision of services to both retail and commercial customers across the continent of Africa. In June 2019, Vivo Energy announced that it was set to take up a 50% stake in KFC in East Africa, in a deal with Kuku Foods East Africa Holdings (KFEAH), the franchise owners. As customers are increasingly demanding for everything under one roof, Vivo Energy wanted to offer more than quality fuel and lubricants by offering other products that meet the needs of refuelling clients. The fundamental premise here is understanding the complete solution of what vehicle refuelling customers need. KFEAH is the region's franchisee of world-renowned KFC outlets, unveiled its initial concept in 2011 at Junction Mall in Nairobi, Kenya, and opened its first outlet in 2013. By the end of 2017, KFEAH had as many as 32 restaurants across the region with Kenya comprising the largest ratio of the company's portfolio. KFEAH prides its success in East Africa on its strong local management team and skilled workforce who are qualified and dedicated to providing outstanding customer service, interacting with customers in a meaningful way and helping the company grow. The company employs over 1000 well-trained team members at both its restaurants and head office level across the region. It continuously invests in developing its staff and provides numerous learning and growth opportunities for each of them.

The JV is expected to help the growth of KFEAH through the opening of new outlets at Vivo Energy's network of service stations across Kenya, Uganda and Rwanda. The JV will manage and operate the restaurants in three markets on behalf of KFEAH who will remain the local KFC franchisee and is expected to leverage Vivo Energy's retail footprint, with more countries to be considered in the future, based on market opportunities.

Commenting on the proposed JV, **Christian Chammas**, **CEO of Vivo Energy**, said: "We are delighted to be partnering with KFEAH to replicate the KFC, joint venture (JV) model, we pioneered in Botswana and Côte d'Ivoire. KFEAG shares our ambition to invest in order to grow the number of restaurants and give more African customers access to the internationally renowned KFC brand. This partnership further demonstrates our ambition to continue to offer more convenience to satisfy the evolving needs of our growing number of African customers".

Derrick Van Houten, Group CEO of KFEAH and Principal Operator of the KFC franchises, added: "Having launched our first KFC in East Africa in 2011, we have successfully grown the business over the last eight years. We are delighted to announce this new partnership with Vivo Energy to continue this growth, bringing our world-renowned KFC products and experience to as many customers as possible".

KFC Africa's General Manager, Tarun Lal concluded: "We are delighted that KFC can leverage the JV entered into between Vivo Energy and KFEAH to continue to grow its network of KFC restaurants in Africa. We are confident that the KFC franchisee will continue to provide customers with a great KFC experience, driving improvements in customer service and quality through its relationship with Vivo Energy".

CASE QUESTIONS

1. Discuss why a JV was preferred to partial acquisitions for this strategic collaborative relationship?
2. Why did Vivo Energy plc choose KFC East Africa than other local restaurants or restaurants chains in East Africa?
3. What are significant knowledge resources both partners will bring for the formation of the JV?
4. What will be the significant challenges the new JV will face?

This case study is compiled from Vivo Energy (2019) press release.

Case Study B

SELECTING PARTNERS FOR JOINT VENTURES IN NIGERIA

Eseck is a small Cameroon-based business that sources natural honey, hot peppers and ogbono seeds (used for soups) from local producers in Cameroon and supplies wholesale quantities to both formal and informal retailers and market traders in Douala, Bamenda and Buea townships.

SUPPORT NEEDS

In the last 3 years, the business has set its sights on entering foreign markets within and outside the African continent. Its primary target on the continent is Nigeria, a neighbouring country with a much larger consumer market. Cameroon has a population size of 25 million, while Nigeria's population is over 200 million people. Other markets of interest are the Middle East and the European Union with which Cameroon is a signatory to the Economic Partnership Agreement (EPA) that guarantees export of honey to the EU at zero import duty. To achieve its market development goals, Eseck, through its founder (Mr Ndashi), sought the support of Smallstarter Africa to penetrate the Nigerian market with its pure honey products.

Smallstarter Africa is an online support base for African entrepreneurs who want to learn and grow. They provide the training, insights and inspiration entrepreneurs need to transform their ideas, dreams and small businesses into successful marvels. They use a combination of curated content, books, basic and advanced business courses, signature coaching programs and private consulting to support entrepreneurs who are at different stages of building their dream business.

THE PROBLEM

Previous attempts to find suitable partners in the Nigerian market were unsuccessful. Poor knowledge of the market, lack of a trusted network and relationships, and loosely structured commercial arrangements were significant contributing factors to the ineffectiveness of earlier market development efforts. Worse still, Eseck struck separate commercial deals with several interested off-takers in Nigeria, which led to a web of complex transactions that increased landing costs and complicated the cross-border logistical task of serving all interested parties.

SMALLSTARTER AFRICA SOLUTION

To facilitate an effective market entry strategy, Smallstarter Africa is working with Eseck to identify a potential joint venture (JV) partner who will act as the sole representative and main distributor of Eseck's products in Nigeria. The partner shall be responsible for determining wholesalers and retailers of the product and coordinate the storage, delivery, transportation and administration of the JV's operational and financial activities in Nigeria.

Before the disruption of economic activities and cross-border trade by the COVID-19 pandemic, Smallstarter had identified two potential partners to represent and coordinate Eseck's market development efforts in Nigeria. As border closures and lockdowns are lifted, it is expected that the JV agreement will be executed with one of the selected candidates.

SUCCESS FACTORS

In selecting potential candidates for the JV, Smallstarter Africa considered business owners and traders who have a good understanding of the honey market in Nigeria and have a strong base of business contacts within the market. Other factors considered were their financial capacity to offtake wholesale volumes of product and feedback from credible references.

CASE QUESTIONS

1. Considering the discussions on JV partner selection, what other essential criteria did Smallstarter fail to consider in its partner selection criteria in Nigeria?

References

Ado, A., Su, Z., & Wanjiru, R. (2017). Learning and knowledge transfer in Africa-China JVs: Interplay between informalities, culture, and social capital. *Journal of International Management*, 23(2), 166–179.

Bartels, F. L., Johnson, J. P., & Ahmed, Z. U. (2002) International equity joint ventures in Ghana and Cote D'Ivoire. *Journal of African Business*, 3(3), 5–30.

Chari, M. D., & Chang, K. (2009). Determinants of the share of equity sought in cross-border acquisitions. *Journal of International Business Studies*, 40(8), 1277–1297.

Chen, S. F. S. (2008). The motives for international acquisitions: Capability procurements, strategic considerations, and the role of ownership structures. *Journal of International Business Studies*, 39(3), 454–471.

Chen, X., Chen, A. X., & Zhou, K. Z. (2014). Strategic orientation, foreign parent control, and differentiation capability building of international joint ventures in an emerging market. *Journal of International Marketing*, 22(3), 30–49.

Dadzie, S. A., & Owusu, R. A. (2015). Understanding establishment mode choice of foreign manufacturing firms in Ghana. *International Journal of Emerging Markets*, 10, 896–920.

Demirbag, M., Tatoglu, E., & Glaister, K. W. (2008). Factors affecting perceptions of the choice between acquisition and greenfield entry: The case of Western FDI in an emerging market. *Management International Review*, 48(1), 5–38.

Ding, D. Z. (1997). Control, conflict, and performance: A study of US-Chinese joint ventures. *Journal of International Marketing*, 5(3), 31–45.

Dong, L., & Glaister, K. W. (2006). Motives and partner selection criteria in international strategic alliances: Perspectives of Chinese firms. *International Business Review*, 15(6), 577–600.

Gómez-Miranda, M. E., Pérez-López, M. C. Argente-Linares, E. & Rodríguez-Ariza, L. (2015). The impact of organizational culture on competitiveness, effectiveness, and efficiency in Spanish-Moroccan international joint ventures. *Personnel Review*, 44(3), 364–387.

Hearn, B. (2015). Institutional influences on board composition of international joint venture firms listing on emerging stock exchanges: Evidence from Africa. *Journal of World Business*, 50(1), 205–219.

Jeanine, C., Jianfeng, W. F., & Bai, X. (2020). Good match matters: Knowledge co-creation in international joint ventures. *Industrial Marketing Management*, 84, 138–150.

Kimberly, M. E., Bruce, T. L., Taco, H. R., & Leon, F. (2015). Mergers and acquisitions in Africa: A review and an emerging research agenda. *Africa Journal of Management*, 1(2), 137–171.

Kotabe, M., & Murray, J. Y. (2004). Global sourcing strategy and sustainable competitive advantage. *Industrial Marketing Management*, 33(1), 7–14.

López-Duarte, C. L., & García-Canal, E. (2004). The choice between joint ventures and acquisitions in foreign direct investments: The role of partial acquisitions and accrued experience. *Thunderbird International Business Review*, 46(1), 39–58.

Oguji, N. (2018). How do entry motives and institutions influence the acquisition strategies of multinationals in foreign markets? Lessons from acquisitions of Finnish multinationals in global markets. *Journal of East-West Business*, 24(2), 81–107.

Oguji, N., & Owusu, R. A. (2017). Acquisitions entry strategies in Africa: The role of institutions, target-specific experience, and host-country capabilities—the case acquisitions of Finnish multinationals in Africa. *Thunderbird International Business Review*, 59(2), 209–225.

Oguji, N., Degbey, W. Y., & Owusu, R. A. (2018). International joint ventures research on Africa: A systematic literature review, propositions, and contextualization. *Thunderbird International Business Review*, 63(1), 11–26.

Rod, M., Lindsay, V., & Ellis, N. (2014). Managerial perceptions of service-infused IORs in China & India: A discursive view of value co-creation. *Industrial Marketing Management*, 43(4), 603–612.

Roy, J. P., & Oliver, C. (2009). International joint venture partner selection: The role of the host-country legal environment. *Journal of International Business Studies*, 40(5), 779–801.

Salavrakos, I. D., & Stewart, C. (2006). Partner selection criteria as determinants of firm performance in joint ventures: Evidence from Greek joint ventures in Eastern Europe. *Eastern European Economics*, 44(3), 60–78.

Sven, D. (2019). Foreign-owned subsidiary knowledge sourcing: The role of location and expatriates. *Journal of Business Research*, 105, 178–188.

Vaaland, T. I., Soneye, A. S., & Owusu, R. A. (2012). Local content and struggling suppliers: A network analysis of Nigerian oil and gas industry. *African Journal of Business Management*, 6(15), 5399–5413.

Vivo Energy (2019, June 20). Formation of joint venture to accelerate growth of KFC franchise portfolio in East Africa [Press release]. Retrieved from https://www.vivoenergy.com/Media-Centre/Press-Releases/Details/Formation-of-Joint-Venture-to-Accelerate-Growth-of-KFC-Franchise-Portfolio-in-East-Africa.

Chapter 11

Buyer–Seller Relationship in Business-to-Business (B2B) Marketing in the African Context

In the context of Africa, there has been a dearth in the literature to extend the body of knowledge on business-to-business (B2B) marketing given the crucial role B2B marketing plays in the development of an economy. This chapter provides insights into B2B marketing in Africa and how a business organisation can leverage it for the performance of their firm and the economy at large. This chapter discusses the meaning of B2B marketing, types and importance of business relationships, how to develop different types of business relationships and harness their potential in Africa, and communication methods in B2B relationships and contract designs in business relationships.

By the end of the chapter, the reader will be able to:

1. Understand the types of relationships in a B2B market
2. Explain the types and importance of alliances in the B2B
3. Understand how to develop different types of valuable business relationships
4. Identify key variables needed to sustain an effective business relationship.

11.1 Introduction

Developing effective marketing programmes that fit the local and international market contexts requires an understanding of the different market segments available to the business organisation (Zimmerman & Blythe, 2017). Within the scope of marketing, an organisation can sell either to other business organisations or to the final consumer. When a product or service is sold to companies, government bodies and other institutions which resell them, use them to produce other commodities or render services to the consumers, such marketing relationship is regarded as Business-to-Business (B2B) (Biemans, 2010), while the marketing of products and service to individuals for personal consumption/use is known as business-to-consumer (B2C) marketing (Biemans, 2010). Zimmerman and Blythe (2017) stressed that B2B marketing transactions have broader implications on a nation's economy than B2C because of the nature and outcome of transactions that exist between stakeholders in the B2B market. Zimmerman and Blythe (2017) further asserted that not only does B2B positively influence the economic status of a nation but also the welfare of the people through employment necessitated by business expansions. Based on these submissions, it is important to manage and understand the value of B2B marketing in the African context as literature has focused more on B2C marketing.

Diverse stakeholders exist in the B2B market whose activities affect the outcome of relationship within the market. In Africa, B2B relationship among stakeholders can be both transactional and relational (Brodie et al., 2008). Transactional marketing involves the exchange of value between two or more parties/organisations, while relationship marketing is premised on enhancing, maintaining and creating a good relationship between the customers and stakeholders associated with the business both internally and externally on a longer-term basis (Ibidunni, 2012; Aka et al., 2016). Relationship marketing aims to keep and improve current customers than acquiring new ones (Zeithaml et al., 2018; Aka et al., 2016). Adopting the two marketing practices shows that businesses do not only want sustenance of their selling relationship but also desire to build a robust industry that would provide the need of the market, by finding solutions to fundamental economic problems. In essence, relationship building is key to the growth of the B2B market. Roberts-Lombard et al. (2019) conducted a study in South Africa to examine the antecedents and consequences of satisfaction in B2B relationships and found trust and commitment as a critical factor that sustains and builds a B2B marketing relationship. Their findings corroborated the findings of previous literature on relationship marketing (i.e. Wang et al., 2015; Lee et al., 2015; Liao et al., 2016) which attest that trust, commitment and satisfaction are important aspects of managing long-term B2B relationships. According to Kempeners (1995), these factors measure the quality of the relationship between a supplier organisation and the customer organisation. Therefore, trust, commitment and satisfaction shared in a B2B relationship are key variables to sustain competitive business advantage.

The context of a B2B relationship requires that one organisation fulfils the needs of the supplier and another the customer. In some cases, an organisation can be in a B2B relationship and also in a B2C relationship. This is attainable if the supplier provides a manufacturing firm with raw materials needed for the production of consumable commodities and at the same time, sells similar materials to consumers who use it for personal consumption. Essentially, the party at the receiving end of any commodity or service determines the nature of the business relationship.

11.2 Understanding the Business-to-Business Market

In the current business market, there is pressure on business organisations to improve efficiency if they are to become effective. In ensuring efficiency, the operational process of the business must utilise the right resources at the right time to achieve the expected outcome with minimal cost. Buyer–supplier relationships strengthen the parties' competitive advantage (Cannon & Homburg, 2001). In addition, Windahl and Lakemond (2006) posited that external relationships with other business organisations are important in providing integrated solutions to business challenges. Ineffective management of stakeholder relationship can negatively affect the image of the business as there can be issues of late deliveries of goods, communication breakdown and quality assurance, among other factors. The B2B marketing relationship is important to the quality of service/product of the business and customer satisfaction.

Bagdoniene and Zilione (2009) assert that B2B marketing involves processes whereby two or more firms create strong and extensive social, economic and technical relationships over time for specific business purposes. In addition, the B2B market is a chain of relationships that flows from top-bottom of the market. Within the scope of the B2B market, the consumer who uses a commodity or service without reproduction intention ends the chain of supply and demand within the B2B. That is, the B2B process comes to an end when a product/raw material gets to a user who has no intention of reproduction or resell. The B2B market is also viewed as long, institutionalised and dynamic stakeholders within the market that generate huge cash flows for business and government.

Accordingly, Zimmerman and Blythe (2017) submit that marketing programmes in the B2B market are always channelled towards increasing sales, reducing costs or meeting governmental regulations as well as avoiding negative public relations. The implication is that B2B marketing relationships exist at the level of strategic top management activities. In the same line, Wright (2004) asserts that the B2B market is a market situation whereby an organisation sells products and services to another organisation for their reproductive or service use, through which a buyer–supplier relationship is built and sustained. This assumption further demonstrates the crucial role B2B market relationship plays, in the product and service rendering process of a business organisation.

The B2B marketing functions require more strategic dealings from organisations involved because the outcome is majorly in the business outputs and not the process. Commenting on business in the African context, Roberts-Lombard et al. (2019) observed that B2B marketing had been affected by the dynamic demand of consumers, environmental instability and technological innovations. Consequently, as observed by the authors, this has defined the kind of relationship, businesses have with other business counterparts within the market.

B2B relationship, particularly practice and operations, differs from what is obtainable in the B2C market in areas such as in advertising, sales strategy, promotion and customer relationships (Swani et al., 2019). Therefore, it will not be advisable for organisations to utilise the same strategy adopted in relating to customers in B2C in the B2B market. Corroborating this position, Brennan et al. (2011) argue that market structure, buying behaviour and marketing practice are different in the two markets. The differences in the nature and structure of the market influence the buyer and seller relationship outcomes in the two markets. To understand the kind of different relationships that exist in the B2B and B2C markets, the categorisation provided by Brennan et al. (2011) explaining the difference in the market practice is shown in Table 11.1.

Table 11.1 illustrates the differences in market practice between the two markets. Hence, different types of relationships exist in the market with strategic importance placed on the role of parties in the relationship.

11.3 Types and Importance of Alliances in the Business-to-Business (B2B) Market

Quality management of business relationships is understood to be the bedrock upon which businesses survive and thrive (Ford et al., 2011; Bagdoniene & Zilione, 2009). Therefore, it is expedient that business organisations effectively manage external relationships with stakeholders. Zimmerman and Blythe (2017, p. 12.) emphasised that "the essence of marketing in business

Table 11.1   Differences in Marketing Practice of the Two Markets

S/No.	Dimensions	Business Marketing	Consumer Marketing
1	Selling process	Systems selling	Product selling
2	Personal selling	Used extensively	Limited
3	Use of relationships	Used extensively	Limited
4	Promotional strategies	Limited, customer-specific	Mass market
5	Web integration	Greater	Limited
6	Branding	Limited	Extensive, sophisticated
7	Market research	Limited	Extensive
8	Segmentation	Unsophisticated	Sophisticated
9	Competitor awareness	Lower	Higher
10	Product complexity	Greater	Lesser

Source: Brennan et al. (2011, p. 2).

is to establish, maintain, enhance, and commercialise customer relationships so that objectives of the parties involved are met". Therefore, effective management of the business relationship between the parties involved, irrespective of the nature of the relationship, is important to business performance.

Webster (1992) categorised the following types of relationships in the B2B market: strategic alliances, joint ventures, transactional, repeated transaction, long-term, buyer–seller partnership and network organisation. Joint ventures and strategic alliances are discussed in Chapter 10 of this book, while transactional, repeated transaction, long-term, buyer–seller partnership, network organisation, commercial enterprise relationship, government agencies and institutions are discussed next.

11.3.1 Transactions

Webster (1992) predicted a new market with various business relationships, which he described as a continuum process. The transaction market relationship is the first in this continuum and is regarded as a form of business transaction between two economic actors (Webster, 1992). Activities within this business relationship are undertaken as discrete, and all information is embedded in the price of the product that is exchanged. This kind of market relationship is not guided by any formal rules of engagement or structures; an organisation transacts with other business organisations to acquire resources for the production of their goods and services which will be sold in a more competitive market. The focus is on obtaining and exchanging value between two organisations based on price, product and cost. The interest is not on loyalty, brand name, recognition of the customer by the seller or credit extension. The interest is on obtaining and exchanging value. Webster regarded this type of market relationship without structure as a pure market transaction.

11.3.2 Repeat Transactions

A step ahead from the transaction relationship is the repeat transaction business relationship, which takes into account various factors that are not crucial in the transactional relationship. The repeat transaction entails frequent repurchase of branded goods, industrial components, and operating supplies for the production of goods and for services. In this type of business marketing relationship, advertising and sales promotion which are not as significant in the transactional relationship are important for marketing success in this system because loyalty and repeat purchase are key.

However, the fact that a repeat purchase is needed in this business relationship between firms and their customers does not always imply that there is a meaningful long-term relationship between them. To ensure repurchase from the perspective of the buyer, there must be trust, credibility and familiarity, and because of technological innovations and discoveries, customers now have direct communication network with the manufacturers and vendors. Continuous repeat transaction as a result of trust in the product and service will result in a relationship marketing that binds the customer with the manufacturers and distributors. Therefore, business relationships are no longer sustained by the traditional one-time transaction with customers but thrive on repeat transactions which are based on trust, credibility and familiarity (Webster, 1992).

11.3.3 Long-Term Relationships

Indeed, the buyer–seller relationship is said to be long term, particularly where there are contractual frameworks that guide the actions of parties. The scenario in the long-term relationship is usually different from buyers seeking low price from other suppliers. In the long-term relationship, prices are the outcome of the negotiation process, which is not determined by market forces. The relationship between manufacturers and customers is mediated by vendors who determine and influence the prices of goods and services within the market. In this relationship, the vendors who play the role of the middleman might inflate prices which are controlled through bidding competition.

Trust, commitment and intention to stay are regarded as the three most critical elements in a long-term relationship. B2B long-term relationships in a variety of industries including manufacturing, advertising and logistics would only blossom and be sustained when trust is cultivated over time. Commitment to a budding B2B relationship is a sine qua non for a long-term relationship. Both or all parties in the B2B relationship must show unwavering commitment in all critical mutual dependencies. Intention to stay (in a long-term business relationship) is borne out of commitment.

11.3.4 Buyer–Seller Partnerships

Buyer to seller partnership is a strategic alliance of business relationship where businesses collaborate among themselves with the commitment of resources (capital, labour, skills, etc.) and with the sole interest of enhancing partners' competitive positions. This form of business relationship is different from the previously mentioned (long-term partnership) because it requires partners' commitments, integrity and loyalty. Partner relationship here is strengthened based on reciprocity of commitment to the business, and this is also shown through small ownership positions in the business of the other to symbolise their long-term commitment. This relationship is not based on financial gains alone but rather adds to the economic value of the quality product and also meets the needs of the market. Here, the parties involved are more interested in achieving customer value, and they want to ensure this through mutual relationship stability. This kind of stability is said to result in information sharing, which promotes long-term growth plans and policies. This model of the business relationship among organisations deviates from the vendor mediated long-term relationship that can be adversarial and finance-conscious. Buyer–seller partnership is more interested in creating value in the product and services and enhancing value to reduce the cost of production in situations of a defect. They believe that quality product sells better and costs less to them in the long run.

11.3.5 Network Organisations

The network organisation business relationship is an outcome of the strategic alliance relations. They are complex and multifaceted in such a way that they partner with other organisations and do not work independently to achieve the strategic business aim. They have been mostly misconstrued as strategic alliance relationship (an agreement between two or more organisations to pursue a goal while they remain independent organisation) which they are not. A network organisation consists of a number of firms working together to create long-lasting value with a centralised source of authority. It was regarded by Webster (1992) as a confederation. The centre with the vested authority has the responsibility of managing financial resources, core competence, building relationship with customers and safeguarding the information that binds the network. A key element of the network organisation is its ability to manage, design and control partnership with distributors, vendors and other customers. It is a relationship built on interdependent strength which is pulled together to form an alliance that creates and sustains value in the market over time.

Snow (1997) posited that it is necessary for B2B marketing relationships to evolve from what he described as the "dyadic paradigm" to the network organisation paradigm. The dyadic model involves a large organisation with considerable resources and influence in a domineering business relationship with a relatively smaller and dependent organisation. The network organisation, on the other hand, involves many organisations (not necessarily with capacity parity) in B2B relationships that are "mutually beneficial" for all parties. Bick et al. (2014) proposed that the future of marketing organisation in Africa, and particularly, South Africa would tend towards the network organisation.

11.3.6 Commercial Enterprise Relationship

There are three types of commercial enterprise relationship identified by Biemans (2010). They are users, original equipment manufacturers (OEMs) and resellers. User's relationship exists when organisations purchase a product or service to create their own products and services, which will be sold to the final consumer. It describes a process whereby an organisation buys a product from another organisation to generate their own product or service. The OEM, on the other hand, is a kind of relationship which describes a manufacturing organisation purchasing a part of its product from another merchant producing similar goods. The product purchased forms "part" of their own manufactured goods with its brand name available for all to see. In these kinds of business relationships, the goods are not treated as a raw material in the production process but as part of the product to be sold. For example, building construction companies will purchase different materials from different suppliers to accomplish their own organisational objectives. In the process of construction, the equipment used still carry the suppliers' brand names, and they form part of the building and not the whole building itself. In essence, OEMs' business relationship occurs when two manufacturers engage in a business transaction to make one party source part of the other's products. Finally, business relationship with resellers under the commercial enterprise describes organisations who buy B2B products and add value to them before selling further to B2B purchasers or final customers. They serve as the link between the suppliers and purchasers. They also add value to the product by giving advice on installation and appropriate usage.

11.3.7 Government Agencies

Governments are major partners and stakeholders in the B2B with a high level of involvement. For example, in Nigeria, the government regulates the market, making policies that will influence demand and supply reactions within the B2B market. The government licenses organisations to operate within this market, and they also have the power to withdraw licenses issued based on set rules and regulations. They are a major partner as they also transact within the market in order to either provide social amenities or improve the standard of living of the people. For example, the government purchases arms, military hardware and other national needs for different agencies from their direct producers and in this process, they become business partners. Furthermore, the government is also the largest employer through service organisations and their institutions. The government makes resources available to these organisations by doing business with other organisations. Government agencies play a crucial part in the B2B market and are therefore key partners to the survival and growth of the market.

11.3.8 Institutions

The B2B relationship with institutions describes the interactions between an institution and a business organisation that supplies the product the institution uses for its day-to-day services. Examples of such institutions are hospitals, schools, nursing homes and trade organisations. These institutions change over time, and such changes affect their purchase behaviour with the other business organisations. Most of B2B products are used in many of these institutions, and they share a strong relationship in terms of product purchase and supply relationship. Most times, the relationship within this category exists for the long term rather than short term. One of the unique attributes of this relationship is that changes within the market would influence a change in the B2B relationship.

11.4 Importance of B2B Relationships

There are numerous benefits which B2B relationships provide the parties involved. Some of these benefits are discussed next.

11.4.1 Enhanced Economic Performance

Through B2B relationships, the economic performance of a nation can be enhanced as the value of the gross domestic product (GDP) increases due to sustained business relationships. Goals of businesses would be met, productivity would be enhanced and the needs of the market would also be made available. When businesses have good relationships with each other, logistic issues that result in the unavailability of goods, high prices, harsh economic conditions on the consumers, inconsistency in the supply of products and low returns on investment are resolved. Through B2B relationships, jobs are also created in product distribution and delivery with quality human capital. If African nations can enhance their B2B market relationships, they could solve part of their unemployment issues. A typical example is the recently created African Continental Free Trade Area (ACFTA) that aims to stimulate trade volume in the continent of Africa. To achieve its aims, African B2B organisations should collaborate not only within their nations but also across other nations. They should collaborate in supply, purchasing, product development, logistics, institutional support, institutional supervision, etc.

11.4.2 Understanding of Customers and Other Market Actors

Through the B2B relationship, organisations get to know more about the need of the market and customers. The need of the market is brought closer to the manufacturers or producers of materials utilised for the production of a particular commodity, especially when there is a change in taste and demand of the consumers. This is done through collaboration with wholesalers, retailers, consultants, foreign trade agents, etc. It will, therefore, afford business organisations the opportunities to shape their products to suit the needs and demands of the market and also to forecast the future consumer needs. B2B relationship is therefore important to the business, customers and stakeholders within a particular market.

11.4.3 Value Creation

B2B relationship among organisations enhances the creation of business value through the usage of quality materials for their products and services. When businesses collaborate in the rendering of service or production of goods, better product/service value is created as well as value-added to the organisation. When a product is made available to the market, and there is a high level of consumer satisfaction from the consumption of such goods and services, the consumer sees the organisation with a lens of value. Hence, businesses working together to achieve business and market goals create value for both the firm and the market.

11.4.4 Reduces Uncertainty, Increases Exchange Efficiency and Enhances Effective Collaboration

Uncertainty in business activities can render the business inefficient and ineffective. The three variables (uncertainty, inefficiency and ineffectiveness) are part of the basic characterisation of a dysfunctional business environment that could affect the availability of products in a market. For so many industries, this is what leads to seasonal fluctuations such as unemployment. The needs of the market would, therefore, be left unmet, which will put consumers in a state of uncertainty about the availability of the organisation's offerings. Arguably, if an organisation does not build a strong relationship with its suppliers or collaborative organisations, they would experience uncertainty, inefficiencies and ineffectiveness with concomitant poor performance.

Accordingly, B2B relationship is meant to enhance the performance of the business in the market through the prompt meeting of needs and provision of quality goods and services.

African organisations must, therefore, understand the importance and role of B2B relationship in the development of a sustainable market and foster the right environment to promote such relationships.

11.5 The Role of Decision-Makers in B2B Context

Good knowledge of an organisation's buying pattern and behaviour is fundamental in developing the right industrial marketing strategy. To achieve effectiveness in the buying/purchasing decision, marketing managers must understand the key participants in the purchasing process. In business purchasing, decision-making involves many people. Each of these decision-makers scrutinises the decision from the perspective of their area of specialisation and expertise.

Fishman (2007) suggests that in a B2B relationships, a marketing executive's purpose is better served when he/she is able to identify this group of persons that make the decision to buy, when to buy and from whom to buy, or not to buy and for what reason. Cultivating trustworthy relationships with these decision-makers in many cases is sufficient to translate to an enduring B2B relationship. This is even more so when the relationship is at the strategic business level, an OEM, such as Dunlop Tyres in Ghana that aims at developing a business relationship with an automobile manufacturing firm like Innoson Motors in Nigeria, would likely be talking through the personal secretaries (gatekeepers), engineers and designers (Influencers) to the CEO at Innoson, who sits in relevant capacity and has the responsibility to make decisions on such strategic relationships. This is so because even the engineers and designers at Innoson know which parts and equipment are best for their product, and the marketing executives at Dunlop know that the decision-makers on such B2B relationships, invariably, are the members of decision-making units (DMUs) that are exceptionally knowledgeable in their trade. The engineers and designers are, by all means, important and are critical parts of the business. The decision-makers need to get necessary technical inputs and participation from the technical team. Still, ultimately, the decision to explore a business relationship with another organisation is up to the top management vested with such responsibilities.

11.5.1 Decision-Making Units (DMUs)

Business purchase decision-making is collective in B2B contexts; therefore, all relevant members whose input is cardinal to the strategic success of such activity must be considered important. According to Kotler and Armstrong (2010), DMU refers to all groups and individuals responsible for the process of decision-making about negotiations of goods and services. The DMU is made up of members with a common goal(s) who decide collectively on issues relating to the purchase(s) of products or services to achieve a predetermined goal. Kotler and Armstrong (2010) outlined six roles the DMU play. The DMU and the roles have been also proposed in marketing literature by Webster and Wind (1972) and Wind and Webster (1972) and is also called "the buying centre" (see also Chapter 4; Lewin & Donthu, 2005). These roles are briefly explained below.

Initiators: These are individuals who identify purchasing/buying problems/needs and attempt to find a solution to fix it. They have been regarded as a very important group in the DMU. This group of people could be the users or other members of the organisation depending on the culture of the business entity.

Influencers: This category of members of DMU are employees who supply information and advice as input in the purchase decision-making process. They influence the purchasing process by way of defining specification and make available relevant information for strategically evaluating options. Technical persons (such as product designers and developers) and outsiders (such as consultants) fall into this category.

Buyers: These are members of the DMU who arrange and negotiate purchase terms and conditions with suppliers. However, in the purchase of technical equipment, technical experts are engaged to undertake this task from the beginning until much later in the process before they are involved. This role is always played by high-level employees who possess the requisite knowledge of this activity.

Deciders: They are also referred to as "Approvers". They are apparently saddled with the responsibility of determining product requirements and selecting the supplier models. Hence, top management sits in this important position in the DMU.

Users: They are the people who work with the purchased products or services. They exert influence in the decision-making process by either initiating the purchase process, developing product requirements or setting both activities in motion.

Gatekeepers: These are employees who control information flow to the purchasing centre. The buying department employees frequently play this role, but it could also be played by the secretaries or receptionists in the organisation.

According to Kotler and Armstrong (2010), the buying centre need not be static. Firms do not need six separate individuals to undertake these six functions. One person may play multiple roles simultaneously. Conversely, more than six persons may be required to execute the tasks in some situations. According to Toman et al. (2017), "the number of people involved in B2B solutions purchases has climbed from an average of 5.4 two years ago to 6.8 today, and these stakeholders come from a lengthening roster of roles, functions, and geographies". In summary, the type of goods and services and the prevailing situation will be the condition under which a buying centre is shaped.

11.6 How to Develop Different Types of Valuable Business Relationship

As discussed above, businesses must develop the right relationship with their stakeholders for efficiency and effectiveness in their business operations. However, developing a sustainable business relationship between the seller and buyer in the B2B context requires that business organisations understand the "how" of developing a business relationship. Sulhaini (2012) discussed the basic methods of developing a B2B relationship. The two factors highlighted by Sulhaini (2012) are intangible firm element and favourable relationship element.

The **intangible firm element**, according to Sulhaini (2012), is where an organisation intends to seek knowledge, sustain the relationship and develop the business organisation. The intangible firm elements are unseen characteristics and factors that distinguish the firm in the market and speaks of their zeal to build a formidable relationship. It is the organisation's learning character that puts them up as a business firm that is willing to add value to the market, learn from other business organisations and improve their marketing outcomes.

The other factor identified by Sulhaini (2012) is **favourable relationship elements** which include satisfaction, trust and commitment. Satisfaction lays emphasis on partners involved in a relationship, ensuring that each partner gets the right outcome from the business transaction and also does everything within their contractual agreement to guarantee the attainment of the collective business objective. That is, a business organisation will be able to develop quality business relationships with other business organisations if they are able to provide a quality satisfaction experience with the other party. Trust, on the other hand, specifies that business organisations must be able to communicate trust in their dealing with each other to secure, enhance and build the right B2B relationship. Where there is no trust, it will be challenging to build, maintain or sustain business relationships. Commitment describes the attitude of a party to a business relationship. It is the degree to which a party shows effort and sense of responsibility to ensure that the business relationship adds value to both parties. Organisations involved in a business relationship must ensure that the right commitment is shown in the process of carrying out their contractual obligations. Businesses are usually curious to work with other business that will show commitment in meeting deadlines and make sure whatever is expected of them is carried out efficiently and effectively.

Overall, developing business relationships with stakeholders in B2B requires that organisations in Africa have the right intangible firm element and favourable relationship element. Businesses are attracted to collaborate with organisations with goodwill, trust and commitment to service/product satisfaction.

11.7 Initiating and Influencing Buyer–Seller Relationship in Business-to-Business Markets

In Chapter 2, we defined business relationship as an interactive exchange relationship between two or more organisations that involves economic and social elements, activities, resources and actors.

We also discussed the participants in the business relationship (buyer and seller organisations and their representatives) and how this interaction process usually begins with information exchange episodes which are followed by social exchange episodes. These business relationships take place over a period of time with several stages and are enforced via certain structures and governance mechanisms. This section introduces how this business relationship is initiated and developed, and how to influence the business relationship development stages.

There are several generic models developed in B2B marketing that described how and the process of inter-organisational business relationships development (see Figure 11.1). These relationship development models are different from the structural and organisational form, and governance structures. While structural and governance mechanisms are a phase in the development of relationships as is evident in the relationship development models below, we define relationship development as the non-sequential stages of an inter-organisational business relationship from conception, initiation, influencing and development.

Figure 11.1 shows four relationship development models developed in B2B marketing. Ford (1980) viewed relationship development in B2B to comprise of five, non-sequential stages that involve pre-relationship stage where the partners are not yet in contact and the company is still searching for a potential new supplier to the early stage where the company starts to negotiate with the supplier. The development stage is the stage where a contract is signed and deliveries with a supplier commence. The signing of the contract reduces uncertainty between the parties, which was in the previous stages. The fourth stage is the stage where the firm has already achieved

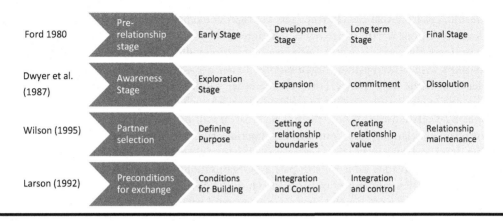

Figure 11.1   Relationship development models.

large-scale deliveries from the supplier over several years with potential cost savings for the buyer. In this stage, the relationship with the supplier is seen as a long-term relationship. After this stage, the relationship enters its final stage characterised with long-established, stable markets and institutionalisation of business norms such as code of practice and business ethics (Ford, 1980).

The Dwyer et al. (1987) model is a four-stage non-sequential model of inter-organisational business relationship development comprising of awareness, exploration, expansion and commitment phases. The awareness stage describes the stage where the firm has not had interaction with the potential partner, but is aware and acquainted of potential brands and merchants that could be a potential partner through their branding efforts.

The exploration stage is the stage that dyadic interaction starts to occur between both firms. In this stage, the firm begins communication and bargaining with the potential partner, developing expectations and norms of the relationships and could also include trial phase with trial purchases, testing and evaluating the products and services in relational exchange. The expansion stage is the stage where there is an increase in benefits of both parties or mutual satisfaction due to their interdependence and continual dyadic interactions leading to the commitment stage where they establish shared values, certainty, trust and governance structures to resolve conflicts and support current and future joint investment relations. The dissolution stage is the stage where there is withdrawal or disengagement of the relationships initiated by either party or a joint decision to terminate the relationship. Wilson (1995) identified five stages of relationship development which comprises partner selection, the definition of purpose, setting relationship boundaries, creating relationship value and maintenance of the relationship. The model integrates 13 relationship variables (social bonds, mutual goals, comparison level of alternative, reputation, performance satisfaction, trust, commitment, cooperation, structural bonds, social bonds, adaptation, non-retrievable investments, shared technology, power dependence) that impacts each of the relationship development stages as shown in Figure 11.2. For example, social bonds, mutual goals, reputation, performance satisfaction, trust, power dependence, shared technology and comparison level of alternative are the most critical variables utilised by the firm at the partner selection stage for selecting a potential new partner.

Larson (1992) developed a relationship process development model consisting of three phases of defining the preconditions for exchange (first phase), specifying the conditions for building the relationship (second phase), and integration and control (third phase) as shown in Figure 11.3. In Larson's model, personal reputation, pre-existing relationships between connected people and the

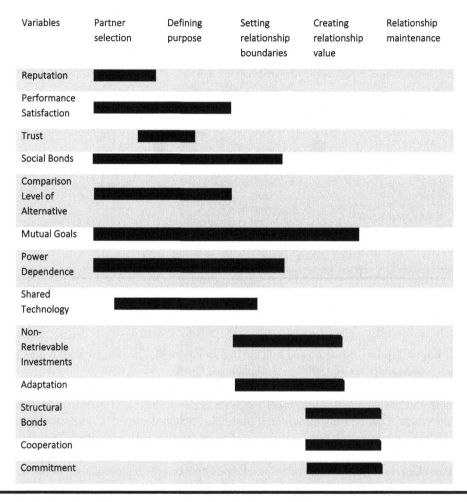

Variables	Partner selection	Defining purpose	Setting relationship boundaries	Creating relationship value	Relationship maintenance
Reputation	■				
Performance Satisfaction	■				
Trust	■				
Social Bonds	■				
Comparison Level of Alternative	■				
Mutual Goals	■				
Power Dependence	■				
Shared Technology	■				
Non-Retrievable Investments			■		
Adaptation			■		
Structural Bonds				■	
Cooperation				■	
Commitment				■	

Figure 11.2   Relationship development model (Wilson, 1995).

reputation of the firm are the historical preconditions for new business relationship formation. The conditions to develop the relationship hinge on the ability or willingness of either firm to initiate or engage in a more collaborative relationship. This is often followed by a trial period where both parties evaluate the mutual economic advantage of the relationship, develop trust and reciprocity norms, clear expectations, the institution of rules and procedures that introduced predictable structure and basis for performance monitoring and the evolution of clear expectations within each alliance.

The third stage consists of the establishment of operational and strategic integration as well as social control. While operational integration enhances communication and connects the back-office of both firms to ensure information exchange (e.g., SAP integration, EDIs), strategic integration involves the integration of value chain between both organisations via the initiation of joint strategic projects such as barcodes and RFIDs. Social control describes how social relations and norms (e.g. trust, norms of fairness, honesty and reciprocity) are embedded in buyer–seller relationships as a control mechanism.

While the relationship development models in buyer–seller relationships capture some aspects of the relationship development cycle, they, however, do not cover the relationship development

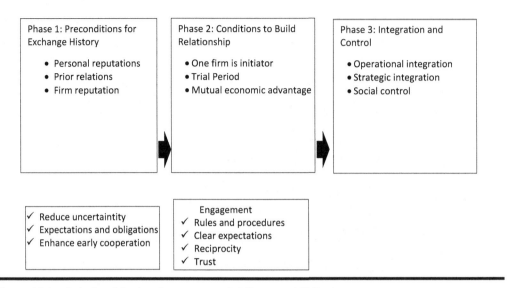

Figure 11.3   Relationship development model (Larson, 1992).

process from conception, initiation and influencing. In Figure 11.4, we describe our model inspired by the work of Mandják et al. (2015) and Ahola et al. (2019).

In the model above, business relationship development starts through conception, initiation, influencing and development. Our model has both organisational and personnel level activities during the stages of conception, initiation, influencing and development. Conception is the origin of the relationship where both organisations have no interaction with each other. There are trigger issues that initiate the business relationship both at the personnel and organisational levels. At a personal level, personal reputation and prior relations between the representatives of the buyer and seller create good evidence or reasons for a referral. The trust the buyer company representative has on the seller company representative motivates the initiation to begin interaction with the seller company. The individual bonding trusts created as a result of the positive reaction of the buyer and seller create organisational level bonding trust that facilitates the birth of new relationship between the buyer and the seller. At the organisational level, one firm often takes the lead in initiating a business relationship. The needs of the firm or market opportunities may create trigger issues for a buyer and seller to initiate a business relationship to co-create value or to co-exploit value. Furthermore, the network position of a company provides the firm closeness centrality and makes it possible for the firm to have access to other network ties which in turn provides the firm access to privileged market information, goodwill, visibility and attractiveness to other members of the networks.

There may be more than one potential partner seeking to initiate or commence a business relationship with the buyer; however, the buyer may seek quotations from several sellers and sellers may enquire for specification from the buyer. In addition to trigger issues, the buyer usually selects a partner that most matches their business requirements, and a contract is signed. Immediately after a contract is signed, the influencing and development path of the relationship starts. During the influencing stage, the initiator creates a joint agenda, establishes communication channels and secures access to critical resources needed to develop the business relationship. Furthermore, the initiator establishes joint decision-making bodies where decisions regarding the

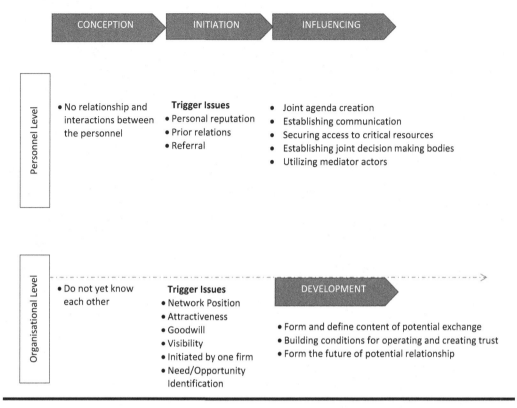

Figure 11.4   A model of relationship initiation, development and influencing.

business relationship will be made and utilise mediator actors whenever necessary to influence key aspects of the decision-making.

The development stage of the relationship involves forming and defining the content of potential exchange in the relationship. What each party brings and gets from the relationship is defined and agreed upon and the conditions to which they operate (e.g. trust, transparency), exchange trust and contents of the relationship is established. Furthermore, the experience from this existing relationship forms a potential basis for future potential relationship.

11.8   Performance of Non-equity Alliance in Africa

In today's marketplace, of which Africa is not an exception, collaborations, strategic alliances and partnership between companies can be highly beneficial. More and more firms are forming part of a new wave of organisations that leverage on effective management of buyers and suppliers' relationship as a channel to the success of supply chain management in firms and the performance of the organisation (Harland, 1996; Ambrose et al., 2010). There are critical suppliers and buyers whose values must be adequately maximised for business success (Chen & Huang, 2004; Ambrose et al., 2010). Given the importance of business relationships, organisations and businesses in Africa must be stimulated to leverage on the benefits in B2B marketing relationship. This chapter proposes B2B relationship as a crucial strategic choice for enhancing organisational value to bridge the gap between the organisation and the market, reduce uncertainty in business transactions and enhance economic performance. The quality of relationship shared by suppliers and customers within a market can result in business expansion, increased profit, larger market audience and new innovative products/services. A marketing relationship between a buyer and a seller is a joint effort of both parties, which would make the relationship yield the expected and right outcomes (Rose, 2018). Within Africa, organisations can leverage cultural similarities and practices to build an effective B2B relationship with other African countries.

The business relationships elements identified can be harnessed to build a formidable business practice between organisations in Africa. An enabling framework for business relationships in Africa can be established through theoretical knowledge of what these business relationships can provide. For example, drawing from the tenets of commercial enterprise, manufacturing organisations in Africa can have a strong and effective commodity exchange market that will give room for cost reduction, quality materials for goods/service and sustained business integration. The end product of organisation "X" can be a key part of the product in organisation "Y" when producing "Z" commodity. Hence, within the African countries/organisations, a supplier–buyer relationship can be created and sustained for the growth of the African business. The B2B relationship in Africa would develop when African businesses patronise each other for their products and service in their production process and not solely partner with foreign organisations abroad. Continuous offshore B2B relationships would increase the cost of production of local goods and price of commodities, and could stagnate the growth of the indigenous firm. Also, Gadde and Snehota (2019) argue that effective relationship management between suppliers and buyers involves three main themes which are interaction in supplier relationships, dealing with supply network interdependencies and the handling of dynamic changes in their supply context. There are benefits for buyers when engaged in an extended relationship with suppliers, and it requires effective interaction. To fully benefit from a positive supplier–buyer relationship, the buying firm must ensure that they possess the right skills needed to react to the dynamics of the market and emerging situations. Adequate skills are required by both parties because there are various issues at different levels of the supply network that require adequate marketing and managerial skills. Therefore, effective purchasing and supply management is conditional on organisational solutions (Gadde & Snehota, 2019). Gadde et al. posit that organisations must pay subtle attention and create conditions that favour them on both the supply and purchasing sides. Organisations must make provisions for learning and development of individual skills that will promote inter-organisational interaction with suppliers and buyers, respectively, depending on the position and status of the firm. Additionally, the authors posit that organisations would benefit more from supplier relationship when the purchase and supply management does not depend on decisions regarding single discrete transactions but shifts towards a much broader perspective, centred on series of simultaneous transactions with various suppliers, at present and in the future. Furthermore, trust and commitment from suppliers and buyers have shown to be a determining factor in firm performance from business relationship (Ambrose et al., 2010), and for performance and satisfaction to be sustained, both parties must perceive that they are gaining as much as they are investing (Narayandas & Rangan, 2004). Another key factor that was recognised for the performance of the business relationship is the reduction of uncertainty by parties (Morris & Carter, 2005). When parties have a feeling of uncertainty in a business relationship, commitment and trust will be affected. In relation to factors that suppliers and buyers should consider in their business relationship for satisfaction and performance, Nyaga et al. (2010) and Ambrose et al. (2010) found that trust, commitment, adaptation and effective communication enhance satisfaction and the performance of business relationships.

11.9 Communication Methods in Business Relationships

One of the most effective strategies to build a significant relationship between buyer and seller within a market is communication (Hung & Lin, 2013; Batra & Keller, 2016; Murphy & Sashi, 2018). Effective communication influences organisational outcomes and also the strength of the relationship between parties involved in B2B relationships. Some scholars (see Johnson & Mena, 2008; Bastl et al., 2012) posits that a buyer–seller relationship demands greater information and knowledge exchange. This increases social bonds and interdependency, and leads to effective supplier–buyer relationship coordination and increased competence and cooperation (Wise & Baumgartner, 1999; Slack et al., 2004; Windahl et al., 2004; Gulati & Kletter, 2005; Windahl & Lakemond, 2006; Bastl et al., 2012). For example, when the seller provides the buyer with an authentic avenue to give feedback on the service/product rendered, the sellers are enhancing the buyers' trust and also have the opportunity to improve product/service quality. In furtherance, effective communication between buyers and sellers could also determine how an organisation competes in the business market (Ramani & Kumar, 2008; Murphy & Sashi, 2018).

Communication between buyers and sellers is paramount to achieving good business relationship, both in the short and long terms. Therefore, organisations and firm must inculcate effective communication methods in the business strategy and be conscious of their communication channels and tools. The intent of B2B communication might vary over time. However, it generally seeks to convey the value which the product offers (Biemans, 2010). Hence, we can describe B2B marketing communication as a process of businesses conveying the value of their products to buyers with the intention to stimulate purchase or build business relationship. From this definition, communication in B2B relationship can be carried out for different reasons which could range from creating awareness to changing the perception of a product and stimulating purchase (Blythe & Zimmerman, 2005). The goal of business communication will determine the methods that will be utilised. For example, the widespread use of the internet and social media provides businesses with the opportunity to communicate their values electronically. Through this platform, demands can be made by buyers to suppliers and delivery effected with ease in a short period of time.

The evolving nature of society and its structure is, therefore, having its effect on supplier–buyer relationship. The effectiveness of communication in B2B can also be determined by the type of communication strategy the organisation utilises. Basically, two types can be practised: one-to-one communication and mass communication (Biemans, 2010). One-to-one communication allows a supplier to communicate with the individual organisation directly through personal selling and direct marketing such as direct mail, telemarketing and internet marketing (Biemans, 2010). It is termed one-to-one marketing because the supplier and buyer have direct communication, and it does not involve a large group of persons or channels. On the contrary, mass communication involves sending and receiving quality information from a supplier to a group of buyers and vice versa. Mass communication focuses on efficiency, and the commonly used tools for this type of communication are advertising, trade shows and public relations (Biemans, 2010).

B2B marketers mostly use the traditional print media to get their message to their audience, with over 89% of B2B marketers using print media (Peter, 2019). However, the changing market structure and audience demand that organisations consider online B2B marketing. Therefore, B2B firms should aim to utilise the most effective social method tools that enhance communication and collaboration. Peter (2019) posits that B2B marketers should consider using more of LinkedIn, video marketing, webinars and social media, and a focus on content marketing if they will keep up with the pace of business competitors. B2B marketing might have excelled through face-to-face interactions previously; however, the trend has changed. It is time for business organisations to embrace and utilise internet marketing as suppliers and buyers are building brand awareness and stimulating sales through content marketing on websites and social media (Peter, 2019).

Businesses in Africa must align with the current trend in the global world by ensuring that their communication is in line with the need of the local market. Language, culture and religion are factors that influence relationships in Africa and business organisations must understand these dynamics. Businesses must communicate the "language" of the people in meeting their needs. The African market must be understood in terms of their needs and capacity to purchase, which should determine the buyer–supplier relationship. If the dynamics of the African market is understood, the right goods and services can be communicated to them in the right language to develop the right relationship.

11.10 Governance Mechanisms in Strategic Alliances

According to Heide (1994), inter-firm exchange involves a multidimensional phenomenon, which includes the initiation, termination and ongoing relationship maintenance between parties. By extension, governance mechanisms are tools utilised to organise these exchange ties effectively (Heide, 1994), and effective management of buyer–supplier relationship requires an appropriate governance mechanism (Clauss & Bouncken, 2019). Buyer–supplier alliances can produce benefits for the parties involved but only when appropriate mechanisms are put in place to manage opportunistic behaviours of partners which seeks to accumulate gains for self at the expense of another party (Huang & Chiu, 2018). Governance mechanism is relevant in B2B relationship management as it enhances smooth interactions between buyers and suppliers, creates joint value among them, fosters quality information exchange, and improves efficiency and competitive advantage for firms (Huang & Chiu, 2018). Governance mechanisms protect and facilitate sustainable and ethical practices in a supplier–buyer relationship so as not to put a buyer at the mercy of the supplier and vice versa. It is also important for establishing trust, which is needed for long-term interaction (Lui & Ngo, 2004). Consequently, governance mechanisms are precautions which industrial organisations put in place to regulate inter-organisational interactions, minimise undue exploitation and protect investments (Jap & Ganesan, 2000; Huang & Chiu, 2018). Firms involved in business relationships wield power which they may desire to use for personal gains, without concrete and well-established governance system; hence, organisations with less vulnerability in the relationship will take advantage of the party with higher dependence in the course of the business dealings. Therefore, a good governance mechanism creates a level-playing field for business partnership in equity alliances.

Governance mechanisms in strategic alliances are necessary to ensure buyer–supplier relationship equilibrium (Benton & Maloni, 2005). Jap and Anderson (2003) consider opportunistic behaviours, divergence of objectives, differences in operational routines and unpredicted market changes as factors that imply the existence of conflict between buyers and suppliers. Cooperative and successful supplier–buyer relationship is ensured through two types of governance mechanism which have been discussed in literature, which are contractual and relational governance (Poppo & Zenger, 2002; Langfield-Smith & Smith, 2003; Lui & Ngo, 2005; Van der Meer-Kooistra & Vosselman, 2000; Cao & Luminuau, 2015). The contractual governance mechanism defines an alliance and describes the rights and duties of parties in a relationship; it gives details on how sensitive information, intellectual property and the procedures for conflict resolutions are to be handled. Also, the liabilities to be implemented in the case of breach of the agreement are stated in the contract of an alliance formed under the contractual mechanism (Clauss & Bouncken, 2019). Hence, contractual governance mechanisms provide binding written documents that guide, regulate and give required directions for the action of parties in the business relationship. In practical terms, the contractual mechanism of regulating business relationship will provide activities and timelines that the supplier will work with, in the delivery of their products and discharge of their contractual responsibilities, which if contravened otherwise will attract a penalty. It is, therefore, important that firms insert this in the contractual agreement clauses to ensure the achievement of their initial alliance goals.

There is also contract specificity as identified by Griffith and Zhao (2015), which is seen as a key element in B2B contract formulation in order to avoid contract violation. Contract specificity is the explicitness, specification and precision a contract poses to avoid misinterpretations and violations (Mooi & Ghosh, 2010; Griffith & Zhao, 2015). Contract specificity is an aspect of the business relationship that sustains and creates a bond between the parties involved. The contract is expected to contain the roles and responsibilities of the partners within the contractual agreement, time duration and reward. The condition for bringing the contract to an end is expected to be stated and also the process of operations. It is strongly believed that when a contract possesses the quality of specificity, it would be of benefits to the parties involved and hindrances to accomplishing their mutual goals would be eliminated.

Relational governance mechanisms, on the other hand, are self-enforcing social mechanisms that often evolve in repeated transactions (Dwyer et al., 1987; Clauss & Bouncken, 2019). This system thrives on commitment, trust, mutual understanding and norms in social exchanges (Tomkins, 2001; Clauss & Bouncken, 2019). The success of this nature of interaction can increase the social bond and reduce uncertainties in alliance transactions. It is an aspect of regulating supplier–buyer relationship through social and mutual norms. Relationship mechanism is created through the relational norm, and it sustains buyer–seller interaction through a social mechanism that focuses on values with the predictability of partner's behaviour (Clauss & Bouncken, 2019). In relationship governance mechanism, contracts are not the foundation and guiding principles but rather relationship values. Opportunistic behaviours are controlled in partners through ostracism (Liu et al., 2009). Relationship governance mechanism thrives on the notion that organisations in the alliance have both social and economic outcomes as the basis for business transactions. Trust and commitment are built through repeated interaction, and firms will reciprocate the right behaviour that is needed to sustain the relationship as exhibited by the other party. Relationship governance, therefore, provides that business relationship be governed based on social and economic norms, which will facilitate trust, commitment and mutual relationship and not just contractual relationship. Quality buyer–supplier relationships allow organisations to make progress in a dynamic marketplace and yield considerable returns for both parties. However, this buyer–supplier relationship may transcend into opportunism and conflict as such; it becomes imperative to govern such relationships on the basis of formal and informal mechanisms as a crucial mechanism for improving the exchange process (Meryem, 2011).

11.11 Conclusion

Businesses do not operate in isolation; they either depend on the demand and changing trend of the market or the availability of internal resources. Essential among exogenous factors that the organisation must take into cognisance to enhance their business performance is the relationship they share with buyers, customers or sellers, depending on the nature of the market. In the B2B context, due to the nature of goods/services, the relationship between the buyers and sellers is different from what is present in the B2C market. The B2B market is the primary market that determines the production, availability and distribution of goods for the actors in the B2C. Hence, businesses in Africa must understand the practice in the B2B market, the type and importance of alliances in the B2B market and how to develop a valuable B2B relationship. This chapter has attempted to provide the basic knowledge, concepts and practices that businesses in the B2B markets need to adopt to build and sustain relationships.

Case and Exercise

STRATEGIC BUYER–SELLER RELATIONSHIP: A CASE STUDY OF ZURAK COMPANY LIMITED

Zurak Company Limited is a major building material supplier in Nigeria with headquarters in the Federal Capital Territory, Abuja, Nigeria. Incorporated in 2001, the company focuses on production and supply of building materials to large construction companies. Over the years, Zurak has grown a reputation for their strong relationship with their buyers, putting them on a firm pedestal in the B2B construction market. In 2019, Rajesh, Zurak's Indian Marketing Manager of over a decade, was approached by Arun, the Marketing Manager of a non-competing product who had heard of their excellent service delivery and wanted to know how they had been able to sustain good customer relationships with major clients over the years. Arun, also an Indian national, was new in Nigeria and had experienced challenges in forging relationships with the different buyers he had dealt with since his arrival the previous year.

Mr Arun met up with Mr Rajesh and posed the question during a lunch meeting to discuss doing business in Nigeria. Rajesh smiled as he explained that Zurak had been able to sustain and enhance business relationships with key buyers by creating positive impressions and trust in their products. Rajesh stated, "we have observed that most B2B relationship in this part of the world do not result in buyer loyalty as it ought to; therefore, we studied the trends of successful business relationships to understand basic factors that sustain these relationships. We observed organisations that have been able to build a robust buyer-seller relationship and how they achieve this and came up with some basic practices which we included in our organisations' daily activities".

Arun was very interested. He looked on as Rajesh continued, "First and foremost, we crafted organisational values that are reflected in the zeal and passion with which we carry out our activities. We ensure that all our business transactions with our client are carried out with a high level of enthusiasm. Yes, this we learnt from other successful business organisation". Rajesh explained further that the second factor is embodied in the tenets of satisfaction, trust and commitment. He stressed, "we make buyers' satisfaction top of our priority, and we do everything within our capacity to ensure that our buyers are satisfied with the product we offer. Trust and commitment of buyers are also what builds and sustains a buyer-seller relationship; your buyers must be able to trust all your delivery schedules and product specifications. If trust is the foundation of business operations between the selling and buying organisations, the buyer's commitment to the selling organisation's product will be sustained".

Over the years, Rajesh stressed, Zurak has sustained buyer loyalty, maintained relationships and ensured commitment to a steady supply of quality raw materials through commitment to its core values evident in transactions with other businesses, giving them a competitive edge in the market.

At the end of the meeting, Arun was impressed. He had other questions on winning key accounts and understanding the decision-making units of companies but would wait. He would request another meeting.

EXERCISE

1. What are the key success factors in the B2B relationship?
2. How important is relationship building and management in B2B transactions?
3. What are the foundational blocks which business relationships are built upon?
4. What other strategies would you propose to organisations to enhance and sustain B2B relationships?

References

Ahola, T., Aaltonen, K., Artto, K., & Lehtinen, J. (2019). Making room to manoeuvre: How firms increase their influence with others in business networks. *Industrial Marketing Management*, 79, 58–70.

Aka, D., Kehinde, O., & Ogunnaike, O. (2016). Relationship marketing and customer satisfaction: A conceptual perspective. *Binus Business Review*, 7(2), 185–190.

Ambrose, E., Marshall, D., & Lynch, D. (2010). Buyer supplier perspectives on supply chain relationships. *International Journal of Operations & Production Management*, 30(12), 1269–1290.

Bagdoniene, L., & Zilione, R. (2009). Business to business relationships: The variables in the context of success. *Social Sciences,* 66(4), 1392–0758.

Bastl, M., Johnson, M., Lightfoot, H., & Evans, S. (2012). Buyer-supplier relationships in a servitized environment: An examination with Cannon and Perreault's framework. *International Journal of Operations and Production Management*, 32(6), 650–675.

Batra, R., & Keller, K. L. (2016). Integrating marketing communications: New findings, new lessons and new ideas. *Journal of Marketing*, 80(6), 122–145.

Benton, W. C., & Maloni, M. (2005). The influence of power driven buyer/seller relationships on supply chain satisfaction. *Journal of Operations Management*, 23(1), 1–22.

Bick, G., Singh, A., & Human, G. (2014). Strategic imperatives as drivers of a network orientated approach to the organisation of marketing in B2B firms. *In 30th IMP-Conference*, Bordeaux, France.

Biemans, W. G. (2010). *Business to business marketing: A value-driven approach*. McGraw-Hill Higher Education, New York.

Blythe, J., & Zimmerman, A. S. (2005). *Business-to-business marketing management: A global perspective*. Cengage Learning EMEA, Andover.

Brennan, R., Canning, L., & McDowell, R. (2011). *Business-to-business marketing*. SAGE Publications Limited, New York.

Brodie, R., Brady, M., Dadzie, K. Q., Johnston, W. J., & Pels, J. (2008). Business-to-business marketing practices in West Africa, Argentina and the United States. *Journal of Business and Industrial Marketing*, 23(2), 84–94.

Cannon, J. P., & Homburg, C. (2001). Buyer–supplier relationships and customer firm costs. *Journal of Marketing*, 65, 29–43.

Cao, Z., & Luminuau, F. (2015). Revisiting the interplay between contractual and relational governance: A qualitative and meta-analytic investigation. *Journal of Operation Management*, 33, 15–42.

Chen, H. L., & Huang, Y. (2004). The establishment of global marketing strategic alliances by small and medium enterprises. *Small Business Economics*, 22(5), 365–377.

Clauss, T., & Bouncken, R. B. (2019). Social power as an antecedent of governance in buyer-supplier alliances. *Industrial Marketing Management*, 77, 75–89.

Dwyer, F. R., Schurr, P. H., & Oh, S. (1987). Developing buyer-supplier relationships. *Journal of Marketing*, 51(2), 11–27.

Fishman, C. (2007). *The Wal-Mart effect: How an Out-of-Town Superstore Became a Superpower*. Penguin, London.

Ford, D. (1980). The development of buyer-seller relationships in industrial markets. *European Journal of Marketing*, 14, 339–553.

Ford, D., Gadde, L. E., Håkansson, H., & Snehota, I. (2011). *Managing business relationships*. 3rd edition. Wiley, Chichester.

Gadde, L. E., & Snehota, I. (2019). What does it take to make the most of supplier relationships? *Industrial Marketing Management*, 83, 185–193.

Griffith, D. A., & Zhao, Y. (2015). Contract specificity, contract violation, and relationship performance in international buyer–supplier relationships. *Journal of International Marketing*, 23(3), 22–40.

Gulati, R., & Kletter, D. (2005). Shrinking core, expanding periphery: The relational architecture of high-performing organizations. *California Management Review*, 47(3), 77–104.

Harland, C. M. (1996). Supply chain management: Relationships, chains and networks. *British Journal of Management*, 7, 63–80.

Heide, J. B. (1994). Interorganizational governance in marketing channels. *Journal of Marketing*, 58, 71–85.

Huang, M. C., & Chiu, Y. P. (2018). Relationship governance mechanisms and collaborative performance: A relational life-cycle perspective. *Journal of Purchasing and Supply Management*, 24(3), 260–273.

Hung, K. P., & Lin, C. K. (2013). More communication is not always better? The interplay between effective communication and interpersonal conflict in influencing satisfaction. *Industrial Marketing Management*, 42(8), 1223–1232.

Ibidunni, O. S. (2012). *Marketing Management: Practical Perspectives*. Concept Publications, Lagos.

Jap, S. D., & Anderson, E. (2003). Safeguarding interorganizational performance and continuity under ex post opportunism. *Management Science*, 49(12), 1684–1701.

Jap, S. D., & Ganesan, S. (2000). Control mechanisms and the relationship life cycle: Implications for safeguarding specific investments and developing commitment. *Journal of Marketing Research*, 37(2), 227–245.

Johnson, M., & Mena, C. (2008). Supply chain management for servitised products: A multi-industry case study. *International Journal of Production Economics*, 114(1), 27–39.

Kempeners, M. A. (1995). Relationships quality in business-to-business relationships. pp. 1629–1638.

Kotler, P., & Armstrong, G. (2010). *Principles of marketing*. Pearson Education, London.

Langfield-Smith, K., & Smith, D. (2003). Management control systems and trust in outsourcing relationships. *Management Accounting Research*, 14(3), 281–307.

Larson, A. (1992). Network dyads in entrepreneurial settings: A study of the governance of exchange relationships. *Administrative Science Quarterly*, 37(1): 76–104.

Lee, D., Moon, J., Kim, Y. J., & Mun, Y. Y. (2015). Antecedents and consequences of mobile phone usability: Linking simplicity and interactivity to satisfaction, trust, and brand loyalty. *Information and Management*, 52(3), 295–304.

Lewin, J. E., & Donthu, N. (2005). The influence of purchase situation on buying center structure and involvement: A select meta-analysis of organizational buying behavior research. *Journal of Business Research*, 58(10), 1381–1390.

Liao, M H., Xu, Y. C., & Sone, H. (2016, July). Old-established companies' traditions and innovations—focusing on e-business of Japan and Taiwan. *In 2016 10th International Conference on Innovative Mobile and Internet Services in Ubiquitous Computing (IMIS)* (pp. 531–532). IEEE, Fukuoka, Japan.

Liu, Y., Luo, Y., & Liu, T. (2009). Governing buyer–supplier relationships through transactional and relational mechanisms: Evidence from China. *Journal of Operations Management*, 27(4), 294–309.

Lui, S. S., & Ngo, H. Y. (2004). The role of trust and contractual safeguards on cooperation in non-equity alliances. *Journal of Management*, 30(4), 471–485.

Lui, S. S., & Ngo, H. Y. (2005). An action pattern model of inter-firm cooperation. *Journal of Management Studies*, 42(6), 1123–1153.

Mandják, T., Szalkai, Z., Neumann-Bódi, E., Magyar, M., & Simon, J. (2015). Emerging relationships: How are they born? *Industrial Marketing Management*, 49, 32–41.

Meryem, B. (2011). Governance mechanisms and buyer supplier relationship: Static and dynamic panel data evidence from Tunisian exporting SMEs. *International Journal of Economics and Financial Issues*, 1(3), 88.

Mooi, E. A., & Ghosh, M. (2010). Contract specificity and its performance implications. *Journal of Marketing*, 74(2), 105–120.

Morris, M., & Carter, C. R. (2005). Relationship marketing and supplier logistics performance: An extension of the key mediating variables model. *Journal of Supply Chain Management*, 41(4), 32–43.

Murphy, M., & Sashi, C. M. (2018). Communication, interactivity, and satisfaction in B2B relationships. *Industrial Marketing Management*, 68, 1–12.

Narayandas, D., & Rangan, V. K. (2004). Building and sustaining buyer–seller relationships in mature industrial markets. *Journal of Marketing*, 68(3), 63–77.

Nyaga, G. N., Whipple, J. M., & Lynch, D. F. (2010). Examining supply chain relationships: Do buyer and supplier perspectives on collaborative relationships differ? *Journal of Operations Management*, 28(2), 101–114.

Peter, V. (2019). An examination of social media practices that improve customer satisfaction in the B2B market in the ICT sector in India.

Poppo, L., & Zenger, T. (2002). Do formal contracts and relational governance function as substitutes or complements? *Strategic Management Journal*, 23(8), 707–725.

Ramani, G., & Kumar, V. (2008). Interaction orientation and firm performance. *Journal of Marketing*, 72(January), 27–45.

Roberts-Lombard, M., Mpinganjira, M., & Svensson, G. (2019). The antecedents and postcedents of satisfaction in business-to-business relationships in South Africa. *South African Journal of Business Management*, 50(1), 1–11.

Rose, C. (2018). Relationship quality in business to business customer-supplier relationships. In *Supplier relationships to family firms* (pp. 7–24). Springer Gabler, Wiesbaden.

Slack, N., Lewis, M., & Bates, H. (2004). The two worlds of operations management research and practice. *International Journal of Operations & Production Management*, 24(4), 372–87.

Snow, C. C. (1997). Twenty-first-century organizations: Implications for a new marketing paradigm. *Journal of the Academy of Marketing Science*, 25(1), 72–74.

Sulhaini, S. (2012). Business relationship development in the context of a high-risk and uncertainty. *Journal of Economics, Business and Accountancy Ventura*, 15(1), 1–16.

Swani, K., Brown, B. P., & Mudambi, S. M. (2019). The untapped potential of B2B advertising: A literature review and future agenda. *Industrial Marketing Management*, 89, 581–593.

Toman, N., Adamson, B., & Gomez, C. (2017, March). The new sales imperative. Retrieved August 6, 2020, from https://hbr.org/2017/03/the-new-sales-imperative.

Tomkins, C. (2001). Interdependencies, trust and information in relationships, alliances. Accounting, Organizations and Society, 26(2), 161–191.

Van der Meer-Kooistra, J., & Vosselman, E. G. (2000). Management control of inter firm transactional relationships: The case of industrial renovation and maintenance. *Accounting, Organizations and Society*, 25(1), 51–77.

Wang, C. L., Shi, Y., & Barnes, B. R. (2015). The role of satisfaction, trust and contractual obligation on long-term orientation. *Journal of Business Research*, 68(3), 473–479.

Webster Jr, F. E. (1992). The changing role of marketing in the corporation. *Journal of Marketing*, 56(4), 1–17.

Webster Jr, F. E., & Wind, Y. (1972). A general model for understanding organizational buying behavior. *Journal of Marketing*, 36(2), 12–19.

Wilson, D. T. (1995). An integrated model of buyer-seller relationships. *Journal of the Academy of Marketing Science*, 23(4), 335–345.

Wind, Y., & Webster Jr, F. E. (1972). On the study of industrial buying behavior: Current practices and future trends. *Industrial Marketing Management*, 1(4), 411–416.

Windahl, C., & Lakemond, N. (2006). Developing integrated solutions: The importance of relationships within the network. *Industrial Marketing Management*, 35(7), 806–818.

Windahl, C., Andersson, P., Berggren, C., & Nehler, C. (2004). Manufacturing firms and integrated solutions: Characteristics and implications. *European Journal of Innovation Management*, 7(3), 218–228.

Wise, R., & Baumgartner, P. (1999). Go downstream: The new profit imperative in manufacturing. *Harvard Business Review*, 77(5), 133–141.

Wright, R. (2004). *Business-to-business marketing: A step-by-step guide*. Pearson Education, London.

Zeithaml, V. A., Bitner, M. J., & Gremler, D. D. (2018). *Services marketing: Integrating customer focus across the firm*. McGraw-Hill, Boston, MA.

Zimmerman, A., & Blythe, J. (2017). *Business to business marketing management: A global perspective*. Routledge, Abindon.

Chapter 12

Building Brand and Customer Loyalty in an African Business-to-Business Context

By the end of the chapter, the reader will be able to:

- Understand the concept of branding in business-to-business (B2B) relationships
- Understand brand positioning strategies in B2B relationships
- Discuss how to utilise social media and internet platforms to build brand and customer loyalty
- Understand systems and required tools to build customer loyalty.

12.1 Introduction

The modern business environment is fast-changing and extremely competitive. This is reflective of the intense struggle for survival through achieving brand recognition, brand loyalty, competitive market share, high sales volume, and profitably achieving organisational goals and objectives (Caxton, 2018). Therefore, most organisations commit to developing strategic brands to increase brand recognition, acceptability and demand for products (Wang et al., 2017). A brand is not just the name of a product but also traits and values it bears, which distinguishes it among similar products in the market. According to Armstrong and Kotler (2016), brands are different from products. Brands are what consumers purchase from the company, while products refer to what the company produce(s). Branding explains all the activities involved in establishing an inimitable distinctiveness among products. It creates the ease of recall of brand names, traits/values, preferences for quick recognition of products in the mind of business partners and target clients (Ogbuji et al., 2014).

The importance of branding in the B2B market cannot be overemphasised (Cassia et al., 2017), with business relationships attracting a series of scholarly literature on the determinants of brand relevance, purchase importance and purchase complexity (see Zablah et al., 2010; Leek & Christodoulides, 2012; Brown et al., 2012; Gomes et al., 2016; Cassia et al., 2017). Key among the practical implications of these studies is the importance of B2B branding in the retention of loyal B2B customers and ensuring positive outcomes for the organisation's sustainable competitive advantage (Guzmán et al., 2012; Reijonen et al., 2015; Hirvonen et al., 2016; Cassia, et al., 2017). Based on these scholars' submissions, B2B organisations are encouraged to invest in branding as a strategy to enhance customers' loyalty (Kotler & Pfoertsch, 2007; Cassia et al., 2017). It is, therefore, crucial that organisations in B2B relationships in Africa begin to look into branding as a strategy for market penetration, customer loyalty sustenance and improved business performances. For this purpose, this chapter documents how B2B (notably, supplier–buyer relationships) in Africa can be significantly improved through branding.

12.2 Building Brands

Business organisations can sustain relationships with their suppliers or buyers through understanding and implementing basic principles. Branding will not only build a positive business image but also enhance business performance. Branding is linked to business performance due to its characteristics of not focusing on the short-term goals alone but more strategically on the long-run operational and business goals of competitive advantage and value creation (Juntunen et al., 2019). Kuhn et al. (2008) describe a brand as providing functional, economic and psychological benefits for end users. Our lives are formed and thrive around branding (Maurya & Mishra, 2012). For this reason, branding is reflected in different situations for different purposes that have influenced the definitions attached to it by marketing researchers. Table 12.1 provides an extracted summary of various definitions attached to branding by different researchers with similar meanings but with diverse scopes of applications.

The classified definitions in Table 12.1 show different emphases on the definitions of branding to explicate its ubiquitous nature in socio-economic life. It traverses culture, personality, tangible and intangible elements and also, corporate organisations which is the centrality of this chapter. Branding is not the resources embedded in the suppliers' products sold to the customer but rather the value and suppliers' marketing communication (Merz et al., 2009; Brodie, 2009; Elsäßer & Wirtz, 2017). The brand of a business establishes its importance in attracting and giving customers experiences that create loyalty. Specifically, Payne et al. (2009) and Prahalad and Ramaswamy (2004) identified branding as key in supplier–buyer relationships. The concept of branding in the context of B2B relationships has not been aligned enough by marketing managers; hence, business organisations and practitioners operating in B2B markets must realise their all-important roles in establishing their brand positioning with customers.

Manufacturing and service organisations in B2B must realise that a strong and unique industrial brand is key to achieving competitive advantage and enhancing industrial performance (Persson, 2010; Elsäßer & Wirtz, 2017). Branding has been well discussed in the B2C context (Kucuk, 2019). However, less focus has been laid on branding to enhance B2B customer loyalty. For businesses to build the right brand in the B2B market, they must consistently have strong brand positioning that will result in customer loyalty.

Table 12.1 Perspectives and Definitions of Brand

S/N	Authors	Perspective	Definition
1	American Marketing Association (2013)	Name/logo	A name, term, symbol, design or any other feature which identifies the seller's good or services as distinct from the offerings of other sellers
2	Van Reil and Balmer (1997)	Corporate identity	A corporate identity which provides a competitive advantage
3	Kapferer (1992)	Identity system	Brand as an identity structure (culture, personality, self-projection, physique, reflection and relationship)
4	Martineau (1959)	Image in consumer's mind	A representation of an image in consumer's mind which commands psychological and functional attributes
5	Woodward (1991)	Relationship	Personality which builds a relationship between brand and consumers
6	Doyle (1994)	Added value	A bundle of tangible and intangible characteristics which increase the attractiveness of a product beyond the functional value
7	Lambin (1993)	Personality differentiation	As a personality differentiation based on functional capabilities
8	Arnold (1992)	Symbolic personality	The symbolic personality that user value provides which is beyond the functional utility
9	Brown (1992)	Connection	A sum of all the mental connections which people have around a product
10	Franzen and Moriaty (2008)	Value system	Values that elicit notable interest

Source: Adapted from Maurya and Mishra (2012).

12.3 Brand Positioning Strategies

Customer repurchase decision benefits businesses that have strong brands (Webster & Keller, 2004; Beverland et al., 2007a; Gomes et al., 2016). Branding helps an organisation to establish a relationship with its target market/audience. It is critical to building trust, confidence and loyalty in a B2B relationship. For a business to have a strong and positive brand that assures customers of positive transaction experiences, the business must have appropriately positioned itself in the market. Through branding, positioning of the business in the minds and consciousness of the target market will be achieved (Keller, 2013; Verster et al., 2019).

The B2C segment has enjoyed many benefits from branding and brand positioning in the marketplace. Since the turn of the new millennium, researchers have increasingly highlighted the benefits of branding in enhancing the competitive advantage of B2B organisations (Leek & Christodoulides, 2012; Verster et al., 2019). Consequently, there has been an increase in publications on B2B relationship marketing with a focus on branding (e.g. Cassia et al., 2017; Anees-ur-Rehman, et al., 2018; Casidy et al., 2018). Although there has been a shift in focus to branding in the B2B literature, there still remains the challenge of building trust in services rendered to the customers due to the intangibility of the product (Glynn, 2012; Verster et al., 2019). The question of quality of service rendered can be well addressed when a business rightly positions itself in the minds of customers as a brand that stands for quality service delivery. Hence, organisations in the B2B market must develop a brand that assures customers of the ability to meet their needs and provides a satisfactory brand experience.

An example is the brand positioning of DAAR communications, a privately owned broadcasting organisation in Nigeria by Nelson Reids, a marketing agency based in Nigeria, for its annual event. DAAR Communications which has been in existence since 1998, hosts an annual event that celebrates Africans who excelled in their respective industries. Nelson Reids had the mandate of branding, promotion, digital campaign and publicity of this event in 2019. The agency designed a logo for this key client adapting a unique, distinctive and relevant feature that showcased the depth of the organisation's Nigerian roots – *an expression that communicates the pride and inimitable African heritage to its customers*. The promotion of the event through social media engagement enhanced the brand's visibility, positioning the event as a world-class celebration of excellence (Nelson Reids, 2019).

Keller (2008) posited brand positioning as designing a brand image that occupies a unique and valued place in the minds of customers. The success of marketing activities hinges on appropriate brand positioning (Blankson & Kalafatis, 2004). A critical criterion for positioning a brand in a market to enhance and sustain consumers' perceived value is to improve benefits and lower costs for customers. In the B2B context where value creation is the centre of attention, Beverland et al. (2007b) opine that factors for positioning a brand must take cognisance of the following criteria: (1) relevance, (2) distinctiveness, (3) superiority, (4) communicability, and (5) imitability and added value. Consequently, B2B organisations can position themselves appropriately in the minds of customers through identified strategies. These organisations can develop a strong brand identity with high-quality services and products, and consequently create a brand perception that provides customer satisfaction and competitive advantage.

From their research, Jalkala and Keränen (2014) propose the following strategies through which organisations operating in B2B markets can build their brands and position appropriately.

12.3.1 Customer Value Diagnostic

Customer value diagnostic is a brand positioning strategy that deals with a supplier's ability to understand customers' needs, trends in the industry and their demonstrable ability/intention to provide value. The customer value diagnostic views the customer as a patient and examines the needs and the business's ability to meet the needs, and makes a conscious effort to provide goods and services as requested by the customer. This strategy places the supplier in the position of a physician who understands customer value and needs, and intentionally puts in place plans to meet the needs or provide solutions to problems. The crux of this strategy is for an organisation to position itself as a solution provider by making conscious efforts to analyse the consumer's need and perceptions of value and consequently make conscious plans to meet them.

12.3.2 Global Solution Integrator

Global solution integrator is a B2B brand positioning strategy that describes an organisation focusing on its capability to create a system that accommodates both internal and external resources to provide a global complex technological service to its customers. Technology plays an important role in this strategy, which entails the organisation operating as a global integrator and provider of complex technological services. The strategy focuses on an organisation creating technological services that meet the needs of the target market and also creating visibility for the organisation in this area of specialisation. In addition, the technological trends and needs of the market play a significant role in this strategy.

12.3.3 Quality Sub-systems Provider

This strategy describes a supplier focusing on developing, building, and delivering high-quality components that will enhance the performance of the buying organisation. It focuses on the organisation providing high-quality technological products which are innovative and dynamic. Hence, it places emphasis on product features and technological capabilities that an organisation has to offer and aligning these capabilities and features to satisfy the target customer. It is a strategy that seeks to position organisations and businesses in the minds of target customers through providing tools, components and variables that will enhance the business performance of buying organisations.

12.3.4 Long-Term Service Partner

The long-term service partner is a positional brand strategy that deals with a business focusing on expressing their excellent service, orientation of their partners and commitment to customers. This strategy promotes the supplier's ability to provide excellent service, take responsibility for the customers and ensure that the part of the buyer's/customer's operation process they are in charge of are upgraded continuously, maintained and innovated. It is a partnership positioning brand strategy whereby organisation A takes charge of activity for organisation B, such that organisation A creates excellence in the discharge of the service, which makes them non-substitutable and unique.

For business organisations to differentiate their brands from other competitors, they must position their brands and communicate the positioning clearly to their customers. Corporate brands can have more than one potential brand position depending on the categories of their products and the target market (Keller, 2003). Organisations must learn to integrate services provided with the needs of the market and design their brand positioning strategy around key capabilities, customer needs and the benefits they are providing to their customers through meeting these needs (Jalkala & Keränen, 2014). With the clear communication and understanding of this proposition, they can successfully say they have positioned their brand.

12.4 Harnessing Social Media and Internet Platforms for Brand and Customer Loyalty

There has been more attention in literature on the usage of social media and the internet in the B2C context (Kaplan & Haenlein, 2010; Gefen & Straub, 2004; Berthon et al., 2012; Laroche et al., 2013; Kohli et al., 2015; Diba et al., 2019), but less in the B2B context (Diba et al., 2019).

In a technology-driven era, organisations in B2B market relationships cannot afford to underutilise the resources available to them via social media marketing. Sales managers and intermediaries are therefore encouraged to utilise the internet and social media to drive the goals of businesses as it provides an avenue for customer loyalty (Zhang & Li, 2019). Despite advocacy for the usage of social media in B2B market relationships, there is still a wide gap in the usage of social media within B2B relationships (Diba et al., 2019).

Twitter, Facebook, WhatsApp, Instagram, YouTube, LinkedIn and WeChat are social media platforms used by business organisations to engage their customers (Juntunen et al., 2019; Zhang & Li, 2019; Diba et al., 2019). Prominently used social media sites by B2B agents are Facebook, LinkedIn and Twitter (Nanji, 2017; Diba et al., 2019). Some of these agents have thousands of followers and use their handles to promote the brands of organisations. Previously, suppliers had no budget for social media marketing (Michaelidou et al., 2011). However, in this current dispensation, it will be an ill-advised strategy for organisations involved in B2B transactions not to make substantial investment in social media and internet marketing. Some reasons for the lack of adoption of social media and internet marketing by B2B firms include lack of executive support, continued scepticism, and low level of preparedness on how digital marketing and sales can change customer behaviour (Agnihotri et al., 2012; Keinänen & Kuivalainen, 2015; Kovac, 2016; Diba et al., 2019).

With the right tactics, social media can be a great tool in B2B marketing. Diba et al. (2019) found trust, integrity, benevolence and altruism as key factors to B2B success in the use of social media. Diba et al. (2019) further emphasised that social media can be used as a tool to enhance buying and the buying process within B2B market relationships. In addition, studies on B2B and social media communications strategies on different platforms have revealed that social media creates sales opportunities, improves relationship management, retailers' performance and boosts buyers' satisfaction (Rodriguez et al., 2012; Rapp et al., 2013; Swani et al., 2014; Agnihotri et al., 2016; Lashgari et al., 2018).

Social media usage in B2B involves the adoption of social media tools to sustain and enhance customer engagement, create value through interaction and build a buyer–supplier relationship for improved business performance (Trainor et al., 2014; Rapp et al., 2013; Andersson & Wikström, 2017; Zhang & Li, 2019). The goal of business organisations using these social media tools in their business relationships with customers is to enhance customer engagement through contents made available on these platforms.

In this digital era, business relationships within the B2B context must take initiatives through technological innovations to meet the needs of their customers, provide quality service, enhance customer loyalty and build thought leadership. To ensure this, business conversations across social media sites should be employed by organisations to discuss and share issues on new developments in the industry, training, online product demonstration, business positioning and generally on how to achieve business success.

The choice of social media platforms to use must be determined by the target audience and the goal of social media marketing. This will inform the basis for the selection of appropriate social media sites. In a survey of the social media platforms used by Fortune 500 companies, LinkedIn ranked as the most popular social network, followed by Twitter and Facebook (Nanji, 2017). Many organisations make use of LinkedIn because of their target audience of professionals or professional organisations. Twitter is one of the commonly used social media tools by companies to build relationships and loyalty. It is ubiquitous, with over 335 million active monthly users and one billion unique monthly site visits, particularly to sites with embedded tweets (Juntunen et al., 2019).

Engagement on social media must be undertaken with specific purpose and clear objectives. The social media platform that works for product "A" might not work for product "B" if there are differences in the category of buyers in the two markets.

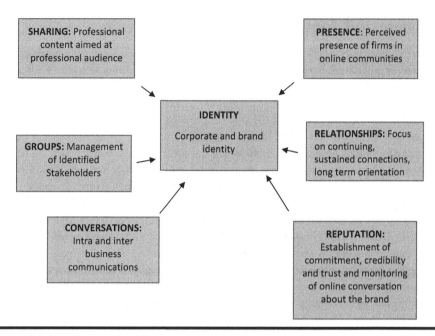

Figure 12.1   The social media functionality framework.

(*Source: Adapted from Kietzmann et al. (2011) – Honeycomb framework.*)

Social media sites have their unique characteristic of of a collaborative marketplace that attracts users; hence, the platforms have become markets on their own where the supplier and buyers meet to have their business transaction. A business must understand the nature of buyers in the market before deciding on the appropriate platform. To ensure that a business takes advantage of the opportunities in the social media platforms, Kietzmann et al. (2011) provide seven functional building blocks of social media to look out for (1) identity, (2) conversations, (3) groups (4) sharing, (5) presence (6) relationships, and (7) reputation. These are represented in Figure 12.1.

From Figure 12.1, identity serves as an organisation's online name and who they want to be seen as. It is the user's information that portrays what they are and stand for. Conversation refers to the content of what is shared and discussed. It is a strategy which businesses use to monitor the responses from the purchase of a particular product. Groups represent the stakeholders the information would be shared with and who will share the information. Sharing is the exchange and distribution of receipts, facts about a service or product on social media with the intent of stimulating orders. Presence is the ability to be aware of other users' availability and online presence to know when to send adverts, promos or new services. Reputation is the extent that users can be aware of the social standing of the business organisation, which is key to their loyalty. If customers on social media have a positive perception of the brand and the content a business makes available, loyalty to product and service will be achieved. Therefore, a business using social media to market products and services to other businesses must address the issue and ask questions relating to each of the parts above. What is our identity? What kind of conversations should we initiate? What should be shared? Who are available (groups) and what reputation and relationship are we building to have loyal customers? How do we strategically create, build and grow our social media presence? These questions are essential to successfully harness the opportunities in social media marketing for customer loyalty in B2B markets.

12.5 System and Tool to Build Customer Loyalty

Businesses need customers to continue to purchase and support their business growth and survival. Low customer patronage will have an adverse effect on business goals and objective. Customer loyalty in the B2B context entails willingness of a customer to purchase the product from a supplier repeatedly to sustain long-term commitment to that supplier (Algesheimer et al., 2005; Zhang & Li, 2019). A loyal customer can be measured on his/her willingness to repurchase the product and services of an organisation. When buyers are loyal to their suppliers, it leads to favourable word-of-mouth communication and helps the company maintain steady stream of revenue (Rauyruen & Miller, 2007).

Social media play an important role in improving customer loyalty in the B2B market. Through social media platforms, customers' engagement can contribute to the quality of service and by this, create a positive brand image and improve corporate reputation (Dijkman et al., 2015; Adeola et al., 2020), generate positive word of mouth, and generally enhance consumer-brand relationships (Hudson et al., 2016). Through social media, supplier–buyer relationships are enhanced as a platform which can be utilised for both parties to meet and relate to issues relating to product, service and trending innovations. To sustain customer loyalty in a supplier–buyer relationship, Zhang and Li (2019) posit that social media usage can enhance trust beliefs, integrity and benevolence of salespeople and supplier organisations. Trust, integrity and benevolence are believed to lead to customer loyalty in B2B markets (Zhang & Li, 2019). Trust is defined as a situation whereby an individual believes in the action of another that he or she will act as expected (Pentina et al., 2013; Zhang & Li, 2019). Before a party attains the trust of another in a business relationship, trust beliefs are formulated during social interaction and exchange. During this process, the individual evaluates and determine whether to trust or not. Zhang and Li (2019) classified trustworthiness into three components which are ability, benevolence and integrity. Ability refers to the capacity of an individual who was bestowed trust upon to meet the need of the individual who bestowed the trust. Integrity, on the other hand, describes an individual who was bestowed trust to keep his/her promise in honesty, and lastly, benevolence is the care and motivation an individual who was trusted displays.

Trust is also categorised into two components, namely interpersonal trust and inter-organisational trust (Huang & Wilkinson, 2013; Zhang & Li, 2019). According to Zhang and Li, interpersonal trust is premised on emotional bonds between individuals in a group. Inter-organisational trust, on the other hand, can be experienced between two organisations in a business relationship. Here, a buyer's inability to see trustworthiness in a supplier will affect customer loyalty negatively. Social media, as a tool for information sharing, provides sellers and buyers with the opportunity to assess the level of trustworthiness of their business associates by observing behaviour while interacting on social media. Importantly, promises and projections of products and services to buying organisations should contain the elements of trust, integrity and benevolence. If a buyer cannot trust a supplier to deliver the products or render the services on time and as promised, the loyalty of such customer cannot be assured. Securing customer loyalty in the B2B market requires the integrity of suppliers/buyers in meeting promises made because a failed supply will have a multiplier effect on the buyers' deliveries, sales and brand image, which businesses cannot afford.

12.6 Customer Relationship Management (CRM): A Tool for Building Customer Loyalty

The intense nature of market competition requires that organisations develop effective strategies that will deliver sustainable advantage if business operations must continue beyond the near future. Customers are the reason business exists; hence, building a special relationship with them is key to organisational survival. Organisations in today's business environment are faced with stiff competition from both existing firms and new entrants resulting in a possible reduction in the market share of individual organisations since competitors provide alternative/substitute products or services (Rodriguez et al., 2012). Based on the foregoing, managers must seek out measures to find and attract new customers/business partners, win their purchase, nurture their interest in the organisation's brand and gain repeat patronage that results in customer loyalty in the long run, which is the core of CRM. The effective implementation of CRM as a strategy will require a synergy of people, process and technology to reduce operations cost and increase the profitability of B2B operations. CRM is defined as a comprehensive strategy and process for the acquisition, retention and partnership with selective customers to create superior value for a business and its customers (Parvatiyar & Sheth, 2004). CRM is a combination of information arrangements used to plan, schedule and control the pre-sales and post-sales activities in an organisation. It encompasses all aspects of dealing with existing and targeted customers, including the sales force, call centre, technical and field service support. Improvement in the long-term growth and profitability of a business through an in-depth understanding of customer behaviour is cardinal to the subject of CRM (Francis, 2016). AMA (2007) defined CRM as a discipline that integrates database and computer technology with service and marketing communication with customers. This definition explains the overriding goal of CRM from the perspective of organisations' ability to apply customers' data (buying history, demographics, industry, etc.) in providing one-on-one or personalised communication with customers. Although there is no generally accepted definition of CRM yet, researchers and marketers in the field of management have identified four sets of activities that can guarantee the success of CRM implementation, including customer identification, attraction, orientation and development. CRM is therefore defined as the coordination of all the resources, processes and activities directed to recognising, attracting, sensitising and developing customers' interactions that enhances organisation–customer/business partner relationships through the integration of organisations' technology and customer database which results in the attainment of predetermined goals and objectives. CRM seeks to achieve effective feedback and facilitate CRM.

12.6.1 Benefits of Well-Implemented CRM

According to Keh and Lee (2006), the general benefit derived from the implementation of a CRM strategy is customer satisfaction that results in customer loyalty. However, the benefits derived from an effective CRM strategy have been classified into two categories: tangible and intangible benefits. From the works of Chen and Ching (2004), the tangible benefits include (1) growth in profit, (2) reduction in marketing cost, (3) increase in labour productivity, (4) effective communication media and (5) good customer services. The intangible benefits are (1) improvement in quality of services provided to customers, (2) effective and easy processes, (3) excellent customer segmentation, (4) good understanding of customer needs, (5) improved customer satisfaction and (6) reduction in the gap between an organisation's capabilities and customer expectations.

12.7 Conclusion

This chapter has shown that branding is key to achieving the goals of an organisation. It is crucial that an organisation properly positions its brand in the market and in the minds of buyers if the business's set goals are to be achieved. Also, an organisation cannot afford to lose out on opportunities to communicate with the target market on internet and social media platforms. It is also important to have a strong online presence to improve customer retention, loyalty and ensure effective relationship management. Social media can be a good marketing platform to engage customers if the business's offerings are well-positioned and the value proposition, adequately communicated. Finally, businesses must proactively build brands that customers are loyal to if they aim to actualise their business goals.

Case and Exercise

BUILDING CUSTOMER LOYALTY: A CASE OF CARRY-YOU NIGERIA ENTERPRISE

Author: Isaiah Adisa, Olabisi Onabanjo University, Ago-Iwoye, Ogun State, Nigeria

Carry-You Enterprise is an indigenous organisation in Accra, Ghana. Established in 2009, the company specialises in distribution, delivery and supply of finished products from manufacturers to sales agents. In 2016, to enhance its visibility in the marketplace, the company embraced social media and began placing advertisements on popular social media platforms such as YouTube, Instagram, Facebook and LinkedIn. In the marketing communications messages across various social media platforms, the emphasis was always placed on the company's fundamental values built around timely response to customer demands, swift delivery of goods, integrity, trust, and benevolence. Over the years, the continuous affirmation of these values attracted customers to the business, making it a preferred organisation in the B2B market.

Early 2019, with increased visibility, Carry-You began to experience challenges in meeting deadlines as the demand for their services increased, and they could not meet up with customer supplies. Consequently, failed deliveries increased, and customers became disappointed and complained online across the various platforms. Carry-You also failed to track online complaints promptly, and customers were dissatisfied with their response time. By mid-2019, Carry-You had urgent delivery requests from two multinational corporations (MNCs) to their key sales agents, which Carry-You drivers misplaced. What belonged to MNC X was given to MNC Y and vice versa. This adversely affected the MNCs' relationships with the receiving sales organisations as they could not meet their customers demand, resulting in loss of income and reputational damage. It took 2 weeks for Carry-You to resolve the issue as the company lacked well laid out procedures to track anomalies as it occurs and also tools to trace deliveries adequately.

The outcome of Carry-You's inability to properly manage its key customers' transactions, despite promises of excellent service delivery made in online adverts across various platforms, affected their brand image and reputation and, in turn, impacted customer loyalty. Carry-You failed to keep to their promise and did not properly handle the market pressure resulting from their well-publicised organisational values and brand promises. The customers were disappointed and withdrew their patronage, moving their businesses to key competitors.

EXERCISE

1. What are the fundamental factors that Carry-You neglected, which made it lose key clients?
2. How should Carry-You ensure that there is a synergy between the brand promise and service delivery?
3. Advise Carry-You on what to do in order to restore customers' trust and loyalty.
4. What should Carry-You do to restore its brand image and properly position the business as a reputable brand in the mind of the customers and the market?
5. What structures should be put in place to build/improve customer loyalty.

References

Adeola, O., Hinson, R. E., & Evans, O. (2020). Social media in marketing communications: A synthesis of successful strategies for the digital generation. In George, B and Paul, J (Eds) Digital Transformation in Business and Society (Theory and Cases) (pp. 61-81). Palgrave Macmillan, Cham.

Agnihotri, R., Dingus, R., Hu, M. Y., & Krush, M. T. (2016). Social media: Influencing customer satisfaction in B-TO-B sales. *Industrial Marketing Management*, 53, 172–180.

Agnihotri, R., Kothandaraman, P., Kashyap, R., & Singh, R. (2012). Bringing "social" into sales: The impact of salespeople's social media use on service behaviors and value creation. *Journal of Personal Selling & Sales Management*, 32(3), 333–348.

Algesheimer, R., Dholakia, U. M., & Herrmann, A. (2005). The social influence of brand community: Evidence from European car clubs. *Journal of Marketing*, 69(3), 19–34.

American Marketing Association (AMA) (2013). Definition of marketing. https://www.ama.org/AboutAMA/.

Andersson, S., & Wikström, N. (2017). Why and how are social media used in a B-TO-B context, and which stakeholders are involved? *Journal of Business & Marketing*, 32(8), 1098–1108.

Anees-ur-Rehman, M., Wong, H. Y., Sultan, P., & Merrilees, B. (2018). How brand-oriented strategy affects the financial performance of B-TO-B SMEs. *Journal of Business & Industrial Marketing*, 33(3), 303–315.

Armstrong, G., & Kotler, P. (2016). *Principles of marketing, global edition*. Pearson Education, Harlow.

Arnold, D. (1992). The handbook of brand management. Century Business, (The Economist Books) Random House Business, New York.

Berthon, P. R., Pitt, L. F., Plangger, K., & Shapiro, D. (2012). Marketing meets Web 2.0, social media, and creative consumers: Implications for international marketing strategy. *Business Horizons*, 55(3), 261–271.

Beverland, M., Lindgreen, A., Napoli, J., Kotler, P., & Pfoertsch, W. (2007a). Being known or being one of many: The need for brand management for business-to-business (B2B) companies. *Journal of Business & Industrial Marketing*, 22(6), 357–362.

Beverland, M., Lindgreen, A., Napoli, J., Roberts, J., & Merrilees, B. (2007b). Multiple roles of brands in business-to-business services. *Journal of Business & Industrial Marketing*, 22(6), 410–417.

Blankson, C., & Kalafatis, S. P. (2004). The development and validation of a scale measuring consumer/customer-derived generic typology of positioning strategies. *Journal of Marketing Management*, 20(1–2), 5–43.

Brodie, R. J. (2009). From goods to service branding: An integrative perspective. *Marketing Theory*, 9(1), 107–111.

Brown, B. P., Zablah, A. R., Bellenger, D. N., & Donthu, N. (2012). What factors influence buying center brand sensitivity? *Industrial Marketing Management*, 41(3), 508–520.

Brown, G. (1992). People, Brands and Advertising. Millward Brown International, Warwick, UK.

Casidy, R., Nyadzayo, M. W., Mohan, M., & Brown, B. (2018). The relative influence of functional versus imagery beliefs on brand sensitivity in B-TO-B professional services. *Industrial Marketing Management*, 72, 26–36.

Cassia, F., Cobelli, N., & Ugolini, M. (2017). The effects of goods-related and service-related B-TO-B brand images on customer loyalty. *Journal of Business & Industrial Marketing*, 32(5), 722–732.

Caxton (2018). *Integrated annual report*. Caxton and CTP Publishers and Printers Limited, South Africa.

Chen, J. S., & Ching, R. K. (2004). An empirical study of the relationship of IT intensity and organizational absorptive capacity on CRM performance. *Journal of Global Information Management (JGIM)*, 12(1), 1–17.

Diba, H., Vella, J. M., & Abratt, R. (2019). Social media influence on the B2B buying process. *Journal of Business & Industrial Marketing*, 34(7), 1482–1496.

Dijkman, R. M., Sprenkels, B., Peeters, T., & Janssen, A. (2015). Business models for the Internet of Things. *International Journal of Information Management*, 35(6), 672–678.

Doyle, P. (1994). *Marketing management and strategy*, Prentice-Hall, London.

Elsäßer, M., & Wirtz, B. W. (2017). Rational and emotional factors of customer satisfaction and brand loyalty in a business-to-business setting. *Journal of Business & Industrial Marketing*, 32(1), 138–152.

Franzen, G., & Moriarty, S. (2009). The science and art of branding. Routledge, London.

Gefen, D., & Straub, D. W. (2004). Consumer trust in B2C e-Commerce and the importance of social presence: Experiments in e-Products and e-Services. *Omega*, 32(6), 407–424.

Glynn, M. S. (2012). Primer in B-TO-B brand-building strategies with a reader practicum. *Journal of Business Research*, 65(5), 666–675.

Gomes, M., Fernandes, T., & Brandão, A. (2016). Determinants of brand relevance in a B2B service purchasing context. *Journal of Business & Industrial Marketing*, 31(2), 193–204.

Guzmán, F., Iglesias, O., Keränen, J., Piirainen, K. A., & Salminen, R. T. (2012). Systematic review on B2B branding: Research issues and avenues for future research. *Journal of Product & Brand Management*, 21(6), 404–417.

Hirvonen, S., Laukkanen, T., & Salo, J. (2016). Does brand orientation help B2B SMEs in gaining business growth? *Journal of Business & Industrial Marketing*, 31(4), 472–487.

Huang, Y., & Wilkinson, I. F. (2013). The dynamics and evolution of trust in business relationships. *Industrial Marketing Management*, 42(3), 455–465.

Hudson, S., Huang, L., Roth, M. S., & Madden, T. J. (2016). The influence of social media interactions on consumer–brand relationships: A three-country study of brand perceptions and marketing behaviors. *International Journal of Research in Marketing*, 33(1), 27–41.

Jalkala, A. M., & Keränen, J. (2014). Brand positioning strategies for industrial firms providing customer solutions. *Journal of Business & Industrial Marketing*, 29(3), 253–264.

Juntunen, M., Ismagilova, E., & Oikarinen, E. L. (2019). B-TO-B brands on Twitter: Engaging users with a varying combination of social media content objectives, strategies, and tactics. *Industrial Marketing Management*, 89, 630–641.

Kapferer, J. N. (1992). *Strategic brand management*. Kogan Page, London.

Kaplan, A. M., & Haenlein, M. (2010). Users of the world, unite! The challenges and opportunities of Social Media. *Business Horizons*, 53(1), 59–68.

Keh, H. T., & Lee, Y. H. (2006). Do reward programs build loyalty for services? The moderating effect of satisfaction on type and timing of rewards. *Journal of Retailing*, 82(2), 127–136.

Keinänen, H., & Kuivalainen, O. (2015). Antecedents of social media B-TO-B use in industrial marketing context: customers' view. *Journal of Business & Industrial Marketing*, 21(6), 404–417.

Keller, K. L. (2003). Brand synthesis: The multidimensionality of brand knowledge. *Journal of Consumer Research*, 29(4), 595–600.

Keller, K. L. (2013). *Strategic brand management, building measurement and managing brand equity*. Prentice Hall, Upper Sadley River, NJ.

Keller, J. M. (2008). First principles of motivation to learn and e3-learning. *Distance Education*, 29(2), 175–185.

Kietzmann, J. H., Hermkens, K., McCarthy, I. P., & Silvestre, B. S. (2011). Social media? Get serious! Understanding the functional building blocks of social media. *Business Horizons*, 54(3), 241–251.

Kohli, C., Suri, R., & Kapoor, A. (2015). Will social media kill branding? *Business Horizons*, 58(1), 35–44.

Kotler, P., & Pfoertsch, W. (2007). B2B brand management. *The Marketing Review*, 7(2), 201–203.

Kovac, M. (2016). Social media works for B2B sales, too. Harvard Business Review, available at: https://hbr.org/2016/01/social-media-worksfor-b2b-sales-too (accessed April 27 2017).

Kucuk, S. U. (2019). Consequences of Brand hate. In S. U. Kucuk (Ed.), *Brand hate* (pp. 87–101). Palgrave Macmillan, Cham.

Kuhn, K. A. L., Alpert, F., & Pope, N. K. L. (2008). An application of Keller's brand equity model in a B-TO-B context. *Qualitative Market Research: An International Journal*, 11(1), 40–58.

Lambin, J-J. (1993). *Strategic marketing*. McGrawHill, London.

Laroche, M., Habibi, M. R., & Richard, M. O. (2013). To be or not to be in social media: How brand loyalty is affected by social media? *International Journal of Information Management*, 33(1), 76–82.

Lashgari, M., Sutton-Brady, C., Søilen, K. S., & Ulfvengren, P. (2018). Adoption strategies of social media in B-TO-B firms: A multiple case study approach. *Journal of Business & Industrial Marketing*, 33(5), 730–743.

Leek, S., & Christodoulides, G. (2012). A framework of brand value in B2B markets: The contributing role of functional and emotional components. *Industrial Marketing Management*, 41(1), 106–114.

Martineau, P. (1959). Sharper focus for the corporate image. *Harvard Business Review*, 3S(1), 49–58.

Maurya, U. K., & Mishra, P. (2012). What is a brand? A perspective on brand meaning. *European Journal of Business and Management*, 4(3), 122–133.

Merz, M. A., He, Y., & Vargo, S. L. (2009). The evolving brand logic: A service-dominant logic perspective. *Journal of the Academy of Marketing Science*, 37(3), 328–344.

Michaelidou, N., Siamagka, N. T., & Christodoulides, G. (2011). Usage, barriers and measurement of social media marketing: An exploratory investigation of small and medium B2B brands. *Industrial Marketing Management*, 40(7), 1153–1159.

Nanji, A. (2017). Social media and blog usage by Fortune 500 companies in 2017. Marketing Profs, https://www.marketingprofs.com/charts/2017/33156/social-media-and-blog-usage-by-fortune.

Nelson Reids (2019). Executing a kick-ass digital campaign for $53m African Media giant. Accessed from https://www.nelsonreids.com/digital-case-study.

Ogbuji, C. N., Kalu, S. E., & Oluchukwu Samson, M. B. A. (2014). The influence of brand extension strategy on marketing performance of soft drinks bottling firms in Nigeria. *American International Journal of Contemporary Research*, 4(1), 1–276.

Parvatiyar, A., & Sheth, J. (2004). Conceptual framework of customer relationship management. In J. N. Sheth, A. Parvatiyar, & G. Shainesh (Eds.), *Customer relationship management: Emerging concepts, tools and applications* (5th ed.). Tata McGraw-Hill Publishing, New Delhi.

Payne, A., Storbacka, K., Frow, P., & Knox, S. (2009). Co-creating brands: Diagnosing and designing the relationship experience. *Journal of Business Research*, 62(3), 379–389.

Pentina, I., Gammoh, B. S., Zhang, L., & Mallin, M. (2013). Drivers and outcomes of brand relationship quality in the context of online social networks. *International Journal of Electronic Commerce*, 17(3), 63–86.

Persson, N. (2010). An exploratory investigation of the elements of B2B brand image and its relationship to price premium. *Industrial Marketing Management*, 39(8), 1269–1277.

Prahalad, C. K., & Ramaswamy, V. (2004). Co-creation experiences: The next practice in value creation. *Journal of Interactive Marketing,* 18(3), 5–14.

Rapp, A., Beitelspacher, L. S., Grewal, D., & Hughes, D. E. (2013). Understanding social media effects across seller, retailer, and consumer interactions. *Journal of the Academy of Marketing Science*, 41(5), 547–566.

Rauyruen, P., & Miller, K. E. (2007). Relationship quality as a predictor of B-TO-B customer loyalty. *Journal of Business Research,* 60(1), 21–31.

Reijonen, H., Hirvonen, S., Nagy, G., Laukkanen, T., & Gabrielsson, M. (2015). The impact of entrepreneurial orientation on B2B branding and business growth in emerging markets. *Industrial Marketing Management,* 51, 35–46.

Rodriguez, M., Peterson, R. M., & Krishnan, V. (2012). Social media's influence on business-to-business sales performance. *Journal of Personal Selling & Sales Management,* 32(3), 365–378.

Swani, K., Brown, B. P., & Milne, G. R. (2014). Should tweets differ for B2B and B2C? An analysis of Fortune 500 companies' Twitter communications. *Industrial Marketing Management*, 43(5), 873–881.

Trainor, K. J., Andzulis, J. M., Rapp, A., & Agnihotri, R. (2014). Social media technology usage and customer relationship performance: A capabilities-based examination of social CRM. *Journal of Business Research,* 67(6), 1201–1208.

Van Riel, C. B., and Balmer, J. M. (1997). Corporate identity: The concept, its measurement and management. *European Journal of Marketing*, 31(5/6), 340–355.

Verster, A., Petzer, D. J., & Cunningham, N. (2019). Using brand identity to build brand equity: A comparison between the South African and Dutch business-to-business architectural industry. *South African Journal of Business Management*, 50(1), 1–12.

Wang, C. L., He, J., & Barnes, B. R. (2017). Brand management and consumer experience in emerging markets: Directions for future research. *International Marketing Review*, 34(4), 458–462.

Webster, F. E., & Keller, K. L. (2004). A roadmap for branding in industrial markets. *Journal of Brand Management*, 11(5), 388–402.

Woodward, S. (1991). Competitive marketing. In D. Cowley (Ed.), *Understanding brands by 10 people who do* (pp. 119–134). Kogan Page, London.

Zablah, A. R., Brown, B. P., & Donthu, N. (2010). The relative importance of brands in modified rebuy purchase situations. *International Journal of Research in Marketing*, 27(3), 248–260.

Zhang, C. B., & Li, Y. N. (2019). How social media usage influences B2B customer loyalty: Roles of trust and purchase risk. *Journal of Business & Industrial Marketing*, 34(7), 1420–1433.

CAPACITY DEVELOPMENT IN THE AFRICAN BUSINESS-TO-BUSINESS CONTEXT

5

Part 5 consists of Chapter 13 only. In this part, we discuss how African B2B organizations can develop sales and marketing capabilities.

Chapter 13

Developing Sales and Marketing Capability in African B2B Context

INTRODUCTION AND OBJECTIVES

At the end of this chapter, the reader will understand and be able to plan strategies regarding

- Developing and designing a strategic sales organisation and sales process in business markets
- How to acquire marketing capability needed to maximise sales and profitability in business markets
- Developing key accounts systems
- Recruiting and training key accounts and sales personnel
- Success factor for sales and key accounts management.

13.1 Developing a Sales Organisation and a Sales Process

13.1.1 Meaning and Evolution of the Sales Organisation

Sales organisation in a B2B setting is a critical unit of the organisation that serves as the front-end or key interface of the company interactions with its customers. Sales organisations are responsible for seeking new business customers, building new relationships, maintaining existing relationships, providing customer support and customer value and providing sales revenue for the organisation.

In today's business environment, the role of the sales organisation is to translate the company's annual strategy and vision to everyday reality. The sales organisation adds value for customers beyond that provided by the products and services by creating competitive differentiation, thereby contributing to the company's profitability (Corcoran, 1995).

The sales organisation has evolved from a traditional sales organisation to a strategic one. Figure 13.1 shows the evolutions of sales organisations and its drivers compiled from Piercy (2010).

The traditional sales organisation is transactional, and the primary focus of the salesperson is to sell products and services (product-centricity) for the organisation's profitability. It is a unit/team or functional department whose primary objective is to use structured sales routine process and design to get more sales from more customers. The strategic sales organisation, on the other hand, is a cross-functional oriented sales organisation whose focus is selling customer solutions via a customer-driven approach. It is strategic, process-oriented and integrated, as it not only translates company visions or objectives into customer solutions but also provides inputs in the development of a company's vision and strategy via market intelligence gathered during sales activities and customer interactions (Geiger et al., 2009).

Over the years, pressures and the need to increase the productivity of the sales functions, drive profitable growth, and gain cost advantage and competitive differentiation have led organisations to reprioritise the role of their sales organisation to have a strategic focus. Companies have begun to see the sales organisation as a source of competitive advantage. They are refocusing their sales approach from customer transaction-based viewpoints into relationship marketing and engaging customers by all possible means (Pansari & Kumar, 2017).

As the salespeople serve as interface and customer touchpoints, they are also a representative of the company's brand and value. Thus, by equipping them with the best-in-class tools, supporting and redesigning their sales approaches, the company not only sells but acquires market intelligence needed to develop superior knowledge-based value propositions for their customers. Sales organisations have begun to see the importance of managing the customer portfolio (Lane & Piercy, 2004) and customer productivity (Leigh & Marshall, 2001). This is because selling should not only aim at pushing products and services but recognise that customer value in terms of, for example, the customer's productivity and cost advantage should be paramount to securing sales and profitable sales growth for the selling organisation.

Before the internet and social media age, the traditional salespersons conveyed products and services of a company to its customers. Although there were traditional catalogues and tools for the sales process, the internet has provided unlimited information banks where business customers can access many details of the company services and products, thus replacing the traditional direct

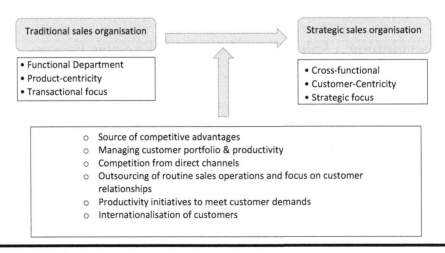

Figure 13.1 Evolution of sales organisation to strategic focus.

channel role of salespersons. Most of the information that is traditionally provided by salespersons via the sales process is increasingly available via the internet. As a result of this technological shift, sales executives have to redesign the role of the sales organisation to add value to the company.

The advent of globalisation has meant that companies can take advantage of low factors of productions in other countries by shifting low-value routine tasks to countries with relatively low cost of production. Sales organisations are not exempted from the pressures of globalisation. This pressure is making sales executives rethink the value of their different sales activities, which ones can be kept in-house and what should be outsourced. So far, sales executives have begun to outsource their routine sales operations and focusing on superior customer relationships. In addition to globalisation pressures, there is also pressure to enhance the productivity of the sales organisation leading to stringent cost-cutting initiatives in several B2B companies. According to Piercy (2010), companies are looking for ways to streamline their sales activities to focus and meet customer demands. To do so, they are changing the role of their sales personnel to be accountable for the desired result of the organisation. Sales personnel should not only understand their business but also need to be the advocate of the customer and understand the customer's business, competences and organisational culture. They should also be reachable and available to solve the problems of the customer by diagnosing, prescribing and resolving customer problems through creativity.

Furthermore, globalisation has also led to the growing internationalisation of business customers. This has put severe pressure on sales organisation about how to develop appropriate responses. Companies are responding by adopting an area, regional or global key account management (AKAM/RKAM/GKAM). To achieve this, B2B companies have to alter prior country-based practices and realign them to serve their global customers. The adoption of AKAM/RKAM/GKAM enables the organisation to negotiate transnational deals centrally while maintaining consistent sales relationships across their geographically diverse locations.

13.2 Developing a Strategic Sales Organisation

Strategic sales organisations are customer-driven in their approach to customers. They seek for customers' solutions, feedback and ways that directly provide solutions in collaboration with their customers and end users. In this section, we discuss how and why strategic sales organisation is part of the organisation's strategy, and we conceptualise and elaborate strategic sales organisation as a customer-centric sales organisation.

Figure 13.2 shows the link between corporate strategy and sales organisation. An organisation's corporate strategy emphasises how the organisation aims to achieve its strategic goals. It sets the direction, commitments and actions to actualise this vision. As a result, the organisation's strategy should drive the role of the sales organisation, their sales strategy and sales process, as well as the objective of the organisation's interaction with the customers and the outcomes of these interactions.

There is a growing emphasis on customer-centricity as part of corporate strategy. Sales organisations are at the interface of the customer interactions and the change transition needed to transition

Figure 13.2 Organisation's strategy and vision as a part of the sales organisation.

the organisation from a product-centric sales organisation to a customer-centric sales organisation. Customer-centric organisations are the opposite of product-centric organisations (Galbraith, 2011). Product-centric organisations are organisations structured around their business areas, with core value propositions centred on the products and services they provide, modifying them to please as many customers as possible (Galbraith, 2011). A customer-centric organisation is structured around customer segments. It focuses on interactive customer relationship management that goes beyond traditional relationship marketing to interactive customer relationship marketing. The customer-centric organisation establishes more intimate customer relationships that favour real integration in the firm via adaptive learning of the customer needs and preferences in the presence of firm-customer trust (Lamberti, 2013). This customer–organisation interaction enables the company to generate customer intelligence to support customised marketing activities that improve customer satisfaction, customer retainment and customer profitability (Rollins et al., 2012).

African companies have been slow to realise this paradigm shift towards customer-centricity. A few examples that have achieved customer-centricity (e.g. Yoco & Capitec) have increased their market share and profitability. Yoco is one of the fastest-growing mobile points of sale players in South Africa. In <10 minutes, customers can sign up to accept card payments. Capitec is one of the largest banks in South Africa due to its ability to give a customer a fully registered bank account in <10 minutes. These companies achieved increased market share and became industry leaders by focusing on customer-centricity.

During a round table discussion with several marketing consultants in Nigeria, they agreed that most companies in Nigeria seem to be product-centric as they utilise sales-driven "push" approach to market their products to different market segments in the country. Although interest in customer-centricity is increasing, however, a fundamental challenge is on how to transition to a customer-centric organisation.

Figure 13.3 shows how companies can develop a customer-centric sales organisation, adapted from Lamberti (2013). In customer-centric sales organisations, the whole marketing process is customised as customers are active players in the marketing process up to how the product and services reach the customers. Thus, the marketing process and value are co-created between the customers and the organisation through participatory decisions (Lamberti, 2013). In customer-centric sales organisations, there is a need for both downstream and upstream integration. The upstream suppliers also play essential roles in co-creating the value. Thus, the supply chain or value chain has to be aligned towards the objective of creating value for all members of the supply chain and ultimately, the customer.

Customer-centric organisations ensure the integration of all customer-facing activities by aligning all firm activities around customer value-adding activities. This requires foremost, to create a customer-centric culture where everyone in the organisation has the goal of giving every customer the quick and most complete answer to their questions and request (Lamberti, 2013). It also requires managing all the customer touchpoints, providing consistent customer management approach and effectiveness across every touchpoint and providing customers with key account managers committed to helping them in their choice (Lamberti, 2013).

13.2.1 Designing the Sales Organisation Unit

B2B firms are more vertically oriented organisations, structured around business functions.

They tend to have both a "marketing" function and a "sales" function, while some others use an integrated marketing and sales function as an integral part of developing market-oriented organisation (Biemans & Brencic, 2007).

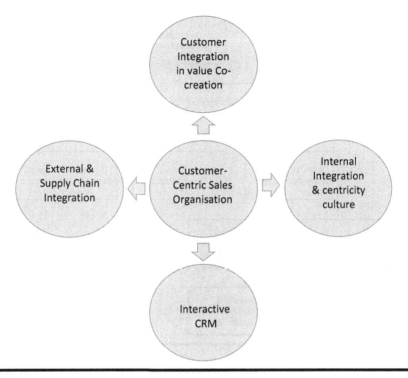

Figure 13.3   Developing a customer-centric sales organisation.

In a modern strategic sales organisation, intimate relationships with customers are very critical in achieving organisational success. Thus, marketing and sales integration, as well as cross-functional relationships and collaboration between departments, is necessary to increase the productivity and competitiveness of their customer management efforts. Therefore, the first step in designing a modern strategic sales organisation is to define what processes that define, create and deliver value to customers (Lane & Piercy, 2009). Often these processes lie within cross-organisational functions (such as production and operations, supply chain, sales, purchasing, customer service, research and development) and increasingly with partner organisations and networks (Lane & Piercy, 2009).

Figure 13.4 shows a model that integrates business intelligence, business development, product and technical support development and the sales team (including account managers and marketing communications) as the organisation's strategic sales organisation function headed by a sales director or key accounts owner.

From Figure 13.4, the role of the key account owner is to integrate and implement corporate strategies into concrete sales approaches and management philosophy as well as use the sales organisation as a vehicle for value co-creation. The key account owner is responsible for designing cross-organisational units that aid in defining, creating and delivering customer value. The business intelligence unit is either in matrix form as part of the strategic sales organisation and overall corporate strategy function whose primary role in the sales organisation is to analyse the key accounts prospects and relational requirements of different customer types, making strategic choices and developing superior knowledge about the customers. The business development translates the excellent knowledge gained from key accounts and product support interactions with

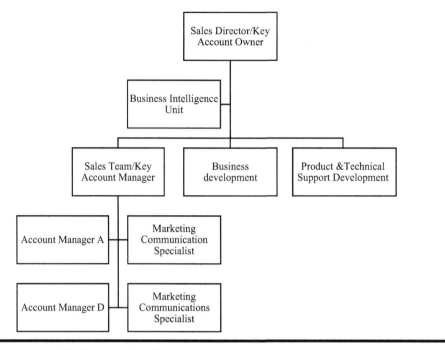

Figure 13.4   A model of a strategic sales organisation.

customers and partner organisations into value propositions for the customers. The communication specialists engage the customer in all customer touchpoints and keep consistent marketing communications in all customer touchpoints as well as promote customer-centric culture across the organisation.

13.3 Developing a Sales Organisation and a Sales Process

KAM is a buyer–seller relationship model for identifying and analysing valuable customers (key accounts) and developing suitable strategies and operational resources and capability to support value co-creation between supplier and buyer organisations.

The key accounts or strategic accounts are the most valuable customers for a company. There are several typologies for KAM, depending on the size and geographical span of the supplier and buyer organisations. KAM can be global (global key account management – GKAM), regional (regional key account management – RKAM), national (national key account management – NKAM) or area (area key account management). However, the underlying principle is that it helps a company to understand how to allocate resources where it is needed and to establish strong relationships with those accounts. Key accounts management supports the overall management philosophy towards the customer-centric organisation and has been conceptualised as a source of dynamic capability for organisations (Ivens et al., 2018).

Companies that seek to move towards customer-centric organisation tend to implement key account management (Lamberti, 2013) to gain more in-depth understanding of their customers and to allocate resources in order of customer needs better. Figure 13.5 depicts reasons for transitioning into key account management function.

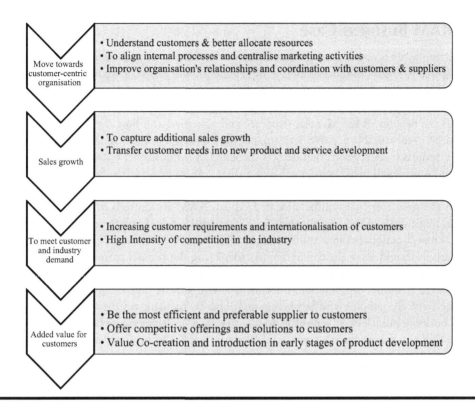

Figure 13.5 Reasons for key account management.

Research in B2B suggests that organisations that move towards customer-centricity tend to adopt key account sales organisation (e.g. Geiger et al., 2009; Ivens et al., 2018). These companies tend to pay attention to their most important critical customers, centralise marketing activities and align their internal processes to improve relationships and coordination with customers and suppliers (Wengler et al., 2006). Although asymmetric relationships can still exist between buyers and suppliers due to power imbalances and differences in strategic intends, through effective KAM, organisations continuously find ways to balance the strategic intents of their customers (Ryals & Davies, 2013).

Key account management helps companies provide added value for their customers through value co-creation. Through KAM, organisations create value with their customers and introduce them early in the process of product and service development. In turn, it enhances the ability to offer customers competitive solutions and becoming their most preferred suppliers.

High intensity of competition in the industry is compelling companies to find a way to differentiate their offerings from competitors. Furthermore, internationalisation of customers and markets entails that organisations should find ways to provide services and support for internationalised customers. Internationalised customers are demanding more coherent, coordinated and centralised purchasing from their suppliers, and KAM has been one of the efficient ways for sales organisations to meet the needs, win and retain their internationalised or global customers (Geiger et al., 2009) and differentiate their offerings from competitors. KAM enables organisations to identify future customer requirements ahead of competitors, sometimes even ahead of the customers, thereby enhancing their competitive position (Ivens et al., 2018).

13.4 KAM Business Case

When setting a key account management framework in a sales organisation, there are four steps to put in place to ensure the success of the implementation of KAM, as shown in Figure 13.6.

One of the first steps in setting up a key account management framework is a good KAM business case that presents a cost-benefit calculation before its implementation. This business case highlights the benefits of KAM, cost, structure and activities, and how the implementation process will lead to measurable positive performance outcomes. First, the business case should involve customer insights from research that depicts the views of the customer on why such a structure is needed and how it will help them in achieving their core strategic goals. Second, KAM incurs a cost, and as a result, the business plan should depict the costs KAM will incur for the organisation as well as the resources that will be allocated. Third, KAM structure is fundamental in achieving the strategic goals of the organisation. Such a structure should reflect the inter-organisational network, cross-functional actors and the responsibilities between the account manager and the KAM team. It should show the contact matrix (depicting the contact patterns between organisations KAM team members and customer representatives) as well as the relationship process and focus with the customer organisation. Successful KAM is those that focus on the value-creating process between the supplier and buyer organisations. By focusing on the value-creating process between both organisations, it is possible to identify value-linkages where both organisations can capture value and future business potential. Fourth, the KAM business case should have measurable monetary and operational goals that include action plans, account-specific actions and opportunity articulation or estimated value capture from the accounts. Finally, top management commitment is needed for the successful implementation of KAM. Guesalaga (2014) suggests that

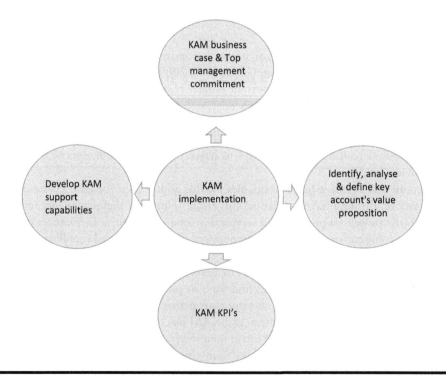

Figure 13.6   Five steps in setting up a key account.

top management can help facilitate the successful implementation of KAM via direct customer contact, decision-making and organisation alignment. He showed that direct customer contact through social interaction with customers is more relevant than business-related interaction. More so, top management can support key account management by aligning the goals and procedures of the different functional areas in the company, and by participating in the decision-making of strategic issues.

13.4.1 Identification, Analysis and Key Account Value Proposition

Several criteria can be used to identify suitable key accounts. This varies depending on the industry and business segments. Extant literature on key account management has identified several factors that organisations can model in other to find suitable key accounts.

Figure 13.7 shows factors identified in the literature for selection of suitable key accounts (see, e.g., Ojasalo, 2001). Most importantly, whatever dimensions a company chooses to incorporate should reflect the volume commitments needed to provide account type service to the customer, an acceptable profit margins, delivery and service requirements (Boles et al., 1999; Ojasalo, 2001).

Each key account identified above should be further analysed in terms of the goal congruency of the partners, switching cost, the company's value propositions, needs, buying frequency, historical buying trends, the cost-benefit ratio of selecting the account and relationship history with the organisation (Ojasalo, 2001). This enables the organisation to be sure that the resource allocated to the account will yield economic value. It is important to note that not all key accounts are equal in all the dimensions which the firms would use to determine its key accounts. Figure 13.8 shows an example of how the key accounts can be segmented into four account pyramids based on customer profitability pyramids developed by Zeithaml et al. (2001). With this pyramid, the sales organisation can know how to allocate resources and operational support to the key accounts based on the level of profitability of the accounts.

Without having such segmentation, the organisation will be forced to deliver the same levels of service to all customers using limited resources and possibly under-serving its most

Figure 13.7   Identification of a suitable key account.

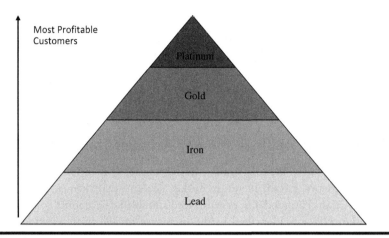

Figure 13.8   Key account segmentation.

profitable customers. The Platinum and Gold customers are the most valued customers and could represent about 1% (50% revenue; 49% profits) and 4% (23% revenue; 25% profits) of total customer accounts (van Raaij et al., 2003). While the Platinum key accounts are the organisation's most profitable customers, they are also large users of the organisation's products and service, and are often not too price-sensitive and are willing to invest in new offerings and solutions. The Gold key accounts are valuable and attractive account segments but with lower levels of profitability compared to the Platinum key account. They also seek more price discounts and have lower levels of commitments compared to the Platinum accounts. The Iron and Lead key accounts are less attractive in terms of profitability, and they are transactional oriented. They are not necessary key accounts but can be considered as other accounts. They may represent about 15% (20% revenue; 21% profits) and 80% (7% revenue; 5% profits) of total customer accounts, respectively (van Raaij et al., 2003). While Iron key accounts are valuable in terms of the volume needed to utilise the firm's capacity, the revenues, loyalty and profitability of this account group do not require special treatment by the key account managers. The Lead account group are the least profitable, take up a lot of the company's resources and cost more than they generate, and may demand more service than they merit given their spending and profitability.

Figure 13.9 shows how the sales organisation can then categorise and allocate their resources based on the key account pyramid as well as define specific value propositions for them. Furthermore, the value proposition has to be set for each specific key account segment as well as the specific key account. The value proposition should be determined by the customer (Vargo & Lusch, 2008). Thus, the organisation needs to identify all benefits the customer can attain from their offerings as well as future opportunities and suggest to the customer how its resources and capabilities (products, services, value chain and processes) can enable the customer to create value (Anderson et al., 2006). It should be a total solution from a single source to the key account consisting, for example, of both standardised and customised offerings bundled with process know-how, consultancy, maintenance, training, etc. (Storbacka, 2012). It should also contain the relationship approach and strategies, goal congruity set and operational-level capabilities to support the KAM.

Figure 13.10 shows an example of how these value propositions, resource allocation and operational-level capabilities can be assigned to the key accounts segments. The sales organisation aligns its goals with the Platinum and Gold key account. In contrast, the Iron and Lead

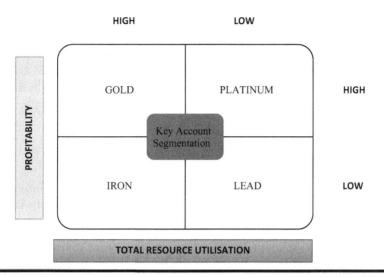

Figure 13.9 **Key account segmentation based on resource utilisation and profitability.**

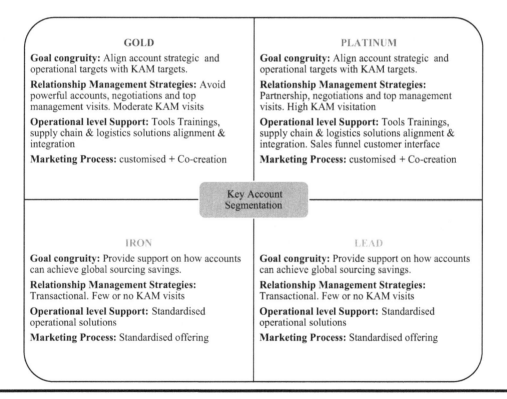

Figure 13.10 **Key account segmentation and value proposition.**

accounts are provided sourcing-related support as they are more price-sensitive accounts than Platinum and Gold accounts. For the Iron and Lead account segments, the sales organisation focuses more on low-cost solutions that will yield more cost savings while allocating few to none visits for the key account managers. These sets of customers are transactional customers, and transactional relationships are encouraged with these account segments. As KAM involves a relationship-driven approach, Iron and Lead customers should embrace the traditional transaction sales process.

Also, while the Platinum accounts require top management visits, the Gold accounts are often powerful. Thus, it is somewhat easier to avoid compelling them to conform to the organisation's practices and, instead, focus on areas where they seek interest in the product and services of the supplying organisation.

13.4.2 Develop KAM Support Capabilities

KAM support capabilities consist of human capability, KAM knowledge management capability and relationship development capability. Each of these capabilities enables the successful implementation and performance outcome of the KAM programme.

Human capability deals with selecting, recruiting and training the right talents for KAM function. Wilson and Millman (2003) suggest that key account managers are political entrepreneurs. They perform boundary-spanning roles of an arbiter by reconciling tensions that exist between self-interest, the key account and the employer. KAM managers perform market sensing for the sales organisation through information acquisition about the accounts and the competitive environment, and provide a signal of upcoming changes in the value of the key accounts (Guesalaga et al., 2018). KAM managers have a broad knowledge of both the employer organisation and the customer, look for synergistic potential between parties and apply diplomatic and linguistic skills with cultural empathy (Wilson & Millman, 2003). It has been suggested that such skills are beyond those of sales personnel. Thus, sales personnel recruited as part of the KAM function would need adequate training that provides knowledge of sales, marketing, cross-cultural intelligence, opportunity discovery, opportunity creation, business development, strategy, skills in operations and other skills that focus on how to build a long-lasting relationship with the customer's organisation (Storbacka, 2012).

KAM also requires knowledge management systems and processes for customer intelligence acquisition and information and knowledge sharing between the organisations. The key accounts use customer intelligence acquisition for understanding customer expectations and satisfaction concerning the KAM programme. It is also used for creating customer value and for the continuous improvement of the KAM programme. We find that companies adopt Salesforce systems linked to their value-creating systems that enable the key account to assign, track and monitor transactions, projects and relationships within their accounts. Some other companies establish sales funnel systems that allow them to store, study and explore all customer-related opportunities. Several researchers have documented such systems and overall knowledge sharing as operational capabilities needed for the successful implementation of KAM programme (Guesalaga et al., 2018; Ivens et al., 2018).

KAM relationship development capability deals with understanding how information exchange, trust and commitment could be improved with the key accounts. Ojasalo (2001) suggests that this requires understanding the key account representative desired style of social interaction. What kind of informal social contacts and events would help in building and enhancing friendship with the key account? Understanding how to be trustworthy in the eyes of the key accounts as well as understanding how relationship routines and quality can be improved is critical. Overall, the participation of key account managers in activities that foster the development of personal networks, and the ability to anticipate and address sources of crises and conflicts, and communicate effectively in crises will improve the account satisfaction, trust and commitment (Guesalaga et al., 2018)

13.4.3 Develop KAM Performance Measure

The KAM performance should consist of measurable outcomes between the KAM organisation and the key accounts. We propose customer-based performance, key account managers performance and KAM team performance (see Figure 13.11).

While the overall stakeholders or cross-functional organisational teams should collaborate to ensure the success of the KAM programme, it is also a critical responsibility of the KAM team to identify gaps and leakages in the KAM process, summon stakeholders meetings and find possible ways to address and continuously improve the process. This requires the KAM team to document issues identified as well as how they have been able to resolve them. The measurement of the KAM programme should incorporate targets for the key account managers. Increased sales, profit margins and the ability of the key accounts to meet customer commitments are suitable performance metrics for key account managers. KAM performance should also measure customer-based performance, which measures how well the customer is satisfied with the overall KAM programme. The amount of customer-initiated projects and jointly initiated projects between the KAM organisation and the customer is a measure of the customer commitments to the KAM programme. It is also essential to measure how well the relationship with the key account has improved or developed in terms of customer perception of trust and commitment of the key account manager to expeditiously resolve problems and maintain communication with the customer account representatives. We see a positive relationship between these measures and the successful implementation of the KAM programme as they capture both customer-centric measures as well as dyadic, team and individual-level factors that impact the KAM process and outcomes.

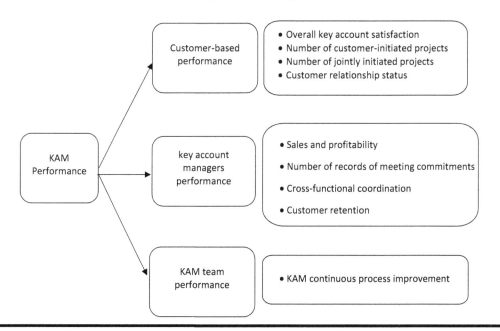

Figure 13.11   KAM performance measures.

13.5 Developing Marketing Capability in Business-to-Business Context

One of the most critical functions of a sales organisation is the development of marketing capability. Marketing capability can be defined as the integrative process that converts resources and market knowledge to explore customer needs and achieve competitive advantage (Yang et al., 2019). Gaining competitive advantage via marketing capability requires that the organisation's resources, routines and processes are valuable, scarce and imitable, and are configured and reconfigured dynamically in response to changes in the market (Yang et al., 2019).

In the previous section, we discussed how key account management programmes help in achieving customer-centricity. By achieving customer-centricity, the key account management programme supports the transforming of the sales organisation towards developing marketing capability through market sensing, customer engagement and inter-functional integration that comes along with its implementation. However, it alone cannot guarantee the efficient development of marketing capability needed for the strategic sales organisation. Figure 13.12 shows inclusive facets of marketing capability development in B2B context.

Market sensing refers to the identification and assessment of an opportunity (Teece, 2012, p. 1396). While the key account manager performs market sensing, the sales organisation broadly have a strategic responsibility to develop tools that aid them for market sensing. This includes predictive analytics tools that enable them to anticipate or proactively identify future customer needs. The ability of sales organisation to proactively identify solutions to customers' future needs has been shown to have a positive effect on key account performance due to its ability to reassuring the key account that the supplier organisation is paying attention to their future needs (Shi & Wu, 2011; Blocker et al., 2011).

Market sensing also requires exploration through proactively and continuously sensing the environment for competitive threats, experimenting and searching to adapt to evolutionary and revolutionary environmental changes (Mu, 2015). It helps sales organisation monitor the market dynamics, business and technological trends in the industry, proactively take advantage of market opportunities before competitors and develop novel products to delight both existing customers and new customers (Mu, 2015). Some organisations have market sensing as part of the role of the business intelligence unit, a matrix function intersecting the sales organisation or a full part of the sales organisation (see Figure 13.4). This unit conducts market research, uses advanced analytics with industry-wide big data and customer information systems to build databases that enable them to predict change, and gain advanced insights on key accounts, competitive threats in pricing and new technologies. Market sensing also involves benchmarking KAM programme to those of their competitors to understand the design of competitor KAM programmes and which competitors use a KAM programme (Guesalaga et al., 2018).

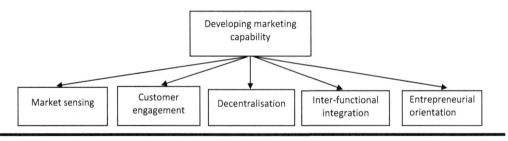

Figure 13.12   Developing marketing capabilities in B2B context.

Entrepreneurial orientation refers to be the ability of the sales organisation to orchestrate resources and adapt organisational processes in recognition and exploitation of business opportunities (Gebauer, 2011; Teece, 2014). While many organisation may conduct market sensing, only organisations that can orchestrate resources and adapt organisational process towards the exploitation of the opportunities discovered via market sensing will possess the marketing capability needed for sustained competitive advantage. This requires the ability of the organisation to be proactive in planning its product mix, target markets and allocate the necessary human resources and investments needed for exploiting the outcome of market sensing (Wu, 2013). It also requires that the sales organisation is strategically agile in terms of its flexibility to allocate and coordinate resources in response to changing environments (Mu et al., 2018). According to Teece (2007, p. 1319), firms with a strong entrepreneurial orientation are not only able to adapt to new market contexts, but also able to shape them through innovation and collaboration with other enterprises, entities and institutions.

Decentralisation of a sales organisation helps the organisation to respond to rapid market changes and to be responsive to customers, competitors and new technologies (Teece, 2007). Decentralised sales organisations are organisations where the key account managers are given the flexibility and substantial autonomy in getting work done, and every "minor" issue regarding customers and competition are not centralised to someone higher in the marketing organisation for decision-making (Mu, 2015). It is evident that innovative new products, processes and ideas are more likely to occur when the sales organisation can draw on a variety of ideas from different sources (Harvey, 2014). The decentralisation of the sales organisation helps to stimulate new directions for creative thinking as ideas and insights are widely distributed to employees, customers and partners; by exposing to and navigating a variety of ideas and insights, the firm exploits the inherent knowledge within its organisation for new market opportunities and new product development (NPD) (Mu, 2015).

Sales organisation has to be inter-functionally integrated into other units in the organisation to achieve decentralisation. This is a unique requirement for customer-centricity as well as for achieving marketing capability in B2B context. Inter-functional linkages mean that all customer-facing activities or customer value-adding activities and functions within the organisation are aligned, integrated, cooperative and coordinated to serve target market needs, jointly solve customer problems, sharing customer information freely across all business functions to create customer value and respond rapidly to market conditions (Mu, 2015). Inter-functional integration plays an essential role in exploiting external opportunities. By increasing both information communication frequency and the amount of information flow in the organisation via inter-functional integration, insights from different sources can diffuse across various units such as R&D and NPD teams. As a result, the firm can turn its market-sensing (exploitation and exploration) activities into new insights for enhancing existing offerings, NPD, and how to serve the customers better and provide superior customer value (Mu, 2015). Inter-functional integration also prevents conflicts and mistrust among functional units as they aim for the same purpose of serving the customer better and are aware of all customer information and customer activities needed to serve the customer better.

Customer engagement refers to the ability of the sales organisation to create intimate relationships with the customers (Park et al., 2010; Mu, 2015). It is achieved by providing reliable and timely responses to customers' needs, proactively responding to customer expectations. It entails attending to customers' ideas and considering customers' viewpoints and reality in designing and improving business process (Mu, 2015). Customer engagement is a facet of customer-centricity, as well as one of the essential roles of key account management. It is also the aim of market sensing as it helps the organisation to detect and adapt to changing market conditions as well as a means to create and maintain customer expectations. Customer engagement is acquired through sustained customer satisfaction that makes the customers identify with and perceive connectedness with the organisation, which in turn increases customer loyalty (Mu, 2015). Organisations that actively engage their customers and can coordinate and deploy both internal and partner resources (e.g. distributors, retailers) to create value for customers, possess marketing capability.

13.6 Developing a Sales Process

Sales in B2B contexts are about taking leads and converting them into revenue for the organisation. A sales process is different from promotion (advertising, branding, public relations, etc.). First, promotion occurs before sales. Second, while promotion is about generating qualified leads, sales process takes the leads and convert them into revenue for the organisation. Therefore, a sales process in B2B context is the process in which a sales organisation understands the customer demands, develops a solution, evaluates the solution with the customer, conducts negotiations and contracts and closes the deal. We discuss the different facets of the sales process as part of the sales funnel toolkit (Figure 13.13) and provide ways and discussions on how customer-centric strategic organisations can utilise it in their sales process to enhance customer engagement and improve the productivity of the key account managers and the sales organisation in general.

According to Davies (2010), the sales funnel is a strategic tool to manage and track:

a. The progress of customers through the sales process (customer progress status)
b. The value of opportunities associated with each customer (opportunity analysis)
c. How long customers take to move down the funnel (customer lead time)
d. How many customers can be found at each step (customer pipeline status)
e. Projected revenue forecasts (potential total revenue).

The sales funnel and sales process apply to both key accounts (Platinum and Gold accounts) and transactional accounts (Iron and Lead accounts). For the key accounts, the sales process and sales funnel are used in addition to the relationship-based value propositions defined for each account segments and key accounts. The sales funnel makes it possible for the sales organisation to have

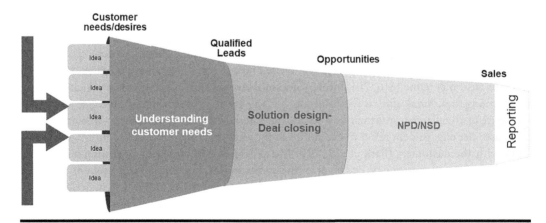

Figure 13.13   A sales process and sales funnel.

deep insight into what customer projects are outstanding, closed and potential revenue. Its working logic is that the deeper a customer project is in the funnel, the more likely it is that deals can be achieved. It is also an interactive tool with customer interface and different functional units within the sales organisation and the rest of the customer-value creating functions. Customers should be able to see and track the status of their projects and have a possibility to expedite or make an upgrade to existing requirements. Functional units can interact with the tool and assign customer projects from one stage or functional unit to another. The tool also makes it possible for all communication concerning a specific customer project to be in one location and timestamps of every status update made to the case/project.

Sales funnel not only allows the sales organisation to forecast future balance sheets, but it also allows for a possibility to track and value resources used in creating customer value. For example, it is possible to estimate how many persons or units are working on a customer project and what kinds of activities are performed by each person/team/unit and how much time it takes to complete the projects. This way, sales organisations can see when they are under-resourced or over-resourced and can estimate their transfer cost proportionally to resource utilised. Below we discuss the different phases of the sales funnel as part of the sales process.

13.6.1 Understanding Customer Needs

At the start of the sales process, the customer or key account has already been identified or known. The sales activity of the key account should be to understand customer needs. Strategic sales organisations are organisations that deploy (1) predictive tools to identify customer needs before they are known, (2) in collaboration with customers jointly identify their needs and (3) respond to customer-initiated needs.

In the age of data analytics and data-rich environment, organisations can proactively gain more insights about their customer needs from several structured and unstructured data sources. Through data analytics, organisations can utilise a wide variety of customer data to gain insights about their customer and increase NPD and sales (Johnson et al., 2017). Recently, there is an emerging theme that not only should organisations use big data analytics to understand customer needs, customers should also be empowered to utilise the data analytics platform to access and analyse the available data to co-develop new products (Zhang & Xiao, 2019). Overall, a common theme in the existing literature is that organisations that are utilising big data analytics are better able to serve customers, co-create value with their customers and gain a competitive advantage over their industry peers.

One crucial role of a key account manager is to collaborate and ensure cooperation with the key accounts. Cooperating with key accounts in solving customer problems has been shown to lead to opportunity creation and value co-creation (Hakanen, 2014). Thus, the continuous interaction between the key accounts and the customer organisation creates a possibility for jointly discovering opportunities. Furthermore, ideas on customer needs and an understanding of its needs can also originate from the customers. This is based on the idea that the customer determines value (Vargo & Lusch, 2008) and decides whether to engage in value co-creation with the provider (Grönroos & Voima, 2012). Thus, customer needs can originate from the customers independently. As a result, the sales organisation has to establish direct and close interaction with the customer to acquire information about their needs and provide ways in which both parties can co-create value.

Whether opportunities are jointly discovered, initiated by the customer or system-based predictive discovery, they are still leads. Customer needs as part of system predictive analytics should be presented to the customer to gain customer interest and possible adjustments. Customer-initiated needs or jointly discovered opportunities require validation to make an informed decision about the business potential and cost impact of customer requirements before proceeding to solution design. This all falls as part of the role and responsibilities of the business intelligence unit discussed in Section 13.1.

13.6.2 Solution Design to Deal Closing

The solution design phase is the next step in the sales funnel/sales process where the sales organisation begins to develop solutions that will meet customer needs before proposing to the customer in the form of prototypes for customer evaluation. The solution would include specific supply chain design such as lead times, packaging and warehousing depending on the B2B context. It would also have a pricing estimate and potential contractual terms. The prototype solution is presented to the customer as a proposal or an incomplete solution that will be refined based on feedback from the customers. There is a possibility the customer will not be willing to pay for it and does not want to continue further with the solution development. At this point, the opportunity is closed as a lost opportunity, and reasons for customer dissent should be documented. If the customer accepts the prototype solution, price and supply chain design matches the customer's value point; then, final solution design should commence immediately.

13.6.3 New Product/Solution Development Opportunities

The final stage of the sales funnel is the opportunities created in terms of a new product or new solution developed. When the final solution agreed with the customer is ready, the customer should be notified immediately, including purchasing process and lead times. The opportunity outcomes can then be closed for NPD/new solution development (NSD). From this stage, the sales organisation can commence a formal process of tracking the sales revenue that will accrue from it.

In summary, we see the sales funnel as a tool for the sales process and also a tool for achieving marketing capability. If we think about the facets of marketing capability, we can rightly observe that sales funnel, if implemented, can serve as an enabler of marketing capability. It can serve as a toolkit or platform that enables the implementation of marketing capability.

13.7 Engaging the Key Account Personnel

Abratt and Kelly (2002) studied customer perceptions of key account management programmes and found that the skills, knowledge and professionalism of their key account managers were the most critical success factors.

Furthermore, Mahlamaki et al. (2019) studied the role of personality and motivation on key account manager job performance. They found that two motivational constructs – learning orientation and performance orientation, play significant roles in the key account manager's job performance. They also found a link between the key account manager's personality traits and their motivations in that personality traits such as extroversion, agreeableness, conscientiousness and emotional stability are found to have significant relationships to the key account manager's motivations. Extroversion and conscientiousness are also linked to both learning orientation and performance orientation. The studies by Abratt and Kelly (2002) and Mahlamaki et al. (2019) provide robust empirical findings on how to engage a key account manager. Figure 13.14 shows

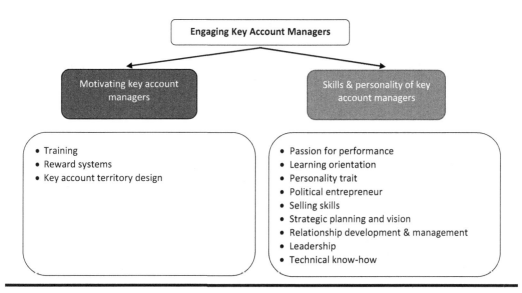

Figure 13.14 Engaging key account managers.

a model of engaging key account managers. A successful KAM program ensures that the right talents are selected for the roles. This is because only those with the right personality traits show signs of motivation which in turn influence their performance in the job (Mahlamaki et al., 2019). Furthermore, Loveland et al. (2015) showed that personality traits (emotional stability, optimism, extroversion, job and career satisfaction) explain the dimensional difference between salespeople and non-sales people and this dimension can be shaped by training and behavioural norms. Thus, you cannot hire a key account manager or train existing employee to become key account managers if they don't initially have the right personality traits for the role. This is a very critical issue in achieving the success of the key account management function. As organisations transform towards the implementation of KAM, they also need to recognise and ensure that only the right employees with the right personality traits are allowed to become key account managers. Thus, personality tests should be conducted for key account managers. Selected key account managers should be those that reflect a high degree of learning orientation, performance orientation, extroversion, agreeableness, emotional stability and conscientiousness as this has been shown to influence the performance of key account managers (Sujan et al., 1994; Mahlamaki et al., 2019). Table 13.1 shows empirical constructs on how organisations can measure the sets of skills when selecting key account managers.

Training is one of the most critical ways of engaging key account managers. The roles of key account managers have been conceptualised as that of a political entrepreneur with boundary-spanning behaviour that has to overcome cultural barriers and circumvent the sensitive political aspects of multiple internal and external interfaces while generating continuous business opportunities (Wilson & Millman, 2003). These require a comprehensive range of skills that go beyond those of a traditional salesperson (Ryals & Davies, 2013). Figure 13.15 shows external and internal training that we have developed for key account managers.

External training should reflect strategies for customer adaptation such as how to adapt to different types of customers and customer settings and situations, how to develop customer relationship, communication typologies and the emotional intelligence needed when dealing with diverse multi-facet stakeholders from internal and external organisations. External training should

Table 13.1 Personality Traits and Skillsets for Key Account Managers

Learning orientation	• It is essential for me to learn new things about my work • I put in a great deal of effort sometimes in order to learn something new • An essential part of being a good worker is to improve your skills continually • Learning how to be a better worker is of fundamental importance to me	Sujan et al. (1994) and Mahlamaki et al. (2019)
Performance orientation	• It is imperative to me that my supervisor sees me as a good worker • I spend much time thinking about how my performance compares with other co-workers • I very much want my co-workers to consider me to be a good worker	Sujan et al. (1994) and Mahlamaki et al. (2019)
Extraversion	• In unclear situations, I usually take control of things • It is easy for me to get to know other people • I usually let others make the decisions • Can talk others into doing things	Mahlamaki et al. (2019)
Agreeableness	• I trust other people • I trust what people say • I like to help others • I believe people usually have good intentions	Mahlamaki et al. (2019)
Emotional stability	• I get very nervous before important meetings • It is easy to hurt me emotionally • It is hard for me to take criticism • I feel that I can handle any situation	Mahlamaki et al. (2019)
Conscientiousness	• I am conscientious about the things I do • I finish my work on time • I am deliberate in my decisions • I obey the rules the best I can	Mahlamaki et al. (2019)
Selling skills	**Adaptive selling** • I experiment with different sales approaches • I adapt selling approaches from one customer to another • I vary sales style from situation to situation **Customer-oriented selling** • I desire to help customers make satisfactory purchase decisions • I help customers assess their needs and offer products that will satisfy those needs • I describe products accurately and avoid deceptive or manipulative influence tactics • I avoid the use of high pressure	Saxe and Weitz (1982) and Schwepker (2003)

(Continued)

Table 13.1 (*Continued*)   Personality Traits and Skillsets for Key Account Managers

Strategic planning and vision	• Ability to set a vision for each key account • Ability to determine and plan joint activities with key accounts representatives • Ability to strategically plan and develop both short- and long-term plans/goals for key accounts • Have sound knowledge of key accounts strategic direction	Ivens et al. (2018)
Leadership styles and negotiation skills	• Transformation leadership • Charismatic • Individualised consideration • Intellectual stimulation • Transactional leadership • Management by exception • Contingent reward	Avolio et al. (1999)
Technical know-how	• Possess knowledge and understanding of the key account customers business • Possess detailed knowledge of product or service, including design and specifications	Al-Husan and Brennan (2009)
Political entrepreneur	• Seeks and exploits business opportunities and synergistic value between buyer and seller • Facilitates the achievement of relational and financial goals between buyer and seller • Builds multi-cultural relationships and promotes meritocracy	Wilson and Millman (2003)
Relationship development capability	• Ability to develop a professional and close interpersonal relationship or social bonds with key account customers • Ability to develop a professional business relationship with key account customers • Ability to develop trust, commitment, cooperation, information sharing, conflict resolution approaches and long-term relationships with key account customers	Haytko (2004), Abratt and Kelly (2002), and Ryals and Davies (2013)

also focus on how to manage internal stakeholders within own organisation, specifically, on how to influence both customers and members of own organisation, organise resources and activities within the operations teams and customer-facing activities. Finally, external training should focus on how to develop the planning orientation of key account managers, for example how to continually conduct market sensing and gather market intelligence as part of their interactions with customers and how to communicate this internally within their organisation to influence future strategy.

It should also focus on how to develop a shared strategy with the customer, in-depth of analysis (e.g. Five Whys) to understanding customer problems and developing and setting targets both short- and long-term goals with the customer.

Figure 13.15   Training key account managers.

Internal training should focus on technical skills, selling skills, IT tools and systems that aid the sales process, enterprise value exchange with customers, tools for analysis, planning, communication and project management. Although there are no boundaries between what constitutes internal and external training, we have created this dichotomy based on areas that are core to the company's business and operations. In reality, this all depends on the training resources an organisation is willing to keep in-house and what to outsource. This also depends on the size of the organisation and the number of key account managers. For large global multinational corporations with global, regional and national key account managers and key account specialists, it is possible that most of the training identified as external training can be made in-house as part of regular training for existing and new account managers.

A structured, measurable and long-term reward system is very critical for motivating key account managers. The reward system should be measurable and should reinforce the contributions of the key account managers in terms of individual performance and team performance. The individual performance should reflect contributions of the key account manager in terms of sales and profitability as well as the number of successful joint projects and initiative carried out with customers, number of records of meeting commitments and how many key accounts have been retained/lost over the period.

The team performance should reflect proactive contributions of the key account manager in improving esprit de corps within the accounts team, special incentive or bravo award for winning together with the account team or excellent leadership displayed in carrying duties of account management. Long-term reward systems should focus on career path rewards for key account managers. As key account managers have a long-term objective and orientation, its account managers should also have long-term rewards. Long-term career path should include both horizontal and upward career mobility path that provides account managers with both intrinsic and extrinsic motivation for their job.

Finally, the design of the key account territory is crucial for the motivation of the key account managers. Existing research has shown that there is a positive relationship between territory design and the motivation of the key account managers (Babakus et al., 1994) and hence the performance and effectiveness of the sales organisation (Piercy et al., 1999). This is because the territory design determines the number of key account customers in the territory, the geographical span of the key accounts, the level of control and empowerment over the key accounts, and the number of budgetary resources (e.g. travel) allocated to the key account manager. Sales organisation should design key account territory such that the account managers have supervisory control over the territory and control over budgetary appropriations allocated to the territory as well as sufficient authority to make crucial decisions over their key accounts. The design should also reflect territories where the key account has specific knowledge or interest in business cultures in those countries and interest in learning local business cultures.

Case Study: Developing a B2B Sales Organisation for FP Agro-Allied

FP Agro-Allied is a manufacturer of a packaged "ready-to-eat" premix product that is made from local cassava flakes ("garri"), milk, sugar and roasted groundnuts. The product is affordably priced and targeted at low-income consumer segments and hygiene-conscious middle- and upper-class consumers who frequently consume the garri staple food. Located in Ibadan, Oyo State (South-West Nigeria), the business currently sells up to 300,000 units of its packaged products monthly and the product has a footprint in other parts of the country, including Katsina, Sokoto and Ogun states.

SUPPORT NEEDS

Nigeria is a leading producer, and consumer of cassava in the world and different processed forms of the tuber crop are widely consumed across the country. Garri, the most widely consumed form of cassava in Nigeria, is a high-demand staple and fast-moving food commodity. FP Agro-Allied expressed a desire to scale up the market footprint for its product to 30 million units in monthly sales. A 100-fold increase in sales volume required a formal, structured and systematic approach to sales that would concentrate on B2B sales, replacing the company's existing strategy that had a significant focus on B2C sales.

FP Agro-Allied engaged Smallstarter Africa to support its development of a sales organisation to spearhead its market penetration efforts. Smallstarter Africa is an online support base for African entrepreneurs who want to learn and grow. They provide the training, insights and inspiration entrepreneurs need to transform their ideas, dreams and small businesses into successful marvels. They use a combination of curated content, books, basic and advanced business courses, signature coaching programmes, and private consulting to support entrepreneurs who are at different stages of building their dream business.

THE PROBLEM

The supply side of the garri commodity market in Nigeria is mainly informal and unstructured, and consists of an interconnected web of small- and large-scale local processors, bulk dealers, wholesalers, market stall traders, hawkers and petty "roadside" traders. In addition to developing a formal and structured sales force to "push" FP's products in the local markets, there was an additional burden of coordinating sales efforts across Nigeria's vast market landscape, spanning three separate regions of the country – the south-west, north-central and north-west. Also, identifying and recruiting the right talent with sufficient levels of motivation and developing a relevant compensation structure to drive the sales team presented considerable obstacles.

SMALLSTARTER AFRICA SOLUTION

Suitable candidates for the sales team were selected on the bases of relevant sales experience in fast-moving consumer goods (FMCGs) and personal attributes that included persuasive ability, ambition, determination, capacity for hard work, resilience and teamwork. The target market area was divided into zones, and sales teams (headed by a sales manager) were assigned to specific zones with full accountability for the sales performance of each zone. To coordinate the sales efforts across the organisation, Smallstarter provided formalised templates including sales agreements, supplier terms and conditions, and sale or return (SOR) contracts, among others.

CASE QUESTION

Considering the discussions on developing marketing and sales capability and setting up a sales organisation, discuss other solutions you would propose to help solve the problem of FP Agro-Allied company?

This case was prepared by Founder & CEO – Smallstarter Africa, John-Paul Iwuoha.

References

Abratt, R., & Kelly, P. M. (2002). Customer–supplier partnerships: Perceptions of a successful key account management program. *Industrial Marketing Management*, 31(5), 467–476.

Al-Husan, F. B., & Brennan, R. (2009). Strategic account management in an emerging economy. *Journal of Business & Industrial Marketing*, 24(8), 611–620.

Anderson, J. C., Narus, J. A., & Van Rossum, W. (2006). Customer value propositions in business markets. *Harvard Business Review*, 84(3), 91–90.

Avolio, B. J., Bass, B. M., & Jung, D. I. (1999). Re-examining the components of transformational and transactional leadership using the multifactor leadership. *Journal of Occupational and Organisational Psychology*, 72(4), 441–462.

Babakus, E., Cravens, D. W., Grant, K., Ingram, T. N., & LaForge, R. W. (1994). Removing salesforce performance hurdles. *Journal of Business & Industrial Marketing*, 9(3), 19–29.

Biemans, W. G., & Brencic, M. M. (2007). Designing the marketing-sales interface in B2B firms. *European Journal of Marketing*, 41(3–4), 257–273.

Blocker, C. P., Flint, D. J., Myers, M. B., & Slater, S. F. (2011). Proactive customer orientation and its role for creating customer value in global markets. *Journal of the Academy of Marketing Science*, 39(2), 216–233.

Boles, J., Johnston, W. & Gardner, A. (1999). The selection and organisation of national accounts: A North American perspective, *Journal of Business & Industrial Marketing*, 14(4), 264–282.

Geiger, S., Guenzi, P., Brehmer, P. O., & Rehme, J. (2009). Proactive and reactive: Drivers for key account management programmes. *European Journal of Marketing*, 43(7/8), 961–984.

Corcoran, K. J. (1995). *High performance sales organisations: Achieving competitive advantage in the global marketplace*. Irwin Professional Publishing, India.

Davies, S. (2010). Building a business-to-business sales process. Open Source Business Resource, (October 2010). http://timreview.ca/article/386

Gebauer, H. (2011). Exploring the contribution of management innovation to the evolution of dynamic capabilities. *Industrial Marketing Management*, 40(8), 1238–1250.

Galbraith, J. R. (2011). *Designing the customer-centric organisation: A guide to strategy, structure, and process*. John Wiley & Sons, Boca Raton, FL.

Grönroos, C., & Voima, P. (2012). Critical service logic: Making sense of value creation and co-creation. *Journal of the Academy of Marketing Science*, 41(2), 133–150.

Guesalaga, R. (2014). Top management involvement with key accounts: The concept, its dimensions, and strategic outcomes. *Industrial Marketing Management,* 43(7), 1146–1156.

Geiger, S., Guenzi, P., Storbacka, K., Ryals, L., Davies, I. A., & Nenonen, S. (2009). The changing role of sales: Viewing sales as a strategic, cross-functional process. *European Journal of Marketing*, 43(7/8) 890–906.

Guesalaga, R., Gabrielsson, M., Rogers, B., Ryals, L., & Cuevas, J. M. (2018). Which resources and capabilities underpin strategic key account management? *Industrial Marketing Management*, 75, 160–172.

Harvey, S. (2014). Creative synthesis: Exploring the process of extraordinary group creativity. *Academy of Management Review*, 39(3), 324–343.

Hakanen, T. (2014). Co-creating integrated solutions within business networks: The KAM team as knowledge integrator. *Industrial Marketing Management*, 43, 1195–1203.

Haytko, D. L. (2004). Firm-to-firm and interpersonal relationships: Perspectives from advertising agency account managers. *Journal of the Academy of Marketing Science*, 32(3), 312–328.

Ivens, B. D., Leischnigb, A., Pardoc, C., & Niersbach, B. (2018). Key account management as a firm capability. *Industrial Marketing Management*, 74(1), 39–49.

Johnson, J. S., Friend, S. B., & Lee, H. S. (2017). Big data facilitation, utilisation, and monetisation: Exploring the 3Vs in a new product development process. *Journal of Product Innovation Management*, 34(5), 640–658.

Lane, N., & Piercy, N. (2004). Strategic customer management: Designing a profitable future for your sales organisation. *European Management Journal*, 22(6), 659–668.

Lane, N., & Piercy, N. (2009). Strategising the sales organisation. *Journal of Strategic Marketing*, 17(3–4), 307–322.

Lamberti, L. (2013). Customer centricity: the construct and the operational antecedents. *Journal of Strategic Marketing*, 21(7), 588–612.

Leigh, T. W., & Marshall, G. W. (2001). Research priorities in sales strategy and performance. *Journal of Personal Selling & Sales Management*, 21(2), 83–93.

Loveland, J. M., Lounsbury, J. W., Park, S-H, & Jackson, D. W. (2015). Are salespeople born or made? Biology, personality, and the career satisfaction of salespeople. *Journal of Business & Industrial Marketing*, 30(2), 233–240.

Mahlamaki, T., Rintamaki, T., & Rajah, E. (2019). The role of personality and motivation on key account manager job performance. *Industrial Marketing Management*, 83, 174–184.

Mu, J. (2015). Marketing capability, organisational adaptation and new product development performance. *Industrial Marketing Management*, 49, 151–166.

Mu, J., Bao, K., Sekhon, T., Qi, J., & Love, E. (2018). Outside-in marketing capability and firm performance. *Industrial Marketing Management*, 75, 37–54.

Ojasalo, J. (2001). Key account management at company and individual levels in business-to-business relationships. *The Journal of Business & Industrial Marketing*, 16(3), 199–216.

Pansari A. & Kumar, V. (2017). Customer engagement – the construct, antecedents and consequences. *Journal of the Academy of Marketing Science*, 45(3), 294–311.

Park, C. W., MacInnis, D. J., Priester, J., Eisingerich, A. B., & Iacobucci, D. (2010). Brand attachment and brand attitude strength: Conceptual and empirical differentiation of two critical brand equity drivers. *Journal of Marketing*, 74(6), 1–17.

Piercy, N. F (2010). Evolution of strategic sales organisations in business-to-business marketing. *Journal of Business & Industrial Marketing*, 25(5), 349–359.

Piercy, N. F., Cravens, D. W., & Morgan, N. A. (1999). Relationships between sales management control, territory design, salesforce performance and sales organisation effectiveness. *British Journal of Management*, 10(2), 95–111.

Rollins, M., Bellenger, D. N., & Johnston, W. J. (2012). Does customer information usage improve a firm's performance in business-to-business markets? *Industrial Marketing Management*, 41(6), 984–994.

Ryals, L. J., & Davies, I. A. (2013). Where's the strategic intent in key account relationships? *Journal of Business and Industrial Marketing*, 28(2), 111–124.

Saxe, R., & Weitz, B. A. (1982). The SOCO Scale: A measure of the customer orientation of salespeople. *Journal of Marketing Research*, 29, 343–351.

Schwepker, C. H. Jr. (2003). Customer-oriented selling: A review, extension, and directions for future research. *Journal of Personal Selling and Sales Management*, 23(Spring), 151–171.

Shi, L. H., & Wu, F. (2011). Dealing with market dynamism: The role of reconfiguration in global account management. *MIR: Management International Review*, 51(5), 635–663.

Storbacka, K. (2012). Strategic account management programs: alignment of design elements and management practices. *Journal of Business & Industrial Marketing*, 27(4), 259–274.

Sujan, H., Weitz, B. A., & Kumar, N. (1994). Learning orientation, working smart, and effective selling. *Journal of Marketing*, 58(3), 39–52.

Teece, D. J. (2007). Explicating dynamic capabilities: the nature and microfoundations of sustainable enterprise performance. *Strategic Management Journal*, 28(13), 1319–1350.

Teece, D. J. (2012). Dynamic capabilities: Routines versus entrepreneurial action. *Journal of Management Studies*, 49(8), 1395–1401.

Teece, D. J. (2014). The foundations of enterprise performance: Dynamic and ordinary capabilities in an (economic) theory of firms. *The Academy of Management Perspectives*, 28(4), 328–352.

van Raaij, E. M., Vernooij, M. J., & van Triest, S. (2003). The implementation of customer profitability analysis: A case study. *Industrial Marketing Management*, 32(7), 573–583.

Vargo, S. L., & Lusch, R. F. (2008). Service-dominant logic: Continuing the evolution. *Journal of the Academy of Marketing Science*, 36(1), 1–10.

Wengler, S., Ehret, M., & Saab, S. (2006). Implementation of key account management: Who, why, and how? An exploratory study on the current implementation of key account management programs. *Industrial Marketing Management*, 35(1), 103–112.

Wilson, K., & Millman, T. (2003). The global account manager as political entrepreneur. *Industrial Marketing Management*, 32(2), 151–158.

Wu, J. (2013). Marketing capabilities, institutional development, and the performance of emerging market firms: A multinational study. *International Journal of Research in Marketing*, 30(1), 36–45.

Yang, Z., Jiang, Y., & Xie, E. (2019). Buyer-supplier relational strength and buying firm's marketing capability: An outside-in perspective. *Industrial Marketing Management*, 82, 27–37.

Zeithaml, V. A., Rust, R. T., & Lemon, K. N. (2001). The customer pyramid: Creating and serving profitable customers. *California Management Review*, 43(4), 118–142.

Zhang, H., & Xiao, Y. (2020). Customer involvement in big data analytics and its impact on B2B innovation. *Industrial Marketing Management*, 86, 99–108.

EMERGING ISSUES IN BUSINESS-TO-BUSINESS MARKETING

6

Part 6 covers emerging issues in B2B marketing, and it consists of Chapter 14 only.

Chapter 14

Emerging Issues in Business-to-Business Marketing

INTRODUCTION AND OBJECTIVES

In this chapter, we discuss emerging issues that are shaping business-to-business (B2B) marketing in Africa. First, we discuss the impact of globalisation on B2B markets in Africa and how African business markets are responding to the changes. Second, we discuss how big data, business analytics and artificial intelligence are transforming the B2B sector. Finally, we discuss servitisation and value co-creation strategies in B2B.

At the end of this chapter, the reader will understand and be able to plan strategies regarding

- The changes in the global and African B2B environment
- The impact of the changes on African B2B markets and how African B2B organisations should strategise for competitive success
- The emergence of big data and how African B2B organisations can benefit from business analytics and artificial intelligence to improve their competitiveness
- Servitisation and value co-creation strategies.

14.1 The Impact of Globalisation on B2B and How Companies Are Responding

14.1.1 Delocalisation of Business Customer

Globalisation has created a rise in delocalisation of customers for B2B suppliers and subcontractors, especially for European, America and Asian multinational corporations (MNEs). This is because as the MNEs move to low-cost locations, their industrial suppliers and subcontractors see their home market dwindling, while simultaneously receiving ever more requests to follow the MNEs to offshore locations (Matthyssens et al., 2008). African MNEs are not as globalised as their counterpart firms in Europe, America and Asia. What is more pronounced in the African continent is Africa-to-Africa internationalisation and African industrial suppliers and subcontractors becoming business beneficiaries of globalisation (Boso et al., 2019). Africa-to-Africa internationalisation creates delocalisation of customers as small and medium-sized enterprises (SMEs) who are industrial suppliers and subcontractors of local MNEs are required to build facilities in several countries to provide the same services and solutions for the African MNE as they internationalise across the African region (Dike & Rose, 2019). Local SMEs have limited resources and challenges arising from African institutional voids, which makes it more challenging for these local SMEs to follow their MNEs to foreign markets (Adomako et al., 2019).

Moreover, several African countries have local content regulations that make it challenging for local SMEs to locate their facilities in other African countries as the MNE is required to show partnership with local firms in parts of their value chain as a pre-requisite for operating in several African markets (Owusu & Vaaland, 2016; Väaland et al., 2012). Globalisation or regionalisation of B2B is creating delocalisation from more developed African markets to less developed African markets as African MNEs expand across the region. As a result, in less developed African markets, small- and medium-scale industrial suppliers and subcontractors are seeking for alliance partners with firms from advanced African countries and as well as from advanced economies of Europe, North America and Asia. These partnerships enable them to serve and meet the demands of both African and non-African MNEs operating in the local markets.

14.1.2 The Globalisation of the Purchasing and Sales Function

MNEs see the potential cost savings in purchasing synergies from economies of scale and scope. As a result, MNEs are centralising their purchasing functions, thereby making the affiliate lose their purchasing mandate. Several SMEs in Africa that supply components or raw materials to MNEs operating in their home country suddenly see a drop in sales from their key accounts as both direct and indirect material sourcing get centralised and purchased from cheaper suppliers in other African markets. Similarly, globalisation has led to the globalisation of the sales function as firms seek to build strong relationships with their global and regional customers (see Chapter 13). African SME industrial suppliers and subcontractors of globalising or regionalising multinationals see the importance of managing and sustaining their relationship with their clients as they globalise or regionalise. The significance of these major global/regional customers to African suppliers and subcontractors has led to growth in the adoption of global account management (GKAM) or national key account management (NKAM). Overall, the adoption of helps the firm in negotiating transnational deals centrally, and maintaining consistent sales relationships across the geographically diverse locations of their major global/regional customers.

14.2 Transitioning to Servitisation and Servitisation Strategies in Business-to-Business

14.2.1 S-D Logic and Value Co-creation

Before discussing servitisation in B2B markets, it is essential to discuss the service-dominant (S-D) logic and value co-creation as they are the antecedents of servitisation. Traditionally, firms have created customer value by focusing on customer needs, mainly satisfied via the manufacturing of products. In recent years, the transition from a product focus to service focus has led to changes in how value is created from the value created from ownership of the product to value creation in the function and use of the products (Howard et al., 2014). Nevertheless, these changes have only had a product-dominant thinking or in other words goods-dominant logic (G-D logic). G-D logic views servitisation as a phenomenon of manufacturing firms "adding value" through the provision of services (Howard et al., 2014). It assumes that the manufacturing firm or producer determines value while the customer is the recipient of the goods (Vargo & Lusch, 2004). For example, some manufacturing firms assume that by just transitioning to services, they have added value and consequently clients are willing to pay more. In reality, "exchange value" that proceeds from the services is just one part of the service value creation process in servitisation and the second level is created after the exchange is complete, that is "value in use." Value in use is all the customer-perceived consequences arising from a solution that facilitate or hinder the achievement of the customer's goals (Macdonald et al., 2016). Thus, the customer and the supplier firm have the responsibility of creating a value-in-use situation while the customer perceives and determines value. S-D logic proposes that a firm can only offer value propositions, which can be achieved only through co-creation with the customer (Howard et al., 2014). Thus, a firm can only collaboratively support value co-creation through facilitating opportunities for the co-creation of value in the customer's use situation (Eggert et al., 2018). To do this, firms must have an in-depth understanding of the customer's role in attaining its value.

14.2.2 Transitioning to Servitisation

One of the prevalent trends in B2B markets is the increasing importance of services in sustaining market share and profitability of manufacturing industries. Servitisation is a recent trend in B2B markets in which manufacturing companies complement their product-based offerings with services or adopt more service components in their offerings (Hakanen et al., 2017). It involves the marketing of bundles of customer-focused combinations of goods, services, support, self-service and knowledge (Vandermerwe & Rada, 1988).

Servitisation requires the development of capabilities and processes in order to shift from selling products to selling integrated products and services (Roy et al., 2009). It provides a means for B2B firms to gain differentiation from their competitors and customer loyalty which in turn provides a competitive advantage. Servitisation shifts the nature of customer interaction from transaction-based to relationship-based, requiring stronger customer orientation and customer lock-in, thereby generating additional revenue and long-term profitability of the business.

To achieve servitisation, firms undergo a shift in their offering content, service operations and processes, customer experience management and service outcome. It also requires that firms develop their service offering according to the characteristics of the local business customers. This may require acquiring new competence either directly or via intermediaries and building a new operating model and processes. While servitisation provides additional cash flow and sustained profitability for B2B markets, companies find it challenging to transform their business into product–service-oriented business for various reasons. First, there is a cultural hindrance in organisations to transition to product–service-oriented business due to product-oriented culture. The product-oriented culture limits interaction between customers and the organisation's employees. Transition to servitisation entails moving away from a transactional exchange to a relationship-based model, thereby increasing the number of customer touchpoints and interactions than previously.

Second, the company has to redefine its offering terms such as contracts, pricing, terms and conditions, and establish clarity of the limits of its offering. This is a core challenge in the transition as customers may misunderstand the value proposition of the organisation's offering.

Third, a lack of internal processes and capabilities limits the ability of companies to transition to product–service-oriented business. To transition to the product–service offering, the organisation needs to access its internal capabilities to design and deliver product–service offerings. Answers to questions such as "do we have the ability to meet our service level agreements?" "What processes and capabilities do we need to meet service level agreements?" "Are our internal processes customer-driven and aligned to meet customer needs?" "What level of servitisation do we now have, or how do we provide the organisation with a blueprint on developing the necessary capabilities needed to transition to product–service-oriented business?" Finally, transitioning to servitisation requires common organisational goals and mindset towards service provision. The organisation needs to speak one language and think like a customer. The common language need not only focus on the organisation; it should also transcend to their suppliers. It requires strategic alignment within the internal and external organisation. The organisation has to increase the degree of cooperation with its suppliers because it is necessary to gain in-depth insight into the problems and applications of customers' problems. To provide integrated offerings, changes in the relationships between product–service providers and their customers should be reflected in the relationships with the provider's suppliers. This requires a high degree of exchange of information and know-how between upstream and downstream members.

Organisations seeking to transition to product–service offering need an understanding of the challenges of servitisation. Next, the organisation needs to design its servitisation strategy. Below we elaborate five steps to help African corporations to transition to the product–service offering.

14.2.3 Servitisation Strategies

In Figure 14.1, we illustrate how companies can transition to the product–service offering. Developing servitisation strategy is one key aspect of the transition. In this section, we discuss four servitisation strategies (service extension, service network transition, customer co-creation and digitalisation strategy) in more detail. African firms could adapt these strategies in their transition to product–service offering depending on their degree of servitisation.

Service Extension Strategy: It is a fact that manufacturing firms may have some degree of services as part of their product offering. Thus, manufacturing firms may have transitioned towards product–service offering yet having a low degree of servitisation. A low degree of servitisation means product-dominant focus where there are still few services offered by the firm, and the share of the revenue from services is minimal compared to product revenues. For this type of companies, a service extension strategy is a viable servitisation strategy. Service extension strategy is focused on building on existing offerings of the provider, integrating an external and new bundle of services to provide more advanced services as part of the overall service portfolio of the company.

Service extension strategy is suitable for companies that have already made some progress towards servitisation as the main aim is to gainer more share of the revenue from services. This is mainly achieved by increasing the number and range of services, introducing new service offering and combining existing services into one service package. This can be achieved via organic growth or acquisition of existing businesses and integrating the organisation's bundle of services. Benchmarking industry players is very important to achieve service extension strategy.

Service Network Strategy: Service network strategy is a transition of networked product-dominant business model into service networks. An automotive firm cannot adopt servitisation without the transition of its entire network of suppliers, distributors, dealers and leasing company. The oil and gas manufacturers cannot transition to services without the evolution of the upstream and downstream operations. Overall, a manufacturer whose business depends on a network of players cannot transition towards advanced service provision without the support and corresponding transition of service network actors. Relationships between these networks of actors are key to enable the smooth transition to services. The challenge of this transition is that it takes time and would require a service model where all network players retain or increase their market share.

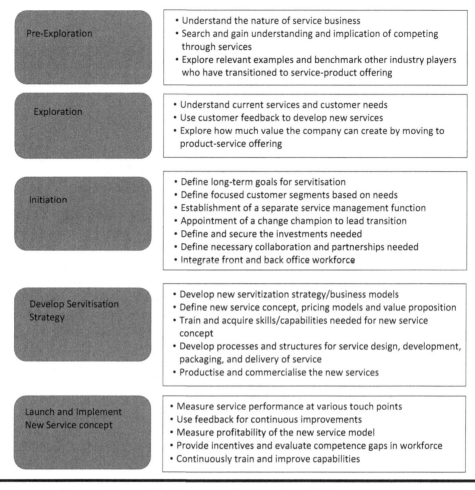

Figure 14.1 Five steps in transitioning to product–service offering.

Customer Co-creation Servitisation: Customers are key players in servitisation as they determine the value and profitability of the service. For a servitisation strategy to be successful, customers need to buy-in before they can engage in the service contract. Narrowing down the service transition to key customer segment within the existing business portfolio could simplify the service package and make the benefit and value proposition more transparent for the customers. The service is usually co-created with the customer segments through collaborating, co-designing, interviews and customer feedback sessions. Customer co-creation servitisation is very efficient as the bundle of services, design and delivery is designed and developed in collaboration with the customer. The company reduces the cost of development, cost of product failures and cost of convincing the customer about the value proposition of the services. One challenge with this servitisation strategy is to be able to identify the key customer segment that will be the focus of the servitisation.

Digitalisation Strategy: Digitalisation servitisation is a strategy in which manufacturing operations transition to services through the application and use of digital applications. Digitalisation strategy requires that organisations digitalise their operations and products using digital technologies to enable the resultant provision of digital services. Digitalisation provides the ability to track machines with telematics and use big data analytics to provide advanced services and meets customer expectation. Digitalisation changes a business model and provides new revenue and opportunities for businesses. Digitalisation strategy reconfigures how value is created, delivered and consumed. For example, the delivery and management of services in a digitisation strategy can be through digital platforms. It could require the bold organisation change and restructuring around centralisation of the service function. We discuss this in more detail in the following section.

14.3 How Digitalisation and Artificial Intelligence Are Transforming Business-to-Business Marketing

In the above section, we discussed the digitalisation strategy as a part of a strategy of transforming to servitisation. In this section, we discuss in more detail how digitalisation and Artificial Intelligence (AI) is altering B2B marketing concepts.

The Digitalisation of Sales Channels: B2B marketing is seeing an increasing trend towards the digitalisation of sales channels as firms aim to increase efficiency and reduce cost. B2B firms are doing this by complementing their sales forces with channels that require online rather than personal interactions. This includes self-service technologies for customers such as online platforms allowing business customers to place an order, track orders and even co-develop products. There is a growing number of trading platforms, e.g. Alibaba.com, platform XOM that allows various suppliers and business customers to exchange services, exchange value, compete and create value.

Sales channel transformation goes beyond the introduction of online sales channels to include transition towards fully automated selling, purchasing and customer service. This has led to a shift in the sales profession, from a focus on selling to focus on value creation for customers such as consulting for complex products, processes and services.

Value Creation and Digitalised Sales Funnels: While there are digitalised funnels in B2C business like Netflix that utilises artificial intelligence to provide personalised offering recommendation to meet customer needs, the B2B marketing is seeing a similar trend as AI technologies is integrated all along the sales funnel. In B2B marketing, AI is used to identify and qualify leads that can benefit from a company's value proposition. For a company that receives more than 1000 leads per week, one of the fundamental questions is how they can turn these leads into actual sales. The number of human resources needed to analyse these leads will be costly. With AI, marketing teams can analyse these leads, score leads that will most likely bring sales for the company in a very short interval. Digitalised sales funnels also include the incorporation of predictive analytics tools into lead scoring. For example, companies are using tools such as Pardot, HubSpot and Marke to track prospects interaction with their company and intelligently nurture them until they are ready to be approached by a salesperson (Järvinen & Taiminen, 2016).

The Digitalisation of Customer Insight: Digitalisation of customer insight includes the digitalisation of activities for creating, codifying, sharing and applying insight about customers. These include what customers purchase, and how and why they make their purchasing decisions and the antecedents of their purchasing decision. Gaining customer insight is critical in serving the customer better, gaining customer loyalty, improving offerings and providing the short and long-term performance of a firm. B2B firms are beginning to introduce various AI platforms to understand their customers better. For example, AI-powered technologies are used to create a comprehensive profile of a company's current and potential customers through analysis of customer behaviour, browsing history, purchase history and interactions with the firm.

Marketing teams are using AI platforms and predictive analytics tools to track prospects across multiple touchpoints and assess how likely they are to buy. A customer who visits a trade show and asks about a product, visits a webshop, registers for marketing email and downloads a product catalogue is providing indicators of likelihood or interest to purchase a product. With AI, at every stage of this customer interaction, the same value proposition is offered, and the customer is provided support at each stage until purchase intention.

Marketing teams are also using AI technologies to understand the personality of the customer in order to adapt their selling strategies. For example, technologies such as JOYai can classify people on LinkedIn by their personality and job responsibilities and then customise messages to each person. Companies are also using NICE (www.nice.com) to match customers to call centre agents with similar personalities.

B2B firms are using AI technologies to analyse users' vast number of datasets on social media platforms to gain insights about user needs, preferences, attitudes and behaviours. Recent technologies can analyse customer feedbacks and provide sentimental analysis of customers. The IBM Watson, for example, has the capabilities to identify sentiment, emotions, values and attitudes expressed in a piece of text.

The Digitalisation of Customer Service Function: Traditionally, customer service function has used telephones and email exchanges to respond to customer inquiries. Recently, B2B firms are introducing AI-powered technologies such as chatbots to manage their customer service function. For example, chatbots are used by B2B firms for marketing, customer relationship management and post-purchase customer support. Chatbots provide quick response to customer inquiries. It is also used for engaging simple conversations with customers such as responding to frequently asked questions and engaging in more complex and advanced discussions with customers. It can book appointments with a firm on behalf of the customers, analyse customer enquiries, generate possible leads and assign to the responsible sales force for more customer follow-up.

References

Adomako, S., Amankwah-Amoah, J., Dankwah, G. O., Danso, A., & Donbesuur, F. (2019). Institutional voids, international learning effort and internationalisation of emerging market new ventures. *Journal of International Management*, 25(4), 100666. DOI: 10.1016/j.intman.2019.04.001.

Boso, N., Adeleye, I., Ibeh, K., & Chizema, A. (2019). The internationalisation of African firms: Opportunities, challenges, and risks. *Thunderbird International Business Review*, 61(1), 5–12. DOI: 10.1002/tie.21977.

Dike, M. C., & Rose, E. L. (2019). Cross-border expansion and competitive interactions of indigenous mobile network operators in sub-Saharan Africa. *Thunderbird International Business Review*, 61(1), 29–42.

Eggert, A., Ulaga, W., Frow, P., & Payne, A. (2018). Conceptualising and communicating value in business markets: From value in exchange to value in use. *Industrial Marketing Management*, 69, 80–90

Hakanen, T., Helander, N., & Valkokari, K. (2017). Servitization in global business-to-business distribution: The central activities of manufacturers. *Industrial Marketing Management*, 63, 167–178.

Howard, M., Caldwell, N., Smith, L., Maull, R., & Ng, I. C. (2014). Servitization and operations management: A service dominant-logic approach. *International Journal of Operations & Production Management*, 34(2), 242–269.

Jarvinen, J., & Taiminen, H. (2016). Harnessing marketing automation for B2B content marketing. *Industrial Marketing Management*, 54, 164–175

Macdonald, E. K., Kleinaltenkamp, M., & Wilson, H. N. (2016). How business customers judge solutions: Solution quality and value in use. *Journal of Marketing*, 80(3), 96–120.

Matthyssens, P., Kirca A. H., & Pace, S. (2008). Business-to-business marketing and globalisation: Two of a kind. *International Marketing Review*, 25(5), 481–486.

Owusu, R. A., & Vaaland, T. I. (2016). A business network perspective on local content in emerging African petroleum nations. *International Journal of Energy Sector Management*, 10(4), 594–616.

Roy, R., Shehab, E., Tiwari, A., Baines, T. S., Lightfoot, H. W., Benedettini, O., & Kay, J. M. (2009). The servitisation of manufacturing. *Journal of Manufacturing Technology Management*, 20(5), 547–567.

Vaaland, T. I., Soneye, A. S., & Owusu, R. A. (2012). Local content and struggling suppliers: A network analysis of Nigerian oil and gas industry. *African Journal of Business Management*, 6(15), 5399–5413.

Vandermerwe, S., & Rada, J. (1988). Servitization of business: Adding value by adding services. *European Management Journal*, 6(4), 314–324.

Vargo, S. L., & Lusch, R. F. (2004). Evolving to a new dominant logic for marketing. *Journal of Marketing*, 68(1), 1–17.

Conclusion

Evolving Marketing Knowledge and Practice

As defined in the introduction, marketing is "the activity, set of institutions, and processes for creating, communicating, delivering, and exchanging offerings that have value for customers, clients, partners, and society at large" (American Marketing Association, 2017). Therefore, marketing encompasses all activities, resources and functions that organisations and companies use to achieve valuable exchange. These activities are undertaken not only by companies (for profit) but also by non-profit organisations, government agencies, institutions and non-governmental organisations.

Marketing has existed since the dawn of humanity, as it is a social activity of exchange. The modern scientific research and practice are dated from the early 1900s by Kotler (2018). According to Kotler, since then, the subject has gone through several stages of evolution. The business world has become more innovative; economies have grown; new communication and analytical technologies and methodologies have been developed; globalisation has expanded. Following these developments, marketers, researchers and consultants have recognised and developed new ways of implementing the marketing mix, the marketing philosophies and achieving competitive advantage (see also Furrer et al., 2020; Grönroos, 2006, 2017; Kotler & Armstrong, 2010; Sheth & Parvatiyar, 1995; Maechler et al., 2016; Vargo, 2019; Zeithaml et al., 2018).

The B2B context has different characteristics compared to B2C. Therefore, B2B-level companies and organisations need to recognise the characteristics of their market and apply appropriate strategies to succeed (Maechler et al., 2016; Möller, 2013). B2B knowledge and competitiveness are not taken for granted or treated as intuitive appendages of B2C by managers any more. Managers, researchers and consultants are developing models and strategies that take cognisance of the special characteristics of B2B markets, B2B relationships, networks, supply chains, clusters and ecosystems (Hadjikhani & LaPlaca, 2013; Keränen & Liozu, 2020; Maechler et al., 2016).

Growing African Markets

In the past two decades, African institutions and businesses have built foundations for the emergence of African markets. With moderate to high average growth rates and fast increasing populations, African markets offer growing demand and opportunities for production: outsourcing; systems and project business; and various forms of B2B collaboration (Amankwah-Amoah et al., 2018; Babarinde, 2009; Leke et al., 2018a,b; Oguji & Owusu, 2017). However, many challenges exist (Asongu & Odhiambo, 2019). African companies and institutions are modernising and internationalising both within and outside the continent (Boso et al., 2019; Ibeh et al., 2018). Thus, the B2B aspect is all the more critical as product development, managerial and technological innovation, application of new technologies, logistics and supply chain management, technology transfer, etc. are mostly done at the B2B level of the economy. African B2B organisations need to achieve their marketing objectives, not through product quality alone but also services quality, servitisation, systems and project business, and other competitive strategies (Kuada, 2016; Mahmoud et al., 2019).

Digitalisation is bringing new challenges and opportunities to B2B marketing. Still, B2B companies have not achieved the potentials provided by digitalisation, both in Africa and the rest of the world (Harrison et al., 2017). While African B2B companies have achieved some success in adopting digital communication within information technologies (Adeola & Evans, 2020; Dike & Rose, 2019; Hinson et al., 2018; Hinson & Adjasi, 2009), there is still a lot to do in the area of developing innovative African technologies in relevant areas like solar energy (Kuada & Mensah, 2020).

Dealing with Covid-19 and Recurrent Crises

How can African B2B companies prepare for and overcome unexpected crises like the financial crisis (2008), and the current Covid-19 situation? According to the International Finance Corporation (2020), the Covid-19 shutdowns will cost African economies between US$37 and US$79 billion in 2020 alone. The pandemic is affecting production, supply chains, international business and the services industry (Jiang & Wen, 2020; Kabadayi et al., 2020; Ratten, 2020). How can African B2B companies come out of this crisis? To deal with the covid-19 crisis, African B2B firms are already responding by adapting and tapping into four broad responses: reputational opportunities; exploiting new business opportunities; digitalisation; rethinking and reconfiguring global supply chains. First, African B2B firms, e.g., Nedbank, Sappi, and Firsthand, have provided relief and support to the most vulnerable in society, thus improving their corporate brand value. Second, covid-19 has led African B2B firms to leverage their capabilities into new markets and exploit business opportunities through using their existing technologies or business models to service new markets or niches that surfaced during the pandemic. Third, Covid-19 has led to several sales operations taking place digitally. Digital sales models have been shown to be just as effective as traditional B2B sales models (Gavin et al., 2020). Finally, the uncertainty and risks created in the global supply chains will undoubtedly make B2B firms in Africa rethink their supply chains and over-reliance on importation from outside Africa for key inputs. African B2B firms should begin to strategically reconfigure their supply chains from too much reliance on imports from outside Africa to favour a mix with local sources to make it feasible for activation during crises. These may favour more collaborative ventures like joint ventures, partial acquisitions etc., which we already discussed in this book.

Dealing with Debt and the Infrastructure Deficit

According to Onyekwena and Ekeruche (2019), Africa is facing a looming debt burden. This is likely to be compounded by the Covid-19 crisis described above. Moreover, African countries have a massive infrastructure deficit. According to Lakmeeharan et al. (2020), almost half of the sub-Saharan African population lack access to grid electricity and the investment requirement is about US$150 billion annually up to 2025. The debt crisis will affect the availability of international credit facilities, exchange rates and the ability of governments to support. Over-indebted countries will lose the ability to bring in foreign financial investments that will enable African industries to invest in innovation and equipment. Their currencies will devalue, leading to higher import prices, but lower export prices in foreign currencies. It could also negatively affect their relationships with foreign partners and the ability to build beneficial networks and supply chains with international partners. These challenges can be overcome first by African economies reducing their reliance on imported supply chain inputs. Secondly African B2B companies should develop innovative marketing management that can expand exporting using the benefit of lower global export prices that result from currency devaluation.

Surviving Global Competition

Global competition is growing from developed and other emerging markets, which reduces the low-cost advantages of African B2B companies and demands innovative strategies to survive (Kuada, 2016; Nkamnebe, 2006; Wenzel et al., 2019). African countries have liberalised, bringing in foreign investment, but at the same time establishing competition for local firms (Dadzie et al., 2018). African and foreign firms entering markets in the continent have implemented both competitive and collaboration strategies (Oguji & Owusu, 2017; Wenzel et al., 2013). To survive, African B2B firms need to appreciate the importance of the totality of marketing by understanding the importance of exchanging value through strategising and implementing the 7Ps of marketing, appropriate marketing philosophies, quality, coopetition, servitisation and digitalisation, among others.

The roles of African and international institutions as enablers and regulators of the business environment have been emphasised as critical for B2B firms (Agbloyor et al., 2016; Musila, 2019). Yet, corruption, inefficiencies and incompetence still exist among African institutions that have the responsibility to create and supervise the business environment (Hansen et al., 2018; Liedong, 2017). On the other hand, many African institutions are implementing policies to deal with the legacy of poor economic governance as evidenced recently by the African Free Trade Area (Etieyibo, 2013; Iheduru, 2015; Mothusi & Dipholo, 2008). An essential policy for ensuring the participation of local African firms in the extractive industries and high resource-demanding sectors of the economy that are often dominated by foreign firms has been local content regulations (Calignano & Vaaland, 2018, 2017; Owusu & Vaaland, 2016; Väaland et al., 2012). Supporting the establishment of sourcing hubs in Africa also holds promise for internationalising African B2B firms (Oguji & Owusu, 2014; Kuada & Hinson, 2015).

Summary of the Book

We have endeavoured to discuss and apply the broad view of marketing that is necessary for successful competition by African firms. We have also discussed specific aspects of marketing, including the 7Ps and the five philosophies. We have delved deeper into strategy formulation and implementation, outsourcing, building niches based on the various marketing principles, services marketing, sales management, emerging challenges and opportunities.

The backbone of the book is established marketing research. Our views and proposals regarding success in Africa are based on many years of research, consulting and practice. As Africans who have studied, taught and worked inside and outside Africa, we also have a wide range of experience of different business environments and cultures. Thus, this book is an integration of the best research findings with practice, consulting and knowledge of the African context.

References

Adeola, O., & Evans, O. (2020). ICT, infrastructure, and tourism development in Africa. *Tourism Economics*, 26(1), 97–114.

Agbloyor, E. K., Gyeke-Dako, A., Kuipo, R., & Abor, J. Y. (2016). Foreign direct investment and economic growth in SSA: The role of institutions. *Thunderbird International Business Review*, 58(5), 479–497.

Amankwah-Amoah, J., Boso, N., & Antwi-Agyei, I. (2018). The effects of business failure experience on successive entrepreneurial engagements: An evolutionary phase model. *Group & Organization Management*, 43(4), 648–682.

American Marketing Association (2017). Retrieved August 8, 2020, from https://www.ama.org/the-definition-of-marketing/. Retrieved August 5, 2020.

Asongu, S. A., & Odhiambo, N. M. (2019). Challenges of doing business in Africa: A systematic review. *Journal of African Business*, 20(2), 259–268.

Babarinde, O. A. (2009). Africa is open for business: A continent on the move. *Thunderbird International Business Review*, 51(4), 319–328.

Boso, N., Adeleye, I., Ibeh, K., & Chizema, A. (2019). The internationalisation of African firms: Opportunities, challenges, and risks. *Thunderbird International Business Review*, 61(1), 5–12. DOI: 10.1002/tie.21977.

Calignano, G., & Vaaland, T. I. (2018). Local content in Tanzania: Are local suppliers motivated to improve? *The Extractive Industries and Society*, 5(1), 104–113.

Dadzie, S. A., Owusu, R. A., Amoako, K., & Aklamanu, A. (2018). Do strategic motives affect ownership mode of foreign direct investments (FDIs) in emerging African markets? Evidence from Ghana. *Thunderbird International Business Review*, 60(3), 279–294.

Dike, M. C., & Rose, E. L. (2019). Cross-border expansion and competitive interactions of indigenous mobile network operators in sub-Saharan Africa. *Thunderbird International Business Review*, 61(1), 29–42.

Etieyibo, E. (2013). Preliminary reflections on the privatisation policy in Nigeria. African *Journal of Economic and Management Studies*, 4(1), 144–152.

Furrer, O., Kerguignas, J. Y., Delcourt, C., & Gremler, D. D. (2020). Twenty-seven years of service research: A literature review and research agenda. *Journal of Services Marketing*, 34(3), 299–316.

Gavin, R., Harrison, L., Plotkin, C. L., Spillecke, D., & Stanley, J. (2020). *The B2B Digital Inflection Point: How Sales have Changed During COVID-19*. McKinsey & Company [Online].

Grönroos, C. (2006). On defining marketing: Finding a new roadmap for marketing. *Marketing Theory*, 6(4), 395–417.

Hadjikhani, A., & LaPlaca, P. (2013). Development of B2B marketing theory. *Industrial Marketing Management*, 42(3), 294–305.

Hansen, M. W., Langevang, T., Rutashobya, L., & Urassa, G. (2018). Coping with the African business environment: Enterprise strategy in response to institutional uncertainty in Tanzania. *Journal of African Business*, 19(1), 1–26.

Harrison L, Plotkin C L., & Stanley S (2017). Open interactive popup. Measuring B2B's digital gap. Available at: https://www.mckinsey.com/business-functions/marketing-and-sales/our-insights/measuring-b2bs-digital-gap. Retrieved: August 20, 2020.

Hinson, R. E., & Adjasi, C. K. (2009). The internet and export: Some cross-country evidence from selected African countries. *Journal of Internet Commerce*, 8(3–4), 309–324.

Hinson, R. E., Osabutey, E. L., & Kosiba, J. P. (2018). Exploring the dialogic communication potential of selected African destinations' place websites. *Journal of Business Research*, 116, 690–698.

Howard, M., Caldwell, N., Smith, L., Maull, R., & Ng, I. C. (2014). Servitization and operations management: A service dominant-logic approach. *International Journal of Operations & Production Management*, 34(2), 242–269.

Ibeh, K. I., Uduma, I. A., Makhmadshoev, D., & Madichie, N. O. (2018). Nascent multinationals from West Africa. *International Marketing Review*, 35(4), 683–708. DOI: 10.1108/IMR-08-2016-0158.

Iheduru, O. C. (2015). Organised business and regional integration in Africa. *Review of International Political Economy*, 22(5), 910–940.

International Finance Corporation (IFC), (2020, May). Covid-19: Impact on sub-Saharan Africa. Retrieved August 20, 2020, from https://www.ifc.org/wps/wcm/connect/05008fd5-a427-4fae-8521-fa6c73d82d88/20200529-COVID-19-Response-Brief-SSA.pdf?MOD=AJPERES&CVID=n9xij1h.

Järvinen, J., & Taiminen, H. (2016). Harnessing marketing automation for B2B content marketing. *Industrial Marketing Management*, 54, 164–175.

Jiang, Y., & Wen, J. (2020). Effects of COVID-19 on hotel marketing and management: A perspective article. *International Journal of Contemporary Hospitality Management*, 32(8), 2563–2573.

Kabadayi, S., O'Connor, G. E., & Tuzovic, S. (2020). The impact of coronavirus on service ecosystems as service mega-disruptions. *Journal of Services Marketing*. DOI: 10.1108/JSM-03-2020-00.

Keränen, J., & Liozu, S. (2020). Value champions in business markets: Four role configurations. *Industrial Marketing Management*, 85, 84–96.

Kotler, P. (2018). Why broadened marketing has enriched marketing. *AMS Review*, 8(1–2), 20–22. DOI: 10.1007/s13162-018-0112-4.

Kotler, P., & Armstrong, G. (2010). *Principles of marketing*. Pearson, Harlow, UK.

Kuada, J. (2016). Marketing, economic growth, and competitive strategies of firms in Africa. *African Journal of Economic and Management Studies*, 7(1), 2–8.

Kuada, J., & Hinson, E. (2015). Outsourcing in Ghana: An integrated perspective. *African Journal of Business and Economic Research*, 10(2/3), 47–86.

Kuada, J., & Mensah, E. (2020). Knowledge transfer in the emerging solar energy sector in Ghana. *Contemporary Social Science*, 15(1), 82–97.

Lakmeeharan, K., Manji, Q., Nyairo, R., & Poeltne, H. (2020, March 6). Solving Africa's infrastructure paradox. Retrieved August 8, 2020, from https://www.mckinsey.com/industries/capital-projects-and-infrastructure/our-insights/solving-africas-infrastructure-paradox.

Leke, A., Chironga, M., & Desvaux, G. (2018a, November). Africa's overlooked business revolution. *McKinsey Quarterly*. Retrieved August 8, 2020, from https://www.mckinsey.com/featured-insights/middle-east-and-africa/africas-overlooked-business-revolution.

Leke, A., Chironga, M., & Desvaux, G. (2018b). *Africa's business revolution: How to succeed in the world's next big growth market*. Harvard Business Press, Boston, MA.

Liedong, T. A. (2017). Combating corruption in Africa through institutional entrepreneurship: Peering in from business-government relations. *Africa Journal of Management*, 3(3–4), 310–327. DOI: 10.1080/23322373.2017.1379825.

Macdonald, E. K., Kleinaltenkamp, M., & Wilson, H. N. (2016). How business customers judge solutions: Solution quality and value in use. *Journal of Marketing*, 80(3), 96–120.

Maechler, N., Sahni, S., & Oostrum, M. (2016, March 3). Improving the business-to-business customer experience. McKinsey & Company, Retrieved August 20, 2020, from https://www.mckinsey.com/business-functions/marketing-and-sales/our-insights/improving-the-business-to-business-customer-experience

Mahmoud, M. A., Hinson, R. E., & Duut, D. M. (2019). Market orientation and customer satisfaction: The role of service quality and innovation. *International Journal of Business and Emerging Markets*, 11(2), 144–167.

Matthyssens, P., Kirca A. H., & Pace, S. (2008). Business-to-business marketing and globalisation: Two of a kind. *International Marketing Review,* 25(5), 481–486.

Möller, K. (2013). Theory map of business marketing: Relationships and networks perspectives. *Industrial Marketing Management*, 42(3), 324–335.

Mothusi, B., & Dipholo, K. B. (2008). Privatisation in Botswana: The demise of a developmental state? Public administration and development. *The International Journal of Management Research and Practice*, 28(3), 239–249.

Musila, J. W. (2019). Anticorruption strategies in Sub-Saharan Africa: Lessons from experience and ingredients of a successful strategy. *Journal of African Business*, 20(2), 180–194. DOI: 10.1080/15228916.2019.1583980.

Nkamnebe, A. D. (2006). Globalised marketing and the question of development in the Sub-Saharan Africa (SSA). *Critical Perspectives on International Business*, 2(4), 321–338.

Oguji, N., & Owusu, R. (2014). Africa as a source location: Literature review and implications. *International Journal of Emerging Markets*, 9(3), 424–438.

Oguji, N., & Owusu, R. A. (2017). Acquisitions entry strategies in Africa: The role of institutions, target-specific experience, and host-country capabilities: The case acquisitions of Finnish multinationals in Africa. *Thunderbird International Business Review*, 59(2), 209–225.

Onyekwena C. & Ekeruche, M. A. (2019, April 10). Is a debt crisis looming in Africa? Retrieved August 8, 2020, from https://www.brookings.edu/blog/africa-in-focus/2019/04/10/is-a-debt-crisis-looming-in-africa/.

Owusu, R. A., & Vaaland, T. I. (2016). A business network perspective on local content in emerging African petroleum nations. *International Journal of Energy Sector Management*, 10(4), 594–616.

Ratten, V. (2020). Coronavirus and international business: An entrepreneurial ecosystem perspective. *Thunderbird International Business Review*, 62(5), 629–634.

Roy, R., Shehab, E., Tiwari, A., Baines, T. S., Lightfoot, H. W., Benedettini, O., & Kay, J. M. (2009). The servitisation of manufacturing. *Journal of Manufacturing Technology Management*, 20(5), 547–567.

Sheth, J. N., & Parvatiyar, A. (1995). The evolution of relationship marketing. *International Business Review*, 4(4), 397–418.

Väaland, T. I., Soneye, A. S., & Owusu, R. A. (2012). Local content and struggling suppliers: A network analysis of Nigerian oil and gas industry. *African Journal of Business Management*, 6(15), 5399–5413.

Vandermerwe, S., & Rada, J. (1988). Servitization of business: Adding value by adding services. *European Management Journal*, 6(4), 314–324.

Vargo, S. L. (2019). From promise to perspective: Reconsidering value propositions from a service-dominant logic orientation. *Industrial Marketing Management*, 87, 309–311.

Vargo, S. L., & Lusch, R. F. (2004). Evolving to a new dominant logic for marketing. *Journal of Marketing*, 68(1), 1–17.

Wenzel, N., Freund, B., & Graefe, O. (2019). Surviving in the BRICS: The struggle of South African business in coping with new partners and investors. *International Review of Applied Economics*, 33(1), 51–70.

Wenzel, N., Graefe, O., & Freund, B. (2013). Competition and cooperation: Can South African business create synergies from BRIC+S in Africa? *African Geographical Review*, 32(1), 14–28.

Zeithaml, V. A., Bitner, M. J., & Gremler, D. D. (2018). *Services marketing: Integrating customer focus across the firm*. McGraw-Hill Education, New York.

Index

Note: **Bold** page numbers refer to tables and *italic* page numbers refer to figures.

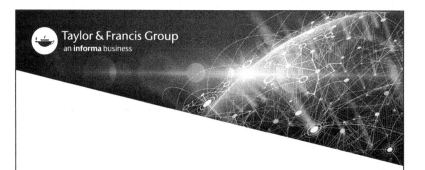